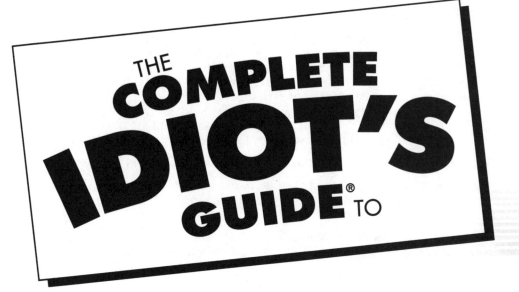

Birdwatching

by Sheila Buff

alpha books

A Division of Macmillan General Reference
A Pearson Education Macmillan Company
1633 Broadway, New York, NY 10019-6785

Copyright © 1999 by Sheila Buff

Macmillan Publishing books may be purchased for business or sales promotional use. For information please write: Special Markets Department, Macmillan Publishing USA, 1633 Broadway, New York, NY 10019.

International Standard Book Number: 0-02863106-4
Library of Congress Catalog Card Number available upon request.

01   00   99   8   7   6   5   4   3   2   1

Interpretation of the printing code: The rightmost number of the first series of numbers is the year of the book's printing; the rightmost number of the second series of numbers is the number of the book's printing. For example, a printing code of 99-1 shows that the first printing occurred in 1999.

Printed in the United States of America

Contents at a Glance

Contents

Foreword

Birdwatching, in some form, is as old as civilization itself, as evidenced by the earliest writings and cave drawings. This interest continued to grow, mushrooming in recent years to more than 50 million people, all claiming to be birdwatchers.

So why the fascination with birds? These feathered bundles of energy amaze us with startling beauty, graceful flight, and intriguing behaviors. They astound us with feather-light skeletons, body temperatures that can exceed 110 degrees Fahrenheit, and heart rates that can reach 1000 beats per minute. Almost everything birds do is captivating, so many of us are simply compelled to watch.

A Black-capped Chickadee lands on your backyard feeder, grabs a sunflower seed, and flies to a nearby branch. It places the seed under a toe and hammers the seed with its bill, splitting the hull and exposing the morsel inside. A quick grab with the bill and its down the hatch. You saw it and smiled. That's birdwatching.

It's also birdwatching when you settle down in your favorite chair and enjoy the antics of a Downy Woodpecker at the suet you provide, or an upside-down White-breasted Nuthatch probing for insects in the bark of a tree. And you can go to great lengths to provide bird feeders, nest boxes, sources of water, and elaborate landscaping to create a wildlife mecca in your backyard that provides unending pleasure. This book will tell you how.

But there's more. It's spring, you're in a wooded park and see movement near the top of a maple tree. You focus your binoculars; the movement takes shape and pops into an opening. It's a red bird with black wings and tail. Beautiful. You just saw your first Scarlet Tanager. That's birdwatching. Or it might be a handsome Hooded Warbler at Pt. Pelee, a diving Peregrine Falcon at Cape May, or a teetering Surf Bird on a jetty near San Diego. And with the growing number of international travelers, it may well be a Turquoise-crowned Motmot in Costa Rica, or a Spangled Cotinga in Peru.

So how do you get started in birdwatching? That's where this book comes in. Fact-filled with a touch of humor, it will bring you up to speed on the ins and outs of birdwatching. The basic equipment, for example, is quite simple-binoculars and a field guide. But which ones? You'll get advice in the book.

Learning to identify birds takes time, but can be readily accomplished with patience and practice. Finding key field marks that allow identification will become second nature. Recognizing songs and calls, while seeming formidable at first, will become automatic with practice. All of this is described inside.

With all this excitement, it's no wonder that birdwatching is the fastest growing outdoor hobby in America. Give it a try. The danger, of course, is that you may get hooked. And then your life will be changed forever. You'll develop a new passion and, maybe, new purpose. You'll certainly have tons of fun, and it's as close as your binoculars. So take the risk, you'll love it.

—Eldon Greij, Ph.D.

Eldon Greij is a native of North Dakota and now lives in Michigan. He studied biology, specializing in ecology and ornithology, and received a Ph.D. from Iowa State University in 1969. He was a member of the Hope College faculty until 1987, when he left to launch *Birder's World* magazine. Greij sold the magazine to Kalmbach Publishing Co. of Waukesha, Wisconsin, in 1995, and continued to serve as editor through October, 1998. He continues in a part-time capacity as a writer, speaker, tour leader, and consultant. Greij teaches a three-day week-end course on bird study entitled "An Appreciation of Birds," at various locations around the country (call toll-free 888-973-2473), and is President of Avian Enterprises, 240 S. River Ave., Holland, MI 49423.

Introduction

Welcome to Birdwatching

If you spend any time outdoors enjoying the natural world, you'll see and hear a lot of birds. Have you been noticing those birds a little more lately? Over the past few years, a lot of people have. In fact, so many people have started noticing that birdwatching is now the fastest-growing outdoor activity in America.

It's Easy—Really

At first, birding might seem awfully confusing. How can you possibly know what bird you're seeing, when it could be one of more than 800 species found in North America? How can you tell one sparrow from another when they all look a lot alike? Relax; it's just not that complicated. Yes, you'll have to do a little studying to get a handle on all the different bird families, and yes, you'll have to practice your observing skills, but there's nothing about birding you can't learn to do. It won't happen overnight, but within a few months of starting to watch birds, you'll be able to identify them a lot better. Remember, for every birder out there who began as a child or teenager, there are a lot more like you: grown-ups who have started watching birds later in life. They learned fast and had a lot of fun doing it—and you will, too.

Enjoy Birds in Your Own Backyard

Your own backyard is a great place to get started in birding. There are probably some birds there already, and with a little effort, you can attract a lot more. Putting up a birdfeeder, providing water, and landscaping to attract birds are all enjoyable aspects of birding. You'll be amazed at how easy and inexpensive it is and at how many more birds you'll start seeing. When the birds discover your backyard, you can practice your observation and identification skills just by looking out your kitchen window.

How to Use This Book

The best way to become a better birder is to do a lot of birding. Explanations and pictures in a book are great—and I hope you'll find this book helpful—but practice and experience are what you need most. That's why I've started this book by getting you right out into the field watching. For now, don't worry too much about identifying the birds; the important thing is to *see* them.

In Part 2, I discuss the ins and outs of identifying what you see. Here's where you'll learn the basic concepts of bird identification and how to put them to use for finding, seeing, and identifying more birds. Part 3 has an important explanation of bird taxonomy—the family tree of birds—and discusses the importance of record-keeping. In Part 4, I explain all about binoculars and other optics, talk about other neat birding stuff, and discuss the importance of listening to the birds. The nine chapters of Part 5 cover some of the largest and most interesting bird families, including hawks, owls, shorebirds, and hummingbirds. Part 6 is a complete guide to backyard birding, from choosing the right feeder to landscaping your yard to putting up houses for the birds. Finally, in Part 7, I take you beyond your backyard and into the world of birding hotspots, tours and trips for birders, volunteer efforts, learning opportunities, and computerized birding.

Throughout this book, I've given you plenty of charts and lists and a lot of great photos, including three separate color sections and a beautiful poster. I also provide a lot of useful information and tips in sidebars.

A Little Bird Told Me...

This box adds interesting bits of information and birding trivia.

Rappin' Robin

This sidebar explains birding lingo and defines important words.

Be a Better Birder

Here's where I give you useful birding tips.

Splat!

Birding is a pretty safe hobby, but there are some pitfalls. These boxes are warnings on how to avoid them.

Acknowledgments

I'd like to thank the many birders who have over the years generously shared their knowledge, their enthusiasm, and their snacks with me. Special thanks go to Eldon Greij, Founding Editor of *Birder's World* magazine, for his interest. Jerome Jackson provided an insightful and very helpful review of the manuscript. So did Alicia Craig-Lich, the resident birding expert at Wild Birds Unlimited.

The wonderful photos in this book come from Cliff Beittel, Daybreak Imagery, KAC Productions, Connie Toops, Tom Vezo, and from these leading manufacturers of birding products: Aspects, Bausch & Lomb, Birder's Buddy, Droll Yankees, Heritage Farms, Natural Technology, Nature Products, Perky Pet, and Wild Birds Unlimited. Special thanks to Barry Van Dusen for the great drawings in Chapter 4.

Finally, thanks again to everyone at Macmillan, including Gary Krebs for once again roping me in, Joan Paterson for keeping me at it, Kris Simmons for outstanding copy editing, and Scott Barnes for handling the production end.

Special Thanks to the Technical Reviewers...

Jerome Jackson, professor of Biological Sciences at Mississippi State University, co-hosts "Mississippi Outdoors," a weekly feature on WCBI-TV, a CBS affiliate. A member of the American Ornithologists' Union and the Association of Field Ornithologists, his area of research expertise is avian ecology, with an emphasis on endangered species, especially the Red-cockaded and Ivory-billed woodpeckers.

Alicia Craig-Lich appears frequently as a guest host on "BirdWatch," a weekly television series on birdwatching and birdfeeding distributed by public television. She is the Senior Nature Education Manager for Wild Birds Unlimited and is the expert behind the "Ask the Expert" area on the Wild Birds Unlimited Web site (**www.wbu.com**). In addition, she coordinates the National Audubon Society Important Bird Areas program for Indiana.

Part 1
Welcome to Birdwatching

The first time I taught someone how to watch birds was years ago in Central Park, the green heart of concrete Manhattan. I started by showing her how to use her binoculars. She focused on a pigeon—the most common bird imaginable. I'll never forget her amazement at how beautiful it was. Next, I got her to focus on a nearby great blue heron. I'll never forget her amazement at how often she had walked through the park and never realized that birds like that were in it all the time.

That sense of beauty and discovery is what gets people started in birdwatching and keeps them hooked. Are you ready to get started? Let's go.

Chapter 1

Why Birds?

In This Chapter

➤ Welcome to birding!

➤ Why birding is the fastest-growing hobby in America

➤ Birding and the environment

➤ Have fun, learn more, and make a difference

Are you new to birding? Good for you! You've joined the 63 million Americans who watch birds. In fact, birding is the fastest-growing outdoor hobby in America, way ahead of other popular activities such as hiking and skiing. What makes birding so popular? It's fun. There's nothing better than getting out and enjoying the sights and sounds of the birds and the beautiful world they live in. And it's easy to get started in birdwatching. You don't need fancy equipment or expensive classes; you can begin in your own backyard right now. Let's get started.

The Joy of Birding

I'm about to spend some 400 pages teaching you how to become a good *birdwatcher,* or *birder,* but it all comes down to this: enthusiasm for the natural world. If you like to be outdoors, if you have a curiosity about the world around you, if you appreciate the amazing intricacy of the environment, *birding* is the hobby for you. The basics of birding are easy to learn, and no other activity gets you out into the field enjoying the natural world faster and more often. So dust off those old binoculars you found in the back of the closet and step outside. You're about to become a birdwatcher.

Today's Birders

The image of a birder as a little old lady in tennis shoes or an eccentric old geezer is long, long past, if it ever had any truth at all. (Watch out for those little old ladies; they can bird rings around some of us younger sorts.) Today's birder is *you*. According to a major 1996 study from the U.S. Fish and Wildlife Service (the people who manage all those fabulous national wildlife refuges), here's what today's birders look like:

➤ They're well educated: 74 percent have at least a bachelor's degree, and 39 percent have graduate degrees.

➤ They're slightly more likely to be men: 44 percent are women.

➤ They're financially well off: More than half have family incomes over $50,000 a year.

➤ They're mature adults: The average birder is 56 years old, although more younger adults are taking up birding.

➤ They're committed to birding: The average birder spends 42 days a year birding, takes about 25 birding trips a year, and travels nearly 3,000 miles a year to do it.

Rappin' Robin

Birdwatching or **birding** is the art and science of observing bird life. People who bird are called **birders** or **birdwatchers**. Which usages are correct? All of them, although the tendency these days is toward birding and birder.

Does any of this sound familiar? Even if it doesn't, welcome to birding. You're about to enter a world of amazingly friendly, amazingly helpful people—people who will be delighted to help you get started in the hobby that gives them so much pleasure.

A Little Bird Told Me...

Because birding isn't a particularly strenuous hobby, many people with physical limitations enjoy it. You don't have to be able to get around much to watch birds from a hawk watch platform, or a jetty, or the road through a wetlands area. In fact, birding from your car is often the best way to see a bird without scaring it off. Many visually handicapped people enjoy birding by ear—listening for birdsongs.

Hobby or Sport?

For some of the more active birders—the type who like to do birdathons, where the object is to see as many birds as possible in 24 hours—birding is a physically demanding sport. For the vast majority of birders, however, birding is a hobby—a leisurely activity they do for pleasure in their spare time. Birding can be as active as is right for you. Some birders are happy to spend all day slogging around swamps or climbing mountain trails; others watch birds from their back porches. They're all birdwatchers and they're all having fun—and the stay-at-homes are probably seeing just as many birds.

The great beauty of birding is that birds are everywhere. You can see a surprisingly large number of them without ever leaving town. If you do get a chance to travel, there are great birds to watch just about any place you go.

The Birds in Your Life

When you stop to think about it, you'll realize you can already identify a lot of birds. Grab a pencil and a piece of paper and start writing them down. Robin, Blue Jay, crow, Bald Eagle, cardinal, pelican, Mallard, pigeon…before you know it, you'll have a list that could easily be 20 or 30 birds long. If you can already recognize so many birds, you can easily learn to recognize more.

I spend a good part of this book explaining how to spot birds and identify them when you see them. That should give you a pretty good grasp of the basics, but experience is what really teaches you best. The more you bird, the better you'll get and the more fun you'll have. To me, the real joy of birding is that it never gets boring or loses its challenge; there's always some interesting bit of behavior to watch, or a new bird to see, or a different place to go birding.

The Science of Birds

You don't need a Ph.D. in biology to move from simply watching birds into studying them. In fact, the science of *ornithology* relies heavily on observations and help from volunteer birders. You sure can't say that about nuclear physics or cancer research. (I talk more about this topic in Chapter 32, "Volunteer Birding.") Even when you're new to birding, your help at a bird-banding station or on

Be a Better Birder

You don't have to live in the country to watch birds. Central Park in urban Manhattan is a great place to see birds. More than 270 different species have been spotted there. Prospect Park, in Brooklyn, has more than 250 species recorded. One of the top places in the country to see birds is Jamaica Bay National Wildlife Refuge, in the shadow of New York City's Kennedy Airport.

Rappin' Robin

The science of birds is called **ornithology,** from *ornis,* the Greek word for bird. Scientists who study birds are **ornithologists**.

an Audubon Society Christmas Bird Count has real research value. It's another example of how easy it is to get involved with birds.

A Little Bird Told Me...

Are birds related to dinosaurs? Actually, that's not the question any more. According to many researchers, birds *are* dinosaurs. That cute little chickadee at your bird feeder may well be directly descended from coelurosaurs, a group of theropod dinosaurs that lived in the Mesozoic age some 200 million years ago. These dinosaurs couldn't fly, but they ran around on two legs, had feathers, and looked a lot like birds in every other way.

Birding and the Environment

For more than a century, birdwatchers have been a major force in the environmental movement. Like the proverbial canary in the coal mine, birds are early-warning signals of environmental problems. The people who watch birds are the first to see the effects on the birds and the first to raise the alarm—as they did when the harmful effects of DDT on birds became obvious in the 1950s.

Today, birders around the country and around the world are active in the environmental movement, especially in efforts to preserve the habitats birds need to survive. As you look for birds in one of the thousands of refuges these volunteers have helped preserve for you and future generations, take a minute to appreciate their conservation ethic and volunteer spirit.

A Little Bird Told Me...

Here's an easy and delicious way to help birds: Buy only shade-grown coffee. Why? The tall trees that provide shade for the coffee bushes on large plantations in Central and South America are excellent bird habitat. When growers cut down the trees to raise more coffee in the direct sun, they destroy bird habitat and damage the environment in other ways as well. Look for coffee with certified shade status; it'll be marked on the label.

As you become more interested in birding, you might find yourself becoming a lot more interested in everything else about the environment as well. If that happens, you'll soon find yourself getting more involved with your community. You'll be volunteering at the local nature center, taking field trips with the local bird club, and being more of an activist than you ever thought possible. Does all this make you a better birder? You bet. It also brings you a lot of new friends and shows you how concerned individuals can make a difference.

Birding Economics

Birders put their money where their binoculars are—and they're big spenders. According to the U.S. Fish and Wildlife Service, in 1996 birders spent more than $29 *billion* on their hobby. That money generated almost $85 billion in economic activity and created more than a million jobs.

Places that attract birders, such as the Gulf Coast of Texas, have caught on to the economics of birding. In 1995, for instance, birders who came to see the Whooping Cranes at Aransas National Wildlife Refuge brought more than $1.2 million into the local economy. (That's not counting the ripple effect that sort of money has.) As you and others become active birders, you're contributing to the economies of the places you visit and encouraging these areas to preserve the habitats that attract birds and birders.

Fun in the Field

Being a beginner in any new hobby has its frustrations, and birding is no exception. Hang on to your perspective and your sense of humor. What matters in birding is not that you see a lot of different birds or identify every bird you see. Not even birders who've been at it much longer than you can manage that. What matters in birding is having an enjoyable time appreciating the natural world. The rest will come. In the meantime, have fun.

The Least You Need to Know

➤ Birding is the fastest growing outdoor activity in America. More than 63 million people watch birds.

➤ Birders today tend to be well-educated, mature adults. Overall, birders spend more than $29 billion every year on their hobby.

➤ It's easy to get into birding. You need very little equipment, and you can find birds to watch anywhere.

➤ You can already identify many common birds—and you can easily learn to identify many more.

➤ Birding is a great way to get outdoors and into the natural world. You'll have fun and learn more about your environment at the same time.

Chapter 2

Getting Started

In this Chapter

➤ Using binoculars, your most important birding tool

➤ How to use your field guide

➤ Understanding field marks

➤ Where are the birds?

➤ Being an ethical birder

Are you ready to take the first steps into birding? I sure hope so because you're about to learn the easy basics of a rewarding hobby. In this chapter, I cover the two fundamentals of birding: how to use your binoculars and how to use your field guide. Once you've got the basic concepts, the rest is simple.

Looking for Mr. Goodbird: How to Use Your Binocs

Pay careful attention here: I'm about to teach you the single most important thing you need to know as a birder. What's that? The right way to use your *binoculars*.

Your binoculars are your single most important birding tool. What you're looking for are binoculars that are 7× or 8× magnification and in reasonably good condition. Chances are good that you or someone in your family already have *bins*; poke around in closets and in the attic to dig them up. (You can save the super-expensive bins for when you're really hooked. I get into the details of choosing the best binoculars in Chapter 10, "Optics: Binoculars and Spotting Scopes.")

Found them? Good. Dust them off and clean the lenses. Next, put the strap around your neck or over your shoulder. Grasp the barrels lightly in your hands, with your index finger on the focus wheel. Find something about 25 feet away to look at—a traffic sign, a flowerpot, anything that's fairly distinct and isn't moving.

Fix your eyes firmly on your target. Now, bring the binoculars up to your eyes in one smooth movement *without taking your eyes off the target.*

Resist the natural tendency to look down at the bins as you bring them up; the secret is in never taking your eyes off the target. Keep at it until you can do this easily and your target appears in your bins every time; it's essential to getting your binoculars on the birds. Take your bins into the backyard or a nearby park and practice, practice, practice. Pigeons make good practice birds.

If you don't get the target into view right away, don't search for it through the bins. Instead, bring the binoculars down, find the target again, and start over. With practice, getting your binoculars on what you want to see becomes second nature; you'll be able to do it easily every time.

Rappin' Robin

Binoculars (*bins* or *binocs* for short) are optical instruments for making distant objects appear closer. Binoculars are two small telescopes arranged side-by-side so that you can look through them with both eyes.

A Little Bird Told Me...

Beginning birders spend a lot of time focusing on broken branches, clumps of leaves, and scraps of newspaper stuck in bushes in the mistaken belief that they're exciting new birds. Your Peregrine Falcons will turn into Herring Gulls, your warblers into chickadees. Last winter I mistook a pigeon in flight for a duck and announced it to friends who used to think I knew something about birds.

Taking a Closer Look

Take a closer look at your binoculars. On all but the cheapest models, you'll see that the eyepiece on the right is adjustable and that there are some markings on it. This is the *diopter adjustment*—a way to fine-tune the sharpness of the image. To set the diopter, focus on a target with both eyes. Then, shut your left eye and look only through the right eyepiece. Rotate the diopter ring until the image is as sharp as you can get it. Once you've set the diopter, you don't have to touch it again.

As you're getting used to your binoculars, you may sometimes get the impression that someone has put a hand over the lens—because the image is blacked out. You need to adjust the eye relief; I explain all the details in Chapter 10. For now, roll the rubber eye cups up or down, as the case may be, until the problem goes away. If it doesn't, you might need to different model of binoculars. (See Chapter 10 for more on the technical stuff.)

Getting on the Birds

In the field, focusing on a bird through your binoculars is called *getting on* the bird. You've been practicing on pigeons in the park. Now, it's time to start looking for other birds.

Here's where birding can be a little frustrating for new birders because you can't focus on a bird to watch until you find one. To do that, look for motion at all levels—on the ground, in underbrush, in the branches of trees, and in the sky. Birds dart around a lot, moving around by hopping, fluttering, or flying. Search for birds using your eyes, not your binoculars; your eye has a much wider field of view than your binoculars do. You might see the movement straight ahead or catch it out of the corner of your eye.

You might hear the bird before you see it; listen for calls, songs, tappings, rustlings, and scratching. When you see or hear something that's likely to be a bird, stop. Watch or listen to pin down more or less where the bird is. If you think the bird is in a fairly small area—a bush, say—look directly at it. Any movement you see among the branches is probably a bird. Once you've got a better idea of where the bird is, use your binoculars to get it in focus.

Rappin' Robin

The **diopter adjustment** on the right eyepiece of your binoculars is used to adjust the image to your personal eyesight. Focus on something through the bins, close your left eye, and rotate the diopter ring until the image is sharp.

Splat!

Always be aware of where the sun is when you're using binoculars. Never look at the sun directly through binoculars; severe eye damage can result!

Rappin' Robin

Getting on the bird is birding talk for seeing the bird through your binoculars. I can modestly say that I'm very good at this. Identifying the bird, of course, is another story....

Be a Better Birder

Because we read from left to right, we naturally scan that way, too. In fact, scanning from left to right is so natural that your eyes might skip right over the bird. Look from right to left; it feels a little weird at first, but I find that it helps me spot the birds faster.

Rappin' Robin

A **field guide** is a compact, illustrated book designed to help you identify birds in the field through pictures, descriptions, and range maps.

Rappin' Robin

A **field mark** is some fairly obvious aspect of a bird's appearance, such as color, bill shape, wing bars, head markings, and so on, that helps you identify the bird as that species and no other.

If the bird is in an area bigger than what you can see in a glance, scan for it. Starting at the top, scan back and forth, from top to bottom, until you spot motion. Then, bring up your bins and focus on the bird. If you don't get on the bird right away but know it's in the area, scan back and forth or up and down a little with your bins to find it. Don't scan in circles, however; you'll make yourself dizzy.

Don't search around for the bird too long. You'll just get frustrated and annoyed—and you might be missing other birds in the meantime. Besides, there's a good chance that what you saw was only the common falling-leaf bird. Give up on it, and look for a real bird instead.

Flipping Through Your Field Guide

Now that you can get your bins on a bird, how do you know what bird it is? You use your next most important birding tool, your *field guide*. These compact books contain illustrations (paintings or photos) and concise descriptions of the birds; they're designed to help you identify the birds you see in the field.

The first true field guide was published by the late, great Roger Tory Peterson in 1934. Before Peterson came along, ornithologists described a bird literally from head to toe, giving equal weight to every part of its appearance. It was all informative but not very helpful unless you were examining a museum specimen.

Roger Tory Peterson, a great artist and a skillful birder, devised a brilliant system for identifying birds by their *field marks*—the colors, markings, and other visual clues unique to each particular bird species. The descriptions and paintings in his book point out the important features of a bird that identify it as that species and no other. The Peterson *field-mark* system is a simple, logical, and natural way to identify birds. It was revolutionary in its time, but today, variations of the Peterson system are used by just about all field guides to the birds and in most guides to other critters as well.

A Little Bird Told Me...

Field guides are so much a part of birding that it's hard to believe these handy little volumes didn't always exist. The birth of the field guide can be pinpointed exactly in time: the publication of *A Field Guide to the Birds,* with illustrations and text by Roger Tory Peterson in 1934, which covered the birds of eastern North America. Organized by bird families, it covered all the birds in a systematic, concise way with illustrations that pointed out the most important identification clues—the field marks that are unique to each bird species. Also, the book was small enough to carry into the field and cheap enough that anyone could buy it.

Playing the Field

A Field Guide to the Birds, also known as just Peterson, is a good choice for new birders, mostly because it's found in every bookstore, it's easy to use, and it's familiar to other birders. It's available in Eastern or Western editions. (For birding purposes, eastern and western North America are divided, a little arbitrarily, at the 100th meridian. A better way to think of it is east and west of the Rockies.)

Aside from Peterson, several other field guides are popular:

➤ *A Guide to Field Identification: Birds of North America,* by Chandler S. Robbins, Bertel Bruun, and Herbert S. Zim. Because this book is published by Golden Press, it's often called the Golden guide. It is illustrated with paintings.

➤ *A Field Guide to the Birds of North America,* from the National Geographic Society. This is often called the Geographic guide. A new, updated edition came out in the Spring of 1999, making it the most current field guide, as of this writing. It's my personal favorite; it's got great paintings and descriptions as well as a lot of room in the margins for making notes. It's a little bigger than the other guides, though, so it doesn't fit into a jacket pocket as easily.

➤ *Stokes Field Guide to Birds* (Eastern and Western editions). These guides come from popular birding personalities Donald and Lillian Stokes. They generally put only one species per page; it is illustrated with photos.

➤ *All the Birds of North America,* by Jack Griggs, sponsored by the American Bird Conservancy. This guide offers a new approach to bird ID, based on habitat groupings instead of family groups. This is an interesting approach, but it's not really very useful. Stick to a more traditional guide.

➤ *The Audubon Society Field Guide to North American Birds* (Eastern and Western editions). This book is organized a little differently. Rather than organize by bird families (taxonomically) the way other guides do, this one uses its own categories, such as gull-like birds, and then organizes the pictures by the color of the bird. Also, the photos and the descriptions are in separate sections of the book. The approach appeals to new birders, but it's fundamentally unsound and you'll outgrow it quickly.

I suggest getting a field guide illustrated with paintings, not photos. Within any bird species, there's naturally a lot of variation in colors and markings. Paintings average out the differences and give you a slightly idealized version of the bird.

Whichever field guide you decide to choose, get the most recent edition you can. Ornithology is a dynamic science, and common bird names, family groups, ranges, and other data change all the time. If you use a musty old field guide you found in the attic of the beach house, you'll be way out of date.

No field guide is perfect. Like most birders, you'll end up with several guides, along with a miscellaneous assortment of specialized field guides to particular bird families.

In addition to whichever field guide you choose, get a copy of *The Birder's Handbook*, by Paul R. Ehrlich, David S. Dobkin, and Darryl Wheye (Fireside, 1988). This indispensable volume has detailed information in field-guide format (but no pictures) about all the North American species, along with fascinating essays about all aspects of birds.

Using Your Field Guide

Start by flipping through your new field guide. Read the introduction and instructions on how to use the book. Get a feel for the way the book is organized, where the range maps appear, and so on.

Be a Better Birder

Keep a field guide handy for those times when you have a few minutes to kill. I keep one in the kitchen and work on my shorebird and sparrow IDs while I wait for a fresh pot of coffee to be ready. After a few minutes of bird study and a caffeine fix, I'm ready to get back to work.

Browse through the pages and get to know the basic bird families. Don't spend long periods reading one species description after another; you'll never remember them. Instead, spend a few minutes at a time studying one group of birds or the birds on a single page.

When you first start birding, finding a bird in your field guide will involve a lot of page flipping. As you get to know the bird families, you'll be able to turn to the right section (usually) and find the right family and even the right species a lot faster. (I get into the details of bird identification and families later, especially in Chapter 4, "May I See Your ID, Please?," and Chapter 8, "Putting the Pigeons in the Right Holes.")

The pictures in your field guide will generally show the bird in a nice profile portrait, with every field mark clearly visible. In real life, of course, the birds don't just sit around posing for you in the clear light of a summer morning. If you keep watching, however, you'll probably get a good view of at least one good field mark and see some sort of behavior—how the bird feeds or flies, for instance. Those are often enough clues to help you find a likely suspect in your field guide and compare the picture to your mystery bird.

Before you decide which bird you've seen, check the range map. If the bird had to be wildly off course to end up in your backyard, it's probably not the bird you think it is. On the whole, birds are extremely predictable; they're usually where they should be when they should be there.

Your field guide will be your constant birding companion. It'll get scribbled in, rained on, and dropped. (It has a mysterious instinct for landing in puddles.) Eventually, it will start to open automatically to exactly the page you need. That's the moment you can be sure (a) you'll lose it; (b) the binding will break and the pages will start to fall out; or a new edition will come out.

I have to admit that I get unreasonably attached to my field guides. I hate it when a new edition comes out and I have to transfer into a new book all the little notes on field marks and songs that I jotted by the descriptions. What's worse is losing a field guide with all those hard-earned notes. Always write your name and address in your field guide. Other birders know how you feel and might return a lost guide if they find one.

Be a Better Birder

To get to certain sections of my field guide faster, I put paper clips on the pages. When I'm off to a beach, for example, the clips go on the start of the gull and sandpiper sections. You can also buy stick-on index tabs and quick indexes for the most common field guides.

Where Are the Birds?

The birds are everywhere; all you have to do is look for them. Start in your own backyard, your neighborhood, and your local parks, greenways, beaches, and preserves. As you learn more about birding, you'll find yourself looking for birds in stranger places— disused railroad tracks, garbage dumps, overgrown empty lots, and even sewage settling ponds.

What are you really doing as you wander around town with your binoculars, peering up into trees and down into drainage ditches? You're looking for birds in a variety of *habitats*. (You're also getting a reputation for being a little strange, but that's something I'm sure you can deal with.) And you're finding those birds because they were there all along; you just weren't looking before now.

Rappin' Robin

A **habitat** is the preferred environment of a particular bird species (or any other living thing). Some birds, for example, are found only at seashores. Some birds have specific habitat needs. Roadrunners are found only in deserts; Snowy Owls prefer open tundra. Other birds aren't too fussy; House Sparrows, for instance, appear virtually anywhere near human habitations.

Many bird species appear only in particular habitats. You wouldn't be likely to see a great Blue Heron on a suburban front lawn, for example, but you'd be likely to see one in a marsh. Knowing a bird's preferred habitat is a big help in finding and identifying it. (I get into this more in Chapter 5, "Location, Location, Location.")

Finding Feathered Friends

One of the best ways to learn more about birding is to take a field trip with an experienced birder. You might already know someone who's an old hand at birding; in fact, you might be reading this book because someone dragged you on a birding excursion and got you hooked. More likely, however, you're on your own. You can find birding buddies right in your own hometown. Once you start asking around, you'll probably learn that there's some sort of birding group in your area. A local chapter of the National Audubon Society or your state Audubon society might be near you; if not, you might find a local or regional birding club. *A Birder's Resource Guide,* the annual directory published by the American Birding Association (ABA), has complete lists of state and local birding organizations. (See Appendix A, "Birding Organizations," for more on contacting these groups.)

All these groups offer regular field trips and bird walks—and new birders are always welcome. You should also check the community events column of your local paper for staff-led bird walks at nearby parks and preserves. Be sure to read the next chapter before you go.

Being an Ethical Birder

You're an ethical person, right? That means you'll want to be an ethical birder as well. What does that mean? It means you respect all wildlife, the environment, and the rights of others. If you do that, you'll always put the welfare of the birds and the environment first.

A Little Bird Told Me...

When it comes to rare birds, even birders who should know a lot better sometimes behave unethically. A good example is the case of the Eared Trogons in 1991. A pair of these birds, usually found only in the mountains of Mexico, was found nesting in Ramsey Canyon in southeastern Arizona. When word got out, birders poured in. Some went too far, trampling the fragile vegetation and blasting the birds with taped calls. The harassment kept the birds from nesting until very late in the season, and the chicks didn't survive. It's a sobering example of why your desire to see a bird should never get the better of your concern for it.

Throughout this book, I talk about how to act ethically while birding. In practical terms, here's what being an ethical birder means:

➤ Don't stress the birds. Be very cautious when you observe or take photos, don't use sound recordings to attract birds, and stay well back from nesting areas and the like.

➤ Don't damage the environment or disturb the habitat. Stay on the trails; don't crash around through the underbrush in pursuit of a bird. You don't want to stress the birds, trample vegetation, and cause erosion and other habitat damage.

➤ Don't trespass. Stay off private property unless you have permission. On public lands, observe all regulations and rights.

Splat!

As a new birder, you might act unethically out of inexperience. For instance, you might accidentally get too close to a nest. That could make the parent bird waste a lot of energy chasing you off or keep the parent from getting to its chicks with food. Be alert. Birds that are making alarm calls or fluttering from perch to perch, for example, are under stress—so back off.

The American Birding Association (ABA), the largest organization in the country devoted to birding, created an excellent code of birding ethics. It's reprinted in Appendix B. Please read it and take it to heart. If you're not an ethical birder, you're not a birder at all.

The Least You Need to Know

➤ Learning to use your binoculars well is essential for birding success.

➤ Use your field guide—a compact book with pictures and descriptions of all birds in a region—as a tool for learning about and identifying the birds you see.

➤ Today, a number of excellent field guides are available. Whichever you choose, buy the most recent edition.

➤ Birds can be identified by their field marks—the unique colors, shapes, and markings that set each bird species apart.

➤ Always be an ethical birder. Put the welfare of the bird and its habitat above your desire to see it.

Chapter 3

Your First Field Trip

In This Chapter

➤ Where to go birding

➤ What to wear

➤ Finding birds in the field

➤ Birding with a group

➤ Bugs and other hazards

Whenever I teach beginners how to watch birds, I spend the first 10 minutes teaching them how to use their binoculars. When everybody has the idea, I then announce that we're going to set off down the trail to find some birds. That usually upsets at least one beginner. "Wait a minute," he says. "You haven't told us how to identify the birds yet." "Details, details," I respond. "You can't identify them if you don't see them." For now, don't worry too much about putting names to the birds you see. Let's just take a field trip and have some fun.

Where to?

The hardest thing about a *field trip* is deciding where to go. I guarantee that there are at least two good birding spots within a half-hour drive of your house, even if you don't know it yet.

Almost all of the good birding spots will be public land of some sort:

➤ **Local (municipal or county) parks, beaches, and marinas:** Even parks managed primarily for recreation usually have nature trails and natural areas that attract birds. Some even have a designated bird feeding area.

➤ **Local refuges and preserves:** Once you start getting to know the natural areas of your neighborhood, you'll be amazed to discover how many are saved and run by dedicated volunteers. A private, nonprofit organization called the Nature Conservancy, for example, has more than 1,300 preserves—the largest private system of nature sanctuaries in the world. The National Audubon Society sanctuary system protects more than 250,000 acres; many thousands more are protected by state and local Audubons.

➤ **State parks, beaches, and marinas:** My home state of New York has more than four million acres of state park land, including the 2.5 million wilderness acres of the Adirondack Forest Preserve. New York City alone has more than 26,000 acres of park land.

➤ **National parks:** The U.S. park system has more than 350 sites covering more than 80 million acres. The Canadian park system includes places such as Wood Buffalo National Park in Alberta, the only place on the planet where whooping cranes nest.

➤ **National wildlife refuges:** The U.S. wildlife refuge system is even bigger than the park system; it has nearly 450 refuges covering more than 90 million acres.

All these places have plenty of accessible trails and an abundance of habitat attractive to birds.

Rappin' Robin

A **field trip** is an outdoors excursion to see birds.

Splat!

Be cautious and considerate when you go birding in residential areas. Don't trespass, and don't turn up too early in the morning. At best, you'll be considered a weirdo and a pest; at worst, you could be mistaken for an intruder, with embarrassing or even tragic consequences.

A Little Bird Told Me...

Physically challenged birders can do plenty of birding. Today, almost all public facilities can accommodate people with disabilities. The fishing areas in many parks, for instance, have docks for people in wheelchairs—and you can see a lot of birds from a fishing dock. Paved nature trails that can handle wheelchairs are fairly common at nature centers, as are trails for the visually handicapped.

Your Birding Wardrobe

Before we go any further on our field trip, let's make some fashion statements. It's crucially important to dress for comfort and for the weather when you go birding. Dress properly, and you'll have fun. Dress improperly, and you'll be miserable. Here's what you want to wear:

➤ **Comfortable footwear with socks:** This is essential; nothing will ruin your birding faster than sore, cold, or wet feet. Wear shoes appropriate for the weather and terrain. (I talk more about footwear in Chapter 12, "Other Cool Birding Gear.") Never wear sandals.

➤ **Sturdy, comfortable, efficient trousers:** You're going to do a lot of walking on trails that may be wet and muddy and lined with thorny undergrowth and poison ivy. Long pants, preferably with lots of pockets, are a must. Don't wear shorts unless you're at the beach.

➤ **Sturdy, comfortable, efficient shirt:** Short sleeves are okay in hot weather.

➤ **Sturdy, comfortable, efficient outerwear:** Sweaters, jackets, rain shells, parkas—you'll need them all, depending on the weather. Make sure you can wear them comfortably in layers. Your parka, for instance, should fit comfortably over a sweater without binding when you lift your arms.

➤ **A hat with a brim:** Hats keep you cool in the summer and warm in the winter. The brim shades your eyes, lets you see the colors of the birds better, and reduces eyestrain.

➤ **Sunglasses:** High-quality sunglasses are essential for birding. They cut the glare, which lets you see the colors and details of the birds better, and reduce eyestrain. If you wear prescription glasses, get prescription sunglasses. The clip-on kind give you annoying reflections and make it hard to use your bins.

Be a Better Birder

Learn from my hard-earned experience: When you arrive at the parking lot for your field trip, put your car keys into a deep pocket that closes with a button or zipper—and make sure the pocket doesn't have a hole in it.

Be a Better Birder

A warm hat makes all the difference in cold weather. Choose the warmest and most comfortable one you can find—never mind how it looks. My husband has a fleece-lined, waterproof hat with fold-down earflaps. We call it his stupid hat. He looks like a member of DENSA (the organization for dumb people) when he wears it, but he's always warm. I prefer a red hood made of thermal fabric; I wear a baseball cap or cowboy hat on top. We're quite a pair.

Choose dark or earth tones for your clothing; camouflage patterns look cool but aren't really necessary. Avoid sequins, metal studs, and anything that's shiny or that clanks (metal canteens, for example). In addition, try to avoid wearing white clothing; white is a warning color for birds, so a white T-shirt or hat will send them flying in the opposite direction.

Dress for the weather. In general, that means dressing warmly in layers because the places you go on field trips tend to be colder than the built-up area you left. If you're not prepared, you'll be cold and miserable in a hurry. Keep an extra sweater in the car just in case.

Other Useful Stuff

I've found an assortment of useful stuff that's handy in the field:

➤ Snacks, lunch, and a lot of water: The expression "eating like a bird" doesn't apply to the people who watch them. A thermos with something hot is a big help in cold weather. Drink plenty of liquids in both hot and cold weather.

➤ Lightweight rain shell with hood: Get the kind that folds up into a little package.

➤ Sunblock: Sunburn is a real hazard to birders. Don't forget your sunblock, and don't forget to put it on the backs of your hands, the back of your neck, and your bald spot (if you have one).

➤ Lip balm: I hate it when my lips get chapped. If you're going out in the sun, get a lip balm with sunblock.

➤ Tissues: This is crucial to successful birding. In addition to considering the obvious uses, remember that you might end up a long way from a bathroom.

➤ Adhesive bandages: These are useful for dealing with the occasional scratch or blister.

➤ Plastic bags: Plastic bags have dozens of uses, including carrying field guides and keeping optics dry.

➤ Old hand towel: On a wet day, a towel is invaluable for wiping you off. For your optics, carry special, non-abrasive lens cleaning paper, or buy a lens cloth.

➤ Pocket knife: The important thing here is the bottle-opener attachment.

Carry all these items in your pockets, a waist pack, or a small backpack.

Finding the Birds in the Field

Now that you're properly dressed and ready to go, let's get out on the trail. You want to get an early start. (As a writer who does her best work late at night, this is the part I hate about birding.) The birds are most active early in the morning, from sunrise to about nine in the morning. Activity slows down quite a bit in the middle of the day; unless it's the nesting season, the birds tend to quiet down and sleep or loaf in the middle of the day. Things pick up in the late afternoon and into dusk, as the birds feed actively and head to their nighttime roosts.

Walk along with your binoculars at the ready; hold them lightly in both hands, ready to bring them up when you spot something. Keep alert for movement all around you, and listen carefully for sounds such as songs and calls, tapping, and scratching. Don't forget to look up to see birds perched on overhead wires and buildings or soaring above.

Move quietly and smoothly, without making a lot of noise or abrupt motions. You don't want to *flush* the birds. Stay on the trail; don't damage the environment by trampling vegetation.

As you walk along, you may notice that the birds seem to be disappearing ahead of you. That's because they've seen you coming and they aren't taking any chances. Stand quietly for a few minutes; disguise your silhouette by leaning against a tree or squatting down. The birds will start again as soon as they realize you're not a threat.

Where are you going to see the most birds? In general, wherever two different habitats come together—where the woods meet a field, for instance. The abundance of birds where habitats meet is called the *edge effect*.

When you're on your field trip, look for edges. When you find one, check out the area carefully for birds. Look especially for birds perched on branches, fence posts, and the like. If there's any water around—a stream or pond, say—look for birds in the vegetation around the edges. Red-winged Blackbirds and Marsh Wrens like to nest among cattails; herons stalk their prey in the shallow water. Ducks may be resting on the shore or paddling around in the water.

For now, don't worry too much about identifying the birds; you just want to get a feel for where they're likely to be and practice getting your binoculars on them. I explain all about identification in the next chapter.

Rappin' Robin

When you **flush** a bird, you're not disposing of a dead one the hygienic way. Rather, you're making the bird fly off suddenly, usually because you've disturbed it in some way.

Rappin' Robin

The **edge effect** happens when different habitats meet—where a field meets the woods or where natural water meets the desert. Because birds that prefer different habitats come together at edges, that's where you'll see the biggest variety.

To PishPishPish or Not to PishPishPish

Pishing or using anything that imitates bird sounds (your voice, tapes, or bird-call devices) is a controversial topic. Here's why. When you pish, you attract birds all right, but you also create unnecessary stress for them. They're responding to your noises as if you were a threat or competition. You might not think you're doing much harm if you pish or play a recording for a few minutes. You might be right, especially if you stop as soon as the birds appear, but what if someone else comes along 15 minutes after you and does the same thing? And someone else comes along 15 minutes after that? In heavily birded areas, that's a realistic scenario. In fact, in many places, birders are now forbidden to use recordings to call the birds. (I talk about this more in Chapter 11, "Birding by Ear.")

If you must pish, do it only if you're sure you're the only birder the birds are likely to see all day. Stop as soon as a bird responds, and don't pish again in that area. If the birds don't respond within a few minutes, stop pishing and move on.

Rappin' Robin

Pishing (also called Spishing) is a way to attract birds by making squeaking or hissing noises with your mouth or with a bird call. Some shy birds will pop up out of the vegetation in response to pishing.

Blinded by the Birds

As you stroll along on the trail, you may come to a *viewing blind* thoughtfully provided by the site management. Check it out. Using a blind is a good way to see birds, especially if you're new to birding, because you avoid a lot of frustration; the blind is where it is because a lot of birds are there, too. Blinds are often placed near ponds or other areas highly attractive to birds.

Enter the blind quietly and close the door behind you. Position yourself comfortably by the viewing window, but don't put your head right up to it; stay back a little bit to avoid scaring the birds. Move quietly and slowly while you're in the blind, and keep talking and pointing to a minimum. Obey any instructions that may be posted in the blind; sometimes, you'll be asked to close the window when you leave.

Rappin' Robin

A **viewing blind**, also called a blind or sometimes a hide (mostly by British birders), is a small, hutlike structure designed to let you view the birds close up without scaring them off.

Follow the Leader

The fastest way to get yourself into the field seeing birds is to join a group of other birders. As I mentioned in Chapter 2, "Getting Started," finding a field trip to join is pretty easy. Most birding groups will have something scheduled almost every weekend all year round. At public parks and preserves, the rangers or naturalists often lead bird walks, especially in the spring.

An organized bird walk or field trip usually has a group leader. If you can, call the leader or park ranger in advance to say you're planning to come along and to get travel directions if you need them. Sometimes, there's a modest fee (only a few dollars).

A typical bird walk at your local nature reserve will be scheduled for early in the morning. Arrive on time, although in my experience, the group rarely sets off on schedule. The walk will probably take anywhere from one to three hours and will cover no more than a mile or two of fairly easy walking. Anyone in modestly good shape can enjoy a bird walk.

Compared to some other hobbies—golf, say—there's not much to birding etiquette, but do follow these guidelines:

➤ Leave small children and dogs at home.

➤ Stay with the group. Don't wander off, and stay on the trail.

➤ Don't get ahead of the leader.

➤ Be quiet. Too much talking, tripping over roots, and banging equipment scares off the birds.

➤ Move smoothly. Be especially careful not to wave your arms around or point too much; you'll flush the birds, to the annoyance of all around you.

➤ Help others. If someone can't see the bird, quietly help him or her get on it.

One final point: Thank the group leader when the trip is over.

There's One in Every Crowd

As a new birder, you may feel a little intimidated and shy around more experienced types. Don't be; birders are friendly and they love to share their knowledge. Sometimes, however, you will run into someone who can only be described as a jerk. This guy (it's almost always a guy) knows it all and doesn't hesitate to remind you that you don't know anything. What especially annoys me about a birding jerk is the way he refers to common birds of no interest to him as "trash birds." With the possible exception of pigeons and House (English) Sparrows, there is no such thing as a trash bird; all birds are interesting, and all birds are worthy of your respect. Besides, his trash bird could be your lifer—a bird you've never seen before.

Sometimes, the members of a birding group can get a little competitive. (That's an ironic understatement if ever I wrote one.) New birder or old, it's important to keep your perspective. What's important is not how many birds are on your life list, how many countries you've "done" in search of birds, or even how many birds you've spotted on this particular field trip. What's important is that you saw some birds, learned a little something about them, and had an enjoyable time experiencing the natural world.

Clocking In

As you're walking along with your birding group, someone will spot a bird. To help the rest of the group get on it, he or she will give directions using the clock system, saying something like, "It's at 10 o'clock in that shagbark hickory." Imagine the tree as a clock face (the old-fashioned kind with hands). The bird is approximately where the 10 would be on the clock face. Of course, there are two sides to the tree—the side facing you and the side the bird is on—but this system will usually help you find the bird. The clock system works best if you can also get some sort of landmark, such as "It's at five o'clock, near that big clump of dead leaves."

There are times, however, when the clock system isn't very helpful, such as when the bird is on the ground. In that case, whoever spotted the bird will use landmarks to guide you to it. Here's the typical sequence: "See the gate? See the leaning fence post on the left? See the big rock next to it? Look slightly past there to the left. Oops, it just flew." It's worse at the shore; there just aren't that many landmarks on a mud flat. There people say things such as "It's just to the left of that dowitcher," which doesn't help a beginner much.

Rappin' Robin

A **finding guide** is a book listing the places to see birds in a particular area. It usually contains discussions of the sites, the birds you can expect to see, the best times to visit, and detailed directions for getting there.

Finding Guides

If you don't already have local knowledge of an area, you can waste a lot of time looking for birds in unproductive places. To find the best places faster, check out a *finding guide* to your area.

Finding guides range from books that cover entire states to those that concentrate on a particular region; I have a good one, distributed by a local birding club, that covers only my county. If a finding guide covers your area, get it. And if you're planning a trip somewhere, don't leave home without a finding guide to that location. For the best selection of up-to-date finding guides, check the sales catalog from the American Birding Association. (See Chapter 34, "Learning More," for details.)

What's Bugging You?

I saved this topic for later in the chapter so you wouldn't get grossed out and stop reading. It's time to talk about bugs. I use the term loosely here to mean any creepy-crawly, insect or otherwise.

If you want to go where the birds are, that means you also have to go where the bugs are. This can be a problem for some new birders. If the sight of a spider sends you into a panic, if you can't stand the idea of touching a caterpillar, or if you're scared of bees, you're going to have a hard time becoming a proficient birder.

Get over it. Bugs are a big part of the natural order of things, and they're a major food for almost all birds. Remember, there are at least 30 million insect species; you're outnumbered billions to one. Beetles alone represent a quarter of all the animals on earth.

Almost all bugs are completely harmless, but a few can put a real crimp into a birding trip. First on the list are mosquitoes, followed closely by such other biting annoyances as black flies and chiggers, to say nothing of ticks.

You can generally deal with mosquitoes by using a repellent that contains DEET; take your pick of the many brands on the shelf at any drugstore or supermarket. Apply it to all areas of exposed skin. DEET works well against mosquitoes and moderately well against ticks. It's useless against black flies, chiggers, and other nasty biters. For the best overall protection against insects, many birders now use permethrin (a popular brand is Duranon), a repellent you apply to your clothing, not your skin. If you'll be in chigger country, I strongly recommend it. (Chiggers, tiny arthropods that burrow into your skin and make welts that itch for weeks, live mostly in grassy areas of the Midwest and South-east. They're the reason the pioneers kept going until they got to California.)

Birders must be especially concerned about ticks. Nasty illnesses such as Lyme disease, erlichiosis, and Rocky Mountain Spotted Fever are carried by ticks. Because ticks live in the same brushy areas that birds do, you're especially at risk. To avoid tick bites, wear closed shoes, socks, long trousers, long-sleeved shirts, and a hat. Stay on the trail; don't go bushwhacking into brushy or grassy areas. Use a tick-repellent spray. Check yourself carefully all over for ticks after a field trip; the deer tick that carries Lyme disease is no bigger than a pinhead when it first gets on you.

If you ever find yourself in a flat field in Texas or the southeastern states and think that climbing up on that little mound will give you a better view, think again. That's a fire ant mound; don't go near it. Likewise, learn to recognize and avoid wasp nests.

Splat!

If you've been infected with Lyme disease or another tick-borne illness, you may get a rash around the bite. If you get sick with a flu-like illness or develop arthritis symptoms within a few of weeks of visiting a natural area, a tick-borne disease could be the culprit. See your doctor immediately. Antibiotics usually clear up things in a couple of weeks. Delay makes tick-borne diseases harder to treat.

Look, but Don't Touch

It's almost impossible to avoid poison ivy, poison oak, and poison sumac if you're a birder. These noxious plants are everywhere the birds are; in fact, the white berries of poison ivy are a major bird food.

Not everyone reacts to the irritating oils on these plants, but you won't know whether you do until it's too late. Even if you're not a reactor now, you may become one. After years of happy disregard for poison ivy, I lost my immunity a few summers ago. I was so surprised that I, who have diagnosed poison ivy in dozens of people, didn't realize at first what it was. It took weeks for the itchy, oozy rash to go away.

Your best approach is avoidance. Learn to recognize these plants and stay away. All parts of the plants—not just the leaves—can give you a rash. For poison ivy, remember this old adage, "Leaves of three, let it be."

The Least You Need to Know

➤ Places to go birding are all around you. Parks, preserves, refuges, beaches, and other public lands are all great places to go birding.

➤ Dress properly for a day in the field with comfortable footwear and clothing that's right for the weather.

➤ For now, work on spotting birds in the field; don't worry too much about identifying them.

➤ You'll learn faster if you go out with experienced birders. Local birding groups have regular field trips; new birders are welcome.

➤ Use insect repellent to keep mosquitoes, ticks, and other annoying insects away. Learn to recognize poison ivy and stay away.

Part 2

Look! Up in the Sky!
It's a Bird!

Yes, but which bird? The heart of birdwatching is identifying the birds you see. To do that, you need to learn some basic skills, but once you've got them down, making those IDs will get easier all the time. As you get to be a better birder, you'll see birds wherever you go, whenever you go. There are plenty of beautiful birds to watch all through the year.

Watching what the birds do is just as important as identifying them—and even more interesting. There are more than 9,000 bird species in the world, and every single one of them behaves differently. You can't get bored watching them.

Chapter 4

May I See Your ID, Please?

Bird   Not a Bird

In This Chapter

➤ What bird is that?

➤ What to look for

➤ Spotting field marks

➤ Watching behavior

➤ Got it!

You're out in the field now, binoculars at the ready. You're seeing birds! All kinds of birds! It's time to take that next, all-important birding step and learn how to identify what you're seeing. As you flip through your field guide and realize that the sparrow-like bird you're looking at could be one of 20 different birds, that might seem a little complicated. Don't panic. Bird identification is basically a matter of systematic observation logically applied. There's nothing magical or mysterious about it, and anyone can learn to do it.

I See It! Now What?

Once you've got a bird in your bins, the most important thing to do is keep watching. You want to observe as much as you can of the bird's appearance and its behavior. You might have only a few seconds to do this before the bird vanishes again—or you might have several minutes or more to observe it at your leisure. In birding, you hardly ever know, so keep watching.

Be a Better Birder

If you lose the bird, don't give up. Even experienced birders spend a lot of time looking at quivering twigs from which a bird has just flown. Small, active birds such as chickadees or warblers move rapidly, but they generally go only a short distance. Stand still and keep looking at the general area where you lost it. Chances are fair that you'll spot some movement or a flash of color and be able to pick up the bird again. On the other hand, if you can't find the bird again within a few minutes, it's time to move on.

Be a Better Birder

Once you get more familiar with the birds, you don't need to see much to identify them. Just as you can identify a close friend in a crowded room by hearing a snatch of his laughter (I once found my father in Grand Central Terminal at rush hour by hearing him sneeze), you will be able to identify familiar birds just by catching a glimpse of them.

Find the Field Marks

What are you looking for? Run down this mental checklist of field marks:

➤ **Size:** How big is it?

➤ **Shape:** Is it chunky, plump, slender? Long legs or short? Long, thin wings or short, rounded ones?

➤ **Color:** Any vivid colors?

➤ **Head markings:** What kind of bill does it have—long and thin, large and heavy, flattened or curved? See any rings around the eye, crests on the head, stripes or patches on the head and throat?

➤ **Body markings:** Any obvious marks, such as wing bars, streaks on the chest, or colored tail feathers?

Remember, a field mark is some fairly obvious aspect of a bird's appearance, such as color, bill shape, wing bars, head markings, and so on, that helps you identify the bird as that species and no other. A lot of times, all you need is one good field mark to be able to make the ID.

You'll also need to bear in mind:

➤ The habitat you're in

➤ Where the bird is within that habitat

➤ What the bird is doing

All are important clues to identifying your mystery bird.

Isn't that an awful lot to try to observe in the three seconds you've got your bins on the bird? Well, yes, but don't worry. The whole rest of this chapter is about the details of what to look for. With a little knowledge and a little practice, you'd be amazed at how much you can notice in a short time. If you've been studying your field guide at all, you should be able to make a pretty good guess about the bird's family—and once you get a mystery bird into the right family, you're on the way to identifying it for certain. (Refer to Chapter 2, "Getting

Started," for more about field guides and how to use them. See Chapter 8, "Putting the Pigeons in the Right Holes," for more about bird families.)

Your Basic Bird

Before I get any further into identification, take a look at the generic bird diagram below and the head diagram on page 34. Get a feel for the basic overall parts of a bird and for the different parts of the head. The crucial field mark you need to see to identify a bird for certain is often on the head—the shape of the bill, an eyestripe, a throat patch. Then again, it might be the streaking on the breast, the shape of the tail, the wing bars, or some other distinctive feature of the bird. If you're familiar with the parts of the bird, you'll know what to look for when the field guide says to look for an eyebrow stripe.

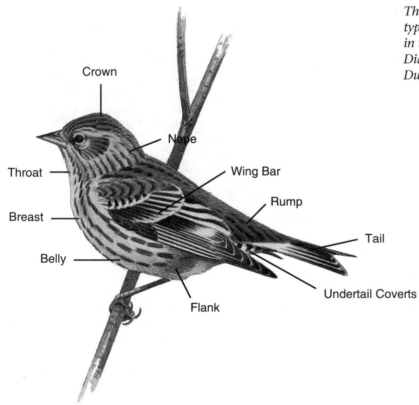

The basic parts of a typical songbird are shown in this drawing. Diagram ©Barry Van Dusen.

Crown

Nape

Throat

Wing Bar

Rump

Breast

Tail

Belly

Undertail Coverts

Flank

The field marks on a bird's head are often useful identification clues. This diagram shows typical marks. Diagram ©Barry Van Dusen.

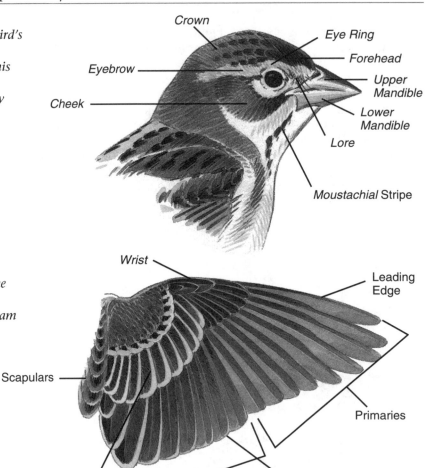

This drawing shows the parts of a typical songbird's wing. Diagram ©Barry Van Dusen.

Size Does Matter

Let's get down to business here. The first thing you need to do when you spot a bird is get a sense of its size. The best way to do that is to compare Bird X to a *reference bird*—a bird you already know well and can use as a handy benchmark for comparing to other birds. You can do this because even if you're brand new to birding, you've seen some common birds, such as blue jays and pigeons, so often throughout your life that you already have a clear mental image of their size and appearance.

Rappin' Robin

A **reference bird** is any bird that you can instantly recognize and use as basis of comparison for other birds.

Ask yourself how Bird X stacks up size-wise against a sparrow, a robin, a pigeon, or a crow. Is it bigger, smaller, or about the same? You just need an impression here, not an exact measurement.

Getting in Shape

After size, the overall shape of the bird is an important ID clue. Compare Bird X to your reference birds, and ask yourself how the bird looks overall. Is it plump, like a pigeon? Does it stand very upright, like a robin? Often, you don't really need a reference bird to describe how the bird looks; words such as slender or stocky will automatically come to mind when you see the bird.

Tailing Off

Checking out the shape and length of a bird's tail provides a good clue to its identity. A short, upcocked tail is a dead giveaway that you're dealing with a wren. Magpies have very long tails, almost as long as their bodies. Barn Swallows have deeply forked tails. When you're tailing a bird (get it?), check out the end. Is it squared off, rounded, notched, forked? Look at the length. Is the tail proportionately very long or short? Check out the colors as well. Are there any bands? Is the tail a different color than the body? When the bird flies, are some of the tail feathers a different color? That's a good clue for juncos and redstarts. While you're looking at the tail, watch for rump patches; the yellow-rumped warbler is a good example.

Take a look at how the bird holds its tail. Many flycatchers pump their tails slowly up and down when they're perched.

Be a Better Birder

Stop and think about it for a minute: You can already identify about 20 different common birds such as robins, Blue Jays, pigeons, and crows. You know these birds from seeing them so often—on your front lawn, in the park, in books and magazines, in cartoons, in movies, on television, and on greeting cards. (Cardinals, chickadees, and Canada Geese seem to be the favorites for Christmas cards.)

A Little Bird Told Me...

One problem with being a birder is that sometimes people corner you at parties, describe a bird they saw somewhere, and expect you to tell them what it is. If they happened to see the right field mark, you can actually do this. It makes a big impression. Once, someone described a bird to me that sounded vaguely like a hermit thrush. When I asked him if the bird had a cinnamon–colored tail, he responded excitedly, "Yes, that's exactly the color. How did you know?" As Sherlock Holmes once said, "You know my methods, Watson."

In Living Color

There's a good chance that what caught your eye about the bird you're watching was a flash of brilliant color. The more obvious the color, the easier it is to identify the bird. A largish songbird that's red all over, for instance, is probably a northern cardinal, but it could also be a summer tanager. Here's where the common name of a bird gives you a lot of clues. Take birds that are blue, for example: Blue Jay, bluebird, Indigo Bunting, Lazuli Bunting, Blue Grosbeak. Sometimes, the color in the common name refers to an important, easy-to-see field mark—the rusty red tail in the Red-tailed Hawk, say, or the bright red wing patches in the Red-winged Blackbird.

Birds are at their most colorful in the spring, when they're in full breeding plumage. Among the brightly colored birds, the males are almost always much gaudier than the females. Male cardinals are brilliant red, but the females are a duller red washed with green. Male Indigo Buntings are bright blue all over, but the females are brown. Male Rose-breasted Grosbreaks are beautiful, with a lovely rosy red chest (though juveniles look more like females); the females look like big, nondescript sparrows.

Be a Better Birder

During the breeding season—spring and early summer—birds pair up. If you spot a male or female, the other partner is likely to be nearby. Keep looking and listen for alternating chirps or clucks as the pair call to each other to keep in touch.

Colors aren't always easy to see when you're birding. That's because a lot of times, the light level is low—when it's very early in the morning or the bird is in deep shade, for example. It's hard to distinguish colors—or any other details, for that matter—in low light. By the same token, it's hard to see colors and details well in very bright light. The brightness and glare wash them out.

Head Trips

If you can look only at one part of a bird, I recommend the head. Why? First, the bird's bill is an important clue that lets you make a good guess about its family. Second, the other markings on the head are also great ID clues. You'll want to look carefully at the bill, the head itself, and the throat area.

Filling the Bill

Let's start with the bill. Here's what to look for:

➤ **Length:** Is it long, short, or in between?

➤ **Thickness:** Is it thin, medium, stout?

➤ **Shape:** Is it curved, flattened, hooked, or unusual in any way?

There's a reason many birds have their bill in their common name. Roseate Spoonbill, Red Crossbill, Blue Grosbeak—all these birds have distinctive bills that are excellent field marks.

The bill is also an easy clue to bird families. Warblers, for instance, have thin, straight, pointed bills; all herons have long, powerful, pointed bills for snatching prey from the water; all woodpeckers have stout, chisel-like bills. For some examples, check out the color picture inserts.

In fact, the bill is so important for ID that you need to know some special descriptive words:

➤ **Beak:** The words beak and bill are really interchangeable, but for some reason, birders usually say bill, except when they're talking about raptors, in which case they usually say beak.

➤ **Beveled:** Chisel-like tip, as in woodpeckers.

➤ **Ceres:** The leathery "saddle" at the base of the upper mandible, as in many raptors.

➤ **Decurved:** The bill curves downward, as in curlews and whimbrels.

➤ **Frontal shield:** A flat extension of the bill up onto the forehead, as in coots and gallinules.

➤ **Mandibles:** Another way of saying jaws. The top part of the bill is called the maxilla; the lower part is the mandible.

➤ **Nail:** A sharp, hard tip on the end of the maxilla (upper mandible). Found in ducks, geese, and swans.

➤ **Nares:** Birder talk for nostrils. Pronounced NAIR-eez.

➤ **Neb:** Another word for bill. Used only in crossword puzzles.

➤ **Recurved:** The bill curves upward, as in avocets.

➤ **Serrate:** The bill has "teeth" along the edges, as in mergansers. Birds don't have real teeth.

➤ **Throat pouch:** A leathery pouch hanging from the lower mandible, as in pelicans.

➤ **Tubenose:** External, tubular nostrils on top of the bill, as in albatrosses and shearwaters.

Markings on the bill and bill color are sometimes important field marks; the Ring-billed Gull is a good example. You can't always get a good enough look at a bird's bill to see the colors. In general, if you don't notice the color right away, it's probably not that important to the final ID. Size and shape are more useful.

A Little Bird Told Me...

Ever wonder how a woodpecker can pound so hard on a tree trunk without hurting itself? A woodpecker's head is specially adapted to take a beating. The bill is shaped like a sharp, extremely sturdy chisel—perfect for chipping holes into wood. Relative to other birds of the same size, woodpeckers have large heads. That's because they have very thick, bony skulls and a thick layer of spongy material between the bill and the skull—perfect for absorbing the shock of repeated pounding.

Making Headlines

All the markings on the head are handy ID clues. Here's what to look for:

➤ **Solid color:** If the bird's head is all or mostly one color—the Red-headed Wood-pecker is a good example—you've got a really useful field mark.

➤ **Crests:** Cardinals, titmice, Blue Jays, Cedar Waxwings, Pileated Woodpeckers, and some other birds have very obvious feather crests on their heads. If the bird has a crest, then it can only be one of a relative handful of birds.

➤ **Hoods and caps:** Hoods are distinctly colored feathers that cover part of the head and neck; the Red-Bellied Woodpecker is a good example. A patch of color on the top of the bird's head is called a cap. The male American Goldfinch has a nice black cap when it's in breeding plumage.

➤ **Stripes:** Look for stripes of contrasting colors; the White-crowned Sparrow is a good example.

➤ **Masks, eyebrows, and eyelines:** Masks make a bird look like it's doing a bandit imitation; check out shrikes and Common Yellowthroats in your field guide to see what I mean. Sometimes, a head stripe makes an "eyebrow" (also called a supercilium, but only by supercilious birders). You can tell a Prairie Warbler, for example, by its bright yellow eyebrow stripe. Sometimes, the bird has a thin line that seems to go through the eye; you see this on a lot of sparrows.

➤ **Patches:** Look for small areas of solid color; often, the patch is on the "cheek" (a malar patch, if you want to be technical) or ears (an auricular patch). The best field mark for the Red-cockaded Woodpecker isn't the teeny little red tufts on the male's head; it's the large white cheek patches.

➤ **Lores:** This is the area between the base of the upper mandible and the eyes. The color of the lores is sometimes given as a field mark, but it's often hard to see. For examples, look at the pictures of the Solitary Vireo in your field guide. Because the lores are the same color as the eye ring, this bird is sometimes said to be wearing spectacles.

➤ **Eye rings:** These are actually fairly easy to spot. Birds such as the Wood Thrush and many flycatchers have conspicuous white rings around each eye—as if they had put white eyeliner all around their eyes. Some birds have dark eye rings, which give them a big-eyed look; the Tufted Titmouse is a good example.

➤ **Eye color:** Usually, eye color is hard to spot unless you get lucky. If it's any color but black, it's a field mark.

➤ **Throat patches:** A contrasting patch of color on the bird's throat is usually pretty easy to see. The White-throated Sparrow is a common example. A spectacularly beautiful example is the fiery orange throat of the male Blackburnian Warbler.

Looking back at this list, I realize it's a lot to remember. Generally, however, there will be one thing about the head that'll really stand out as a field mark; you'll probably see it right away. Take the White-throated Sparrow, for instance. You can't miss the white throat patch. To see what I mean, take a look at the color picture inserts.

The Body of Knowledge

After the head, check out the bird's breast, sides, belly, and the rest of the body. You're looking for contrasting colors or for patches, streaks, stripes, and spots that are good ID clues. The American Tree Sparrow, for instance, has a clear gray breast with a conspicuous dark spot in the middle. The male Chestnut-sided Warbler, as you might have guessed, has chestnut patches on its sides. Just guess what color the Red-breasted Nuthatch has on its breast. (If you got that one, here's another: What color was George Washington's white horse?) The Canada Warbler has a black "necklace" on a solid yellow breast. No matter what the bird is, try to pick up something distinctive about the body.

On the Wing

When a bird is perched, look for horizontal (more or less) bars on the wings or for patches. These are often useful field marks, especially for warblers and the more troublesome members of the flycatcher crowd.

When a bird is in flight, you want to watch for two separate things: the appearance of the wings and the way the bird flies. You'll see what I mean when you look at the color pictures.

Spreading Your Wings

When they spread their wings, some birds show off very visible patches or bars. You can easily see this in the Northern Mockingbird, which flashes large white patches on each wing when it flies. The wing and tail markings on a bird in flight are especially important when you're looking at the shorebirds; I discuss that in Chapter 16, "Sorting Out the Shorebirds." How the wings look from underneath is also helpful for figuring out hawks because that's how you're most likely to see them. I talk more about that in Chapter 14, "Hawk Watching."

It's helpful to know the names for the various parts of a bird's wing—you want to hold your own in any learned discussions of the color of the secondary feathers near the leading edge. Check out the drawing on page 34 to learn the parts of the wing.

Flight Plans

How a bird flies is a good clue for what family it's in. Most hawks soar high in the sky; sparrows flutter around close to the ground. Woodpeckers fly in an undulating, up-and-down pattern, like riding a rollercoaster; they flap a few times, fold in their wings against their bodies and sink, and then flap again. Mockingbirds fly with very slow wingbeats. With experience, you'll be able to ID a bird just from the way it flies. Practice; you wouldn't believe how much this impresses nonbirders.

A Feeling for Feet

I'm doing this mostly to explain some mystifying terminology; you don't really get too many chances to get a good look at a bird's feet. If you do, however, look first for color; it's a helpful field mark, especially for gulls and shorebirds.

Birds have four toes (a few have only three, and ostriches have only two), usually with three toes that point forward and one that points back (anisodactyl, to use the technical term). Each toe ends in a claw.

In a typical perching bird—a robin, say—each toe is separate. The feet are ideally adapted for perching on branches.

Of course, there are plenty of other foot designs; a lot of water birds have webbed feet, for instance.

There's nothing like slinging around technical foot terms to make you sound like a real birder. Memorize this list:

> ➤ **Zygodactyl:** Two toes pointing forward and two pointing backward—as in woodpeckers, parrots, and owls (although owls can move one toe forward or backward).

Be a Better Birder

Here's a question someone's bound to ask you: Why don't birds fall off the branch when they fall asleep? A bird's feet are actually in their normal relaxed position when they're grasping a branch. The answer to "Why don't their bare little feet freeze?" is that the veins and arteries in a bird's legs and feet run parallel and right next to each other; warm blood from the arteries warms up the cooler blood returning in the veins.

➤ **Lobed or lobate:** Flat, paddle-shaped toes, as in grebes and coots.

➤ **Palmated:** Having webbing between the forward-facing three toes, as in ducks, geese, and gulls.

➤ **Totipalmated:** Having webbing between all four toes, as in cormorants and pelicans.

➤ **Semipalmated:** Having partial webbing between the forward-facing toes, as in some plovers and sandpipers.

➤ **Talons:** The strong, sharp, curved claws of birds of prey.

Got all that? Good—here's two more: *Pamprodactyl* means a bird with all four toes facing forward—as in some swifts. *Syndactyl* means having the toes fused along part of their length, as in the forward-facing toes of kingfishers.

A Little Bird Told Me...

The 10 members of the *Empidonax* group of flycatchers (plus a few related birds) are a real challenge to even the most experienced birders. All these drab little birds look a lot alike. Telling them apart is tough; you have to look for field marks such as the bright orange lower mandible of the Western Flycatcher or compare the eye rings of the Willow and Alder Flycatcher. Another way is to listen for the subtle differences in their calls—assuming they don't decide to stay obstinately silent while you're around.

Where Are You?

I'm not asking where you are this very minute; obviously, you're sitting in a comfy chair engrossed in this book. What I mean is where are you in terms of *habitat* as you watch the bird. Are you in a swamp? At a beach? Along a lake shore? What part of the country (or the world) are you in? Where you are gives you some important clues about what birds you're seeing. For instance, you wouldn't expect to see a Prairie Chicken or a Roadrunner in the Great Swamp of New Jersey. (That's a real place, not just another way of referring to the whole state.) These birds would be impossible in terms of both geography and habitat. What you're more likely to see are birds that like freshwater ponds and shrubby vegetation—birds such as Belted Kingfishers, Great Blue Herons, warblers, and Wood Ducks. Likewise, some gulls, such as the Herring Gull, are found everywhere. Other gulls, such as the California Gull, are found only on the west coast. I discuss all this a lot more in Chapter 5, "Location, Location, Location."

Where's the Bird?

Where's the bird within the habitat? Is it on the ground, at the edge of some water, floating on the water, flitting around in the shrubbery, or high up in a treetop? Within a *habitat*, different birds are found in different places. That's because they're each finding food, nesting places, and other important necessities, such as good singing perches, in different *niches* within the habitat.

Rappin' Robin

A bird's **habitat** is the particular part of the environment it prefers to live in—grasslands, say, or a freshwater marsh. Technically, a bird's **niche** is the role it plays within its habitat, including its preferred place within the habitat—in treetops, say, or on the forest floor.

By looking at where the bird is within the habitat, you can eliminate a lot of possibilities right away. If the bird is floating on the water, for instance, you know you'll find it some place toward the front of your field guide, in there with the ducks, grebes, geese, and other water birds. If it's a large, chicken-like bird walking around in the woods, you know it has to be a member of the grouse and ptarmigan family (which includes Wild Turkeys).

Birds move around a lot within their habitat, of course, but on the whole, they stick to the level and niche they prefer. You're very unlikely to see a red-eyed vireo on the ground; they're always way up in the treetops. Towhees, on the other hand, are ground-dwelling birds; you can often hear them scratching through the leaf litter in the woods. By having at least a vague idea of where a bird is generally found within its habitat, you can eliminate a lot of possibilities and keep your guesses within the bounds of reality.

What's It Doing?

Watching a bird's behavior is every bit as important for getting an ID as field marks are. In fact, because female birds are often less colorful and have fewer distinctive markings, it's sometimes more important. Ditto for the songs, calls, chirps, chips, and other sounds a bird makes. They're so important, in fact, I've given them their very own chapters. Be sure to read Chapter 7, "Understanding Bird Behavior" and Chapter 11, "Birding by Ear." I also talk a lot about behavior in the chapters in Part 5.

I Can Resist Everything Except Temptation

As soon as you spot a good field mark and an interesting bit of behavior, you might be overtaken by an overwhelming urge to stop watching and start looking for the bird in your field guide. Resist! Keep watching. Paging through your field guide is no substitute for careful observation. The longer you watch, the more field marks and behavior you'll see and the more identification clues you'll have. The more clues you have, the better the chances that you'll look in the right section—maybe even the right page—of the field guide when you do open it.

Keep track of your clues by jotting them down in a small notebook. (I like the 5 × 8 spiral-bound kind.) You might also make rough sketches as a visual reminder of what you saw. Note everything you can about the bird's appearance, behavior, and the habitat you saw it in. Save the search through your field guide for when you're back home from your birding trip.

Here's where you are going to put all the clues together and come up with your ID—or at least get close. Think over everything you've learned about Bird X from observing it. Make your best guess about what it is—by family if not by species. Then—and only then—turn to the right section of your field guide and look for a picture of the bird. There's a reasonable chance that your family guess was pretty good and you'll find your bird quickly. There's also a reasonable chance that several pictures look a lot like Bird X. Here's where behavior, location, and habitat come in. Which of the possible birds comes closest to being in the right place? Use the field guide descriptions and the range maps to figure it out.

When you first start doing this, you'll be doing a lot of page-flipping, head-scratching, and under-the-breath swearing. You might never really be able to identify a lot of the birds you see. Keep at it; you'll be surprised at how quickly you learn. The day will come when you catch a quick glimpse of a bird out of the corner of your eye and, to your own surprise, automatically identify it.

Be a Better Birder

Always carry your notebook and at least two ballpoint pens with you on a field trip. (Marker pens run when the paper gets wet, as it inevitably will.) In cold weather, use pencils; the ink in the pens may freeze. Use a couple of thick rubber bands to hold the notebook pages down.

The Least You Need to Know

➤ Always watch a bird as long as you can. Don't stop watching to look up the bird in your field guide. Spot as many clues from field marks, behavior, and habitat as you can.

➤ The overall size, color, and shape of a bird are valuable clues for identifying it.

➤ Look carefully at the bird's head. Check out the size and shape of the bill and look for colorful caps, patches, stripes, and other markings. These field marks are helpful for identification.

➤ Look for colors and markings on the bird's body—a spot or streaks on the breast, for instance. The size and shape of the bird's tail can be a helpful clue.

➤ Check out the wings for bars, patches, and feathers with contrasting colors.

➤ Take notes, make rough sketches, and put your ID together after the field trip by comparing your notes to the field guide pictures.

Location, Location, Location

The great Louis Pasteur, founder of the modern scientific method, said in 1854, "In the fields of observation, chance favors the prepared mind." (If you'd like to say that in French, it's "Dans les champs de l'observation le hasard ne favorise que les esprits préparés.") Boy, did he get that right. When you're out in the field, you'll see a lot more birds—and be able to identify them a lot better—if you know what you're looking for.

Ranging Afield

What are you looking for when you go birding? Birds, of course—but not every bird that happens to be in your field guide. You're looking for the birds you would expect to see in that particular habitat in that particular part of the country at that particular time of year. If you look hard and have a bit of luck, those are exactly the birds you will see. How can I be so sure? Every bird species has its preferred range, habitat, and niche.

Home on the Range

The broadest geographical category for a bird is its *range*—the large area in which the species is normally found. Just as importantly, a bird species isn't usually found outside its normal range. Migratory birds actually have three ranges—their breeding range, their wintering range, and their range where they are simply transients, though they can be found in these areas for one month or more each year.

Each bird's range is shown in your field guide with a little map. Be sure to read the introductory section of your field guide; that's where the explanation of the colors and symbols used in the map appears. Overall, the map will show you the rough boundary for sightings of each species. It will also show the breeding (spring and summer) range of the species, its year-round range, and its winter range. As you'll see, the seasonal ranges sometimes overlap—and sometimes are widely separated. (I talk more about migration in the next chapter, "Birding Through the Year.")

Rappin' Robin

A bird's **range** is the geographic area in which it's normally found.

Rappin' Robin

A bird's **habitat** is that special part of the environment in which it prefers to live. For example, the Bridled Titmouse is found in the mixed juniper, oak, and pine woodlands of the mountains in southern Arizona, New Mexico, and Mexico. You are unlikely to find it in any other sort of habitat.

Range maps are useful for figuring out what bird you're seeing. Birds are sometimes found outside their normal ranges, but on the whole, they're pretty predictable. Let's say you're in Maine and you see a really big, black bird soaring around with its wings held in a V shape. You're pretty sure it has to be a vulture, especially because there's something dead nearby, but is it a Turkey Vulture or a Black Vulture? By checking the range map, you can eliminate Black Vulture; they are not known to get that far north. That leaves you only with Turkey Vulture. (You never gave any serious consideration to the California Condor, did you?)

Get in the Habitat Habit

The bad thing about range maps is that they're a little misleading. First, the birds get scarcer toward the edges of their range. Second, the birds aren't found everywhere within the range. Instead, they're found only in their preferred *habitats*.

If you know which habitat a bird prefers, you can eliminate some suspects when you're trying to identify a bird. Let's say you spot a wren of some sort in the shrubby underbrush in Rock Creek Park, a good birding spot in the middle of Washington, DC, in January. Turning to your field guide, you realize it could be one of nine possible species. A quick check of the range maps eliminates the Cactus wren, Rock wren, and Canyon wren; they're all found only in the western part of North

America. The Sedge Wren and the Marsh Wren are possibilities based on their ranges, but the habitat rules them out; these birds would only be found in reedy or marshy areas.

Based on range and habitat, now you're down to four possibilities: Bewick's, Carolina, Winter, and House. By looking at the winter ranges and habitats, you see that the House Wren and Bewick's Wren are possible but very unlikely.

Now, you're down to just two choices: Winter Wren or Carolina Wren. Both like shrubby underbrush in wooded areas, and both are found in the DC area in the winter. Winter Wrens are on the secretive side—you just don't see them all that much—so your bird's most probably a Carolina Wren. To be sure, you'll need to keep watching for a good field mark. Look for the bold white eyebrow, or listen for its cheerful song.

A Little Bird Told Me...

Some birds are found in a wide range of habitats; the Great Horned Owl, for example, is found everywhere in North America except the Arctic region. Swainson's Hawk is a bird of the prairies and plains; it's rarely seen on the West Coast or in the eastern half of North America. Other birds are much fussier. The California Gnatcatcher, for instance, is found only in dry, shrubby coastal slopes in southern California—land that is rapidly being turned into shopping malls and housing developments.

Birding by Habitat

Range maps and habitat are useful tools for eliminating possibilities when you're identifying a bird, but let's take a more proactive approach. You can use your knowledge of range and habitat to predict the birds you're likely to see on a birding trip. That's a big help. If you know what you're likely to see, you're a lot more likely to see it—and you're a lot more likely to identify it quickly.

If you're planning a visit to an ocean beach in the Northeast, for example, use your field guide to work out in advance what birds you're likely to see. Ditto for any other specific habitat, such as a salt marsh or grassland. It's a good way to learn new birds in a manageable way that also gives you some insight into the ecology of a particular habitat.

Be a Better Birder

Any good book on ecology will give you a useful overview of habitat types. One I like because it has great illustrations is called *Habitats,* edited by Tony Hare (Macmillan, 1994).

A Niche for Everyone

As you watch several different kinds of shorebirds feeding on the same mud flat, ask yourself how so many birds can all share the same habitat. The answer is that within the habitat, each species has staked out a particular *niche*, or preferred place within the habitat.

Rappin' Robin

A bird's **niche** is the role it plays within its habitat: where and how it eats, nests, lives, and its preferred place within the habitat.

In the case of the shorebirds, look more closely at their bills. The tiny Sanderlings have short, stubby bills, whereas the Long-billed Curlews have long, slender bills some nine inches long. Both birds can share the same habitat because they occupy different niches within it. The Sanderling feeds on tiny crustaceans it finds just below the surface of the sand right where the waves ripple in and out; the Long-billed Curlew feeds on worms it pulls from deep burrows higher up the beach in the mud flats.

A Little Bird Told Me...

The classic research on niches was done by the distinguished biologist Robert MacArthur in 1958. MacArthur studied five warbler species—Cape May, Yellow-rumped, Black-throated Green, Bay-breasted, and Blackburnian—that all seemed to share the same niche of mature spruce, fir, and pine trees. Because by definition a niche can't be shared, MacArthur took a closer look. He discovered that each species foraged for insects in a *different part* of the tree. They shared the same trees in the coniferous forest habitat but occupied distinct niches within it.

Edges and Hedges

Rappin' Robin

The **edge effect** is the increase in the number of different birds that happens wherever different habitats meet.

I talked a little bit about the *edge effect* in Chapter 3, "Your First Field Trip." Any sort of border area where habitats meet—where a field meets the woods or where natural water meets the desert—will have a lot of different birds. Why? Where habitats meet, there's a larger variety of vegetation at different levels above the ground. That means more different kinds of foods (such as nectar, seeds, berries, and the insects they attract) and more places to nest and shelter, which in turn means more bird species. When you're out birding, look for tangles of mixed vegetation and you'll find birds.

Swamps and Marshes

Swamps and *marshes* are really productive places to go birding. They have a variety of vegetation at different heights, and they're rich in the insects and other creepy-crawlies birds like to eat.

From a new birder's point of view, swamps and marshes have two advantages: a lot of birds and easy watching. At many preserves and refuges, boardwalks take you through the area slightly above the ground. You walk along easily without getting your feet wet or disturbing the vegetation. For an outstanding boardwalk that's more than two miles long, visit Corkscrew Swamp, a National Audubon Society sanctuary near Naples, Florida. The boardwalk winds through virgin stands of bald cypress, slash pine, and saw palmetto, giving you great views of birds such as wood storks—and also all the other fascinating plant and animal life.

Some wetlands are manmade or have been modified by humans, often in the name of flood or mosquito control; Merritt Island National Wildlife Refuge in the shadow of the Kennedy Space Center is a good example. Dikes in this saltwater marsh make an easy driving loop; you can see the birds without ever leaving your car. Another good example is one of my favorite places, Jamaica Bay National Wildlife Refuge in New York City. The smooth, broad path around West Pond lets you amble along for almost two miles and easily enjoy some of the finest birding in the Northeast.

Rappin' Robin

Swamps and **marshes** are both **wetlands**—low-lying areas that are saturated with water. The difference between them is mainly in the vegetation. A swamp has shrubby vegetation such as buttonbush and arrowwood and moisture-loving trees such as red maple, alder, and black willow. A marsh has mostly grasses, sedges, and rushes such as cattails and phragmites.

Be a Better Birder

It's counterintuitive, but sometimes, you'll see more birds if you stay in your car. Birds don't seem to realize that a car contains people, so you can use it as a portable blind—one that comes with heat and air-conditioning.

When you visit a wetlands, don't forget to look up. You'll see raptors such as kites, Northern Harriers, Ospreys, and Kestrels silently gliding and hovering as they prowl for their next meal. You'll also see flocks, strings, and wedges of waterfowl coming and going, herons flapping and gliding, and warblers and sparrows flitting around.

Rappin' Robin

A **hotspot** is a place that, because of its rich habitat and geographic location, is particularly attractive to birds—and birders.

Hotspots: Where the Birds Are

Birds are everywhere, especially once you get a little experience and know where to look. Even so, some places have more birds than others—and some places reliably have a *lot* of birds. In birder talk, a place where a variety of birds is found in abundance is called a *hotspot*. As I discuss more in Chapter 6, "Birding Through the Year," and Chapter 29, "Hotspots and Rare Birds," there are tons of great birding hotspots all over North America; chances are good there's one near you. Once you get to a hotspot, you'll see why it's so attractive to the birds. The habitat is usually rich in the food, water, and shelter birds need.

The Least You Need to Know

➤ A bird's range is the broad geographical area in which it's found. Some birds have separate summer and winter ranges.

➤ Within its range, a bird will be found in its preferred habitat—a particular part of the environment, such as a desert or marsh.

➤ Within its habitat, a bird will be found in a part of the habitat it prefers, such as the reeds around a pond.

➤ You can use your knowledge of a bird's range and habitat to help identify it.

➤ By knowing which birds you're likely to see in a particular habitat, you have a better chance of spotting them.

➤ Hotspots are areas of rich habitat that attract a variety of birds in large numbers.

Birding Through the Year

One of the best things about birding is that unlike many other outdoor hobbies—skiing or golf, say—you can do it all year right in your own neighborhood. Watching the seasonal changes in bird life is a fascinating aspect of birding. Bird activity peaks during some seasons of the year, but no matter when you're watching, there's always something interesting to see.

Understanding Migration

Aristotle, the first writer about the natural world, seriously believed that swallows spent the winter hibernating in the mud at the bottom of ponds. He was writing in the fourth century B.C., of course. Even so, it wasn't until the 1700s that anyone's ideas about bird *migration* got more advanced.

Bird migration is an extremely interesting subject, one that I could write a whole book about. You'll be glad to learn that here, I talk about it only in the practical sense of how migration affects the birds you see.

Rappin' Robin

Migration in birds is the seasonal movement of some species from their summer breeding areas to warmer wintering areas.

Be a Better Birder

Not all birds that are supposed to migrate actually do. Most of the robins in your area will probably head south for the winter, but a few will stay, switching from eating bugs to eating fruit and other foods. In recent years, Canada Geese that decide to stay put for the winter have become increasingly common. Why? Nobody really knows.

Who Migrates?

About 80 percent of the birds in North America are migratory to a degree. Most species don't travel all that far. As you'll see when you look at the range maps in your field guide, most migratory species are still in North America over the winter. The ones that migrate farther mostly end up in Mexico and the rest of Central America, but some go as far south as South America, and a few go all the way, ending up in the southern tip of South America and even the Antarctic region. As a general rule, birds that need open water for feeding, such as ducks, geese, herons, sandpipers, plovers, and other wading birds and shorebirds, are highly migratory. So are insect-eating birds such as warblers, swallows, and thrushes. Some hawk species, especially the buteos, are migratory.

What makes migration so interesting to birders is that you get to see a lot of birds that aren't usually found in your area. As they pass through on their way further north or south, migrant birds stop to rest and feed—and give birders a glimpse of them. During migration, you also get to see some birds in large numbers. Swallows, blackbirds, and some other species form huge migratory flocks, sometimes with tens of thousands of birds. Waterfowl such as ducks and geese migrate in large groups, and shorebirds such as Red Knots move through in large waves. (I talk more about migration for raptors, shorebirds, and other species in Part 3, on bird families.)

A Little Bird Told Me...

Migrating birds perform amazing feats of endurance. The Arctic Tern, for instance, breeds in the Arctic and winters in the Antarctic, flying as far as 11,000 miles *each way* to get back and forth—the long-distance record. Red Knots aren't far behind. They nest near Baffin Island and winter in Tierra del Fuego, the southern tip of South America, for a journey of 8,000 miles one way. The Blackpoll Warbler travels from the northeastern coast of the U.S. to the Caribbean coast of South America, a journey that takes almost 90 hours of nonstop flying.

Migration north begins as early as March for some species, but it peaks as the weather warms up in April and May. On the return trip south, some of the shorebirds that nest in the Arctic start heading back as early as July, but most birds wait until into September and October to begin their journey.

Flyways and Migrant Traps

By definition, migration is a seasonal event, but it's actually spread out over a few months in each direction. That's for two reasons. First, each species is on its own schedule, so some migrate sooner or later than others. Second, it takes time for the birds to make their way in each direction. From the time migrating songbirds arrive on the Alabama coast, for example, to the time they arrive in New England can be two weeks or more.

Migrating birds tend to follow the major north–south features of North America. They travel along four major *flyways*—the Atlantic and Pacific coasts, the Mississippi River, and the central region (roughly paralleling the Rockies). Try not to think of flyways as bird highways. The birds don't stick to narrow lanes; they fan out across a broad front along the way.

If you happen to be along the flyway during migration, you'll get to see a lot of birds as they pass through. Many birds migrate at night, when they can't feed and when they're less vulnerable to predators, and land during the day to rest and feed. One big exception to this is hawks, who mostly soar along during the day on the warm air currents. (I talk more about this in Chapter 14, "Hawk Watching.") Birds that catch insects on the wing, such as swallows, also migrate during the day.

When daybreak comes, hungry, tired birds look for some place green to put down. All along the flyways, birders know that *migrant traps* will reliably attract a lot of birds. Migrant traps are everywhere along the flyways; some, such as Cape May in New Jersey and Point Pelee in Ontario, are extremely well-known.

Rappin' Robin

A **flyway** is a major migratory route for birds, usually running along a highly visible geographic feature such as a coastline, river valley, or mountain range. Flyways are more useful for tracking waterfowl and raptors than for song birds, which usually don't follow flyways.

Rappin' Robin

A **migrant trap** is an attractive place along a migration route where birds land to rest and feed before moving on again.

A Little Bird Told Me...

A bunch of very cool web sites let you track bird migration paths using satellite data and interactive and animated maps.

To learn about albatross migration, visit

> The Albatross Project
> **www.wfu.edu/albatross**

To track the migrations of the endangered Whooping Cranes, log on to

> Texas Whooping Cranes
> **www.electrotex.com/aoc/**

You can track Mallard migration at

> Mallard Tracker
> **www/ducks.ca/**

The migrations of cranes and raptors around the world are followed on

> Bird Tracks
> **sdcd.gsfc.nasa.gov/ISTO/Birdtracks/**

You can follow eagles, loons, and other birds as they journey north on

> Wild Wings Heading North
> **north.audubon.org/**

Wood Storks and can be tracked at

> Wildlife Conservation Society
> **www.clark.net/pub/wcsweb/wcssat**

Hummingbird migration can be tracked at:

> Hummingbirds!
> **www.derived.net/hummers**

And for a lot of good information about bird migration in general, check out:

> Smithsonian Migratory Bird Center
> **www.si.edu/natzoo/zooview/smbc**

Migration and the Weather

When the weather's right during migration times, you can get ready for a day of good birding. When it's wrong, you might as well stay in bed. In the spring, good birding weather happens when the winds are from the southwest, pushing the birds north on a wave of warm air. When the winds are against them or the weather is cold and gray, migrating birds tend to stay where they are. That can make them back up along the flyways, just the way a blizzard can strand passengers at the airport. When the birds are stalled or forced down by bad weather, it's called a *fall-out*. If you're at a migrant trap during a fall-out, you can hardly move for all the birds.

When the weather does clear, all those waiting birds take off—sometimes in numbers so large they get picked up on radar screens. That's a bonanza for birders because waves of warblers and other birds will pass through. (I talk more about this in Chapter 19, "Warblers, Warblers, Warblers!") The same thing happens in reverse in the fall. Strong winds from the northwest send waves of hawks heading south.

Spring: Welcome Back

I said at the start that birders can have fun year-round, but I have to admit that spring birding is something special. The birds are in their breeding plumage, which makes them easier to see and identify. Although everything's in bloom, all the leaves haven't come in yet, so the birds are easy to spot in the trees and bushes. The birds are also singing their little heads off as they stake out territory and try to attract a mate. If you manage to catch a warbler wave on a sunny, mild day in May, you'll be in birder heaven.

The spring shorebird migration gives you an opportunity to see one of nature's most amazing spectacles. Every spring, hundreds of thousands of shorebirds gather at *staging grounds* to rest and feed before heading farther north. Places such as the Copper River delta in Alaska, the pothole region of the prairie states and provinces, and the shores of Delaware Bay are crucial to migrating shorebirds.

Rappin' Robin

A **fall-out** happens when migrating birds get stalled along the way by bad weather. The birds back up in large numbers as they wait for the weather to improve.

Rappin' Robin

A **staging ground** is an area where birds, especially shorebirds, gather in large numbers to rest and feed during migration.

Staging a Protest

For a few weeks every May, up to a million shorebirds such as Red Knots, Ruddy Turnstones, and plovers arrive on the shores of Delaware Bay after flying nonstop for 2,000 miles. In an exquisite bit of timing, they hit the beach just as the horseshoe crabs are coming ashore to lay their eggs. The birds gorge on the protein-rich eggs, rest, and then move on. It's a spectacle that's very much worth a visit—and is also very much in danger. Commercial harvesting of horseshoe crabs in the bay has reduced their numbers, which in turn has reduced the amount of food available to the birds at this critical time in their migration. In the past few years, birding and conservation organizations such as the New Jersey Audubon Society have put so much pressure on the officials in Delaware and New Jersey that as of this writing, there's a ban on harvesting the crabs. The ban is a good example of birding economics at work. Thousands of birders come to the area in May to see the sight—and they spend a lot of money while they're there. The ban isn't yet permanent. It will only get that way if birders like you stay involved.

The Lazy Days of Summer

Summer is a pretty quiet time for birders. The birds have found their mates and settled down to nesting and raising their chicks. They've stopped making such a racket, and they've stopped being so visible. In fact, they've gotten downright secretive. In my neighborhood, the Blue Jays, who are usually all over the place making noise, practically disappear during the nesting season.

Summer is a good time for seeing shorebirds. The birds that breed in the high Arctic are already finished with their domestic duties and have started heading south again. The males are often still in their breeding plumage, which makes them a lot easier to identify. (I get into the ins and outs of shorebird ID later in Chapter 16, "Sorting Out the Shorebirds.")

Fall Farewell

By September, the birds are moving into migration mode. This is a good time to be watching. There are a lot of birds to see because all the young that hatched that summer are now fully grown and on their own. The weather is good, the bugs are less annoying, the leaves are coming down, and there's interesting behavior to watch.

For a few weeks before they take off, the birds eat like crazy to stock up on the body fat that fuels their trip. Amazingly, during this time a bird can pack on as much as 10 percent of its body weight in fat every day. Some birds, such as the Blackpoll Warbler, practically double their weight.

Come fall, birds such as swallows, kingbirds, and many others start flocking together, first in smaller groups and then in flocks that may have many thousands of birds. Watching and listening to a massive flock of Red-winged Blackbirds as it swirls in and roosts for the night is an amazing experience.

Pelagic birding—watching birds far out on the ocean—is at its best in the fall as well. That's when you'll see the most species and the largest numbers as the oceanic birds start moving to their winter homes. (Check out Chapter 22, "Birds of the Ocean Blue," for more on this.)

Fall is *the* time of year for hawk watching. Because hawks migrate during the day along uprising currents of air, they tend to follow predictable and visible migration paths. Hawk watches all along the flyways let you see the incredible sight of thousands of hawks soaring past in a day. (I get into this in detail in Chapter 14, "Hawk Watching.")

Winter: Birding in the Cold

With all the migrant birds gone, you might think winter is a quiet time for birding. Not at all. Remember, south is a relative term for a lot of birds. In the Hudson Valley where I live, for instance, winter is when we see Bald Eagles and loons, Dark-eyed Juncos and Snow Buntings. In the summer, these birds are farther north.

Winter along the coastlines also brings some pelagic birds, such as Harlequin Ducks and Oldsquaw, farther south and closer to shore. With a good spotting scope and a bit of luck, you can see them from the beaches.

As the leaves come down in late fall and winter, start looking around for empty nests. I'm always amazed as I look around and see nests that I walked past all summer long and never spotted.

Enjoying Irruptions

Sometimes, the winter brings a special treat for northern birders—an *irruption*. Not to be confused with an eruption (or an eructation, which is just a fancy word for a burp), an irruption is an unusual, irregular movement of birds out of their normal range.

The most common irruptive birds are owls, hawks, and finches such as redpolls and crossbills that are normally found in the northern pine forests and tundra of the subarctic region. (Check out the chart for a more detailed list.) They head south when their normal food supply fails for some reason. Snowy Owls, for instance, eat mostly lemmings and other small rodents. The lemming population tends to build up over a few years and then crash dramatically. When it crashes every fourth year or so, birders get to see Snowy Owls as far south as New Jersey. The finches irrupt when the conifer seeds they depend on fail, usually after a dry summer. Check your local rare bird alerts over the winter; if there's an irruption going on, it'll be reported. To see animated maps of irruptions as they happen, check out the Web site for Project FeederWatch at **http://birdsource.cornell.edu**.

Splat!

Hypothermia and frostbite are hazards for birders who spend time outdoors in cold weather—during a Christmas Bird Count, for example. Hypothermia is a dangerous drop in body temperature caused by prolonged exposure to cold, windy, or wet weather. Frostbite means that the skin and tissue beneath the skin have frozen. These serious conditions need immediate medical care. Refer to any good book on first aid.

Rappin' Robin

An **irruption** is an unusual, irregular movement of birds out of their normal range usually due to a food shortage.

Irruptive Birds

Owls

Great Gray Owl
Hawk Owl
Long-eared Owl
Short-eared Owl
Snowy Owl

Hawks

Northern Goshawk
Rough-legged Hawk

Finches

Cassin's Finch
Common Redpoll
Hoary Redpoll
Pine Grosbeak
Pine Siskin
Purple Finch
Red Crossbill
Rosy Finch
White-winged Crossbill

Jays

Clark's Nutcracker
Pinyon Jay
Steller's Jay

Other Birds

Bohemian Waxwing
Boreal Chickadee
Evening Grosbeak
Northern Shrike
Red-breasted Nuthatch

Crazy Mixed-Up Birds

Sometimes, a bird turns up where it's really not supposed to be. It might have gotten off course in migration or been pushed around by a storm. (Some birders look forward to hurricanes for the birds they bring in.) Sometimes, the bird is a young one with an adventurous streak or maybe just a lousy sense of direction. Whatever the reason, we're beyond irruption now. These stray birds are known as vagrants or accidentals. It's not that uncommon for a vagrant to be a little out of its normal range, but sometimes vagrants are off by thousands of miles. When they're spotted, they cause such a sensation that I have to talk about it in another chapter; check out Chapter 29, "Hotspots and Rare Birds."

The Least You Need to Know

➤ Migration in the spring and fall affects the majority of North American birds.

➤ During migration, birds that aren't normally found in your area might pass through. You can also see birds in large flocks.

➤ Birding is a year-round hobby. The birds are most visible and abundant in the spring and fall.

➤ In the summer and winter, the birding is still good. Summer is a good time for shorebirds, and winter brings some birds of the far north farther south.

Chapter 7

Understanding Bird Behavior

In This Chapter

➤ How bird behavior helps in identification

➤ How and what birds eat

➤ Understanding breeding behavior

➤ Territorial behavior

➤ Birds in flight

What makes birding so interesting isn't just seeing and identifying birds. It's *watching* them—seeing what they do and trying to understand why. You'll be amazed at the way you zoom up the learning curve when you start behavior watching. There's nothing like seeing a bird do something interesting to help you identify it and remember it—so you'll identify it again faster the next time you see it. Even if you're seeing birds you've seen a zillion times before, watching their behavior keeps them interesting.

Table Manners

Birds have more unusual ways of feeding than a set of three-year-old quintuplets. In fact, different birds have such specific ways of feeding that watching how a bird eats is an excellent clue for identifying it. Because birds spend a lot of time looking for food, you get to spend a lot of time watching them do it. Let's take a closer look at feeding strategies.

Feeling Peckish

Pecking—picking up food such as seeds and insects from the ground—is one of the most common feeding strategies. If you want to see it in action, just toss out your sandwich crust the next time you eat lunch in a park. You'll see pecking behavior in a hurry as the pigeons, starlings, and House Sparrows descend on it. In the woods, sparrows such as towhees and White-throated Sparrows use their feet to stir up the leaf litter and reveal hidden food. When you're out birding, listen for the rustling noises these birds make as they toss the leaves around.

Be a Better Birder

Many birds that peck have conical beaks—and birds with conical beaks are usually grosbeaks, buntings, sparrows, or finches. Large gallinaceous (chicken-like) birds such as grouse and Wild Turkeys also peck. In addition, blackbirds and corvids (crow-like birds) have somewhat conical bills and also peck somewhat. If the bird pecks while feeding, you can narrow down the possibilities of which family it's in.

Probing into Things

When you see a robin walk across your lawn, stop and stab its beak into the ground, and come with a worm, you're seeing probing in action. Birds such as thrushes probe for their food—usually insects, worms, and other creepy-crawlies—with long, pointed bills. Nuthatches and Brown Creepers use their long, thin bills to probe into crevices, such as in tree bark, in search of insects and other food. (Nuthatches also store seeds in crevices and come back later to find them.)

As you might expect from their long, thin bills, the champion probers are the shorebirds. You can easily see this as you watch sandpipers poking their bills into the sand and mud to catch little crabs and other critters. The way a shorebird probes is an identity clue. Dowitchers, for instance, probe rapidly up and down; they look exactly like sewing machines. Plovers and willets, on the other hand, tend to probe slowly and deliberately.

Perch-Gleaning

Warblers, chickadees, titmice, kinglets, and some other birds find insects, insect eggs, spiders, and other good stuff by foraging rapidly among the leaves and twigs of trees and bushes. The birds perch on a twig, quickly poke around for food, and then flit to the next twig. In general, when you see a small bird moving energetically through the trees and underbrush, you're seeing it perch-glean. This is a useful way to distinguish between warblers and other small, acrobatic birds and other tree-hugging birds such as vireos.

To see perch-gleaning close up, watch the chickadees at your feeder. They swoop in, grab a sunflower seed, and then fly off to hammer it open someplace else.

On the Fly

Flycatching (also called *hawking*) for prey is common among insect-eating birds. Naturally, members of the flycatcher family, such as phoebes, have perfected the art. They perch quietly someplace, sometimes pumping their tails slowly up and down, and then suddenly dart out, grab a flying insect, and return to their perch or one nearby.

Other birds, such as Red-eyed Vireos, Cedar Waxwings, and American Redstarts, also catch bugs on the wing.

If you want to see flycatching in action, check out an overgrown field on a warm summer morning. You're almost certain to see a kingbird, phoebe, or some other member of the flycatcher family zoom out from a handy perch on a branch, fence post, or utility wire.

Rappin' Robin

Birds such as phoebes *flycatch* or *hawk* to catch flying insects. These birds perch somewhere, zoom out and catch an insect, and then land on a nearby perch again. Birds such as swallows and swifts catch their prey by *aerial pursuit*—they chase flying insects on the wing, without perching in between catches.

Plucky Little Birds

Many birds eat fruits, berries, and seeds that they pluck directly from the plants. Cedar Waxwings, for instance, love to eat berries, wild grapes, and wild cherries. In my yard, small flocks of these elegant birds land on my mulberry tree and eat their fill, sometimes politely passing the berries to each other. Likewise, goldfinches land on the seed heads of thistles and glean the seeds. A great way to see this sort of behavior is to stake out a food source, such as a patch of ripe berries, and wait to see which birds come along.

Eating Like a Bird

Birds eat in plenty of other ways. Turnstones, for instance, use their thin, slightly upcurved bills to flip over shells and pebbles on the beach and then snatch up whatever they uncover. You can't miss this sort of feeding behavior when you see it. Here's a rundown of other behaviors to watch:

➤ **On the wing:** Birds such as swallows, swifts, and nighthawks catch insects on the wing. Watch for swallows swooping to catch bugs wherever there's an open field, pond, lake, or swampy area.

➤ **Plunging:** Kingfishers, terns, pelicans, and Ospreys plunge into the water from the air to catch fish and other prey. If you're birding near fresh water and hear a loud splash, look around for a kingfisher perched somewhere nearby. Many raptors use the same behavior over land, only in this case it is referred to as stooping.

➤ **Grazing:** Geese, including Snow Geese and Canada Geese, graze on grass and other vegetation by pulling it up or biting it off. If you see a large bird that seems to be nibbling the ground, it's a goose.

A Little Bird Told Me...

If you've ever used the phrase "She eats like a bird" to describe someone who's a very light or picky eater, think again. Relative to their size, birds eat a lot. A Bald Eagle eats on average about two pounds of fish a day, or about a quarter of its body weight—the equivalent of 30 pounds of food for a 120-pound human. And although some birds are more than a little fussy about what they eat—the Snail Kite eats only apple snails—there's hardly anything that some bird doesn't eat. Great Horned Owls even eat skunks!

➤ **Dabbling:** Surface-feeding ducks such as mallards dabble; they upend themselves in the water and feed on underwater vegetation, insects, and invertebrates such as snails while waggling their rumps in the air. How a duck feeds is such an important identity clue that I talk about it more in Chapter 18, "Ducks and Geese."

➤ **Diving:** Diving birds float on the water's surface and then submerge completely in pursuit of food, usually underwater vegetation and small critters such as insects, snails, crayfish, and clams. Diving ducks—ducks usually found in open water—do this. In places where several duck species share the water, watching how they feed is a good way to get started in sorting them out. Other diving birds include grebes, anhingas, and cormorants. Grebes are fun to watch; they don't dive so much as just sink slowly out of sight, like submarines.

➤ **Stalking:** Some herons and egrets stalk their prey—fish, frogs, snakes, and the like—by standing in the shallows or moving slowly and silently along the edge. To me, herons are the Zen masters among birds. A Great Blue Heron stands for moments on end in the shallow water, motionless but deeply intent, and then darts with lightning speed and unerring accuracy to snatch its prey from the water.

➤ **Surface feeding:** Gulls, shearwaters, and other sea birds pluck their food, mostly small fish and crustaceans, from the surface of the water. You can easily see this by tossing anything remotely edible to a Herring Gull. (For more on sea birds, see Chapter 17, "Terns and Gulls," and Chapter 22, "Birds of the Ocean Blue.")

➤ **Piracy:** The dark side of birds. Some birds get their food by stealing it from other birds. Gulls do this now and then, but the aptly named Parasitic Jaeger is the absolute master. This bird feeds almost entirely by harassing a tern until it drops the fish it's carrying.

➤ **Scavenging:** Vultures, crows, and gulls are nature's clean-up crew. These birds eat carrion—dead animals. Vultures eat pretty much nothing but carrion; Bald Eagles often eat carrion, especially dead fish. Gulls and crows are more flexible and will eat any sort of garbage. In fact, once you get to be a fanatic birder, you'll make a special pilgrimage to the dump in Brownsville, Texas, just to see the Mexican Crows that fly across the border to eat the trash.

➤ **Commensal feeding:** An interesting aspect of feeding behavior, *commensa feeding* happens when one bird species finds food as a result of another's activity. A good example is the way cormorants at the shore stir up prey when they dive; other birds, such as Snowy Egrets, follow along and snatch up the food dislodged by the cormorants. Likewise, Cattle Erets follow cows and catch the insects the animals stir up with their hooves.

Rappin' Robin

Even humans get into the act of **commensal feeding**. Watch your lawn the next time you mow it. When you're done, robins and other birds will come in to eat the bugs you stirred up.

The Birds and the Bees

Forget the bees; let's stick to birds. Attracting a mate and raising a family takes up a major part of a bird's life. As you'd expect, it also leads to a lot of interesting behavior. All that singing, for instance, is often an important part of breeding behavior; in fact, it's so important that I talk about it more in Chapter 11, "Birding by Ear." For now, bear in mind that male birds are basically saying two connected things with their songs. The first is the obvious one: "Ladies, I'm over here—and look how gorgeous I am. Don't you want me to father your children?" The second is a little more subtle: "Hey, you guys, this is my territory; keep out! And ladies, see what a great territory I have? And see how well I keep those other guys from muscling in? Don't you want me to father your children?"

In most cases, the female birds listen to all this, check out the territory, check out the other male birds, and make their choice. When you hear a male bird singing, then, there could be a female bird nearby. Keep looking and you'll probably spot her.

In some birds, the courtship process is a little more complicated. Here are a few bits of behavior you might spot:

➤ **Courtship feeding:** Some male birds show females what good providers they are (at least that's the way humans tend to interpret it) by bringing them food. You

Rappin' Robin

A **lek** is an open area where male birds such as ruffs, grouse, Prairie Chickens, and even some hummingbirds gather to compete with each other in displays before the females. The display behavior is called lekking behavior.

can spot courtship feeding easily if you have a bird feeder. Watch the cardinals, chickadees, and Mourning Doves carefully in the spring. You might see a male gently place a sunflower seed in the female's mouth. Some warblers, herons, terns, and gulls also do courtship feeding.

➤ **Lekking:** Some birds, most notably Prairie Chickens, put on a sort of group dance performance. The male birds gather in an open area called a *lek* and "dance" for the females, who gather on the edges and watch. The most energetic couple of dancers get to mate with the females; the wimpier males are ignored.

➤ **Aerial displays:** Male hummingbirds attract females by zooming around in front of them and showing off their flying ability. Male woodcocks also do spectacular aerial displays. At dusk, a male woodcock sits out in an open field making distinctive *peent* sounds. After a while, he takes off and flies in an upward spiral that can take him up to 200 feet above ground. As he flies up, his wing feathers make a distinctive whistling noise. At the top of the spiral, the woodcock circles for a bit and then comes down in steep dives and starts the whole thing all over again. Other birds that do aerial displays of various sorts include Chimney Swifts, Mourning Doves, plovers, and American Goldfinches. Many raptors, such as Bald Eagles, do spectacular aerial displays that include steep dives and flight acrobatics.

A Little Bird Told Me...

Great Blue Herons nest in colonies called heronries. As part of the mating ritual, the male heron brings a nice stick to the nest, presents it to the female, does a little jig, and then flies off in a short loop. It's a spectacular sight. There's a heronry not far from my house that can easily be seen from the side of a fairly busy road if you have a spotting scope. I often stop by in early spring. Every time, at least two people stop to ask what I'm looking at. Of course, I show them. I can't tell you how many times someone has said, "I've driven past here for years and never noticed."

➤ **Dances:** This is a pretty general term for the many ways birds do ritual movements as part of forming pair bonds. Gulls, albatrosses, cranes, and others do "dances" to attract females and strengthen the pair bond. Dancing birds are unmistakable. No matter what motions are involved—bowing, bill movements, stretching, and the like—they're very exaggerated.

➤ **Swimming displays:** Some waterbirds, such as grebes and loons, form pairs and race madly through the water together in a special upright posture. These birds, and also many ducks, also do elaborate courtship displays and dances in the water. Once you see this sort of thing, you'll finally understand why some people go in for synchronized swimming (although I still don't understand why it is an Olympic sport).

Most birds don't have elaborate courtship displays, but as you get more attuned to bird behavior, you'll start to notice the subtler stuff. Even if you don't spot the courtship behavior, you're likely to see birds with twigs, grass, and other nesting material in their mouths.

Birds get very cautious during the nesting season. They'll take roundabout routes to get to their nests and won't go to them at all if they think someone's watching. If you notice a bird behaving nervously—sitting very erect, flicking its wings and tail, wiping its bill, or doing other fidgety things—chances are good the nest is nearby. You're keeping the bird from taking care of business. Leave quietly.

Keep Off!

Staking out and defending a *territory* takes up a lot of a bird's time. Territorial behavior is extremely interesting—and very easy—to watch. Take the common Red-winged Blackbird, for instance. The male bird has handsome, glossy black feathers with brilliant red shoulder patches. (The females are a streaky brown and white—they look like overgrown sparrows.) Especially in the spring, you can easily watch a male patrolling his territory. The bird will glide slowly from perch to perch around the boundaries, flashing his red patches the whole time. Any other male who dares to invade will be chased off, with much flashing of patches. Flight displays such as this are common, especially among birds of open areas where they're easy to see. Watch for flight displays when you're looking at shore-birds. Don't stop watching when the bird lands. The display sometimes continues, with strutting around, head bobbing, and other behavior.

Splat!

If you notice a nesting bird, stay away. Checking on the nest stresses the birds. It also gives it away to predators such as raccoons, foxes, crows, and cats.

Rappin' Robin

A bird's **territory** is an area it stakes out and defends against other birds of the same species. Territories are usually used as feeding and breeding areas.

Singing is another way of defining a territory. A male bird will perch somewhere conspicuous, sing loudly for a bit, and then fly off to another conspicuous spot along the perimeter of its territory and repeat the performance. If you watch long enough, you'll get a pretty good idea of the size and shape of the territory.

Once you know what to look for, you'll see territorial behavior everywhere. Even those cute little chickadees chase off interlopers. Generally speaking, if you see one bird chasing another of the same species or of the same sex, you're seeing a border skirmish. The fighting is usually limited to flying at each other, chasing, and squawking, but sometimes it escalates into a real tussle; feathers may even fly. Don't worry and don't interfere. It's very rare for either of the birds to be hurt.

Don't Distract Me

Here's a scenario that scares the daylights out of beginning birders. You're birding along in an old field when you notice an injured Killdeer, dragging one wing pathetically and giving pitiful chirps. You follow along for a hundred yards or so, making plans all the while for taking the bird to the local animal rescue center, when suddenly the bird flies off. What happened? The Killdeer was doing a *distraction display*—in this case, faking an injury to lure you away from her nest. Worked pretty well, didn't it?

Rappin' Robin

To lure predators away from their nests, many ground-nesting birds do **distraction displays**. They distract the predator by pretending to be injured or imitating a rodent.

Pretending to be injured is a common distraction display among ground-nesting birds such as Killdeer, Nighthawks, sandpipers, and many shorebirds and waterfowl. Another common distraction display is called rodent running. The bird distracts a predator such as a fox away from the nest by darting off through the grass just like a field mouse. A lot of shorebirds do this; so do some songbirds.

What Big Eyes You Have

Birds have really sharp eyesight. It's hard to make an exact comparison with human eyesight, but most ornithologists agree that a typical bird can see at least twice as well as a typical human. The main reason is that birds have very large eyes. A starling's eyes, for instance, take up about 15 percent of the weight of its head; your eyes are only about 1 percent of the weight of your head. In fact, although a Great Horned Owl is considerably smaller than you, its eyes are as large as yours. Ostriches, the largest birds on earth, also have the largest eyes of any vertebrate animal—larger than those of whales and elephants.

You'll often see a bird cock its head or bob its head up and down. Head-cocking might seem as if the bird is listening because that's what humans do when they want to locate a sound. Actually, the bird is tilting its head to focus the fovea of its eye—the area of sharpest vision—on whatever it's looking at. Songbirds do this a lot. Waterfowl, shorebirds, pigeons, and some other birds such as turkeys bob their heads a lot, probably to get greater depth perception. Some birds, such as the Spotted and Solitary sandpipers, bob and teeter constantly.

Birds see colors far more intensely than humans, and they can also see into the ultraviolet spectrum. The next time you're feeling philosophical, imagine what that must be like.

Preening and Cleaning

Birds spend a lot of time *preening* to keep their feathers in good shape. You can easily see this when a bird seems to "nibble" its feathers or run its bill along them. The bird is smoothing the feathers, reconnecting the barbs that hold them together, and removing dirt and annoying parasites such as ticks and fleas. Most birds have special glands at the base of their tails that produce an oily substance. The birds use their bills to spread the oil over their feathers. Especially in the case of waterbirds, the oil probably helps waterproof the feathers, but ornithologists still aren't really sure if that's the only purpose of the oil. Whatever the reason, when a bird ducks its head under its tail and then preens, it's spreading the oil on its feathers.

An interesting feather behavior you might spot is called *allopreening,* or mutual preening. This happens when one bird preens another of the same species. Usually mated pairs allopreen, but sometimes unrelated birds do it. Allopreening is fairly common, but you're most likely to spot it among the waterbirds such as ducks and geese. A lot of other birds, including herons, gulls, crows, blackbirds, and jays, also do it.

Birds also take baths—in water or in dust—to clean off excess oil and get rid of feather pests. To learn more about their bathing behavior, check out Chapter 26, "Wet and Wild."

Birds on the Wing

Birds take such good care of their feathers because they're essential for flying. Whole books have been written about bird flight (a good one is *How Birds Fly,* by David Goodnow), so I stick to the real basics here.

Rappin' Robin

Preening is how a bird maintains its feathers in good condition by cleaning, smoothing, and arranging them with its bill. **Allopreening** is the preening of one bird by another of the same species.

Be a Better Birder

How a bird flies is a clue for identifying it, especially when it comes to larger birds such as ducks and geese. Look for the position of the head relative to the wings. Swans fly with their heads extended, whereas loons fly with their heads lower than their bodies. Whistling Ducks, ibises, herons, and some other birds fly with their feet hanging out beyond their tails.

A bird's wing is often described as an airfoil; seen in cross-section, the wing is shaped like an elongated tear drop, with the narrowest part at the back, or trailing edge, of the wing. (Actually, because evolution invented the wing long before humans invented the airfoil, the comparison should really be the other way around.) As the bird moves horizontally through the air by flapping its wings, the leading edge of the wing "splits" the air. This makes the air flowing over the curved upper surface of the wing travel a longer distance than the air flowing under the bottom of the wing. The air flowing over the top surface of the wing moves faster, which means it exerts less pressure. (You might remember this from learning about Bernoulli's law back in high-school physics class.) The higher pressure underneath the wing forces it up, providing lift. When the lift is equal to or greater than the bird's weight, the bird flies.

Although the basic principles are always the same, there's a lot of variation in wing shape and flight styles among bird species. The shape of the wings and how the bird flies tell you a lot about the bird. Check out a flying bird to see what I mean. Look at the wing shape (the aspect ratio, if you want to get technical). Birds with long, narrow wings (a high aspect ratio) are good at high-speed gliding; watch a gull to see what I mean. Birds with short, rounded wings (a low aspect ratio) are better at quick take-offs and maneuverability; watch a Ruffed Grouse for a good example. Generally speaking, birds found in open areas—kestrels and swallows, for example—have wings with pointed tips. This design is fast and efficient because it has very little drag, but it's not particularly maneuverable. Wings designed for soaring, as in hawks and vultures, have easily visible slots between the primary feathers at the wingtips. Air gets forced upward through the slots, which improves lift by reducing turbulence, letting these birds soar for hours with very little effort.

The Least You Need to Know

➤ If you don't know what bird you're seeing, keep watching. How a bird behaves gives you a lot of clues to its identity.

➤ How and what a bird eats tells you a lot about it. Feeding behavior is an excellent identity clue.

➤ Breeding behavior, including singing and various kinds of displays, is distinctive. Every bird species has its own particular way of attracting a mate.

➤ Birds stake out and defend feeding and breeding territories. Watching this behavior can help you identify the bird.

➤ The way a bird flies helps you easily figure out what family it's in and is often a good hint for deciding what species it is.

Part 3
Keeping Track

Has your family ever had one of those giant reunions, the kind where everyone from your sister to your great-great-aunt to your fourth cousins once removed show up? If you have, you know how confusing all those relations can be. Checking out the family tree makes it a lot easier to understand who's related to who and how.

It's the same with all the bird families. Once you understand how the different families are related, and how the birds within the family relate to each other, you'll be able to identify the birds you see a lot better.

Keeping track of the birds you see is one of the more creative areas of birding. Start with your basic life list—a list of all the birds you've ever seen—and take it from there.

Chapter 8

Putting the Pigeons in the Right Holes

In This Chapter

➤ Understanding bird families

➤ Species and subspecies

➤ How birds get their names

➤ Lumps, splits, and changes

When I was kid, we used to play the guessing game Twenty Questions in the back seat on long car rides. (I think it drove my parents a little crazy to have to listen to it.) You remember how the game goes. The traditional first question is, "Animal, vegetable, or mineral?" From there, you ask questions that narrow down the possibilities more and more, until finally you come up with the answer—whatever it was the other person had in mind. Well, playing Twenty Questions is good training for understanding bird taxonomy.

Nine Thousand Ways to Be a Bird

Worldwide, there are about 9,700 bird species. That's a lot of birds. How can you keep track of them all, much less identify them? The answer lies in *taxonomy,* the scientific system used to classify all living things.

Taxonomy works by placing all living things into an exact spot in a hierarchical system. It's the basic filing system for all biology. Stick with me here as I explain the system from top to bottom:

➤ **Kingdom:** The broadest taxonomic classification. Birds belong to the animal kingdom.

➤ **Phylum:** Birds belong to the phylum Chordata, meaning animals that have a notochord, a rodlike structure that's a primitive backbone or from which the backbone develops.

➤ **Class:** Here's where all birds, living and extinct, literally get into a class of their own—Aves, from the Latin word for bird. Taxonomically, we've reached the definition of a bird: a warm-blooded animal with feathers and wings that lays large, yolky eggs with chalky shells. To sum it up, if it has feathers, it's a bird— and if it's a bird, it belongs in the class *Aves*.

➤ **Order:** The class *Aves* is divided up further into about 30 orders, or groups of families.

Rappin' Robin

Taxonomy (pronounced tax-ON- oh-mee) is the standard hierarchical system used to classify and arrange the birds (and other animals and plants), based on their similarities and differences and their degree of evolutionary closeness. The word comes from the Greek word *taxis*, meaning arrangement, and *nomos*, meaning law.

Be a Better Birder

The concept of family is important to birding. Once you have a firm grasp of the various bird families and their characteristics, you can probably make a good guess at the family an unfamiliar bird is in. Once you've got a bird into the right family, you've on the way to identifying it.

➤ **Families:** A family is a group of broadly related birds. A good example is Picidae, or the woodpecker family. (I explain what those funny scientific names mean a little later in this chapter.) By observing their physical appearance and their behavior, you can easily see that all the woodpeckers are related. All told, there are about 160 bird families.

➤ **Genus:** Families are divided up into *genera* (that's the plural of *genus*), or groups of closely related species. Let's take the woodpeckers again. If you look at all of the 210 or so members of the family, some will seem more closely related than others, just as you're more closely related to your brothers and sisters—and look and act more like them—than you are to your third cousins, even though you're all genetically related. All the different sapsuckers, for instance, are a genus within the woodpecker family.

➤ **Species:** Here's what this whole long list has been aiming at. The *species* is the fundamental unit of taxonomy. A bird species is one that is closely related to other members of its genus but can't interbreed with them. Within the sapsucker genus, in North America there are four separate species. Each species is unique unto itself, both in appearance and behavior, and doesn't inter- breed with any other sapsucker species.

➤ **Subspecies** (sometimes called races): Some species have subspecies—a population within

Color Clues

A male Mountain Bluebird preens a wing. The beautiful turquoise blue of this bird is hard to miss. Photo by Cliff Beittel.

The male Scarlet Tanager has a vivid red body and jet-black wings and tail. Photo by Kathy Adams Clark/KAC Productions

Bill Collecting

Herons have long, spearlike bills, the better to snatch fish, frogs, and other prey from shallow water. An adult Great Blue Heron such as this can stand four feet tall. Photo by Cliff Beittel.

How does the Long-billed Curlew get its name? Guess. The decurved (down-curving) bill can reach eight inches in length. Photo by Cliff Beittel.

If a description of the bill is part of the common name, look for it, as in this Roseate Spoonbill. Photo by Richard Day/Daybreak Imagery.

The Crowning Touch

The Tufted Titmouse is one of the most common visitors to bird feeders. The tufted crest is easy to see. Photo by Richard Day/ Daybreak Imagery.

A Pileated Woodpecker feeds its young at the nest. The brilliant red head crest on this crow-sized woodpecker is an easy field mark. Photo by John and Gloria Tveten/KAC Productions.

Heads Up!

Eyestripes are a bit hard to see at first, but with a little practice you'll pick them up quickly. This Chipping Sparrow has a white eyebrow stripe and a black eyeline stripe. Photo by Cliff Beittel.

The Red-headed Woodpecker has a solid red head (you were expecting some other color?). Look carefully at this picture and you'll see the zygodactylic toes—two facing forward and two facing backward. Also note the way the bird braces itself with its tail feathers—this is very characteristic of woodpeckers. Photo by Richard Day/ Daybreak Imagery.

You know this bird is in the wren family from the upcocked tail. The very conspicuous white eyebrow stripe tells you it's a Carolina Wren. Photo by Cliff Beittel.

The vivid black and white stripes on the head of the White-crowned Sparrow are easy to spot. Look also for the pinkish bill. Photo by Connie Toops.

The American Tree Sparrow has a rufous (rusty red) crown, a rufous stripe behind the eye, and a faint rufous moustachial stripe. The breast is gray, with a dark central spot. Photo by Richard Day/ Daybreak Imagery.

The well-defined white patch under the chin tells you this is a White-throated Sparrow. Photo by Richard Day/Daybreak Imagery.

Everything about the Painted Bunting is a vivid color, including the eye ring. Photo by John and Gloria Tveten/ KAC Productions.

Practice spotting eye rings on the very common Mourning Dove. Photo by Richard Day/Daybreak Imagery.

Body Parts

The Northern Mockingbird has large white patches on its wings and tail—they're unmistakable when the bird is in flight. This bird is carrying nesting material in its mouth. Photo by Cliff Beittel.

Markings on the breast (chest) are good identity clues, as in the red triangle on this male Rose-breasted Grosbeak. Other good field marks for this bird are the large, heavy bill and white wing patches. Photo by Richard Day/Daybreak Imagery.

The Golden-winged Warbler has bright yellow wing patches and a bright yellow crown that contrast beautifully with its gray plumage. Photo by John and Gloria Tveten/KAC Productions.

Warblers are small, active, brightly colored birds. This Yellow-rumped Warbler gets its name from the bright yellow patch above the tail. Look also for the small, thin warbler bill and the bright yellow patches on the wings and head. Photo by Richard Day/Daybreak Imagery.

Where Are You?

Where you are helps you figure out what the bird is. This heavily barred bird is wren-like, with a thin bill and conspicuous white eyebrow stripe, and it's standing on a saguaro cactus. What bird is it? Cactus Wren. Photo by Richard Day/Daybreak Imagery.

Sparrows, like this Song Sparrow, are generally found low to the ground, in the grasses, underbrush, shrubs, and lower tree branches. Song sparrows are very variable, with more than 30 subspecies. Look for the broad gray eyebrow stripe—all the subspecies have it. Photo by Richard Day/ Daybreak Imagery.

What's the Season?

Birds are at their most colorful in the spring, when they're in their bright breeding plumage. This male American Goldfinch is hard to miss. No other bird is bright yellow with black wings and a black cap. Photo by Connie Toops.

Is this khaki-colored bird also an American Goldfinch. Yes—it's a male in winter, nonbreeding plumage. Photo by Richard Day/ Daybreak Imagery.

the species that shows some variation, usually because of geographic separation. The differences aren't enough to keep the subspecies from interbreeding where they meet.

Still with me after all that? I know it's a little complicated, but you can see how important it is. If you understand taxonomy, you understand how the different bird species are related. Your field guide starts to make a lot more sense. That's because it's organized taxonomically by order and then by family, genus, species, and subspecies. The sequence of the birds starts with the most primitive—the oldest in the evolutionary sense—and ends with the most recently evolved birds.

Name That Bird

The whole hierarchical concept of modern taxonomy was laid down by the great Carl Linnaeus in 1735. In Linnaeus' time, every educated person knew Latin and Greek; they were the universal languages of science. Not surprisingly, then, Linnaeus used Latin suffixes to indicate the different levels in his system. Here's how it works:

> **Orders** always have the suffix *-iformes*.

> Example: Passeriformes, the order of perching birds. Orders are always capitalized, never italicized.

> **Families** always have the suffix *-idae*.

> Example: Woodpeckers are all members of the Picidae family. Families are always capitalized, never italicized.

Rappin' Robin

A **genus** (the plural is genera) is a group of organisms with closely similar characteristics. The word comes from the Latin meaning birth, race, or kind. **Species** (the word is both singular and plural) is the fundamental unit of taxonomy. A species is made up of organisms that can interbreed. The word comes from the Latin meaning particular sort or kind.

Be a Better Birder

How do you pronounce those complicated scientific names? It's easier than it looks. Pretend you're speaking Spanish; pronounce every letter, including the ones at the end of the word. Vowels are generally long; in other words, pronounce the letter i as eye. Always put the accent on the next-to-last syllable.

In the Linnaean system, every bird species has a unique, binomial (two-part) name in scientific Latin. The first part of the name is always the genus (always capitalized, always italicized); the second part of the name is the species (always lowercased, always italicized). The Yellow-bellied Sapsucker is, scientifically speaking, *Sphyrapicus varius*. To make life a little simpler, you write out the full binomial the first time you mention the bird; after that, you can abbreviate the genus name to the first letter, as in *S. varius*.

If you have trouble remembering the full binomial names of the bird species, join the club. As I discuss in the next section, common names are a lot easier to remember. Do try to get a feel for the genera names. Birders often talk about larids, for instance, when they're discussing gulls. If you know the genus name, you won't be so mystified. Getting a handle on the genera names is also helpful when you're trying to understand a large family. Knowing the genera helps you break the family into manageable groups and makes the relationships among species clearer.

Common Names

A bird's common name is the name it's usually known by in ordinary colloquial English (or whatever language you happen to speak). Common names used to vary quite a bit, especially in different regions of the country, but today birders use the standardized common names for North American birds set out by the American Ornithologists' Union. Common names are a lot easier to deal with than scientific names. Which name are you more likely to remember, *Pooecetes gramineus* or Vesper Sparrow?

Common names often include important clues to the bird's appearance in them. Red-headed Woodpecker, for instance, tells you a lot about how this bird looks; so does Three-toed Woodpecker. Don't rely too much on the common name, however. The Red-bellied Woodpecker has a red belly, but it's difficult to see between the bird's legs— a much better field mark for this bird is the solid red crown and nape in the male.

Watch out for place names in common names. The Philadelphia Vireo is rarely if ever found in that city; the Tennessee Warbler, a bird that's easy to confuse with the Philadelphia Vireo, is rarely if ever found in Tennessee. Just to confuse you further, the scientific name for the Mourning Warbler is *Opornis philadelphia,* which literally means "a bird passing through Philadelphia." Because this bird is usually found much farther north, the name is probably based on a specimen that was captured as it passed through the city during migration.

A Little Bird Told Me...

The beauty of the binomial system is that the scientific name of a species is always the same, even when the common name changes. For example, the American Woodcock is also sometimes called a timberdoodle or bogsucker, but scientifically speaking, it's always *Scolopax minor.* Likewise, whether the bird is called a yellow-rumped warbler, a myrtle warbler, an Audubon's warbler, or a butter-rump, scientifically it's always *Dendroica coronata.*

Why do birds get such misleading names? The person who first identifies a new species gets the honor of naming it scientifically. Often, the name refers to where the original specimen was collected; the binomial for the very widespread Red-tailed Hawk is *Buteo jamaicensis* because the first specimen to reach Europe came from Jamaica. Often, the scientific name refers to some aspect of the bird's appearance or behavior. When the bird was new to science, whoever named it was often guessing, which is why completely misleading information about a bird is often immortalized in its name. The binomial for the Laughing Gull, for instance, is *Larus atricilla,* which refers to the black band on the tail—but the band is found only in juvenile birds.

Sometimes, the bird was named in honor of its discoverer or in honor of someone else. Bachman's Warbler and the Black Oystercatcher (*Haematopus bachmani*), for instance, were named by John James Audubon in honor of his dear friend the Rev. John Bachman. Two of Audubon's sons married two of Bachman's daughters. Tracing the history and meanings of common and scientific bird names is a lot of fun. You'll learn a lot about ornithological history as you look up the names in one of the many good reference books and dictionaries of bird names. (See Appendix F, "Your Basic Birding Bookshelf," for some titles.) Bird names are also great for trivia questions. Here's one, if you can remember it. What's the bird with the longest scientific name? *Griseotyrannus aurantioatrocristatus,* or Crowned Slaty-Flycatcher; it's got 35 letters.

Being Specific

The taxonomic order seems pretty solid, doesn't it? Actually, it's not; taxonomists shuffle the birds around all the time as they learn more about them. To take a good example, for centuries the North American vultures were thought to be members of the order Falconiformes, which also includes hawks, eagles, kites, and falcons. Recently, after a lot of research and discussion, ornithologists have decided these birds are really members of the order Ciconiiformes, which includes the storks. There will be more of this to come as DNA studies tell us more about the evolutionary relationships of the birds.

Rappin' Robin

A **morph** or **phase** is a normal variation in color or some other aspect of appearance or anatomy within a species. It's enough to be noticeable but not enough to count as a subspecies.

Within a species, there's a certain amount of natural variation that's not quite enough to qualify as a subspecies. Normal variations are called *morphs.* (Sometimes, the term *phase* is used instead.) Many birds have different color morphs. Many hawks, for instance, have dark and light color morphs.

It's Splitsville

Even though a species is the most basic unit in taxonomy, scientists can change their minds about it. Based on studies of a species' range and appearance, researchers might decide that a single species

Rappin' Robin

When ornithologist decide to divide a species into two or more separate species, it's called **splitting.** When they decide to combine two separate species into one, it's called **lumping.**

is really two different species. Alternatively, they might decide that two separate species are really so alike that they're one species.

When a species gets divided, it's called *splitting*; when two species get combined, it's called *lumping*. Sometimes, after deciding to lump or split species, the researchers change their minds. A classic example of this happened with the Baltimore and Bullock's orioles. In 1973, the two species were lumped into the Northern Oriole—only to be split apart again in 1995. In 1997, the Solitary Vireo was split into three species: Blue-headed Vireo, Plumbeous Vireo, and Cassin's Vireo. The Rufous-sided Towhee was split into the Eastern towhee and the Spotted towhee. Now do you see why it's important to use an up-to-date field guide?

Needless to say, splits and lumps can really get your life list tied into knots. If you saw a Plain Titmouse before 1997, you'll have to go back to your field notes and check if you saw it west of the Sierra Nevada, in which case it's now the Oak Titmouse, or in the interior, in which case it's now the Juniper Titmouse. (Better common names for these new species might be plain and plainer titmouse. You'll know what I mean if you ever see them.)

Rappin' Robin

When birds of two species interbreed, the young they produce are **hybrids**, crosses between the two species. About 10 percent of all North American birds can hybridize with a closely related species.

A big reason for deciding to split or lump a species is whether different populations interbreed. The Bullocks' Oriole, found in the west, is pretty different in appearance from the Baltimore Oriole of the east. The rationale for lumping the two was that where the two species meet on the Great Plains, they interbreed and produce *hybrid* young. Ordinarily, hybrids can't reproduce, but in the case of the orioles, the offspring were fertile. Logically, then, that meant the two birds weren't really separate species. The two species had to be lumped. But closer study showed that the hybrid offspring, although fertile, didn't survive as well as purebreds, and eventually, the species was split back.

A Little Bird Told Me...

Not all the birds in the world have been discovered yet. A new species gets discovered once every year or so. The latest find was a species of antpitta found in the Andes Mountains of Ecuador in 1998. Antpittas are secretive, long-legged, short-tailed birds that are found on temperate forest floors ranging from Mexico to Argentina. As the name suggests, antpittas mostly eat ants and other invertebrates that they find on the ground. As of this writing, the new antpitta hasn't been named by its discoverer, ornithologist Robert Ridgely.

Who's in Charge Here?

Who decides all this stuff, anyway? For the birds of North and Central America, it's the American Ornithologists' Union (AOU), which periodically updates its *Checklist of North American Birds*. Distinguished ornithologists on the AOU Checklist Committee review all the evidence for taxonomic and name changes and make their decision, which is then adopted in North America. The changes are published in *The Auk*, the official AOU journal. You can get the latest edition at most large public libraries, or you can buy the whole 883-page checklist from the AOU; it's in its seventh edition.

For birds worldwide, you have your choice of two standard lists; I won't go into the technical differences between them. The first is *Birds of the World: A Check List*, by James F. Clements. Known simply as Clements, this is the official checklist of the American Birding Association. It's now in its fourth edition. The other standard list is *A World Checklist of Birds*, by Burt L. Monroe and Charles G. Sibley, known as Sibley-Monroe. I find Sibley interesting because it's based on DNA evidence, but take your pick—or get both.

> **Be a Better Birder**
>
> The AOU, Sibley, and Clements/ABA checklists are available online from
>
> Birding on the Web: The Next Generation
> **www-stat.wharton.upenn.edu/ ~siler/birdlists**

The Least You Need to Know

➤ Taxonomy is the science of classifying and organizing the 9,700 bird species of the world.

➤ Under the taxonomic system, birds are divided into increasingly smaller groups, until finally we reach the fundamental unit of taxonomy, the species.

➤ Every bird species has a unique two-part scientific name. Birds also have common, or colloquial, names. For example, the bird known scientifically as *Cyanocitta cristata* is known by the common name Blue Jay.

➤ Sometimes, after considerable research and discussion, a bird species is moved in the taxonomic order, combined with another species (lumped) or divided into two species (split).

Chapter 9

List Mania

In This Chapter

➤ Checklists and field notes

➤ The value of listing

➤ Your life list

➤ Lists and more lists

➤ Your birding journal

On the surface, birders are a congenial bunch. You wouldn't think they'd have much in the way of philosophical differences. They all like birds, right? What could they possibly find to argue about? Well, there's always the merits of various binoculars brands, but for a real brouhaha, get a bunch of birders started on listing. Some will passionately defend it. Others will say, with equal passion, that listing gives birding a bad name. Why does listing cause such controversy? Read on.

Check!

Before I get into the ins, outs, and maybes of *listing,* let me explain *checklists,* also known as *field cards.*

In its most basic form, a checklist is simply a list, in taxonomic order (see Chapter 8, "Putting the Pigeons in the Right Holes," for more on bird taxonomy), of all the birds ever found in a particular region or site, with a space or box next to each species. You check off (or tick, if you're from the U.K.) each bird when and if you see it on that particular birding trip.

Rappin' Robin

Listing is the practice of keeping ongoing permanent records of the birds you have seen. A **checklist** or **field card** is a preprinted booklet or folded card listing all the birds known to occur in a particular region or birding site.

Often, a checklist is more complex than a simple list, but this is one of those rare instances where complexity is better than simplicity. That's because a good checklist can be very, very useful for helping you figure out which birds you're seeing; a thorough checklist is crammed with valuable information.

As you'll see from the examples on pages 83 and 84, a checklist generally gives you some idea of when in the year you're most likely to see a particular bird, how abundant it's likely to be, and whether it breeds in the area.

There's usually an explanation or symbol key somewhere at the start of the checklist. Even so, some of the terms are a little confusing, so let's take a closer look.

The Four Seasons

Actually, in birding, there are five or six seasons. The fall migration really has two parts: August and September, when the shorebirds, warblers, flycatchers, and some other birds have already started south, and October and November, when the waterfowl, hawks, and finches are on the move. Many checklists break fall into early fall and late fall; some also break spring into early and late. The seasonal headings on a checklist tell you how likely you are to see a bird at a particular time of year. Migratory birds that are just passing through, for instance, would only be in the area for a relatively brief period in the spring and fall (not necessarily both).

Here's how the seasons usually break out on a field card:

➤ **Spring:** Abbreviated as Sp or s, spring is usually March through May.

➤ **Summer:** Abbreviated Su or S, summer is usually June through August, but in areas with significant shorebird migration, summer is often only June and July.

➤ **Fall:** Abbreviated F, fall is usually September through November.

➤ **Early fall:** Abbreviated eF, early fall means August and September.

➤ **Late fall:** Abbreviated lF, late fall means October and November.

➤ **Winter:** Abbreviated W, winter means December to March.

Birds don't carry Filofaxes, so they might not be exactly where they should be on any particular date. It's not uncommon to see early birds arriving ahead of schedule or to find stragglers hanging around when they should already have left. The seasonal information on any checklist is approximate, but it's still a good guide to what to expect at any given season.

Checklist example. (Also see page 84 for a second example.)

KINGLETS - THRUSHES - THRASHERS

___ Golden-crowned Kinglet	u		u	o
___ Ruby-crowned Kinglet	o		o	o
___ Blue-gray Gnatcatcher	u	o	u	
___ Eastern Bluebird	r	r	r	r
___ Veery	u		o	
___ Gray-cheeked Thrush	o		o	
___ Swainson's Thrush	u		o	
___ Hermit Thrush	u		u	u
___ Wood Thrush	u	o	u	
___ American Robin	c	c	c	u
___ Gray Catbird	c	c	c	r
___ Northern Mockingbird	c	c	c	u
___ Brown Thrasher	u	u	u	r

WAXWINGS - SHRIKES - STARLING

___ Water Pipit			o	r
___ Cedar Waxwing	o	o	o	o
___ Northern Shrike	r		r	r
___ Loggerhead Shrike			r	
___ European Starling	a	a	a	o

VIREOS - WOOD WARBLERS

___ White-eyed Vireo	u	u	u	
___ Solitary Vireo	o		o	
___ Yellow-throated Vireo	r		r	
___ Philadelphia Vireo			o	
___ Red-eyed Vireo	u	u	u	
___ Blue-winged Warbler	u	o	u	
___ Golden-winged Warbler	r		r	
___ Tennessee Warbler	o		r	
___ Nashville Warbler	o		r	
___ Northern Parula	u	o	u	
___ Yellow Warbler	c	c	u	
___ Chestnut-sided Warbler	o		o	
___ Magnolia Warbler	u		u	
___ Cape May Warbler	o		o	

SEASON

s - Spring	March - May
S - Summer	June - August
F - Fall	September - November
W - Winter	December - February

RELATIVE ABUNDANCE

a - abundant	a species which is very numerous.
c - common	certain to be seen or heard in suitable habitat
u - uncommon	present, but not certain to be seen.
o - occasional	seen only a few times during a season.
r - rare	seen at intervals of 2 to 5 years.

Species	B	Sp	Su	eF	lF	W	#
Loon							
Red-throated		R			R	R	
Common		U			U	R	
Grebe							
Pied-billed	Co	U	U	U	U	R	
Horned		C			C	C	
Red-necked						R	
Eared		▼			▼	▼	
Cormorant							
Great					U	U	
Double-crested		A	C	A	C	U	
Bittern							
American	✳	R	R	R	R	R	
Least	Co	R	R	R			
Herons and Egrets							
Great Blue		U	R	U	C	U	
Great Egret	Co	C	C	C	U	R	
Snowy Egret	Co	C	C	A	C	R	
Little Blue	Po	U	U	U	R	R	
Tricolored heron	Po	U	U	U	R	R	
Cattle Egret	Co	U	U	U	R		
Green	Co	U	U	U	R		
Night Heron							
Black-crowned	Co	C	C	C	C	U	
Yellow-crowned	Co	U	U	U	R		
Glossy Ibis	Co	A	A	A	U	R	
Swan							
Tundra					R	R	
Mute		C	A	A	C	C	
Snow Goose		A	R	R	A	A	
Brant		A	R	R	A	A	
Canada Goose	Co	A	A	A	A	A	
Wood Duck		U	R	U	U		
Green-winged Teal	✳	C	U	C	C	U	
Black Duck	Co	A	A	A	A	A	
Mallard	Co	A	A	A	A	A	
Pintail	✳	U	R	U	C	U	
Blue-winged Teal	✳	C	U	C	U	R	
Northern Shoveler	Co	C	R	U	C	R	
Gadwall	Co	C	C	C	C	U	
Wigeon							
Eurasian		R			R	R	R
American	✳	A	R	C	A	A	
Canvasback		C	R	R	A	U	
Redhead	Co	R	R	R	R	R	
Ring-necked Duck		R			R		
Scaup							
Greater		A	U	U	A	A	
Lesser		U			U	U	
Common eider				R			
King eider		▼	▼			▼	

HOW TO USE THIS CHECKLIST

Seasonal Headings:

B Breeding: species confirmed breeding on the NY Breeding Bird Atlas Project 1980-82 (and to date) are coded Confirmed **Co**, Probables **Pr**, and Possibles **Po**. Other birds known to have bred prior to 1970 are marked with an ✳. Presently, most of the herons, American Oystercatcher, all the gulls and Common Terns nest on remote is lands scattered about Jamaica Bay.

Sp Spring: principally April and May, but in a broader sense, the spring migration.

Su Summer: June and July, the breeding season. Southbound shorebird migration begins in July.

eF Early Fall: August and September. Early fall migrants including shorebirds, flycatchers. vireos, and warblers.

lF Late Fall: October and November. Late fall migrants including waterfowl, hawks and finches.

W Winter: December to March.

Status Symbols:

A Abundant: more than 30 individuals are usually recorded every visit.

C Common: 10 to 30 individuals usually recorded every visit.

U Uncommon: 1 to 9 individuals per visit, some times missed.

R Rare: only one or a few individuals recorded throughout the season, often missed.

▼ Very rare: recorded sporadically, not seen every year.

Status Symbols

In this case, a status symbol isn't the latest high-end spotting scope, it's an indication of how common the bird is during each season. Status categories tend to be a little loose, but here's what the symbols usually mean:

➤ **Abundant:** Abbreviated A or a, abundant means that numbers of the bird (10 or 20 or more) are easily observed at any time. Abundant is another way of saying you can't miss this one.

➤ **Common:** Abbreviated C or c, common means that the bird is very likely to be seen or heard. It would be hard to miss seeing at least one.

➤ **Uncommon:** Abbreviated U or u, uncommon means the bird is there, but you might not see it. If you do, you'll probably see only a few individuals.

➤ **Scarce or occasional:** These terms aren't used that much, but when they are, it means the bird is seen only once every few years.

➤ **Rare:** Abbreviated R or r, rare means the bird is usually not there. If it is seen, only one or a few individuals are spotted throughout the season, and the bird might not be seen at all some years. You probably won't see it.

➤ **Accidental:** Usually indicated by an asterisk or some other symbol. Accidental means the bird has only been spotted a few times over many years.

Sometimes, the relative abundance of a species is given not with abbreviations but by a horizontal bar across the seasons. The thicker the bar, the more abundant the bird.

Remember, all status terms assume you're looking in the right habitat at the right time of year. At Merritt Island National Wildlife Refuge near the Kennedy Space Center in Florida, for instance, the Roseate Spoonbill is uncommon in the spring, common in the summer, occasional in the fall, and rare in the winter.

Breeding Status

Checklists usually tell you whether a bird is known to breed in the area. That's useful information because if the bird breeds there, you know that it will be hanging around for a while. If you miss it on one visit, you have a good chance of spotting it on a return trip. You might even spot some interesting breeding behavior or see young birds. If a bird is known to breed in the area, it's usually indicated by an asterisk. Sometimes, the checklist will include more information about the breeding status as a note or in a separate column.

Checking It Out

Now, let's put all the information on the checklist to some practical use. Before you start your field trip, glance over the checklist for the site. You'll get an idea of what to expect, which will help you recognize the birds when you see them. If you know that

Bank Swallows, for instance, are common in the area but Rough-winged Swallows aren't, you're less likely to be confused about what you're seeing. (But you still need to see the dark breastband to be sure it really is a Bank Swallow.)

Once you're out in the field, use your checklist to eliminate some of your wilder guesses about what a bird might be. Let's say you're birding at one of my favorite places, Jamaica Bay National Wildlife Refuge. (This outstanding hotspot is in New York City—the borough of Queens, to be precise—quite literally in the shadow of Kennedy Airport.) It's July, and you get a glimpse of a wren of some sort in the phragmites.

Based on the habitat, it could be a Sedge Wren or a Marsh Wren. A quick look at the checklist tells you that Sedge Wrens are very rare here, whereas Marsh Wrens are common. It's very unlikely (although still possible) that your bird is a Sedge Wren.

Let's take a tougher example. It's August at Jamaica Bay, and you think you're looking at a Wilson's Phalarope. The checklist says this bird is uncommon at this time of year. It might indeed be a Wilson's (much stranger things have happened at Jamaica Bay). Then again, this bird is easy to confuse with the Stilt Sandpiper—which your checklist tells you is common at this time of year. Now what? Keep watching, take notes, and work out the ID later with your field guide. (Hint: Wilson's Phalarope has a needlelike bill.)

Important Checklist Abbreviations

Out in the field, you can't always be certain of a bird's identification. You might be sure you saw a dowitcher, for instance, but you might not be sure about the species. Was it Long-billed or Short-billed? Put it down in your notes and on your field card as dowitcher sp., short for species (spp. for the plural). If you can't even be sure it was a dowitcher, put it down as sandpiper sp. Don't hesitate about this; birders far more experienced than you do it all the time.

Particularly as a new birder, you need to know some other important abbreviations:

➤ **BVD:** Better view desired—use when you haven't got the faintest idea.

➤ **LBB:** Little brown bird.

➤ **LYB:** Little yellow bird.

➤ **LBJ:** Little brown job—use for variety when you get tired of LBB.

➤ **BBB:** Big brown bird.

➤ **SCB:** Small chirpy bird—my personal favorite because I use it so much.

Again, don't hesitate to use these abbreviations or invent your own. Trust me, people who've been birding for years use them, too.

The Value of Listing

Listing—keeping records of the birds you see—is one of the most interesting, enjoyable, and controversial areas of birding. Just about every birder keeps a *life list*, but listing can go far, far beyond that; you can come up with all sorts of imaginative ways to classify the birds you see. If your personality tends in that direction, birding is definitely the hobby for you. Even if you're more the haphazard sort, listing has its points. It's always interesting to compare lists—from the same month on different years, say, or from the same place at different times of the year. Also, listing keeps you involved. Even the most ordinary birds gets more interesting if it means a check mark on your list of birds seen on every lawn in a five-block radius from your house.

Where listing gets controversial is when it starts to take over a birder's personality. In their lust for a check mark on a list, some birders forget about good birding ethics. Listing can also make some birders just a tad competitive. They catch a quick glimpse of a bird, check it off, and rush on to check off the next bird. That's fun now and again, as I discuss in Chapter 31, "Birding Events," but you won't learn much about the bird or see any interesting behavior.

Rappin' Robin

Your **life list** is a list of all the bird species you have seen since you started watching birds.

A Little Bird Told Me...

The world champion birdwatcher is Phoebe Snetsinger of Missouri. As of 1999, her life list stands at 8,600+ birds seen around the world over the past few decades; she broke the 7,000 mark in 1992. To see all the species in the world, she only has about a thousand birds to go. To put that in perspective, a serious birder who's been at it for a dozen years might have a life list of about 500 North American birds. Birders who have topped 600 in North America are considered in the elite.

You and Your Life List

Your life list is a list of all the birds you've ever seen. When you see a new bird for the first time, you're seeing a *life bird,* or lifer. When you start your life list, here's what to count:

➤ Only birds you've seen since you started your list.

➤ Only birds that are unrestrained, native, and living count. Captive or dead birds are out, as are escaped pet birds.

➤ Only birds that you've seen and positively identified for yourself. Don't count a partial glimpse of a bird that someone else identifies.

➤ Only birds seen under ethical conditions. (See Appendix B, "American Birding Association Code of Ethics," for details.)

Rappin' Robin

A **life bird** or **lifer** is a bird you've seen and identified for the first time.

Listing works on the honor system; there's no life list police to haul you off if you break the rules. In all aspects of listing, let your conscience be your guide.

What about birds you've heard but not seen? Yes, you can list them according to the ABA, if you're absolutely certain about your ID. No, you can't list them, according to many birders, because you can't be absolutely certain unless you also see the bird. I deal with this controversy more in Chapter 11, "Birding by Ear." If you can't make up your mind, keep a separate list of heard-only birds.

A Little Bird Told Me...

Every birder has a nemesis or hex bird—a bird you just can't get to see, no matter how hard you try. Strangely, nemesis birds often aren't particularly rare. It took me four trips to Arizona to spot a Scott's Oriole. My current nemesis bird is the Golden Eagle. I've arrived at a hawk watch not once, not twice, but three times just a few minutes *after* a Golden Eagle passed by.

Checklist Areas

Most birders actually keep two basic life lists: an American Birding Association (ABA) area list and a world list. Let's stick to the ABA list for now because as a new birder, you're probably not traveling the world yet on birding trips.

The ABA checklist area includes Canada and the 49 continental United States, plus their adjacent waters to a distance of 200 miles or half the distance to a non-included area, whichever is less. The southern offshore limit is the latitude of the Mexican border. Hawaii, the Arctic, the Caribbean, and Mexico and the rest of Central America aren't in the ABA area.

There are other ways to define regions, but I won't get into the gory details here. If you want to know more, check with the ABA and the American Ornithologists' Union. (See Appendix A, "Birding Organizations," for details.)

List Lust

As a new birder, your life list is in two figures; it might even still be in the teens. Not to worry. Just by birding in your area, you can raise your total in a hurry with only a couple of field trips a month. In one spring morning in the woods, for instance, you could easily add a dozen new birds; a trip to a wetlands area during the fall waterfowl migration could add a dozen more.

Once you've seen all the easy birds, of course, the growth in your life list will slow down. Depending on where you live, you'll probably have to do some traveling to raise your list much over a hundred. In my home state of New York, for example, 451 species have been recorded, but in my home county of Dutchess, only 245 species are regularly found. To get up to the elite level of 500 or more birds, then, by definition I'd have to travel well beyond New York and even the mid-Atlantic region. Once you're that committed, of course, you'll be constantly plotting ways to go birding in distant places.

Lots of Lists

Even birders who say they're not really into listing usually keep at least a few beyond their life list. As you get more into birding, you might want to keep basic lists along these lines:

➤ **Regional list:** Based on your geographic region—New England, for instance.

➤ **State list:** All the birds you've seen in your state.

➤ **Neighborhood list:** Define neighborhood however you like.

➤ **Property list:** Birds seen on or over your property. I'm hoping to break 100 soon.

➤ **Bird feeder list:** Birds attracted by your feeder, including hawks that pick off small birds.

➤ **Site lists:** Birds seen at birding spots you visit.

Keeping birding lists can go far, far beyond your life list. Many birders keep lists of birds they've seen in various places, such as states or regions they've visited, in zoos and aviaries, at a particular hotspot, by county, on campus, and so on. Some people keep lists of birds they've seen on TV and in the movies.

You can also keep lists by date. It's traditional to make a note of the first bird you see on New Year's Day, for example, and some birders will go to considerable lengths to make sure that bird is something unusual. (My first bird of 1999 was an American Tree Sparrow under my feeder. Not a life or property bird, but a first for my feeder list and also the first time in 10 years that my first bird of the year wasn't a Black-capped Chickadee.) Many birders keep lists of birds seen by year, season, and month, along with records of Big Day counts (see Chapter 31, "Birding Events," for more on this) and other special occasions. You can keep records of birds seen on your birthday, or on the Fourth of July, or the first day of spring, or whatever other dates you choose.

Getting a little weirder, you can keep records of dead birds, stuffed birds, birds you've dreamed about, birds you've seen on Christmas cards or postage stamps, birds on all the kitchen towels, potholders, jewelry, and other doodads people keep giving you—anything.

What's the most important list of all? I thought you'd never ask. Your list of lists, of course.

Listing Software

One traditional way to keep track of your life list is to use one of those nice little books you see in nature stores, with a list of all the birds, little boxes for checking them off, and maybe space for some notes. Never buy one of these. As your interest in birding becomes known to your friends and family, you'll start getting them as gifts.

Be a Better Birder

Listing software offers a major advantage: updates. Bird taxonomy is dynamic, and bird classifications do get shifted around a bit now and then. If you keep your lists by hand, you'll have to do a fair amount of reorganizing every couple of years. If you keep your lists on your computer, software updates do the reshuffling for you and keep your lists accurate.

Another method is to keep track of the birds on index cards filed in a shoe box or to check them off on a field card with the date and keep notes on the sighting in your journal. (I discuss journals in just a little bit.)

Definitely the coolest way to keep your lists is on your computer. As I discuss more in Chapter 33, "Virtual Birding," listing software is inexpensive and easy to use. What I like best is not only that you can keep extensive notes, all sorts of lists, and combinations and permutations of lists. You can also use the software to analyze your lists—to see which of the warblers of the Pacific coast you haven't seen yet, for instance. Let's say you're planning a trip to southern Arizona. You can analyze your past trips to see which birds are and aren't on your list for the region. You can even use the software to make target lists. Most programs will automatically update all your lists. If you see a Painted Redstart in Madera Canyon (south of Tucson), for instance, and enter it on your life list, it will also be entered on all other relevant lists.

Birding Journals

When you come home from a field trip—or better yet, while you're still in the field and your observations are fresh—it's time to take the information from your checklist and your field notebook and combine it all into your birding journal. Whether you keep it on a computer or in a large notebook, your journal is a complete record of your birding experiences. This is the place to record the details of seeing a life bird or something unusual, interesting, or beautiful. It's fun to keep a journal and even more fun to look back over it and see how you've improved as an observer.

As with life list books, at least once a year you're certain to get a gift of a beautiful nature notebook. It might have handmade paper, quotations from great nature writers, or a leather cover (maybe even all three). Thank the giver politely and put the notebook to some other use. For your birding journal, you want something a little bigger and a lot sturdier. Most people don't bring their journals into the field, but they do take them along on trips and they do use them a lot. Check out your local stationery and art-supply stores for diaries and sketchbooks and pick one that's a comfortable size and shape for you. If you like to sketch, pick a book with blank pages; otherwise, ruled pages are fine.

The Least You Need to Know

➤ Checklists—taxonomic lists of all the birds that can be seen at a birding site—are useful tools for keeping track of your sightings.

➤ Checklists also help you identify the birds you see by eliminating the unlikely or impossible birds.

➤ Just about every birder keeps a life list—a list of all the birds he or she has ever seen.

➤ Most birders keep at least a few other lists, such as a state list, backyard list, or feeder list.

➤ Listing software is inexpensive and easy to use.

➤ In addition to a life list, most birders keep a journal of their birding experiences.

Part 4
Tools for Birding

Birding is basically a simple hobby; grab your binoculars and you're ready to go. But like all hobbies, the more you get into it, the more enjoyably complex it gets. Complexity means a lot of cool gear. You'll soon move from watching birds through binoculars to wanting the extra power of a spotting scope. From there, you might get into one of the most popular, challenging, and gear-filled aspects of birding, bird photography.

For all the constant talk about binoculars, birding isn't only a visual hobby. Listening to the songs and sounds of birds is not only a lot of fun, but also it's an important part of identification.

Chapter 10

Optics: Binoculars and Spotting Scopes

In This Chapter

➤ Binoculars: your most important birding tool

➤ Understanding birding optics

➤ Choosing the right binoculars for you

➤ Spotting scopes: getting closer

You'll know you're hooked on birding when you feel naked leaving the house without your binoculars. Most serious birders have several pairs strategically placed around the house. One or two are near the windows facing the yard and birdfeeder. The current favorite pair is right by the door, ready to be grabbed on the way out. And of course, another pair is in the glove box of the car, ready for emergency roadside birding.

Binoculars: Don't Leave Home Without Them

Your *binoculars* are your most important birding tool, so it pays to understand how they work. There's nothing mysterious about them once you grasp the basic binocs lingo.

Magnification: Up Close and Personal

The whole point of using binoculars is to make distant things look closer. Just how much closer is the *magnification*—also known as the power. Take a look at your bins. Someplace on them—usually by the focusing wheel—are numbers such as 7 × 40, 8 × 42, or 10 × 50. The first number is the magnification, so 8 × 42 binoculars make whatever you view seem eight times closer. A bird that's 80 feet away, then, would seem only 10 feet away through the binoculars.

What's Your Objective?

The second number in the equation tells you the diameter of the *objective*—the lens at the wide end. On a pair of 8 × 42 binoculars, then, the objective is 42 millimeters across (about $1^1/_5$th of an inch). Generally speaking, the bigger the objective, the more light it can gather, the brighter the binoculars will be, and the better you'll be able to see through them in dim light. Also, big objectives let you see more details. On the other hand, the bigger the objectives, the bigger and heavier the binoculars.

The eyepiece or small end of your binoculars is sometimes called the *ocular* because you hold it to your eyes.

Rappin' Robin

The word **binoculars** ("bins" to birders) comes from the prefix bi–, meaning two, and oculars, meaning optical devices. Basically, binoculars are two small telescopes arranged side-by-side so that you can look through them with both eyes—an idea that dates back to World War I. Before binoculars, the most common way to get a good look at a bird was to shoot it.

Field of View

You'll see a mystifying phrase that reads along the lines of "365 ft at 1000 yds" marked on your binoculars. This indicates the *field of view*, or the horizontal width of the area you can see when looking through the binoculars. In other words, if you look through your binoculars at the horizon a thousand yards ahead of you, you can see a piece of it that's 365 feet wide.

For birding, you want a wide field of view—250 feet at a minimum—so you can see as many birds in one look as possible. Field of view is related to magnification; the bigger the magnification, the smaller the field of view. In general, a wider field of view is better for following moving birds or scanning an area to find them.

Exit Pupil

No, it isn't what the teacher says when throwing you out of class. The *exit pupil* is the column of light that comes through the binoculars and hits your eye. You can see it by holding your bins up to the light. See that little circle in the center of each eyepiece? That's the exit pupil. On good binoculars, the exit pupil is round and centered. The bigger the exit pupil, the brighter the image will be, especially under low-light conditions.

Oh, What a Relief It Is

You'll often see the phrase "long eye relief" in ads for binoculars. To understand why *eye relief* is a big selling point, imagine looking through a keyhole into a room. The closer your eye is to the hole, the more you can see. It's the same with binoculars. The problem is, you can't hold the eyepiece right up against your eyeball. In fact, if you wear eyeglasses, you automatically have extra space between the eyepiece and your eye. The eye relief for a pair of binoculars is the distance your eye can be from the eyepiece and still see the whole image. Eye relief is measured in millimeters. Long eye relief is anywhere between about 14 and 23 millimeters. If you normally wear eyeglasses while birding, try the binoculars before you buy to make sure the eye relief is good for you.

A Little Bird Told Me...

How can you tell whether the eye relief on a pair of binoculars is right for you? Look through the bins and move them around a little. If the view through one or both tubes suddenly seems blocked off, as if a shutter has come down, the eye relief isn't right; the exit pupil isn't falling directly onto the pupil of your eye. Change the eye relief by adjusting the eye cups on the eyepiece up or down. (You'll probably have to adjust them down if you wear glasses.) If that doesn't work, don't buy that brand.

Coats of Many Colors

When light passes through a lot of glass, as it does in binoculars, all sorts of distortion, refraction, and reflection happen. To prevent this, manufacturers use special glass, coatings on the lenses, and a variety of other technical fixes. Today, all high-quality optics have coated lenses. All sorts of technical jargon, such as low-dispersion glass and apochromatic correction, is thrown around in the ads. You can safely ignore it all.

A Little Bird Told Me...

For a lot of excellent, up-to-date information about birding optics, check out these web sites:

Optics for Birders
www.optics4birding.com

Better View Desired (the online version of a newsletter)
www.biddeford.com/~sing/BVD.html

Raising the Roof

For complicated optics reasons, your binoculars have prisms inside them. The prisms in high-quality binoculars come in two flavors, Porro and roof:

1. **Porro prisms:** If the binoculars have the eyepiece offset from the objective, they have Porro prisms inside (invented by Mr. Porro of Italy in the middle of the 19th century).

2. **Roof prisms:** If the binoculars look like the letter H, with the lenses positioned inline, they have roof prisms inside.

Roof-prism binoculars. Note the H-shape; the eyepieces are in a direct line with the objectives. (Photo courtesy Bausch & Lomb.)

What's the difference? In general, Porro prisms will give you somewhat better depth perception. In the middle price range, they are excellent buys. Roof-prism binoculars, however, are more streamlined and compact. High-end roof-prism bins are more field-worthy; they're usually fogproof and waterproof. Also, in porro prism binoculars, the ocular lenses move in and out on lubricated metal tubes as you focus. The lubrication is exposed and accumulates dust—then focusing gets more and more difficult until it is nearly impossible. With roof prism binoculars, the moving parts are all inside where they can't get gummed up. Roof-prism bins are more expensive, mostly because they're harder to manufacture.

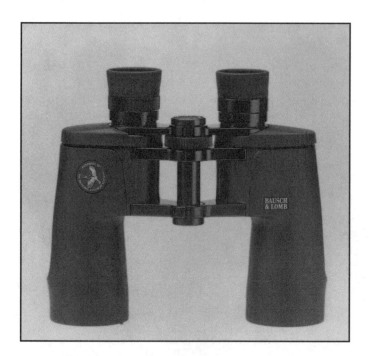

Porro-prism binoculars. The eyepieces are offset from the objectives, giving the binoculars sort of a Z shape. (Photo courtesy Bausch & Lomb.)

Choosing Binoculars

Things a little slow at the hawk watch? Say something assertive—good or bad, it doesn't matter—about a brand of binoculars, and things will get lively in a hurry. You'll hear a lot of strong opinions expressed, but in the end, choosing the right binoculars for you is an individual decision. The binoculars a friend adores may not feel right in your hands, for instance. No matter which binoculars you end up choosing, you have to consider two basic ideas: cost and comfort.

Let's look at cost first. Good binoculars are expensive—around $250 for a worthwhile pair of Porros, around $350 for very good Porros or roofs, and well over $500 for the spectacularly good high-end roof prisms. Yes, that's a lot of money—and yes, it's worth it. A good pair of binoculars will last for many years and make a real difference in how well you see the birds. As you become a better birder, you'll quickly outgrow your clunky, dim, color-distorting, cheapo binoculars. Skip the frustration and wasted money, and go straight for the high end. If you're on a tight budget, let it be known to all who matter that contributions to your binoculars fund will make good birthday and holiday gifts.

Be a Better Birder

Today's high-end binoculars can focus as closely as eight feet away—fabulous for watching birds in thick brush and great for butterflies. At a minimum, choose bins that focus to 15 feet.

The second big factor is comfort. You want bins that fit your hands, don't weigh too much, and give you the right eye relief.

In general, birders stick to 7× and 8× binoculars. Although 10× binoculars give you a lot of magnification, they also weigh a lot; you'll have a hard time holding them steady. Remember that the magnification not only magnifies the object you are looking at, but also the shakiness of your hands. Binoculars that are too powerful have to be mounted on a tripod.

Lightweight bins are a trade-off between power and weight. Lightweight bins are easier to hold, especially if you are carrying anything else. (Photo by Cliff Beittel.)

Splat!

No-name or "house brand" binoculars are cheap, but they're no bargain. You'll soon be frustrated by the poor quality of the image, especially the color distortion. As with any expensive purchase, be an informed consumer and shop around, but buy only reliable brands from reputable dealers.

The only way to tell whether the bins fit your hands comfortably and give you the right eye relief is to try them, preferably in a situation where you can compare several different brands. Binoculars manufacturers advertise heavily in the birding magazines, and hardly an issue goes by without an article about optics. Read the articles and the ads, and then contact the manufacturers for details. (See Appendix E, "Optics Manufacturers," for a list.) Finally, visit a well-stocked optics store and do some comparisons.

Before you fork over your money for new binoculars (or as soon as the bins arrive from a mail-order source), check the alignment of the lenses. Focus the binoculars on a horizontal line, such as a countertop or porch railing. Slowly move the binoculars away from your eyes until you can see two separate images—one in each ocular. If the images aren't on the same level in each, the prisms are out of whack—don't but the bins or send them back.

Birding with Your Bins

In Chapter 2, "Getting Started," you learned how to use your binoculars to find and focus on birds. Here's a quick refresher: While keeping your eyes firmly fixed on the bird, bring your binoculars up to your eyes. In birding as in baseball—keep your eye on the bird! With a little practice, this becomes second nature and you can get on any bird quickly.

You'll be able to see the birds better if your lenses aren't encrusted with grime. Clean them every now and then, using a commercial lens-cleaning fluid and a microweave cleaning cloth. Using a compressed air can, gently blow away any obvious grit. Put a drop of the fluid on the cloth and gently wipe the lens clean, moving in a circle outward from the center of the lens.

Splat!

Never look directly at the sun through your binoculars or spotting scope. You could cause serious eye damage.

Binocular Extras

Most binoculars come with a thin plastic neck strap designed to slice off your head at the neck. Throw this away at once and buy a broad neoprene strap. The broad strap spreads the weight and doesn't cut into you; it makes carrying your bins much more comfortable.

You can try the fancier support straps that fit over your torso. They don't work too well if you're wearing bulky clothing such as a parka, but they're fabulous for shirt-sleeves birding. The idea is to reduce the fatigue you get from hauling your bins around all day.

Your bins will come with a soft case of some sort. Use the case for storage and for travel, but leave it behind when you go into the field. Ditto for the lens caps.

Splat!

The worst thing you can do to your expensive binoculars is drop them. Here's a good rule: If the binoculars are in or even near your hand, the strap should be around your neck.

Scoping Out the Right Spotting Scope

After a couple of frustrating birding trips trying to see the birds huddled on a distant sandbar, you'll want to consider buying a spotting scope. Basically a small telescope, a spotting scope is a fabulous birding tool.

Splat!

Birders are an amazingly honest group. Alas, the same cannot be said for the rest of the world. Mark your binoculars and other optics clearly with your name, and keep a record of the serial numbers. Store optics and their telltale cases out of sight when you park your car.

The lingo for scopes is a little different than for binoculars:

➤ **Aperture:** Scopes are usually described in terms of their aperture—another way of saying the diameter of the objective. Most scopes have an aperture somewhere between 60 and 80 millimeters.

➤ **Focal length:** The focal length is the distance, in millimeters, from the objective to the point where the image is formed. That's why spotting scopes have long tubes; the longer the focal length, the bigger the image.

➤ **Magnification:** This gets a little tricky because you have to add an eyepiece to the spotting scope. The magnification is determined in part by the focal length of the scope and in part by the eyepiece. It's a little too complex to discuss here, but in general, the magnification from a spotting scope and eyepiece will be about 20× or more.

Be a Better Birder

Spotting scopes are expensive; they cost as much or more than high-end binoculars, plus you'll have to buy an eyepiece or two and a good tripod. If you're lucky enough to have a scope, share it. If you don't have a scope, make friends with someone who does.

Be a Better Birder

Spotting scopes are ideal for situations when the birds are very distant—ducks far out on the bay, for instance. They're also great for when you're observing a single spot such as a nest for a long period. When it's too dark to bird, you can use spotting scopes for skygazing.

Like binoculars, spotting scopes come in two flavors, straight-through and angled:

1. *Straight-through scopes* have the eyepiece mounted inline with the front lens, so you look straight ahead to see the bird.

2. *Angled scopes* have the eyepiece mounted pointing up at a 45 degree angle, so you bend over to look into it.

I have to say that I really hate straight-through scopes. Because the eyepiece has to be at eye level, they're hard to share; you have to constantly adjust the tripod for people of different heights. Because I'm on the short side (okay, I'm 4'11"), I not only always have to adjust the scope down, but also I have to listen to a lot of remarks.

As with binoculars, there are a lot of other considerations in a spotting scope. Read the reviews in the birding mags, get the manufacturer's literature, and look through as many scopes as you can before you buy.

Eyepieces for Scopes

Eyepieces for spotting scopes are usually sold separately. The important thing to know is that eyepieces are straight magnifiers. The shorter the focal length, the more powerful they are. The more powerful the magnification, however, the smaller the image and the narrower the field of view. The solution? Buy several eyepieces or a high-quality zoom eyepiece. Use the lower power when you're scanning for birds and the higher power when you want to zero in.

Tripods

Spotting scopes are way too heavy to hold; you need a high-quality, sturdy tripod that won't tip over or vibrate in the wind. On the other hand, you have to haul that tripod around all day, so you want one that's not too heavy.

I strongly recommend getting a video tripod with a fluid head. The tripods are sturdy, and the fluid head lets you move the scope around easily and smoothly in any direction with just one handle.

An alternative to a tripod is a rifle-style shoulder stock. I find it hard to hold the scope steady this way, but some birders I know swear by it. If you have a straight-through scope, try it.

Another useful accessory for your scope is a window mount, also called a carpod. Basically a tripod head that clamps onto your car window, a carpod lets you use your vehicle as a viewing blind.

Traveling with Optics

Years of business travel have taught me one major lesson: Never check your luggage unless you absolutely have to. You'll waste precious birding time waiting for your bag at the carousel. If your bag is lost, so are your optics. Always put your bins in your carry-on luggage. Spotting scopes and tripods don't always fit comfortably into carry-on luggage, however, and they can sometimes arouse suspicion at airport security. (Shoulder stocks really get the security people worried.) Especially when traveling overseas, pack the scope in your suitcase and check it through. Within the U.S., I sometimes ship my scope and tripod ahead, but do this only if you know there's someone reliable on the receiving end.

Making a Difference

Your old binoculars can make a difference. Instead of throwing them away or selling them at a yard sale, donate them to Birders' Exchange. This valuable program recycles old bins and other birding equipment (even books) by sending them to educational programs in the Caribbean and Central and South America. Birders' Exchange is a joint program of the Manomet Center for Conservation Sciences in Massachusetts and the American Birding Association. For more information on how you can help, contact:

> Paul Green
> American Birding Association
> P.O. Box 6599
> Colorado Springs, CO 80934
> (800) 850-2473
> **paulgrn@aba.org**

The Least You Need to Know

➤ Binoculars are your most important birding tool; buy the best you can afford.

➤ The best binoculars for birding are 7× or 8× power. Anything less doesn't magnify enough; anything more is too hard to hold steady.

➤ Choose the binoculars that fit your price range and feel most comfortable to you.

➤ Spotting scopes—small telescopes—are great for times when you need more magnification.

Chapter 11

Birding by Ear

In This Chapter

➤ Listening to the birds

➤ Understanding birdsong

➤ Identifying the birds by song

➤ Learning bird sounds

What could be more delightful than waking up in the morning to the sound of birds singing? Waking up to the sound of Leonardo diCaprio saying, "Breakfast is ready, darling." And then he says…what was I talking about? Oh, yeah, birdsong. What could be more delightful than waking up in the morning to the sound of birds singing? Nothing.

Learning to Listen

Learning to identify birds by the sounds they make is called *birding by ear*. It's an important birding skill because a lot of times you'll hear the bird long before you see it—if you see it at all. Being able to home in on the bird gets you closer to seeing it. Even if you never catch a glimpse of it, the bird's song and other noises are clues to its identity. In fact, in some cases, you really can't decide what the bird is until you hear it.

Being able to bird by ear is an acquired skill. Start by listening carefully for bird sounds. This can be difficult. Most of us are constantly surrounded by endless noise; true silence is rare. We learn to tune out most of the noise, but that means we sometimes have trouble tuning in. Also, when you're outdoors, there's a lot of noise that doesn't come from birds. The alarm squeak of a startled chipmunk, for instance, can sound a lot like the call of a towhee. Squirrels making *chuk chuk* calls in the woods can sound like jays. With experience, you'll learn to tell the difference.

Be a Better Birder

Sometimes, you need to hear a bird sing to know what it is. Unless a Lesser Yellowlegs happens to be standing right next to a Greater Yellowlegs on the beach, even experienced birders can't tell the difference until the birds call. The Greater Yellowlegs has a clear, three-note whistle: *Whew! Whew! Whew!* The Lesser Yellowlegs has a one- or two-note *yew* or *yew-yew*.

Be a Better Birder

A reminder: The ABA rules say you must see or hear any bird under ethical conditions before you can count it. That could rule out hearing a bird that's responding to a tape.

In fact, with practice, just about anyone can learn the songs and calls of the most common birds. Having said that, I have to add that some people are naturally better at hearing and recognizing birdsong than others. Your hearing might naturally be more or less acute than someone else's. Age plays a role here: Older adults generally can't hear very soft or high-pitched sounds as well as they used to. Musical ability also plays a role, although I know people who can't carry a tune in a bucket but can identify every bird they hear.

Do Heard Birds Count?

Count on what? Your life list, of course. Check back to Chapter 9, "List Mania," for the really long answer to this sticky question. Here, I just give the short answer: No…and definitely yes. According to the American Birding Association, heard-only birds *don't* count on your life list, but they *do* indeed count, if you're sure of the identification, on every other list, such as your trip list, annual list, area list, state list, and so on.

There's no mistaking the sounds of some birds—owls and rails are good examples—so you'd be okay to list them if you heard them only. On the other hand, unless you're a real expert, the call note of a songbird—a sparrow, say—doesn't tell you enough to ID the bird. You'd want to hear it sing to be certain. Bear in mind that some birds, such as jays and starlings, are good mimics, and that it's hard to distinguish the songs of some birds. Even so, the sounds of many birds are distinctive, and with a little experience, you can be sure of the identity just by the song or call note.

How to Home In

You know the bird is nearby because you can hear it singing. If only you could figure out where the song is coming from, you could spot the bird. Here's how to home in on the song:

➤ Stand still and really *listen*. If you're with other people, get them to do the same.

➤ Turn your head slowly from side to side as you listen. You should hear the bird more loudly toward one side or the other.

➤ If that doesn't work, move to your left or right and listen again. You can also cup your hands behind your ears to pull in the sound a touch more.

➤ Once you've got a better idea of where the bird is, start scanning for it with your binocs. Especially in the spring, songbirds tend to sing from fairly visible perches. (I explain why later in this chapter.)

Just as you think you're homing in on a singing bird, it clams up. Chances are the bird has noticed you and has decided to pipe down until the "threat" is past. Lean against a tree or squat down to disguise your silhouette. Wait quietly for a few minutes, and the bird will probably start to sing again, perhaps after flying off a short way.

Songs, Chips, and Chirps

Birds make all sorts of sounds, or *vocalizations*. Most of them fall into two main categories: *songs* and *calls*.

Singin' a Song

Birdsong usually means loud, complex, musical sounds made mostly by passerines, the perching birds. (Check Chapter 8, "Putting the Pigeons in the Right Holes," for more on the passerines.) That's why this large bird family is sometimes loosely called the songbirds. With some exceptions, birdsong is a guy thing; in most species, male birds do the singing. It's also a seasonal thing, done mostly during the breeding period in the spring.

Why do male birds put all that energy into singing? Two interlocking reasons: to define their territory and to attract a mate. The males stake out their territory by singing from prominent points on the borders. That's why you often see songbirds trilling away on an exposed branch or fence post.

They're telling other males in the neighborhood to stay away. The singing attracts females, again for two interlocking reasons. The bigger and better the territory the male has, the more likely he is to be a good mate—likewise for the louder and better he sings.

Rappin' Robin

Birdsong is often used as a general word for all the sounds made by birds, but a better word is **vocalizations**. **Song** usually refers to the complex, loud, musical sounds made by birds. Some birds also make sounds with their bills or wings. These are called nonvocal sounds.

Be a Better Birder

Once you get the hang of noticing birdsongs, you don't have to get up early to go birding. Leave the windows open as you go to sleep on a spring night. When the birds start singing at dawn, lie comfortably in your bed and tick them off. My personal best is 22 species one May morning in the Hudson Valley. Roger Tory Peterson once topped 40.

The best time of day to hear birdsong is early in the morning. Some birds sing more or less all day (and mockingbirds have been known to sing all night), but you'll hear the most songs in the couple of hours after sun-up. If you're an extra-early riser, you'll get an extra treat. Very early in the morning in the spring and early summer, just before sunrise, some birds start the day with special dawn songs. The sound is indescribably beautiful.

Although they're small birds, wrens sing with surprising loudness. This bird is a Bewick's Wren. (Photo by Cliff Beittel.)

Call Me

Almost all birds make *calls*—short, simple sounds—of some sort. Among the songbirds, calls are usually one or two short notes in a wide range of chips, chirps, tseeps, whistles, and other sounds. Among other birds, the calls may be longer, or they may be hisses, grunts, quacks, and other sounds. Both males and females make calls all year round. *Contact calls* are used to keep in touch with other birds, while feeding or while in a migrating flock, for example. *Alarm calls* are just that—calls given to alert other birds to danger. With some practice, you can learn the calls of common birds, such as cardinals, chickadees, jays, and crows. A lot of times, however, even experienced birders can't tell what bird is making the chips coming from a brushy area. If you can't ID the bird by ear, use the sound to home in for a look.

Birds such as the bitterns, Prairie Chickens, and some grouse make a range of weird sounds, including booming and cooing noises, using air sacs in their throats. Once you've heard these sounds, you'll remember them.

Rappin' Robin

Calls are short, simple sounds made by almost all birds. They make contact calls to keep in touch with each other and alarm calls to warn of danger.

Bring in da Noise

In addition to singing and calling, birds also make nonvocal sounds—noises made with parts of their bodies. Woodpeckers drum with their bills to attract mates and define their territory. For maximum resonance, they usually drum on hollow trees. Some woodpeckers discover they can get extra reverb by drumming on other things, such as aluminum siding, pipes, or even cars. You can figure out the species by listening to the rhythm of the drumming. Other birds, such as nuthatches, tap on tree trunks in search of food; you'll often hear this on a quiet winter day in the woods.

Some birds use their wings to make noise. Mourning Doves, for instance, make a whirring noise with their wing tips as they take off. During the breeding season, male Ruffed Grouse use their wings to make a noise that sounds a lot like a distant motorcycle being started.

Learning Bird Sounds

As you leaf through your field guide, you'll notice descriptions of the various songs and other sounds. It's hard to put sounds into words, of course, so the descriptions are only a rough idea of what the birds actually sound like.

A Little Bird Told Me...

The late, great Roger Tory Peterson was a pithy writer, able to capture the essence of a bird's appearance or song in a memorable phrase. In *A Field Guide to the Birds*, he says of Bell's Vireo that it "sings as if through clenched teeth." Of the Northern Parula Warbler, he says the song is "a buzzy trill or rattle that climbs the scale and trips over at the top." Once you've heard these birds, you'll realize that Peterson's descriptions are perfect—and you'll never forget them.

The easiest bird sounds to remember are the ones made by the name-sayers—birds whose sounds are also their names. A classic example of this is the *chicka-dee-dee-dee* call of the Black-capped Chickadee, which sounds exactly as it's written. Another good example is the harsh call of the Blue Jay, which sounds like *jay jay jay*. A little less obvious, to my ears, are name-sayers such as the Bobwhite and Killdeer. Then, there's the Mute Swan, which gets its name because it supposedly doesn't make any sounds at all. (They do hiss, however, when threatened.)

Be a Better Birder

Learn the song of the American Robin; a lot of other birdsongs are compared to it. The Scarlet Tanager sounds like a robin with a sore throat, whereas Roger Tory Peterson says, rightly, that a Rose-breasted Grosbeak sounds "as if a robin had taken voice lessons."

Other songs and calls aren't so simple. Songs are often described as melodious, clear, whistled, slurred, thin, wiry, cheerful, and so on. Calls may be described as a harsh chatter, a buzzy trill, or a rattle. Songs and calls are also often transliterated as a burry *teeooo*, raspy *churr*, or simple *chip, tseep, ik* or even *chjjj*. How the heck are you supposed to know what *chjjj* sounds like? What exactly is the difference between sounds that are buzzy, burry, and raspy? And how are you supposed to pronounce the *woika-woika* of a Red-bellied Woodpecker?

The best way to answer all these questions is to actually hear the real bird make the sound. Theoretically, you'll be out birding, and you'll find and identify a bird, hear it vocalize, and remember the sound forever after. Yeah, right. You need help.

A Little Bird Told Me...

Even the experts disagree about how to describe bird sounds. For example, Roger Tory Peterson says the song of the Acadian Flycatcher is "a sharp explosive *pit-see*," whereas other guides describe it as *PEET-sah, peet-suh*, and *flee-see*. The authors of the National Geographic guide say the Willow Flycatcher makes "a sneezy *fitz-bew*," while the authors of the Golden guide say it's "*fitz'bew*, a whistle superimposed on a buzz." Actually, all the flycatchers in the Empidonax genus are notoriously hard to identify by sight; you really have to hear them, and even then....

Birdsong Mnemonics

A mnemonic is a phrase that helps you remember something. *Birdsong mnemonics* generally capture the rhythm and cadence of a bird's song in a catchy way so you'll remember it. Trust me; once you've learned a mnemonic such as this one for the Warbling Vireo, "When I see one, I shall seize one and I'll squeeze it 'til it SQUIRTS!" you don't forget it. Once you've actually heard the bird, the mnemonic makes sense. Check out the chart for a list of some traditional mnemonics for common birds.

Birdsong Mnemonics

Bird	Mnemonic
Acadian Flycatcher	Pizza!
American Goldfinch	Potato chip, potato chip
American Robin	Cheerily, cheerily, cheer up
Barred Owl	Who cooks for you?
Black-throated Blue Warbler	I am so la-zee
California Quail	Chi-CA-go!
Carolina Wren	Tea kettle, tea kettle, tea kettle, tea
Chestnut-sided Warbler	So pleased, so pleased, so pleased to meet cha *or* I want, I want, I want to see Miss Beecher
Eastern Meadowlark	Spring of the year
Eastern Towhee	Drink your tea!
Golden-crowned Sparrow	Oh dear me
Indigo Bunting	Fire! Fire! Where? Where? Here! Here! See it? See it?
Magnolia Warbler	She knew she was right yes, she knew she was right
Olive-sided Flycatcher	Quick! Three beers!
Ovenbird	Teacher, TEACHER, TEACHER
Red-eyed Vireo	Here I am. Where are you? Here I am. Where are you? (Repeated endlessly all day long.)
Song Sparrow	Sweet, sweet, sweet, sweet
Warbling Vireo	When I see one, I shall seize one and I'll squeeze it 'til it SQUIRTS!
White-throated Sparrow	*For Americans:* Poor Sam Peabody, Peabody, Peabody *For Canadians:* Sweet, sweet Canada, Canada, Canada
Yellow Warbler	Sweet, sweet, sweet; I'm so sweet
Yellow-throated Warbler	Sweetie, sweetie, sweetie

When you're listening for birdsong, remember that birds don't necessarily start their songs at the "beginning." Quite often they begin in the middle of a phrase or add a note or two before getting down to the real song. The American Goldfinch, for example, often says "Chip, potato chip." Birds generally repeat their songs over and over, sometimes dozens of times in a minute. Also, birds sing variations on their songs and even variations on their variations. Some birds are more variable than others. Most Tufted Titmice sound pretty much the same, for instance, but every Eastern Towhee I've ever heard has had a different version of the basic "Drink your tea" call.

Mnemonics aren't necessarily song imitations. Sometimes, they're comparisons to other sounds. The Red-breasted Nuthatch, for example, makes a *yank yank* call that sounds as if it's coming from a toy horn. The Belted Kingfisher make a rattling call that sounds exactly like a baby's rattle. Then, the "song" of the Black and white Warbler sounds exactly like the squeaky noise of a rusty gate being opened. As you learn the sounds of the birds, you'll come up with your own comparisons.

Easy Listening

An excellent way to learn bird sounds at home is by listening to recordings. A lot of recordings are available on both tape and CD. Some are organized bird by bird, from the front of the field guide to the back. I think the ones that organize the birds into learning groups by their sounds are a lot more helpful. You can get recordings of only warblers, owls, and other bird families or recordings of the birds of a particular region.

I like to listen to bird recordings while I'm driving or doing something around the house. After about 10 minutes, however, I tend to tune out. Other birders have told me the same thing, so I suggest listening for short periods—while the recording goes through a particular group of birds, say—and then stopping. Pick up where you left off the next time you get a chance. Here's a tip: Don't play birding tapes for the carpool gang; they're not what most people want to hear on the way to work.

Be a Better Birder

The mockingbird gets its name from the way it imitates other birds (and doorbells, fire sirens, car alarms, barking dogs—anything) in its song. Mockingbirds, Brown Thrashers, and Gray Catbirds are all members of the *Mimidae* family, or mimic thrushes. Here's how to tell the difference: Mockingbirds repeat their borrowed phrases at least six times before switching; thrashers repeat the phrase twice; and catbirds don't repeat at all.

Birdsong Recordings

A lot of birdsong tapes and CDs are available. They're all good, but if I had to make a choice, I'd pick the Lang Elliot Know Your Bird Sounds recordings. He's also done, with Marie Read, a good little book/CD set called *Common Birds and Their Songs* (Houghton Mifflin, 1998). The book has great pictures and an informative text covering 50 common birds; the sound clips on the CD are excellent and long enough so you can really hear the song. To purchase them, contact:

Lang Elliot/NatureSound Studio
P.O. Box 84
Ithaca, NY 14851
Phone: (607) 257-4995
Email: lang@naturesound.com
Web site: www.naturesound.com

Houghton Mifflin also publishes several other good birdsong recordings, including the Birding by Ear series by Richard K. Walton and Robert W. Lawson, and the Peterson Field Guide series, which is keyed to the pages of the field guides.

Donald and Lillian Stokes have a good recording called Stokes Field Guide to Bird Songs (Eastern Region), available from Time Warner AudioBooks.

A Little Bird Told Me

If you're a visually or physically handicapped birder, don't hesitate to count a heard-only—or even felt-only—bird on your life list. To learn more about birding by ear, check out the two-cassette recording "A Birdsong Tutor for Visually Handicapped Individuals," by Lang Elliot. You can get it from the National Library Service for the Blind and Physically Handicapped of the Library of Congress and from the Canadian Institute for the Blind.

CD-ROMs for your computer are a great way to learn birdsongs because you also get to see the bird and learn some other facts about it at the same time. A lot of good programs are now available; I talk about them more in Chapter 33, "Virtual Birding."

A Little Bird Told Me...

Several web sites have great audio clips and pictures of the birds—which are excellent for practicing your ID skills. Check these out:

Library of Natural Sounds at Cornell Laboratory of Ornithology
www.birds.cornell.edu/LNS

Patuxent Wildlife Research Center, U.S. Geological Survey
www.mbr-pwrc.usgs.gov/bbs

Nature Sound Studio
www.naturesound.com

North American Bird Sounds Web Page
www.naturesongs.com

For excellent links to bird sounds from around the world, as well as sounds from a wide range of other animals, check this site:

Guide to Animal Sounds on the Net
www.io.com/~hmiller/AnimalSounds

Tapes, CDs, and software programs are all helpful for beginners, but the best way of all to learn bird sounds is to get out into the field. What you see and hear there will stick with you far better than anything you see on a screen or hear through a speaker.

Eavesdropping on the Birds

You can use a range of electronic devices to pull in bird sounds from a distance. For active birding, parabolic mikes and "hearing aids" are sometimes helpful.

A hand-held parabolic microphone for recording birdsong is light enough to carry with you into the field. (Photo courtesy Natural Technology Industries.)

A Little Bird Told Me...

Making your own recordings of birdsongs is now one of the more interesting aspects of birding. Until fairly recently, the equipment you needed was heavy, cumbersome, and expensive, plus you needed an advanced degree in engineering to operate it. Today, the equipment is a lot lighter and easier to use, although it's still pricey at the high end. I don't have space to discuss it all here, but if you're technically minded, check out the web site for the Library of Natural Sounds at the Cornell Laboratory of Ornithology (**www.birds.cornell.edu/LNS**) for more information.

Frankly, I don't know any birders who use the mikes only for listening. They're bulky, and you have to haul a power source and speaker with you. Hearing-aid style earpieces are a lot more convenient for individuals. I don't like them; they amplify everything, not just the bird sounds, and they take a lot of getting used to. They are good if you're having trouble hearing the higher frequencies. If you can't hear Cedar Waxwings, give the hearing aids a try.

Bird monitors are a lot more fun. These include mikes designed to be placed near your birdfeeder and speakers designed to be placed in your living room. You can listen to the birds in your backyard with the windows closed.

The Least You Need to Know

➤ Learning to identify birds by their sounds is called birding by ear. It's an important birding skill.

➤ The more birds you hear, the more you'll see.

➤ Birding by ear takes practice and a certain amount of natural ability, but it's easy to learn the songs of the most common birds.

➤ You can easily learn to recognize other bird sounds, such as the drumming of woodpeckers.

➤ The best way to learn birdsongs is to see and hear the bird in the field. To learn faster, listen to birdsong tapes, CDs, and software programs.

Chapter 12

Other Cool Birding Gear

In This Chapter

➤ Choosing the right footwear

➤ Special clothing for birders

➤ Backpacks and other carrying gear

➤ High-tech gear for birding

What's a hobby without a lot of cool gear to go with it? I mean, look at all the great equipment mountain climbers get to use. Compared to them, birders look pretty paltry; all we need is a pair of binoculars. Cheer up. Birding is so simple that it's easy to make it more complicated. There's plenty of neat birding stuff out there. Even better, you can spend many happy hours looking for it in camping stores and catalogues.

Voting with Your Feet

Next to your binoculars, your most important birding purchase should be comfortable, sturdy footwear appropriate for the season and terrain. Depending on where you live, that could end up meaning four or more pairs of shoes and boots. Here's what's in my closet:

➤ **Ordinary walking shoes/sneakers:** Perfect for a morning bird walk around the neighborhood, down a country road, or on flat, well-groomed trails.

➤ **Lightweight day hikers:** Day hikers are a good overall choice for rougher terrain, such as open fields or hilly trails.

➤ **Heavy-duty hiking boots:** If you're doing serious hiking on rough trails, you need heavier boots.

➤ **Rubber wellies:** For slogging around in wet, muddy areas, all-rubber wellington boots are perfect; you just hose them down to clean off the muck. Wear them and you too can look like a member of the British royal family. Wellies are worn over thick socks, not shoes, so check the fit carefully when you buy them.

➤ **Snow sneakers:** Insulated walking shoes meant for cold weather. They're great when the ground is dry, but they're water-resistant, not water-proof. Your feet will eventually get wet if you tramp through a lot of puddles or snow.

➤ **Extra-warm winter boots:** Cold, wet feet will ruin your birding trip faster than anything I know. Wear waterproof, insulated winter boots if you're doing serious winter birding, such as a Christmas Bird Count.

Be a Better Birder

For winter wear, look for boots made with Thinsulate. When you're buying winter boots, try them on wearing thick socks. For the rest of the year, look for footwear made with Gore–Tex; it's waterproof and breathable.

All your footwear should fit properly; you don't want blisters or squished toes slowing down your birding. Buy the best quality you can afford. Good footwear will last a long time.

Birding Vests and Other Clothing

Hunters, fishers, and photographers have vests with all sorts of convenient pockets— and so do birders. The best thing about birding vests is that they have roomy front pockets just the right size for a field guide. They have other pockets for pencils, note-books, lunch, snacks, and all the other paraphernalia you carry with you. Vests are a good way to distribute the weight of your gear and keep it handy; there's a separate pocket for everything. The drawback to vests designed for fly fishers and other outdoorsy types is that they're generally meant to be worn over a shirt or light jacket. They don't fit well over bulky outerwear, which means they're not much help on, say, a Christmas Bird Count.

Check out the vests designed specifically for birders. Birder's Buddy, (800) 955-1951, is a popular brand because it has open sides held together with adjustable straps. That means you get ventilation in hot weather and can still wear the vest over a parka in the winter.

As you get more into birding, you'll find yourself outdoors in cold or wet weather a lot. Be prepared with the right clothing. Today, there's all sorts of great cold-weather stuff made from fleece and waterproof and windproof materials. (Check Chapter 3, "Your First Field Trip," for more information on dressing for the weather.)

Be prepared for unexpected cold or wet weather. I strongly recommend carrying a lightweight, wind-resistant, water-resistant shell in your pack at all times. Shells made of Supplex work great and fold down into packets when you're not using them.

Whatever you buy, be sure it's roomy enough so that you can move your arms without any binding. This is especially important for outerwear such as parkas.

Birding vests fit comfortably over your clothing and have a lot of convenient pockets. Look for a vest that has a pocket large enough to hold your field guide. (Photo courtesy Birder's Buddy.)

Packing It In

Birders often carry light backpacks or fanny packs in addition to or instead of birding vests. There are zillions of these packs in all shapes and sizes; I've been on a quest for the perfect day pack for years. You'll inevitably end up owning several. In my experience, a lot of small packs are too small. You need one at least big enough to hold your field guide, notebook, water bottle, and lunch. I like packs that have tie-down straps so you can strap your jacket or sweater to the pack as the day gets warmer. I also like packs that have external holders for two water bottles; that way, a leaking water bottle can't ruin your field guide or worse, your lunch. If you do bird photography, check out photo stores for lightweight field bags that are still rugged enough to protect your gear. You'll have a lot of choices.

Roger, Over

Deadly serious birders use radios, cell phones, and pagers to keep in touch with fellow birders in the field and to get and give instant updates on rare birds. Frankly, a lot of the reason I go birding is to get far away from my telephone, so I'm not a big fan of this approach. It does have its uses, however. If you spot something unusual, you can call your birding friends and get them to race right over—or they can call you. Phones and radios are helpful if you're birding with a partner or small group and you want to spread out but still keep in touch. This is important, especially when there's been a change of plans about which restaurant to meet at for lunch. If you carry a cell phone or a pager, however, make sure it is one that vibrates instead of rings—nothing will scare the birds faster than a ringing telephone.

Weather Radios

I keep talking about how you should dress for the weather. To find out what the weather really is, you need more than the brief report on your local radio or TV station. Every birding household needs a dedicated weather radio that tunes in to the three different National Oceanographic and Atmospheric Administration (NOAA) frequencies. You can buy these inexpensively at any electronics store. Get a portable, battery-powered model you can carry with you to get on-the-spot reports.

Rappin' Robin

The **Global Positioning System** (GPS) is an array of navigation satellites originally created strictly for military use. Today, the system has been "civilianized" and can be used by anyone with a receiver for the signals. GPS receivers are hand-held devices that can locate your position anywhere on land or sea and even set a course to a new location. The cost? Under $300.

Other Cool Stuff

Here's just a sampling of the coolest electronic gadgets for the techie birder:

➤ **GPS receivers:** Thanks to the end of the Cold War, the future of outdoor activity is here. GPS receivers tap into the *Global Positioning System* satellite net overhead and give you an instant fix on your position—the electronic equivalent of a trail of breadcrumbs. GPS receivers are fabulous for telling you precisely where you—or the birds—are, down to seconds of longitude and latitude. You can also hook your GPS receiver into a laptop computer loaded with map software and get a detailed map showing you how to get from here to there. This stuff used to be expensive and cumbersome, but it's amazingly small and cheap now—and getting better all the time.

➤ **Mini video cameras:** Definitely the best new toys I've seen recently. You can set these up to observe or videotape nesting birds or your bird feeder. You need to get the camera pretty close, and of course, you need to be very cautious about disturbing nesting birds, but you can get some great close-up views with these setups. They're surprisingly inexpensive and easy to use.

➤ **Leatherman tool:** This handy all-in-one tool combines pliers, knife blades, screwdrivers, and the all-important can and bottle opener. I find it more useful than a Swiss Army pocket knife for fixing balky tripods and broken binocular straps in the field. Makes a great gift; hint around long enough and you're sure to get one.

➤ **Night vision scopes:** These scopes are also getting better and cheaper all the time, but that doesn't mean they're good or cheap. They do extend your night vision, which I guess could be useful when you're on an owl prowl, but the image is a little hard to read, the color is weird, and they only magnify about two times. If you have a spare thousand dollars or more and you're not happy unless you have the latest gadget, go ahead.

➤ **Portable computers:** As discussed earlier, laptop computers are useful when combined with a GPS receiver. (For more about computers and birding, refer to Chapter 9, "List Mania," and skip ahead to Chapter 33, "Virtual Birding.") If you can't wait to get home to update your life list, you can carry a palmtop organizer with you right into the field (for serious obsessives only).

Remember that all these electronic goodies run on batteries. Bring plenty of spares.

The Least You Need to Know

➤ The right footwear can make the difference between success and misery on a birding trip. Wear shoes that are appropriate for the weather and terrain.

➤ Birding vests and lightweight day packs are useful for carrying your extra gear comfortably.

➤ Be prepared for cold and wet weather with the right clothing.

➤ Electronic devices such as portable phones, weather radios, and GPS receivers make it easy to get valuable information right in the field.

Chapter 13

Basics of Bird Photography

In This Chapter

➤ Equipment for bird photography

➤ Capturing the birds—on film

➤ Being an ethical bird photographer

➤ Where to buy bird slides

Here's how to get started in bird photography: Use your simple point-and-shoot camera to take a picture of a bird. When you get the film back, look carefully at the pictures. When you realize that the beautiful bird you saw is nothing but a blurry speck in the photo, you're ready to get serious about bird photography.

Join the Crowd

A lot of birders prefer seeing their birds through a camera's viewfinder. That's because bird photography is fun and challenging—a true test of your skills as both a birder and a photographer. You don't have to be the next Eliot Porter to enjoy bird photography. A lot of birders take pictures just for fun or to document their sightings. Warning: The next time you see a birder staggering along with 40 pounds of cameras and lenses around his neck, a tripod over one shoulder, and a overstuffed gear bag over the other, remember that he too once took pictures "just" to document his sightings.

Investing in Your Camera

Your point-and-shoot Ph.D. (Push here, Dummy) camera just doesn't cut it when it comes to birds. You'll need to invest in a high-quality 35mm SLR (single-lens reflex) camera. Why? As I explain in a little bit, you need a rugged camera that can take different lenses. You also need a camera that lets you control the exposure by setting the aperture and shutter speed yourself. If your camera comes with a built-in motor drive to advance the film, listen to it before you buy. Some of today's motor drives are actually quieter than the manual film advance, but some aren't; choose the quietest.

Competition is so intense today that all SLR cameras from well-known manufacturers are high quality; crummy ones don't stand a chance. Read the ads and reviews in the photography magazines, send for the manufacturer's literature, and buy the best you can afford. As with any expensive equipment, stick to well-known, reliable manufacturers. Avoid no-name and house-brand equipment.

Cameras and lenses are expensive and a little delicate; you really need to keep them clean and dry. By definition, that's not always so easy when you're birding. You probably won't want to be photographing in a rainstorm, but weather happens. Be prepared. Carry plastic bags in assorted sizes for keeping gear dry, along with soft cloths for wiping it down.

Be a Better Birder

To learn more about bird photography, I suggest taking a photo workshop. There's no substitute for hands-on experience and a good teacher. Introductory photo workshops are easy to find; check your local adult education programs. Numerous nature photography workshops are offered all the time all over the country. Check out the listings in specialty magazines such as *Outdoor Photographer*.

Which Film?

Not an issue of a photo magazine goes by without an article on film. Most nature photographers use daylight color slide film from Kodak, Fuji, or Agfa. That's because professionals need to provide slides for publication. Amateurs like slides, too, because you can put together slide shows. But if you want the pictures for your photo album, to hang on the wall, or for identification and record-keeping, shoot color print film.

Beyond that, your film choice will depend a lot on the speed you need. (In general, the dimmer the conditions, the faster you'll want the film to be.) Every film brand is a little different in the way it captures color, so experiment and find the films you like.

L-o-o-ong Lenses

There's no way you can do bird photography without really long, really good lenses. That means spending really serious money. A good 300mm lens runs hundreds of dollars—and as the lenses get longer, so do the price tags. Don't cheap out. If your lens is crummy, your pictures will be crummy, no matter how beautifully you compose the shot. Never buy a no-name or "bargain" lens; I guarantee you'll regret it the minute you get your first roll of film back. Save the money toward a high-quality lens from a reputable manufacturer.

Bird photography requires really long lenses and a sturdy tripod. (Photo by Connie Toops.)

For serious bird photography, a 300mm lens is on the short side, although you can still get good pictures if you can get close enough to fill the frame with your subject—if you're photographing birds at your feeder from a nearby window, say.

For anything else, you really want a 400mm lens, and even that's good mostly for bigger birds. For smaller or more distant birds, you'll need a 500mm, 600mm, or even 800mm lens.

Lenses that long are a little tricky to use; you're way beyond point-and-shoot now. You'll need to shoot a lot of film to learn how to get sharp, well-exposed pictures. If you're just getting started in photography and you don't want to invest in long lenses, use a camera adapter on your spotting scope instead. The lousy results will persuade you to buy a good lens.

Lean on Me

Long lenses are heavy and cumbersome. You can just barely hand-hold a 300mm lens if you have strong arms and very steady hands, but a sturdy tripod to support the camera and lens combo is a vital tool for bird photography. Another useful tool for nature photography is a car pod—a mount for your camera that clamps onto a car window. A bean bag is handy for situations too awkward or low to the ground to use a tripod. Rest the lens on the bean bag to hold it steady.

Be a Better Birder

To learn more about nature photography in general, I recommend *The Essentials of Nature Photography* by Milton Heiberg (Tern Book Company, 1997). A good basic book on bird photography is *Wild Bird Photography* by Tim Gallagher (The Lyons Press, 1994). If you're serious about your pictures, get *The Art of Bird Photography: The Complete Guide to Professional Field Techniques* by Arthur Morris (Watson-Guptill, 1999)

Shoulder stocks that mount the camera and lens like a rifle are useful for shooting fast-moving birds. They're also great for taking pictures from any sort of moving platform, such as a boat.

I'm Ready for My Close-Up Now

What about filming and videotaping birds? That's way too complicated to discuss here. You'll need really good equipment to make it worthwhile. The average camcorder, for instance, is meant for taping your kid's birthday party, not for capturing birds in action. The first problem is that most of these cameras don't work well in any sort of low light, although some now come with a low-light switch that compensates. The so-called long lenses on camcorders don't work all that well in general; they rely on digital enhancement, not actual magnification, to pull in distant subjects. Camera shake shows up obviously when you use the magnifying switch on a camcorder; you'll have to use a tripod. Of course, you'll be seeing the bird in black-and-white through the viewfinder.

Setups for bird photography can get pretty elaborate, as this arrangement for hummingbird photography shows. (Photo by Connie Toops.)

Hunting with Your Camera

How do you find birds to photograph? Use your basic birding skills, along with these techniques:

➤ **Walk and stalk:** Walk along with your camera and tripod until you find a bird. Slowly get close enough to take a picture. That usually won't be very close, which is why you need those long lenses. This technique works best for shore birds, ducks, and wading birds such as herons, especially if there's some sort of barrier—water, a boardwalk, a jetty—between you and the birds.

➤ **Bait and wait:** Attract birds with food or water, set up your camera, and wait for the birds to come in. Your backyard birdfeeder is the simplest approach to this. This approach works well for smaller perching birds. It's how most pictures of hummingbirds are taken.

➤ **Blinds:** A *blind* lets you get close to the birds in a natural setting without being seen and without disturbing them. This is the best and most ethical approach to photographing behavior, especially breeding behavior and nests. A lot of refuges have permanent blinds near strategic spots such as ponds. Check with the refuge in advance about regulations and fees. Portable blinds (which you can buy or make on your own) let you set up exactly where you want, but again, check with the refuge management before you start. The best portable blind of all? Your car.

The beauty of a blind is that you can set up a lot of expensive equipment without scaring off the bird. Reflections glinting off lenses and equipment can frighten the birds. A blind cuts down on that quite a bit. It also keeps your gear out of the wind, so you don't have to worry as much about vibration and tripods crashing over, and it keeps your gear dry in wet weather. Depending on the situation, you might be able to leave your equipment in place for a few days, which saves a lot of hauling.

Rappin' Robin

A **blind** (hide if you're British) is a structure, either permanent or temporary, for observing wildlife without being seen.

The important thing in bird photography is to avoid flushing or stressing the birds. Be cautious, move slowly, and turn off all the noisy beepers on those fancy cameras. Most of all, be patient. For every stunning bird image you see in books and magazines, the photographer took a *lot* more pictures.

A Little Bird Told Me...

Here's what my friend Milton Heiberg, author of *The Essentials of Nature Photography*, has to say about cars: "My favorite way to use a car as a blind is to let my wife drive while I play General Patton from the sunroof of my car with head, shoulders, and elbow at car roof level and a 400mm lens with a bean bag resting on the roof as a camera support."

Ethical Photography

The quest for the perfect photo has been known to make bird photographers take an elastic approach to birding ethics. It's easy to cause a lot of stress to the birds you're trying to photograph. Here's how to do it ethically:

➤ Obey all regulations regarding photography on public lands. Avoid unpleasant surprises by asking in advance.

➤ Stay well back—at least 30 feet—from nesting sites, roosts, display areas, and feeding areas. *Never interfere with the birds' activities.*

➤ If you must get close, use a blind.

➤ *Never disturb the habitat.* Breaking off a branch to get a clearer view of a nest, for example, gives predators a clearer view of the nest as well.

➤ Use artificial light such as flashes cautiously. The closer you are to the bird, the more cautious you should be.

Be a responsible birder at all times. If you're in doubt, don't photograph.

What to Do with Your Pictures

Once you get started in bird photography, it's hard to stop. What can you do with all those pictures? Well, you're a birder, so you can spend many happy hours organizing and categorizing them. Then, you can post them on your home page or arrange them into slide shows and show them to anyone you can get into a dark room. Photo night is always a popular event for birding clubs. You can also enter your pictures into any of the many, many local and regional photo contests. If your pictures are very, very good, consider donating them to VIREO (mentioned later in the chapter).

Are you so good you're thinking of turning pro? Don't quit your day job. I've been a professional photo editor and researcher for years. I've had the great pleasure of working with many professional nature photographers. And I can tell you, this is a very, very tough way to make a living. The competition is intense. Your pictures have to be truly outstanding, not just very good. No matter how good your pictures are, without a good understanding of how the marketplace works, you're sunk.

Be a Better Birder

If you're serious about turning pro, get this book: *John Shaw's Business of Nature Photography: A Professional's Guide to Marketing and Managing a Successful Nature Photography Business* (Amphoto, 1997).

Buying Pictures

Sometimes, you'll want bird pictures you can't take yourself. You might want to study gull plumage, for instance, or prepare for a trip someplace by looking at slides of the birds you're likely to see. You can buy excellent individual 35mm color slides or sets of slides from:

Visual Resources for Ornithology (VIREO)
Academy of Natural Sciences
1900 Ben Franklin Parkway
Philadelphia, PA 19103
(215) 299-1069
Fax: (215) 299-1182
www.acnatsci.org/vireo/
VIREO@acnatsci.org

Cornell Laboratory of Ornithology
Division of Visual Services
159 Sapsucker Woods Road
Ithaca, NY 14850
(607) 254-2450
Fax: (607) 254-2415
www.birds.cornell.edu/closlides/index.html
djw16@cornell.edu

Sea and Sage Audubon Bird Slides
P.O. Box 5447
Irvine, CA 92616
(949) 261-7963
users.deltanet.com/users/adv/seasage/index.html

VIREO is the largest collection of bird slides in the world. All the pictures in these collections come entirely from donations by both professional and amateur photographers.

The cost to buy slides is minimal, just a few dollars apiece. Remember, however, that these slides are for your personal, nonprofit use only; you can't reproduce them or use them in any commercial way. It's okay to show the slides at a meeting of your local bird club, Scout troop, and the like. In fact, you can buy slide sets complete with scripts and even soundtracks designed for giving talks.

The Least You Need to Know

➤ Bird photography is an important aspect of birding and an enjoyable hobby in itself.

➤ You need good equipment to take good bird photographs. A high-quality camera and long lenses (at least 300mm) are musts.

➤ Finding birds to photograph is a lot like finding birds to watch. Photographing from blinds is a particularly useful way to get good shots.

➤ When photographing, always follow good birding ethics. When in doubt, don't take the picture.

129

Part 5
That Family Feeling

You might not know much about birds, but you know a hawk—and a hummingbird, a gull, a heron, a duck, and an owl—when you see one. Congratulations; you're on your way to being a good birdwatcher. You've already grasped the concept of bird families.

Understanding bird families is the first big step toward being a better birder. If you can get a bird into its family, you're on the way to identifying it; the rest is just details.

Chapter 14

Hawk Watching

In This Chapter

➤ Meet the hawk family

➤ Secrets of hawk identification

➤ Finding hawks to watch

➤ Hawks and migration

For many birders, hawks represent everything wild in nature. These powerful, agile birds are perfectly adapted to a life of hunting on the wing. Once you've seen a Peregrine Falcon come screaming down in a 200-mile-an-hour dive to seize an unsuspecting pigeon in a cloud of feathers, everything else in birding seems a little, well, tame.

Wrapped Up in Raptors

Birds that chase and kill animals or other birds to eat are generally known as *raptors,* or birds of prey. In general, the word raptor refers to hawks, falcons, eagles, and owls. These birds are magnificent fliers and have long, wickedly sharp talons and long, curved beaks. Because owls are nocturnal raptors—they're active at night—they need a chapter all to themselves. (See Chapter 15, "Owl Prowls.") In this chapter, you'll learn about *diurnal* raptors: day-flying birds of prey.

Worldwide, there are 205 diurnal raptor species. About 22 species are commonly found in North America.

A Little Bird Told Me...

The Harpy Eagle, found in the rain forests of Central and South America, is the raptor you'd least like to meet in a dark alley. Weighing in at 20 pounds or more (roughly twice the weight of a Bald Eagle) and with a wingspan of more than six feet, the harpy eagle is the largest and most formidable raptor in the world. Because of massive rain forest destruction, it's also one of the most endangered.

Know Your Hawks

Broadly speaking, you can call all day-flying birds of prey hawks, but that's like calling every sort of aircraft an airplane. Just as some aircraft are two-seater prop planes and others are jumbo jets, hawks come in a variety of sizes and shapes. Just about all the North American raptors fall into one of five main groups, but a few raptors are in categories all their own. Read about the hawks here, and then take a look at the color picture inserts.

Rappin' Robin

Raptors are birds of prey, members of the hawk, falcon, eagle, and owl families. The word comes from the Latin word meaning "one who seizes," which is a pretty good description of how these fierce birds behave. **Diurnal** raptors are birds of prey active during the day—basically, all the raptors except for the owls.

Kites: Poetry in Motion

Slim, light-bodied, medium-sized raptors, kites eat mostly insects, reptiles, amphibians, and small mammals such as mice. Kites are extremely graceful and acrobatic in flight, with long, pointed wings and long tails. In North America, kites are found mostly over open spaces in southern parts of the country. Unlike many other raptors, kites tend to be very sociable, flocking together and migrating in groups that may contain several hundred birds.

A Little Bird Told Me...

The Snail Kite is one of pickier eaters in the bird world. This bird eats almost nothing but apple snails. To pry the snails out of their shells, the Snail Kite uses its very long, curved, slender beak. Snail Kites live in fresh-water marshes throughout Central and South America. They were once found widely throughout Florida, but because of habitat loss, today they're pretty much restricted to the Loxahatchee Wildlife Refuge on Lake Okeechobee.

Accipiters: Hawks of the Forest

Birds of the forest, accipiters prey mostly on other birds and on small mammals. Accipiters are built for speed and maneuverability, with long tails and short, rounded wings. There are only three accipiter species in North America: the Sharp-shinned Hawk, the Coopers Hawk, and the Goshawk. If you see a hawk pick off a bird at your bird feeder, you're probably seeing a Sharp-shinned Hawk. In old books, accipiters are sometimes called chicken hawks or pigeon hawks.

Buteos: Soaring on the Wind

When you think of a hawk, you're most likely thinking of a member of the buteo family. These birds have chunky bodies, broad, rounded tails and large, broad wings. They soar effortlessly high in the sky, wheeling in large circles. The 12 North American buteos are pretty diverse in size, range, and appearance. The most common buteo is the red-tailed hawk, which is found in just about every habitat across North America.

A Little Bird Told Me...

Hawks usually hunt alone or in pairs, but the Harris's Hawk, found in the Southwest and Latin America, hunts in packs much as wolves do. Like wolf packs, the "hawk pack" is a family group of about five individuals. The birds work as a relay team to chase down their prey (usually rabbits) and then share the food. When one of the females in the group has chicks, all group members, not just her mate, bring food to the nest.

Get to know the Red-tailed Hawk (take a look at the picture), and use it as your reference bird when you're hawk-watching. A Red-tail is a large, stocky bird, with a wing span of about four feet. Seen from below, its body is light-colored. When this bird is soaring, you can usually spot the short, rusty red tail quite easily (except for young birds, who don't have their red tails yet). Another good field mark is the patagial bar on each wing, a dark streak on the leading edge of the wing that reaches from the body to the wrist.

Eagles: Size Does Count

When is a hawk an eagle? When it's *big*. Eagles are the largest raptors in North America; the Bald Eagle can have a wingspan of up to 7.5 feet. Worldwide, there are about 60 eagle species, but only the Bald Eagle and the Golden Eagle are commonly found in North America. In fact, the Bald Eagle is found *only* in North America. You're most likely to see one along coastal areas, large inland lakes, and rivers.

Falcons: Masters of Flight

The sleekest, fastest hawks, falcons have swept-back, pointed wings, long tails, and slim, compressed bodies. These fierce birds are supremely good flyers and generally capture their prey on the wing. Falcons generally eat other birds, but smaller falcons such as the American Kestrel also eat a lot of grasshoppers, small rodents, and other small prey. In old nature books, peregrines are sometimes called duck hawks; Kestrels are sometimes called sparrowhawks or windhovers.

You can find Peregrine Falcons today in just about any major city. After all, a skyscraper ledge or bridge tower is just as good a nesting site as a cliff face, and cities are full of complacent pigeons that make easy meals. That these magnificent birds are found in major cities today is a direct result of conservation efforts that reintroduced captive-bred birds. The introduced birds have generally done so well that they've raised families of their own.

A Little Bird Told Me...

In the 1940s, there were some 275 active Peregrine nesting sites in the northeastern United States alone. By the 1960s, poisoning from the pesticide DDT had affected the Peregrines so severely that not one of those nests was in use. When DDT was banned in 1972, the Peregrines began to recover, helped along by captive breeding and reintroduction programs. Today, there are more than 1,500 breeding pairs of Peregrine Falcons across the U.S. and Canada, and the birds are about to be taken off the endangered species list.

Peregrine Falcons are favorite birds for *falconry,* the ancient sport of hunting with hawks. In the U.S., you must have a permit to own a raptor for falconry. Unfortunately, in other parts of the world, the rules are lot looser, and there's big money to be made. The demand for wild-caught birds is a big reason for illegal trapping of wild raptors.

Northern Harrier: the Hawk of the Marshes

There are 13 members of the harrier subfamily worldwide, but only the Northern Harrier is found in North America. This slim, long-tailed bird has slender wings; the males are pale gray, whereas the females are rusty brown. The Northern Harrier is easy to identify when it's flying: It glides along low to the ground, and you can see a distinctive white patch on its rump. Look for it especially in open, marshy areas; that's why in older books, it's called the marsh hawk.

Rappin' Robin

Falconry, or hunting with tamed raptors, especially Peregrine Falcons, is an ancient sport dating back more than 4,000 years. In the past—and in large part, today—the birds used in falconry are wild birds that have been trapped and trained.

Osprey: Fish Tales

The Osprey is in a subfamily all its own—*Pandionidae.* This large raptor is found on every continent except Antarctica. Its long, crooked wings span anywhere from four to six feet. Ospreys are exclusively fish eaters. They hover over water until they spot a fish and then dive down and plunge feet first into the water to grab it. Not surprisingly, older common names for Ospreys include fish hawk and sea eagle.

Vultures: the Raptors That Aren't

Birds such as the Turkey Vulture and the Black Vulture sure look like raptors: They've got awfully large, sharp bills, and they fly by soaring high in circles. Recent research shows, however, that New World *vultures* aren't raptors at all; they're really members of the stork family.

Vultures are part of nature's clean-up crew. They eat mostly carrion, or dead animals, and don't usually kill their prey themselves. These birds are big, with wingspans of six feet, and quite common. They're easy to ID. A Turkey Vulture holds its wings in a V shape, and the bird tilts and rocks as it soars. Black Vultures have shorter tails and broader wings. They fly with a series of rapid flaps and then a short glide.

Rappin' Robin

Vultures are often incorrectly called buzzards. The word buzzard comes from the French word *busard,* meaning hawk, and is used in Europe today to refer to soaring hawks, or buteos. Here in the U.S., it doesn't really mean anything.

In all this talk about hawks, I haven't mentioned the common nighthawk. Why? This bird isn't a raptor at all; it's a member of the insect-eating goatsucker or nightjar family, along with the whip-poor-will and several other species. Goatsuckers have tiny bills, incredibly large mouths, and very short, weak legs. They're generally most active at dusk and at dawn.

North American Raptors

Raptor Group	Species
Kites	Mississippi Kite
	American swallow-tailed Kite
	White-tailed Kite
	Snail Kite
	Hook-billed Kite
Accipiters	Sharp-shinned Hawk
	Cooper's Hawk
	Northern Goshawk
Buteos	Harris's Hawk
	Common Black-hawk
	Gray Hawk
	Red-shouldered Hawk
	Broad-winged Hawk
	Red-tailed Hawk
	Swainson's Hawk
	Rough-legged Hawk
	Ferruginous Hawk
	White-tailed Hawk
	Zone-tailed Hawk
	Short-tailed Hawk
Eagles	Bald Eagle
	Golden Eagle
Falcons	Crested Caracara
	American Kestrel
	Merlin
	Aplomado Falcon
	Prairie Falcon
	Gyrfalcon
	Peregrine Falcon
Harriers	Northern Harrier
Ospreys	Osprey

A Little Bird Told Me...

There's a reason we use expressions such as "eagle-eyed" or "watching something like a hawk." Raptors have extremely good eyesight; as a rough rule of thumb, a hawk can see about two to three times as well as a human. In part, that's because a hawk's eye is proportionately much larger than a human's eye. A Bald Eagle's eyeball, for instance, is larger than a human's—even though a bald eagle generally weighs only about 10 pounds. A soaring bald eagle can spot potential prey on the ground from hundreds of feet in the air.

Hawks in Flight

Hawks are awesome flyers; everything about them is designed for flight. When you watch hawks, you'll see several different kinds of flight:

➤ **Soaring**: When sunshine warms the ground, columns of warm air called *thermals* rise up. Hawks catch the rising thermals and use them to soar effortlessly upward on outstretched wings. Likewise, hawks soar on wind that is deflected upward along mountain ridges. A group of hawks using the same thermal to spiral upward is called a *kettle*.

➤ **Gliding**: Once a hawk gets up to the top of a thermal, it can move along to the next one by gliding—tucking its wings in partway and gliding downward at an angle. By soaring and gliding, a hawk can go for miles with hardly a wing flap. Buteos are particularly good at this.

➤ **Flight**: When there aren't any thermals to ride, hawks have to fly actively by flapping their wings. Because this takes a lot of energy, hawks generally combine flapping and soaring—usually a few flaps and then a glide.

➤ **Hovering**: When something on the ground catches a hawk's interest, it may hover with beating wings over the spot to take a closer look. Kestrels do this a lot; so do Ospreys.

➤ **Kiting**: Instead of hovering, larger hawks such as Red-tails kite when they want a closer look. They face into the wind and hang still in the

Rappin' Robin

Soaring birds use **thermals**, columns of air warmed by the sun that rise up from the ground, as an easy way to gain altitude. A **kettle** is a group of hawks using a thermal to climb upward. Kettle also means any large group of hawks. A bunch of hawks soaring up on a thermal look like the bubbles in a pot of boiling water.

Be a Better Birder

Experienced hawk watchers can identify raptors in flight from great distances. How? Every raptor species flies in a different way. Once you get the idea, telling the raptors apart gets a lot easier. For expert advice, I strongly recommend the bible of the field, *Hawks in Flight*, by Pete Dunne, David Sibley, and Clay Sutton (Houghton Mifflin, 1988).

air, just like a kite on a string. If you can get your binocs on a kiting hawk, you'll be able to get a really good view of all the field marks. Watch long enough, and you might see the bird stoop, or dive down to seize prey.

Finding Hawks to Watch

Compared to say, chickadees, you'll see a lot fewer hawks. That's because hawks aren't particularly sociable birds—they don't usually flock together—and because they're territorial. A hawk pair will chase away any other hawks that wander into their territory. The hawks are there, however, and once you know where to look, you'll easily spot them.

When you're out birding, the best way to find hawks is to go where the hawks like to be. In general, hawks need room to soar, so they're more likely to be found around open areas such as grassy fields, beaches, and marshes. Whenever you're birding in these areas, keep an eye out for hawks. Look up, of course, to see any soaring birds on patrol over the area. Also be sure to check out the edges; look for hawks perched in the branches of trees bordering fields, for instance. American Kestrels are often found perched on a fence post, stump, or wire along the edge of an open field or even on a grassy median strip by a highway. From there, they can easily spot and pounce on their favorite foods, grasshoppers and small rodents—a technique known as perch-hunting. Sometimes, kestrels will hover over a promising patch of ground. (These little hawks will nest in human-provided nesting boxes. See Chapter 27, "Equal Opportunity Housing," for more information.)

Any place with a high concentration of shorebirds or waterfowl, such as beaches, marshy areas, and wetlands, will also be attractive to raptors, such as Northern Harriers and Peregrine Falcons, that prey on these birds.

Be alert to the behavior of the birds around you. If you suddenly see all the songbirds dropping out of the sky and diving for cover, for example, chances are good that a bird-eating hawk such as a Peregrine Falcon is in the area. Likewise, if you see a flock of larger birds such as mallards suddenly take off, look for a hawk—especially if the birds have flown off in all directions.

Perched hawks are often harassed by other birds; crows love to do this. If you notice a bunch of crows dive-bombing a tree and making a ruckus, check the branches for a hawk. (Keep an open mind; as you'll learn in the next chapter, they could be attacking an owl instead.) Once you spot the hawk, keep watching. It may get so fed up with those pesky crows that it flies off.

A Little Bird Told Me...

The Peregrine Falcon was saved and reintroduced in North America through the efforts of The Peregrine Fund and other conservation organizations. Worldwide (including North America), birds of prey are still in trouble. For information on how you can help support research and captive breeding and reintroduction programs, contact:

The Peregrine Fund/World Center for Birds of Prey
5666 West Flying Hawk Lane
Boise, ID 83709
(208) 362-3716
Fax: (208) 362-2376
tpf@peregrinefund.org
www.peregrinefund.org

The Peregrine Fund also has a captive breeding and release program for the endangered California Condor, a bird that would be extinct today without the Fund's efforts.

Sometimes some of the small birds in the area gang up on a hawk (or an owl), a type of behavior called *mobbing*. Why would a bunch of little chickadees and sparrows take such a risk? Good question—researchers aren't really sure. Some believe that the smaller birds are telling the hawk they know it's there. By mobbing it, they're in effect saying to the hawk, "We're on to you, big guy. You're not going to catch one of us by surprise. Why don't you just forget it and leave quietly?"

Bald Eagles will often concentrate in areas where food is easy to find. A famous example is the Chilkat Peninsula in southern Alaska, where the eagles gather by the hundreds every winter to feed on salmon. To a lesser degree, eagles will also gather near reservoirs and dams where the water stays open all winter. Local birders can usually tell you about eagle concentrations.

Migrating Hawks

During the fall migration, hawks are among the easiest of birds to watch. That's because their migration paths tend to follow the air currents along north–south mountain chains, ridge lines, rivers, and coastlines—paths that funnel the hawks past well-known observation points, or hawk watches. During the peak migration period, thousands of raptors may pass overhead every hour.

The famous hawk-watch platform at Cape May Point, New Jersey. The tally board keeps count of the species that pass overhead. (Photo by Cliff Beittel.)

Visiting a hawk watch site is a great way to learn a lot about hawks in a hurry. All the well-known hawk watches, such as Hawk Mountain in Pennsylvania and Cape May Point in New Jersey, are staffed by professional naturalists and enthusiastic volunteers. They're there to keep count of the birds and to educate the public, and they'll be delighted to introduce you to the birds they love. After seeing several thousand birds of the same species go past, you'll have a pretty good idea of how to identify it on your own the next time. You might also get a chance to see some hawks up close because a lot of hawk watches have nearby banding locations. Captured birds are sometimes brought to the watch site for demonstrations and then released.

The fall hawk migration season begins in late August and lasts into late November. Years of observation at hawk watches show that different species have fairly predictable peaks; you'll see some hawks at any time during the migration period, but you'll see some species in spectacular numbers only at certain times. At the Hazel Bazemore County Park hawk watch in Corpus Christi, Texas, for example, you could see nearly a million Broad-winged Hawks pass overhead in flying rivers from late September to early October—thousands in an hour—to say nothing of the 18 or so other hawk species you might see.

A Little Bird Told Me...

There are dozens of well-known hawk watches across the United States and Canada—and more are being discovered all the time. To find a hawk watch near you, contact:

Hawk Migration Association of North America (HMANA)
377 Loomis Street
Southwick, MA 01077
www.hmana.org

HMANA is a nonprofit volunteer group that keeps track of the various hawk watches. The Web site has a comprehensive listing of North American hawk watches.

Where are all those hawks going when they migrate? It depends. Swainson's Hawks move from their breeding grounds on the prairies to their wintering grounds in the pampas of Argentina—a distance of about 7,000 miles. Broad-winged Hawks go as far south as Peru. Most raptor species are partial migrants; some individuals stay put year round, whereas others move south out of their usual range.

The ideal weather for a day at the fall hawk watch? A clear, blustery day—preferably after a day or two of rain—with winds from the north. In the spring, it's the same, except you want winds from the south. Either way, the weather's likely to be cold; dress warmly in layers. Bring along a thermos, snacks, lunch, and a cushion to sit on. To help you keep count, bring a notebook and pencil or, better yet, a hand-held clicker. (You can get these at well-stocked stationery stores.)

Hawk watching is exciting, but it's not exactly strenuous. You mostly stay in one place as the hawks pass by. Often, you don't even have to go far; at Cape May Point, the hawk watch platform is

Splat!

A day at the hawk watch is usually a day in cool temperatures but bright sunshine. You can get a nasty sunburn if you're not prepared; don't forget the sunblock. Hawk-watching is also tough on the eyes. Wear high-quality sunglasses and a hat with a visor. Even so, be prepared for red, tearing eyes by the end of the day. Over-the-counter eyedrops often help.

just yards from the parking lot. At the Butler Sanctuary in Mount Kisco, New York, you have to walk about a quarter of a mile from the parking lot to get to the tiers of bleachers at the hawk watch.

A lot of other migrating birds fly past at the hawk watch. Hawk watchers call these birds tweetie birds, dicky birds, or hawk food.

The Least You Need to Know

➤ The raptors, or birds of prey, include hawks, falcons, eagles, vultures, and owls. The words raptor and hawk are loosely interchangeable.

➤ About 22 day–flying raptor species are found in North America, including kites, accipiters (bird hawks), buteos (soaring hawks), eagles, falcons, the Northern Harrier, and the Osprey.

➤ Although vultures are traditionally considered raptors, recent research shows they are really members of the stork family.

➤ All raptors are magnificent flyers; look for them high in the air above open fields, marshes, and beaches.

➤ During the fall and spring migration, raptors pass overhead in large numbers at predictable points along the migration paths. Visiting a hawk watch is a great way to see a lot of birds.

Chapter 15

Owl Prowls

In This Chapter

➤ Owls: masters of the night

➤ My, what big eyes—and ears—you have

➤ Listening for owls

➤ How to see an owl

Whenever a movie director wants to make a nighttime scene seem really scary, you can be sure owl hoots will be on the sound track. The effect is wasted on birders; they know better. Owls are mysterious and fascinating, but scary? Never.

Owls: The Eyes Have It

When the sun goes down, there's a shift change among the raptors. The hawks and eagles settle down for the night, and the *owls* take over. Owls are nocturnal raptors, fearsome hunters perfectly adapted for nighttime existence. Owl flight is distinctive because the wings flap high up and well below the body, sort of like a moth. When an owl flies, its flat head, short neck, and stocky body make it look a little like a speeding bullet going backward.

Except for Barn Owls, which belong to the family *Tytonidae*, all owls are members of the family *Strigidae*. There are about 148 owl species worldwide; 19 species are found in North America. Check out the table for a list of North American owls.

Owls of North America

Common Barn Owl	Whiskered Screech-Owl
Short-eared Owl	Flammulated Owl
Long-eared Owl	Elf Owl
Great Horned Owl	Ferruginous Pygmy Owl
Barred Owl	Northern Pygmy Owl
Great Gray Owl	Northern Saw-whet Owl
Spotted Owl	Boreal Owl
Snowy Owl	Northern Hawk-Owl
Western Screech-Owl	Burrowing Owl
Eastern Screech-Owl	

Owls have very large eyes, usually with yellow or orange irides, and that are sensitive to light. They're also forward-facing instead of on either side of the head as in all other birds; that, combined with their short bills, is why owls look so "human." Owls can see extremely well even in near total darkness. Because their eyes face forward, owls have binocular vision, much as humans do. This gives them excellent depth perception and lets them judge the distance to their prey with great precision.

Rappin' Robin

Owls are birds of prey active mostly at night or twilight. In general, owls are stocky birds with forward-facing eyes, large heads, short bills, and short tails. Owls can fly silently because their feathers are very soft and generally cover even the legs and feet; there's almost no air resistance to make noise.

An owl's hearing is just as sharp as its eyesight. Owls have large, highly developed ears with big openings. In many species, the ears are asymmetrical; one ear is slightly higher than the other. Owls also have flat faces with the feathers arranged in a disk shape. The facial disk acts sort of like a satellite dish to reflect sound waves to the ears, whereas the asymmetrical ears help the bird triangulate on prey. The end result? Barn Owls can catch mice in total darkness, finding them through sound alone.

Many owls have "ear tufts" that stick up from their heads. Calling these feathers ear tufts is misleading. An owl's ears are on the sides of its head and can't be seen. The tufts are actually just part of the owl's camouflage; they make the bird look more like a mammal.

A Little Bird Told Me...

Despite myths to the contrary, owls can see perfectly well in daylight. At night, they can see easily 10 to even 100 times as well as a human. Like most other birds, owls can't move their eyes in their sockets. To see to either side, an owl has to move its whole head. That's the basis of the myth that owls can rotate their heads in a complete circle. They can't, but they come close at 270 degrees in either direction.

Who-o-o-o Are You?

You're more likely to hear an owl than see one. These nocturnal birds call fairly often through the night, especially during the breeding season. Each owl species has a distinctive call, so you can easily learn to identify the species by ear.

In most of North America, the most common owls are the Great Horned Owl, the Screech-Owl (Eastern or Western species), the Barred Owl, and the Common Barn Owl. Here's what to listen for:

➤ **Great Horned Owl:** The usual call is five or six deep hoots or *whoos*, repeated several times. A good mnemonic that captures the rhythm is "Who's a-wake? Me t-o-o." Often the calls are between mates or other Great Horned Owls in the area, so listen for the answer as well. If you hear an answering *whoo, whoo,* you're probably hearing the female of the pair.

➤ **Screech-Owls:** The Eastern Screech-Owl makes a soft, tremulous sort of whinny or whistle that slides down the scale. It also makes trilling calls on one note; these can go on for several seconds. The Western Screech-Owl makes a whistling sort of call, a series of short, spaced notes that start slowly and speed up in tempo.

➤ **Barred Owl:** The call of the Barred Owl is a series of deep hoots that follow this rhythm: "Who cooks for you; who cooks for you a-a-a-l?"

Be a Better Birder

Mourning Doves, one of the most common birds in North America, make a sad, five-syllable call that goes *oo-ah, whoo, whoo, whoo.* Because the last three notes are on the same pitch, beginning birders often mistake them for the hoots of an owl. If you're in doubt, check the time. If you hear the call during daylight hours, it's probably a Mourning Dove. Owls only sometimes call during the day in early morning or late afternoon.

Splat!

Some birders have good luck luring owls in by imitating the squeaks of an injured mouse. If you do it cautiously and stop the moment you see the owl approach, squeaking is okay. Luring owls by imitating their calls or playing tapes isn't. Calling causes unnecessary stress to the bird and is forbidden in most refuges. The only time calling is acceptable is for research projects.

➤ **Barn Owl:** These owls don't hoot at all, but they do make a lot of other noises, including a shriek that's terrifying until you realize what it is. The more common sound is a short screech. Young Barn Owls make a lot of raspy, almost barking sounds as they demand food from their parents.

Owls are territorial, so if you hear one, chances are it's a resident of the area and will call some more. During the breeding season, the female tends to stay close to the nest while the male moves around. You'll hear one owl calling from different places while the response comes from roughly the same place. Listen carefully, and you might get an idea of where the nest is. Crashing around in the woods at night isn't the best idea, however, so you'll have to come back in the day to find it for sure.

Seeing Owls

You know there are owls out there somewhere because you've heard them. The next step—and it's a big one—is to see them.

Owls are so hard to find because they're masters of camouflage; they're hard to see even when you're looking right at them. As you can see from the pictures in this chapter and on the color pages, owls usually come in shades of brown, tan, and white, arranged in patterns of streaks, bars, and spots that let them blend in perfectly with tree trunks and branches. Even when someone else has focused a spotting scope exactly on an owl, you might have to stare for several minutes before you see it. You're hardly alone; even experienced birders have trouble spotting owls. I was once with a group of birders trying to find a Long-eared Owl we knew for a certainty was perched in a Japanese black pine. All six of us circled the tree for at least 10 minutes before someone finally spotted the ear tufts sticking up. Even then, it took several more minutes of direction-giving before everyone saw the bird. On the other hand, I once saw a Great Horned Owl perched at dusk on a TV antenna atop a suburban split-level. That's the fun of owls; you never know when you'll get lucky.

The best way to see an owl is to find a nest or roosting spot. That's a lot easier said than done, but you can improve your odds by knowing what to look for. You've found a roosting spot when you see:

➤ **Whitewash:** The polite way of saying bird droppings, whitewash looks just like it sounds—like splashes of thick white paint on the trunk and lower branches of favorite roosting trees and on the ground below.

An Eastern Screech-Owl perches next to a tree trunk. The ear tufts make a potential predator think it's seeing a mammal. (Photo by Connie Toops.)

➤ **Pellets:** Where there's whitewash, there's likely to be owl *pellets*. Look for little heaps of them on the ground below a roost. Unlike other animal droppings, owl pellets are dry, compact, and rough; they're often gray or whitish. They vary in size from tiny (Screech Owls) to huge (Great Horned Owls) and contain obvious bits of fur, bones, and feathers.

➤ **Bones, skulls, or feathers on the ground:** Sometimes, an owl will drop a piece of its prey—a wing or a leg—on the ground. Also, when pellets decompose, bits of bone and whole skulls are often left sitting on the ground. If you see a neat circle of feathers on the ground, however, you've found the remains of a hawk's kill.

Rappin' Robin

Owls don't have enough stomach acid to digest bones, feathers, and fur from their prey. Instead, they form these waste products into solid **pellets** and regurgitate them, usually at the rate of two a day.

149

Owls often use the same roost over and over again, so keep your eyes open in the woods and look for the telltale whitewash. Also look—and listen—for agitated song-birds or jays or crows making a ruckus. They might be mobbing a roosting owl or hawk.

A Little Bird Told Me...

Dissecting owl pellets is an interesting way to learn about what owls eat. Collect some pellets—they're odorless and safe to touch—and break them up gently with your fingers. You'll see a lot of fur and feathers and a lot of teeth, small bones, and bone fragments. You'll even see whole skulls of small rodents and birds.

If you're very, very fortunate (I've only ever seen this once), you might spot wing marks in the snow made by an owl snatching its prey.

Another good way to spot an owl is to spot a nest. Owls don't make nests themselves, so you'll have to look for likely nesting sites:

➤ **Stick nests in treetops:** Some large owls, such as the Great Horned Owl, take over abandoned stick nests made by other birds such as hawks or crows. You can find these nests fairly easily by scanning the treetops, especially along the edges of fields and meadows.

➤ **Cavities:** Smaller owls such as Screech-Owls are cavity nesters; they use holes in tree trunks and even fence posts and utility poles. The holes are easy to spot, but seeing the owl—assuming one is there—is tough because the owls blend in so perfectly. The best advice I can offer is to check out every possibility, preferably from several angles. Look especially in large, old trees with natural cavities and in tree stubs with old flicker holes in them.

➤ **Ledges:** Barn Owls will nest in cavities, but they seem to prefer ledges inside barns and other large, open buildings. They also like bridge girders and similar sites like microwave towers.

➤ **Nest boxes:** Smaller owls such as Barn Owls and Screech-Owls will sometimes nest in boxes put up just for them (or for kestrels).

If you do find an owl nest, don't get too close. It's unethical to disturb or harass the bird—and annoyed owls have been known to attack over-curious birders.

Going on an Owl Prowl

The best time for owling is between midnight and about 3 a.m., which can certainly complicate your life if you have a day job or a family who likes to see you now and then. Wait for a moonlit night without much wind. The best season for owling is late summer to early winter. Stay out of the woods during the breeding season, which for owls is basically from January to April.

If you're new to owls, go on an owl prowl with an organized group. Local bird clubs often arrange informal evening owl prowls to visit known roosts and nest sites in the area. Owl prowls are also regularly scheduled at some well-known birding sites such as Cape May. By going with a group, you'll get a feel for what to look for—and you'll probably see an owl or two.

The drawback to going with a group is that all the noise you make may spook the owls. I much prefer going on an owl prowl by myself or with just one or two other people.

Alone or in a group, you need to be aware of your movements as you approach an owl. Moving rapidly or making a lot of noise will send the owl flying off silently before you get close enough to spot it. Move very, very quietly and very, very slowly. When you see the owl, freeze for a few moments. Then, slowly and quietly, crouch down or lean up against a tree trunk; the idea is to disguise your silhouette and seem less threatening. If you're fortunate, the owl will relax and stay put, letting you slowly bring up your binoculars and get a good look.

Some owls, such as the Great Horned Owl and the Barn Owl, are found pretty much everywhere across North America. Most are fussier about their habitats. The Spotted Owl of the Pacific Northwest is so fussy that it won't live anywhere but old-growth forests—a major reason the government halted the logging of these magnificent forests. The Elf Owl appears only in the deserts of the Southwest. Some owls, such as the Snowy Owl and the Great Gray Owl, are generally found well north of the Canadian border. Almost every winter, however, a few of these northern owls find their way as far south as Washington DC, although northern Minnesota and Michigan are more likely spots. When these owls turn up, birders come running for the chance to see them.

Be a Better Birder

When you go into the woods at night, bring a large, high-quality flashlight with fresh batteries. Bring a compass and a map and stay on the trail; it's easy to get disoriented in the dark. Dress warmly in cold weather; put on a lot of bug spray in warm weather.

The Least You Need to Know

➤ Owls are birds of prey perfectly adapted for nighttime activity. They have keen eyesight and hearing.

➤ Owls are heard much more often than they're seen. The calls are easy to learn.

➤ To see an owl, locate a favorite roost or nest site. Owls are so well camouflaged that they're hard to spot even when they're in plain sight.

➤ Some owl species, such as the Great Horned Owl, are widespread and relatively easy to find. Others, such as the Elf Owl, are found only in certain kinds of habitats; you'll have to make a special trip to see one.

Chapter 16

Sorting Out the Shorebirds

In This Chapter

➤ Sorting out the shorebirds

➤ Identifying plovers and sandpipers

➤ Learning the other shorebirds

➤ Understanding shorebird migration

For the average person, a day at the beach means you lounge around in the sun, work on your tan, go for a swim, and maybe get a hotdog or ice cream at the food stand. For the average birder, a day at the beach is something very different. It starts at dawn, when the birds are most active and the food stands are still closed. You don't get to lounge around much either; when the birds are active, you have to be, too.

A Day at the Beach

Beaches and shorelines are really productive for birding; you're sure to see some interesting birds at any time of year. Of all the birds at the beach, however, the most interesting and challenging are definitely the *shorebirds*—those drab little birds you see running along by the water's edge or standing around on sandbars and mudflats.

Rappin' Robin

Shorebird is a general term used mostly for birds in the plover (*Charadriidae*) and sandpiper (*Scolopacidae*) families—birds found mostly along ocean and bay shorelines. European birders often say *waders* instead of shorebirds. In the U.S., however, waders usually refers to larger birds such as herons, storks, and ibises.

Be a Better Birder

Especially during the spring and fall migrations, you can see plenty of passerine birds at the beach, including warblers, sparrows, thrushes, swallows, and flycatchers. Find these birds by moving inland to the belt of coastal vegetation just behind the dunes. To find larger wading birds such as herons, visit any nearby fresh or saltwater marshes.

At first glance, the shorebirds might all look the same, but the fun of birding is taking that second glance and realizing how diverse the birds really are. What looks like a bunch of the same little brownish birds turns into several different species when you know how to look.

Shorebird ID can be a little tricky. Shorebirds come mostly in subtle shades of gray, brown, white, and tan. They don't usually have the distinctive colors and field marks that make it easy to tell the difference between, say, a cardinal and a scarlet tanager. There's also not usually much difference in appearance between males and females.

To sort out the shorebirds, you'll rely on plumage plus some other hints. Start by looking at the overall shape of the body; this is probably the most important clue. Is the bird dumpy or slender? Does it teeter along on extra-long legs? What's the shape and size of the bill? How and where is it feeding? Look also for the pattern of white and black that flashes on its wings as it flies—and check whether the bird has a white rump patch. You'll also have to listen; the most reliable way to tell some shorebirds apart is by their calls. Finally, you'll need to understand shorebird migration patterns. (I discuss that later in this chapter.)

You can actually check all these features because shorebirds are fairly easy to watch. They tend to stay more or less in one place for short periods and then fly a little ways. You can generally get good looks at them as they feed or stand around and then get good looks at them as they fly. You'll also be able to hear them easily; many shorebirds call as they fly or land. By putting together all the clues—appearance, behavior, and sound—you'll be able to work out the ID.

154

A Semipalmated Plover, one of the most common shorebirds. The compact rounded body, short bill, and short legs are all clues that the bird is in the plover family. (Photo by Cliff Beittel.)

A Marbled Godwit, one of the largest members of the sandpiper family. Note the long slightly upcurved bill; only godwits have bills like this. (Photo by Cliff Beittel.)

155

A Little Bird Told Me...

When you look closely at the subtle colors of shorebirds, you'll see that these birds tend to be darkest along their backs. Their flanks are lighter, and they often have pure white on their bellies. Countershading, as this is called, helps conceal the birds from predators, especially airborne predators such as hawks. Seen from above, the bird's dark back blends in to the darker water or ground. Seen from below when the bird is in flight, the light underparts blend in to the light sky. Seen from the side, the bird's shadow darkens the underparts, while the sun lightens the back—the bird blends in to the landscape.

Birding at the Beach

The best time to see shorebirds is early in the morning or at low tide; they'll be actively feeding then. At high tide, the birds tend to rest huddled together on sandbars or above the high-water mark. To learn the tide schedule for a site you want to visit, check the tide tables in the local paper (it's usually near the weather map) or call the site. The best season for seeing shorebirds is in July and August. The birds have finished their breeding chores up north and are on their way back to their wintering grounds. They're still in their breeding plumage, however, so they're easier to tell apart. The young birds hatched that year are also in the southbound crowd, so there are a lot of birds on the beach.

A Little Bird Told Me...

Shorebird identification can be tricky even for experienced birders, much less for beginners. Sometimes, you just can't be sure what the bird is. Don't let it bother you. Remember what Henry David Thoreau, who was both a pretty good philosopher and a pretty good birder, wrote in his journal for November 1, 1853: "Saw three of those birds.... They must be either sandpipers, telltales...or plovers (?) Or may they be the turnstone?"

You'll definitely want to bring your spotting scope to the beach. The shorebirds are wary; you can't always get close enough with binocs to see them well. Sandbars and mudflats usually have tons of resting and feeding shorebirds on them, but again, you'll need your scope to see them.

Shorebird Families

The two main shorebird families are the sandpipers and the plovers. In your field guide, the descriptions of the species in each family go on for page after intimidating page of birds that all look alike. They appear not only in breeding and winter plumages but also juvenile plumage.

Well, shorebird ID can be tricky, and I'll admit it's my weakest area as a birder. (Actually, I'm so bad at it that I'm a big joke to my birding friends. They only come with me to use my spotting scope.) Even so, I usually manage to eventually work out the right ID, and you can, too. In fact, with a little practice, you'll probably do it a lot better than I do. Let's start by looking at the two main families.

Plowing Through the Plovers

All told, there are 64 plover species worldwide, but only about 14 usually appear in North America. The typical *plover* is a plump shorebird with a large head, nearly vertical forehead, and large eyes, a short bill (shorter than the length of the head), and a short neck. A plover's legs are roughly as long as its body from belly to back; if the bird has long legs, it's not a plover. Plovers tend to move in spurts. They'll run quickly for a little bit and then stop suddenly.

Be a Better Birder

You can get detailed information about tides, currents, and other interesting ocean stuff online from the Oceanographic Products and Services Division of the National Oceanographic and Atmospheric Administration (NOAA). The web site is **www.co-ops.nos.noaa.gov**.

Rappin' Robin

Plovers get their name from the Latin word *pluvia*, meaning rain. I have yet to find a convincing explanation of what rain has to do with these birds. *Charadriidae*, the scientific name for the plover family, comes from the Greek word *charadra*, meaning gully. This name makes a little more sense because it refers to the nests plovers make, which are little more than scrapes in the ground.

Get to know the semipalmated plover *(Charadrius semipalmatus)* as your reference bird. The semipalmated is one of the most widespread plovers; you'll see flocks of them on beaches and mudflats. During the breeding season, look for the bright orange patch at the base of the stubby bill and the bright orange feet. All year round, look for the black band around the neck. When the bird flies, look for the narrow white wing stripe.

Sorting Out the Sandpipers

Boy, does the sandpiper topic get complicated. You could be looking at one of about 40 different birds. Not only that, it is a diverse family; snipes and woodcocks are actually sandpipers.

Fortunately, the family's diversity actually helps you sort them out. That's because you can categorize into the various family groupings—and once you've done that, you're a long way toward figuring out the species. Take a look at the chart to get a feel for the most common sandpiper subfamilies.

The Common Sandpipers

Genus	Common Name
Tringa	Greater Yellowlegs
	Lesser Yellowlegs
	Solitary Sandpiper
Catoptrophorus	Willet
Actitis	Spotted Sandpiper
Bartramia	Upland Sandpiper
Numenius	Whimbrel
	Long-billed Curlew
Limosa	Black-tailed Godwit
	Hudsonian Godwit
	Marbled Godwit
Arenaria	Ruddy Turnstone
	Black Turnstone
Aphriza	Surfbird
Calidris	Red Knot
	Sanderling
	Semipalmated Sandpiper
	Western Sandpiper
	Least Sandpiper
	White-rumped Sandpiper
	Baird's Sandpiper
	Pectoral Sandpiper
	Purple Sandpiper
	Rock Sandpiper
	Dunlin
	Curlew Sandpiper
	Stilt Sandpiper
Tryngites	Buff-breasted Sandpiper
Limnodromus	Short-billed Dowitcher
	Long-billed Dowitcher

A typical sandpiper (if there is such a thing) is a slender bird, with a long, thin bill, sloping forehead, long neck, slender body, and long, pointed wings. As you can see from the chart, a lot of the sandpipers fall into the *Calidris* group. In general, these sandpipers are small, stocky birds with short legs and short, straight (or straightish) bills. They have long, pointed wings and usually feed by probing in the mud or wet sand with their bills.

Your field guide and other books on the shorebirds are full of field marks and behavior tips to help you tell the sandpipers apart. Some of the ID tips aren't much help to beginning birders, especially when they compare one bird to another. My advice? Focus on one bird and keep watching it for as long as possible; don't get distracted by the other birds. If you keep watching, you'll gather a lot of useful information, including where it's feeding on the beach, how it feeds, how it looks when it flies, and how it sounds. These clues are as valuable as the field marks for getting the right ID.

There's so much variation among the sandpipers that you can't really pick a single species as a reference point. Instead, sort them out by their more obvious characteristics into the categories listed in the chart. Once you've got the birds narrowed down, you can concentrate on the other clues to get the identification. Warning: This is a pretty subjective chart—you could just as easily put the turnstones in the plump category—so feel free to disagree and make your own categories.

Splat!

The Piping Plover nests on sandy beaches above the high-water line or in the dunes. This bird, which breeds along Atlantic beaches from southern Canada to North Carolina, is seriously endangered by habitat loss and off-road vehicles. The Snowy Plover, which breeds along the Gulf coast and on the West Coast, is similarly endangered. As part of conservation measures, plover nesting areas are fenced off. Do not enter the nesting area!

Be a Better Birder

Despite all the attention given to describing the feet and legs of a shorebird, these field marks aren't much help; it's really, really hard to get a good look at a shorebird's feet. As for color, there's a lot of natural variation, and the legs are often covered with mud or other stuff. If you can't get a good look, forget the feet and stick to other ID clues.

Sorting Out the Sandpipers

Sandpipers with Really Long Bills

Long-billed Curlew
Whimbrel
Hudsonian Godwit
Marbled Godwit
Long-billed Dowitcher
Short-billed Dowitcher

Sandpipers with Really Short Bills

Ruddy Turnstone
Black Turnstone
Surfbird

"Peep" Sandpipers

Sanderling
Baird's Sandpiper
Least Sandpiper
Semipalmated Sandpiper
Western Sandpiper
White-rumped Sandpiper

Long-Legged Sandpipers

Greater Yellowlegs
Lesser Yellowlegs
Solitary Sandpiper
Stilt Sandpiper
Upland Sandpiper
Wandering Tattler
Willet

Plump Sandpipers

Dunlin
Red Knot
Buff-breasted Sandpiper
Pectoral Sandpiper
Purple Sandpiper
Rock Sandpiper
Spotted Sandpiper

Peeping at the Peeps

The Sanderling and the Baird's, Least, Semipalmated, Western, and White-rumped Sandpipers are often lumped together and called "peeps." That's because they're small, stubby birds that look very much alike, especially in their winter plumage. With practice, you can learn to tell at least some of these birds apart. It's pretty easy to identify a Sanderling, but even experts have trouble with the Semipalmated and the Western. Don't worry if you have trouble, too.

Strange Sandpipers

All birds sometimes wander from their usual routes and end up far from where they should be (I'll talk more about this in Chapter 29, "Hotspots and Rare Birds.") Sandpipers seem to be more prone to this wandering than other birds, so almost every year, an unusual one shows up somewhere. At the very least, the bird ends up on the local rare bird alert. On slow news days, it may end up on national TV, complete with video of goofy-looking birders and a tiny speck of a bird way, way in the distance. Stray sandpipers tend to hang around, sometimes for days or even weeks, so you'll have a good chance of seeing it. It will be easy to find; just look for all the other birders who have come from miles away. Someone's bound to have a scope on it.

Other Shorebirds

Plovers and sandpipers are the main shorebird families, but members of several other families are also often seen:

➤ **Oystercatchers:** Two species appear in North America: Black Oystercatcher and American Oystercatcher. Look for large, chunky birds with large, bright red or orange bills. You'll often see them on rocky areas, looking for mussels and oysters. They should really be called oyster eaters. I mean, how hard is it to catch oysters? It's not like they run away.

➤ **Stilts and avocets:** These are slim, graceful birds with very long legs, long necks, and long, very slender bills. The plumage is boldly patterned in black and white. Look for the Black-necked Stilt near shallow ponds and open marshes. A stilt's legs are easily six inches long; in relation to its body, the stilt's legs are the longest of any bird. The American Avocet prefers wet meadows and open pastures.

➤ **Phalaropes:** You'll probably see these graceful birds swimming as often as you'll see them walking or wading. In the water, phalaropes spin like tops while stabbing at the water with their thin, straight bills; they're catching the little critters they stir up. Three species are found in North America: Wilson's, Northern, and Red-necked. You're most likely to see the Wilson's Phalarope at the shore.

Oystercatchers, stilts, avocets, and phalaropes are distinctive and easy to identify; they can't be anything else.

Technically, I should have discussed the common snipe and the American Woodcock when I talked about the other sandpipers. These stocky birds with their long, heavy bills aren't much like typical sandpipers, however, and they're hardly ever seen at the shore. Look for them in marshes and bogs.

Shorebird Migration

Most of the shorebirds we see on the beaches and grasslands of North America are just passing through on their way to or from their breeding grounds. In the early spring, they're on their way north to their breeding grounds across the prairies, tundra, and even Arctic regions of Canada and Alaska. They raise their young there through the very long summer days and start heading south to their winter homes as early as the beginning of July.

The migration patterns of the shorebirds are a clue to their identification. Take the Hudsonian Godwit. This largish sandpiper nests way up north, along the Arctic coast of Alaska and around Baffin Bay. It spends its winters in Argentina. That's a long way to go, so this bird doesn't spend a lot of time hanging around at stopping points along the way. Your chances of seeing it, then, happen only during the short migration windows as it moves up from the Texas coast to the Great Lakes and beyond.

Be a Better Birder

You don't have to be a beach bum to see shorebirds; you can see them in any part of North America that's got short grass, open fields, and fresh or brackish water—prairies, marshes, and wet meadows, for instance. Shorebirds such as Spotted Sandpipers, Upland Sandpipers, Hudsonian Godwits, Marbled Godwits, and Wilson's Phalarope are so common away from beaches that birders often call them "grasspipers."

A Little Bird Told Me...

Most of the shorebirds found in northern North America during the breeding season spend the winter in Central or South America. The little Sanderling, for instance, makes an amazing circuit every year. In the spring, the birds head up the West Coast of North America to their breeding grounds in the Arctic regions across the top of North America. Breeding chores over, the birds head home by flying down the East Coast back to their wintering grounds in Chile and Peru. Even the shorebirds we commonly see all winter long breed far, far to the north. The Dunlin, for instance, winters along the east and west coasts but breeds in the Arctic.

We mostly see the shorebirds while they're en route one way or the other during migration. Fortunately for birders, at that point they're still in their breeding plumage and are relatively easy to identify. Shorebirds don't generally molt into their duller, paler winter plumage until they get to their winter homes.

All the World's a Stage

Every year, 20 million shorebirds migrate through the U.S. on their way to their northern breeding grounds. Along the way, they gather in vast numbers at critical *staging grounds* to rest and feed before starting another long leg of the journey. There are five major staging grounds in North America: the Copper River delta in Alaska, Gray's Harbor in Washington, Cheyenne Bottoms in Kansas, the beaches lining Delaware Bay in Delaware and New Jersey, and the Bay of Fundy in eastern Canada. The birds gather here by the thousands—sometimes hundreds of thousands—as they pass through over a period of just a few weeks. Any staging ground is an amazing spectacle, one that attracts birders from around the world. It's well worth the trip.

Rappin' Robin

A **staging ground** is an area where birds gather to rest and feed during migration.

The Least You Need to Know

➤ Most shorebirds are members of the plover and sandpiper families. North America has about 14 common plover species and about 61 common sandpipers.

➤ Shorebirds are generally small, drab birds that come in subtle shades of brown, tan, gray, and white. Identifying these birds can be challenging.

➤ Bill size, body shape, voice, and behavior are as important as plumage for identifying shorebirds.

➤ Most shorebirds are only passing through on their way to and from their breeding grounds in the subarctic and Arctic and their wintering grounds in Central and South America.

Chapter 17

Terns and Gulls

In This Chapter

➤ Spotting terns and gulls

➤ How to know the terns

➤ Basics of gull identification

➤ Visiting nesting colonies

Remember the book *Jonathan Livingston Seagull,* by Richard Bach? Sure, you do; for a while back in the '70s, it was hard to escape. Enjoyable as the philosophical Jonathan was, I have some sad news for you: There is no such bird as a seagull. (I can't tell you how many times, in my years as a book editor, I've corrected that mistake.) There are about 45 gull species, and not one has the common name seagull. That's because gulls are frequently found far from the sea and they like fresh water as much as salt. (Can you call gulls that like shallow bodies of saltwater bagels?) Variety like this is one of the things that makes gulls and terns, their close relatives, so interesting.

Meet the Larids

Gulls and *terns* belong to the *Laridae* family—the larids, as birders call them. Within the family, almost all the gulls belong to the genus *Larus,* and almost all the terns belong to the genus *Sterna.* These birds are a lot of fun. They're very active and vocal, they're fairly common, and they're easy to watch. They tend to land and take off a lot, so you can get good looks at standing and flying birds. If you lose sight of one bird, there's almost always plenty of others from the same species to focus on. Gulls and terns aren't especially colorful—they come mostly in shades of white, gray, and black—and they don't have particularly vivid markings. By watching long enough, though, you can usually see enough field marks and behavior to work out the ID.

One Good Tern Deserves Another

Terns are very much birds of the water. They're always found near oceans, lakes, rivers, and sometimes marshes. Although terns are so closely associated with water, most aren't good swimmers; they don't rest on the surface of the water. Terns are also fussy eaters; most are strictly fish eaters, although some catch insects and even frogs. Unlike gulls, they stay away from garbage.

Terns are graceful birds with long, narrow wings, notched or strongly forked tails, short necks, short feet, and thin, pointed bills. The front three toes of their feet are webbed.

Rappin' Robin

Terns have always been called terns; their name goes back to an Old Norse word. **Gulls** probably get their name from the Latin word *gula,* meaning throat. We get the words gullible, gulp, and gullet from the same word, so gull might refer to the way these birds will eat just about anything. The family name *Laridae* comes from the Latin word *larus,* meaning gull.

Be a Better Birder

Where there's one gull, there's lots of gulls—ditto for terns. And where there's one gull species, there's likely to be others—again, ditto for terns. Comparing the different species first hand is a great way to learn their field marks.

Terns generally feed by diving from the air for fish just below the surface of the water. Watching terns catch a meal is really fun. They hover over the water and then plunge down head first to grab a fish. They don't really go under the water, though; they come up quickly and hardly seem to get wet.

Worldwide, there are some 40 tern species, but only about 14 breed in North America. The most widespread tern in North America is the Common Tern. You'll see this graceful bird up and down the East Coast and well inland, especially over large lakes. Common Terns are also seen on the West Coast, but there, you're more likely to see the closely related Forster's Tern. The Common, Forster's, and Arctic Terns all look a lot alike. They're so hard to tell apart that when birders can't decide whether they're seeing a Common or Arctic Tern, they split the difference and call it a "comic" tern.

Even so, the Common Tern makes a good reference bird to learn. Look for the bright red-orange bill with a black tip and the dark wingtips.

During the summer breeding season, terns have black "caps" on their heads that help you tell them apart. You'll know you're seeing a Least Tern (the smallest tern in North America) when you spot a white patch between the bill and the cap. In the winter, the caps mostly molt away to white or gray smudges. Fortunately, most terns migrate south for the winter, so you usually get to see them in their more identifiable breeding plumage.

Juvenile terns take a year or sometimes two to get their adult plumage. Until then, their feathers are much darker and their markings are less distinct.

The bird you're most likely to see at the beach—a Herring Gull. (Photo by Cliff Beittel.)

A Little Bird Told Me...

The Arctic Tern has the longest annual migration of any bird in the world—more than 12,000 miles *each way*. In the spring, this elegant bird heads north to the shores of the Arctic Ocean and the northernmost Atlantic to breed under the midnight sun. After the breeding season, the birds head south, all the way to the edge of the Antarctic pack ice, for the winter (the Antarctic summer). Even more amazing, the terns do most of the trip by flying nonstop over open water.

Where the Gulls Are

Gulls are big, sturdy birds with long, pointed wings, large, hooked bills, and squarish tails. They have webbed feet. They don't usually dive for their food. Instead, gulls float on the water and grab whatever comes by. They're equally happy to feed on land, scavenging anything dead and feasting on garbage.

Gulls aren't just birds of the beach; some species are often found far inland away from salt water. The best spot in the country for seeing gulls is Niagara Falls, where you could easily see 14 species in the winter. Gulls are often seen floating on the water, but they're equally comfortable on land. Franklin's Gull, for example, is often seen on prairies. Ring-billed and Herring Gulls are seen anywhere there's a garbage dump.

Gull Plumage: The Wonder Years

Young gulls go through several variations of streaky brown plumage before they reach adult plumage—a process that takes three or four years. There are so many possible plumage variations that birders watching gulls spend most of their time wondering what they're seeing. Because there are roughly 25 gull species regularly found in North America, and because each gull can have three or four different plumages depending on its age, and because adult gulls have winter and breeding plumages, you'd have to know nearly 200 different variations to identify every gull. If you start considering the various stages of molt and feather wear that the birds go through before reaching their full adult plumage, the number of possible combinations and permutations could reach more than a thousand.

Be a Better Birder

Here's a surefire way to tell a tern from a gull: Terns fly with their slender, sharply pointed bills "terned" down. A slightly less surefire way is to look at the tail. Almost all terns have forked tails; hardly any gulls do.

For some reason, new birders find the idea of learning all that just a tad intimidating. The good news is that you can always find plenty of adult gulls to identify. Ignore the juveniles until you feel ready enough—or interested enough—to take on the challenge.

Guessing at the Gulls

If you stick to adult gulls in their regular plumage, you've got a pretty good chance of identifying them. Narrow the field by focusing on these field marks:

➤ **Hood:** During the breeding season, dark-headed gulls such as the Laughing Gull have black hoods. Unfortunately, in the winter, the hood molts away and the birds have white or smudgy gray heads.

➤ **Wing color:** This is a good way to get started on your ID. Are the wings pale gray all over? Are they mostly black all over? Or are they darker gray with some black at the wingtips?

➤ **Wingtip pattern:** The pattern of white, gray, and black on the wingtips is a good ID clue. The Herring Gull has dark gray wings; the wingtips are black with white spots. Ditto for the Ring-billed Gull, the Mew Gull, and the California Gull.

➤ **Size:** The Great Black-backed Gull, the largest gull in the world, is easy to spot just because it's so big; look for a gull that's as big as a hawk and has a really large, heavy bill. The dark-headed gulls are the smallest gulls.

➤ **Bill color and shape:** Gulls in general have large, heavy bills that tend to be yellow, but there's a lot of fairly visible variation among species. The Herring Gull, for instance, has a "typical" gull bill that's large and yellow—but it also has a distinct red spot on the lower mandible. The California Gull looks a lot like the Herring Gull, but it has red and black spots on the lower mandible. Look also for rings on the bill; the Ring-billed Gull is a good example. Heermann's Gull and the Laughing Gull have red bills.

➤ **Leg color:** Gulls legs vary in color from pink to yellow to black. Try to spot the leg color when the bird perches or flies.

Gulls aren't especially shy, so you'll usually be able to get close enough to see field marks such as bill spots and leg color.

Get to know the Herring Gull as your reference bird. Herring Gulls will eat just about anything, so they're found in a lot of different habitats, not just shores. Herring Gulls will let you approach very close, so it's easy to get to know their field marks. Note the red dot on the lower mandible of the bill and the pink legs. Get a good feel for the pattern of white dots on the black wingtips. In the summer, get a good look at the lovely yellow eyelids. When Herring Gulls fly, they soar gracefully like hawks. The loud, bugle-like call is one of the most common bird sounds at the beach; you'll know it the instant you hear it. Herring Gulls are a bit smarter than the average bird. Among other tricks, they open clams by flying up with them and dropping them down on rocks to smash them open.

If you're in the southern part of the country, get to know the Ring-billed Gull as your reference bird. Look for the yellow bill with a black ring near the tip, the yellow legs, and the two white spots on the tips of each wing.

Be a Better Birder

Ask yourself where you are when you're identifying gulls. Some gulls are strictly east or west coast residents. On the East Coast, for instance, a large gull with black wings could only be the Great Black-backed Gull; on the West Coast, the bird could only be a Western Gull.

An easy clue to start identifying this Laughing Gull is the black hood on the head. (Photo by Robert McKemie/Daybreak Imagery.)

Larids on the Lam

Larids sometimes "tern" up in the wrong place. As with any vagrant bird that's where it shouldn't be, this causes great excitement among birders. Because these birds are hard to identify, vagrant larids can also cause controversy. When an Aleutian Tern showed up in England a while back, the birders who first reported it were accused of having "Aleutianations." It was the bird who was on a bad trip, though; it was thousands of miles off course.

Sometimes, gulls get a little mixed up about their mates. When a gull of one species mates with a gull of another, the result is a *hybrid*. Gulls that share ranges, such as the Herring and Glaucous Gulls in the Northeast, hybridize fairly often. When a hybrid gull shows up, it sends the gull experts into raptures, but it's tough on us ordinary birders; we get even more confused. Then, there are the gulls that are just unusual—unusually small or dark, say. Talk about confusion!

What do you do if you think you're seeing a vagrant, hybrid, or weirdo gull? At times like this, I give up on trying to identify the bird and watch the birders instead. If you're lucky, you'll get to see one of those indescribable birding moments—six deadly serious birders standing around on a beach in a high wind and drizzle, having an arm-waving discussion of the mystery bird while wrestling with field guides, notebooks, journal articles, and their personal collections of gull pictures. Treasure the moment.

Rappin' with the Raptors

One look at this fearsome beak tells you this is definitely a raptor—a bird of prey. In fact, it's a Red-tailed Hawk. Photo by Susan Day/Daybreak Imagery.

The broad wings and rounded tails tell you right away this raptor is a buteo, or soaring hawk. The easily seen rusty red tail tells you it's a Red-tailed Hawk. Photo by Richard Day/Daybreak Imagery.

The American Kestrel is a small falcon no bigger than a Blue Jay. It's often seen just like this, perched on a fence post keeping a keen eye out for grasshoppers and mice. Photo by Richard Day/Daybreak Imagery.

Ospreys are the only raptor that actually plunges into the water to grab a fish. Compare the size of the fish in the bird's talons to its wings—the wingspread of an Osprey can reach six feet. Photo by Cliff Beittel.

On the Owl Prowl

The big ear tufts and very large yellow eyes tell you this is a Great Horned Owl. Photo by Richard Day/Daybreak Imagery.

The Barred Owl has a rounded head with brown eyes and no ear tufts. The body is chunky, with dark barring across its upper chest and vertical streaks on the belly. Photo by Cliff Beittel.

You might have to look carefully to spot the gray-phase Eastern Screech-Owl in this photo. The ear tufts are part of the natural camouflage that helps this bird blend in perfectly to its background. Photo by Richard Day/Daybreak Imagery.

Birds by the Sea

The Semipalmated Sandpiper is a very common shorebird, but telling it from the other peeps can be hard even for experienced birdwatchers. When the bird is standing, try to see its legs. Semipalmated Sandpipers have blackish legs. Photo by Richard Day/Daybreak Imagery.

In flight, Semipalmated Sandpipers still look a lot like other peeps. You'll have to identify them by ear. Listen for the soft chet *call the bird makes in flight. Photo by Richard Day/Daybreak Imagery.*

Sanderlings are those little birds you see running in and out among the waves on sandy beaches. This bird is in bright breeding plumage; in the winter, sanderlings are much paler. Photo by Cliff Beittel.

Life's a Beach

Get to know the Herring Gull—you'll see it everywhere. Look for the white head, pale gray back, black wingtips, and orange-pink legs. Look also for the red spot near the tip of the bill. Photo by Cliff Beittel.

The elegant Arctic Tern. Note the black cap, dark red bill, and matching feet. In flight, the wings have a thin black border. Photo by Cliff Beittel.

During the breeding season, Laughing Gulls have a black hood; during the winter, the head is white with just a smudge of black behind the eye. All year round, this bird has a dark bill and a dark back. Photo by Robert McKemie/ Daybreak Imagery.

The Black Skimmer feeds by skimming along just above the water. Its lower mandible, which is about a third longer than the upper, slices through the water picking up small fish and other goodies. Photo by Cliff Beittel.

It's Just Ducky

A male (drake) and female (hen) Mallard—the most common of all ducks in North America. The male is the one with the colorful green head and white necklace. Photo by Richard Day/Daybreak Imagery.

With its brilliant colors, red bill, red eye ring, and distinctive head crest, the male Wood Duck in breeding plumage is hard to mistake for any other bird. Photo by Richard Day/Daybreak Imagery.

A parent Canada Goose sails along leading a string of goslings. Look for a white chin strap on any large waterbird in flight—if you see one, you're seeing a Canada goose. Photo by Richard Day/Daybreak Imagery.

Dabbling ducks such as this male and female pair of Northern Shovelers feed by dabbling their bills just below the surface of the water or upending themselves. Photo by Richard Day/Daybreak Imagery.

Wood Warblers

The Yellow Warbler is very common and easy to identify. It's a small, active bird that's yellow all over. Because it doesn't have any head markings, the black eyes seem larger than they actually are. Photo by Richard Day/Daybreak Imagery.

The black mask and bright yellow throat and chest of the male Common Yellowthroat make it easy to identify this little warbler. Look for it along streams and anyplace that's marshy, swampy, or just damp. Photo by Richard Day/Daybreak Imagery.

This portrait of a Cerulean Warbler gives you a good look at the typical warbler bill—long and thin. Photo by John and Gloria Tveten/KAC Productions.

Spotting Sparrows

The most widespread feeder bird in North America, the Dark-eyed Junco has a distinctive pink bill and flashes two white tail feathers when it flies. Photo by Connie Toops.

Snow Buntings are members of the sparrow family. In their winter plumage, they look brown on the ground, but in flight they look almost white. Look for the large white wing patches when they fly. Photo by Richard Day/Daybreak Imagery.

Hummers!

A male Ruby-throated Hummingbird feeds on bee balm. The vivid coloring is seen best when the light strikes the bird at an angle. Photo by Connie Toops.

A hibiscus blossom attracts this Broad-billed Hummingbird. Most of the orange bill is deep inside the flower. Photo by Richard Day/ Daybreak Imagery.

Nesting Colonies

Terns and gulls are *colonial nesters*. They nest in very large, very noisy, and very smelly colonies. Terns generally prefer isolated beaches, but gulls will nest in dunes, on offshore gravel banks, sandbars, and islands, and on rocky cliffs. To protect the birds during the breeding season, nesting colonies are generally closed to the public. You can sometimes arrange a visit through a local nature group or through the site manager.

Offshore islands and cliffside nesting colonies have a lot of species on them, including terns, gulls, and other fabulous seabirds such as gannets and puffins. These colonies are best seen by boat. Don't try to do this by yourself; these sites are off-limits to unofficial visits. In some places, commercial boats take you out to the sites, often as part of a general nature trip that also might include seeing seals and whales. For some sites, you'll need to arrange a visit through the site management.

Visiting a seabird colony is a real experience, but it's not for the faint of heart—or stomach. The ride out can be a little rough, and once you get there, the stench of bird droppings and rotting fish can be overwhelming. The endless ruckus made by thousands and thousands of nesting birds—none of them noted for their melodic calls—is deafening. If you're allowed to land, you'll probably have to wear a hard hat to protect you from dive-bombing birds. Memories of your trip to the nesting colony will definitely remain with you.

Rappin' Robin

Colonial nesters are birds that breed in large groups, or colonies, of the same species. Many water birds, such as gulls, terns, pelicans, herons, and cormorants, are colonial nesters.

Splat!

Protected nesting colonies are often marked with signs or fencing. Do not enter!

Royal Terns at a nesting colony. They're in their breeding plumage, so they have tufted black caps. (Photo by Connie Toops.)

171

How Gullible Are You?

It's easy to be fooled by some of the gull-like birds at the beach. Let's take a closer look:

➤ Jaegers and skuas: These large birds are related to the gulls; in fact, they're in the *Laridae* family. They don't have a lot of family feeling, however. Jaegers and skuas are most commonly found stealing food from gulls and other birds or eating their eggs and chicks. These birds hardly ever come ashore, but they can often be seen off beaches, especially if there are a lot of gulls around to steal from.

➤ Black skimmers: Skimmers are also members of the *Laridae* family. They look a little like giant terns, but they have large red and black bills with the lower mandible much larger than the upper. As skimmers fly along just above the surface, their lower mandible slices through the water until something edible comes along. Then, the upper mandible snaps shut on the meal. I really enjoy watching these interesting birds crisscross the water.

Keep your eyes open at the beach. I was once birding at Torrey Pines near San Diego when I noticed a large gull that seemed to be flying differently than the others. Watching more carefully, I saw my first Northern Fulmar.

The Least You Need to Know

➤ Gulls and terns are very common birds, especially at seashores. Some gulls and terns are also found inland.

➤ Because gulls and terns are fairly common and are generally found in large numbers, they're not too hard to find and identify.

➤ Terns have long, pointed wings, long and thin bills, and forked tails. During the breeding season, they have black caps on their heads.

➤ Gulls are robust birds with large, heavy bills, pointed wings, and squared-off tails.

➤ Juvenile gulls go through several confusing plumage changes before they reach their adult plumage.

➤ Terns and gulls nest in huge, noisy colonies. Visiting a nesting colony is a worthwhile birding experience.

Ducks and Geese

Even if you're brand new to birding, you know a lot about waterfowl. This big bird family includes the ducks, geese, and swans—birds that are familiar to just about everyone. You've been seeing Mallards, Canada geese, and Mute Swans all your life, even if you didn't know their names, and you can easily tell the families apart. After all, if it looks like a duck...

Waterfowl Facts

Ducks, geese, and swans are all *waterfowl*, aquatic birds that have flattened, blunt-tipped bills with a hard *nail* on the tip of the upper mandible. Waterfowl have stout bodies covered with thick coats of dense, waterproof feathers. They have long necks and narrow, pointed wings; most are strong fliers. Waterfowl have short legs placed far back and wide apart on their bodies—that's why they waddle when they walk—and webbed feet.

All waterfowl are members of the order *Anseriformes* and the family *Anatidae*. In all, there are about 148 species in the *Anatidae* family; 57 are commonly found in North America. Because this family is so big and complicated, it's divided further into eight *tribes*. Geese and swans are each one tribe, but the ducks have six. Keep reading; sorting out the waterfowl isn't as complicated as it sounds.

Rappin' Robin

Waterfowl is an overall word for ducks, geese, and swans. British birders use the word *wildfowl* in much the same way. The flattened bills of waterfowl have a hard, hooked tip called a **nail** on the upper mandible. Just to confuse you, all birds also have toenails, but they're called claws.

Rappin' Robin

A bird **tribe** is a taxonomic grouping that falls between a subfamily and a genus. Tribe names are used to group related species within a varied subfamily. Names for tribes always ends in the suffix *-ini*. The surface-feeding ducks are grouped into the Anatini tribe. (For more on how the birds are classified, refer to Chapter 8, "Putting the Pigeons in the Right Holes.")

Duck!

You already know a lot about ducks. Remember those Daffy Duck and Donald Duck cartoons? More to the point, remember tossing bread to the ducks in the park when you were a kid? The ducks that came crowding around were of two kinds. The big white ones with large orange bills—the real-life Donald Ducks—were domesticated Pekin ducks, probably released a few weeks after Easter when they stopped being cute little chicks. The smaller, dark ducks were mallards—the real-life Daffy Ducks (sort of).

Mallards are the most widespread ducks in North America. They're found on just about every freshwater lake, pond, and marsh and can become very tame. In a lot of parks, they'll come close to anyone feeding them. Studying mallards is a good and easy way to learn about ducks in general.

The first thing you'll notice about the mallards is that they come in pairs—a brightly colored male with a vivid green head, thin white "necklace" and rich brown chest and a much drabber female with streaky brown plumage. Look carefully at that drab female. She—and the male—has a patch of colorful blue feathers bordered in white on each wing. Most ducks have a *speculum,* as the patch is called, on each wing.

The next thing you'll notice about the mallards is the way they feed, at least when they're not gobbling the bread crusts you toss to them. They tip their rumps up into the air and their heads below the water. That brings me to a convenient way to divide the ducks: by how and where they feed.

The Northern Pintail duck gets its name from the way its tailfeathers come to a point. (Photo by Richard Day/Daybreak Imagery.)

A Little Bird Told Me...

Domesticated waterfowl can cause a lot of confusion to birders. Domesticated ducks often escape (or are turned loose) and end up in the same water as wild birds. Large white ducks with orange bills are Pekin ducks. A large, dark duck with warty red growths all over its face (as if the bird had really bad acne) is a Muscovy duck. Mallards are the ancestor of all domestic ducks except the Muscovy, so they easily hybridize. If you see a weird-looking duck that's not in your field guide, chances are good that it's a hybrid of a domestic duck and a mallard.

Dabbling Ducks

Dabbling or surface-feeding ducks such as the mallard feed with their heads and necks underwater and their rumps up in the air. Even when they don't upend themselves, they dig around, or dabble, with their bills to get their food. Dabblers are strong flyers. They take off with a jump straight out of the water. Because they take off and land almost vertically, dabblers are often found on small, shallow bodies of water; that's why they're sometimes called puddle ducks. More scientifically, the dabblers are all members of the genus *Anas*. This family includes the teals, Northern Pintail, Gadwall, and wigeons. Look for mallards on inlets, lakes, ponds—even swimming pools—and

Rappin' Robin

Most but not all ducks have colorful secondary feathers on their wings. (Refer to Chapter 4, "May I See Your ID, Please?" for more on feather structure.) The feathers form a patch called a **speculum**. Looking at the speculum, especially when the bird is in flight, is a good way to get a handle on the bird's ID. Green-winged and Blue-winged Teal, for instance, get their names from the color of their speculums.

marshes. Generally speaking, male dabbling ducks are much more colorful and distinctly marked than females.

Divers, Sea Ducks, and Sawbills

Diving ducks dive completely under the surface of the water to get their food. They're generally found in deeper water than the dabblers. Because they need to patter along the surface of the water for a while to get airborne, they're found on larger bodies of water than the dabblers.

The diving ducks can be divided further into bay ducks and sea ducks. Bay ducks such as scaups prefer protected water such as lagoons, inlets, lakes, and estuaries. These ducks often have light-colored bodies and dark heads; they don't have a speculum on the wing. To be technical about it, bay ducks have a lobed hind toe.

Sea ducks such as buffleheads are mostly found along coastlines and in large, deep lakes. These birds generally have bold patterns of black and white, especially on the heads and wings.

Stiff-tailed ducks are small, diving ducks such as the Ruddy Duck. As the name suggests, they have stiff, upright tails. They don't exactly dive; ruddy ducks just sink slowly beneath the surface, sort of like submarines.

Sawbills are mergansers—ducks with a difference. Instead of the usual flattened bill, mergansers have long, thin, wicked-looking bills with serrated edges, the better to catch fish with.

Wood Ducks and Whistlers

The beautiful Wood Duck is one of the most common breeding ducks in the eastern U.S. Wood Ducks nest in tree cavities, but they'll happily come to nest boxes put up along quiet lakes, ponds, and swamps. Wood Ducks have a distinctive crest on the head. Males have a red bill, bold white patterning on the face, and a spectacular red eye ring. Wood Ducks often nest in cavities 10, 20, or even 50 feet off the ground. When the chicks hatch, they're too young to fly. Instead, they jump, one by one, from the hole and land unhurt on the ground below.

Whistling ducks are large birds with long necks and very upright posture; they're ducks, but they act a lot like geese. The two North American species—Fulvous Whistling-Duck and Black-bellied Whistling-Duck—aren't that common. You're most likely to see the fulvous in open marshlands or on flooded rice fields in southern California and coastal Texas. The Black-bellied is most often seen in southern Arizona and southern Texas.

Digging Up Ducks

You can see mallards just about anywhere there's open water all year round. The best time to see most ducks, however, is in the fall, winter, and early spring. Most North American ducks breed on the prairies and subarctic tundra along lakes, ponds, potholes, wetlands, and marshes. The ducks that breed farther south on the continent are still hard to spot during the breeding season because they conceal their nests and keep a low profile while raising their chicks.

Another reason ducks are scarce in the summer is *molting.* In the late summer, most male ducks molt their colorful breeding plumage and grow new feathers in much duller colors. The new plumage is so much dimmer, in fact, that it's called *eclipse plumage.* The ducks lose so many feathers at once that they can't fly for several weeks. For most of August, then, almost all ducks are extremely secretive, hiding deep in marshy areas until their new feathers grow in. They'll stay in the eclipse plumage for anywhere from one to three months. After that, they gradually grow new, more colorful feathers as the breeding season begins again. For ducks, that means the winter.

In the fall, ducks and other waterfowl migrate south; they head back in the very early spring.

As I explain a little later, "south" is a relative term. Plenty of waterfowl head only as far south as the New England coast for the winter. In general, when winter arrives, ducks become a lot more visible. They look for open water along coastlines, estuaries, harbors, lakes, ponds, lagoons, marshes, and other sheltered places. They tend to form large flocks, or rafts, that sometimes contain thousands of birds.

Rappin' Robin

Molting is the process of shedding feathers and growing new ones. Just before the breeding season begins, birds molt into their brightly colored breeding plumage. When the breeding period is over, they molt again, usually into duller colors.

Rappin' Robin

The timing of the molt varies widely among bird species. In ducks, the males molt rapidly into their winter plumage at the end of the breeding season in August, stay in their dull **eclipse plumage** for a few months, and molt back into bright breeding plumage by the winter.

You can see ducks easily in the winter, although you'll probably need a spotting scope to see the birds rafting offshore. (You'll also need to dress very warmly.) Amazingly, sea ducks such as Surf Scoters and Harlequin Ducks spend the winter in the frigid waters off the New England and mid-Atlantic coastline. To see these birds in winter, take your scope out to a rocky jetty along the coast; the birds are attracted to the shellfish that attach to the rocks.

Be a Better Birder

You might have trouble telling the colors when the ducks are on the water; light reflections and sunlight can wash out the colors. Look not only at the colors, but also at the overall shape of the duck (especially its head and bill), its behavior, how it flies, and its wing markings when it flies.

Ducks are fairly active all the time, and you should be able to get good looks at them as they loaf on the land, float on the water, feed, and fly. (Bay ducks tend to laze around and sleep on the water during the day; they mostly feed at night.)

You should be able to spot enough field marks to work out identifications for the males, but female ducks are much trickier. For now, stick to the males. When you feel ready to take on the females, remember that they have the same head, bill, and body shape as males of the same species. If you see a male duck, keep watching—there's a good chance that its mate is nearby.

Whenever you see ducks, especially in large numbers, look carefully. A big flock almost always has several different species in it.

Getting Goosed

Geese are biggish birds with stout bodies and long necks. They're usually found on or near open water. Like ducks, they have webbed feet set far apart and far back on their bodies, so they waddle when they walk. Their bills are large, but they're not as flat as ducks'; goose bills are much deeper at the base. Most geese are vegetarians that graze on grasses and other plants, including water weeds of various sorts. They're as comfortable walking and feeding on land as they are swimming and feeding on water.

Worldwide, there are about 27 goose species; about 7 species are commonly found in North America. Of all the geese, the most widespread is the well-known Canada Goose. This very large, black-and-white goose has a distinctive white "chin strap" on the head. Males and females look alike.

A Little Bird Told Me...

Canada Geese are found all over North America. Migrating geese generally return to the same breeding sites year after year. Natural genetic variation among the birds at the sites has led to at least 11 different races or subspecies, with distinct physical differences. Some are noticeably larger or smaller; others have short necks or make cackling sounds. When the various subspecies come together, the differences can sometimes be obvious, but researchers still disagree about exactly how to classify them.

You can see this goose just about anywhere; in fact, you may be wondering how to get rid of them. In recent years, Canada Geese have been multiplying rapidly and staying put instead of migrating. That means they're hanging around in large numbers in parks, golf courses, beaches, fields, and lakes, making a lot of noise—Canada Geese are very vocal—and leaving a lot of large droppings. Why this is happening and what to do about it are open questions.

Once you've learned to recognize the Canada Goose, picking out other geese such as Snow Geese and Brant will be easy. Don't look for Brant inland, however; these geese are strictly coastal.

The Canada Goose is one of the most easily recognized waterfowl. This large bird has a distinctive white chin strap. (Photo by Connie Toops.)

Swanning Around

Swans are the largest waterfowl; in fact, they're among the largest birds, period. These graceful, long-necked birds are closely related to geese. In North America, there are only three species: the native Trumpeter and Tundra Swans and the introduced Mute Swan. All three birds are white all over, with black feet.

The Mute Swan has become a common bird on ponds and lakes in parks. It's the swan you're most likely to see year round. In the winter, you can often see Tundra Swans along the coastline in the Pacific Northwest, New England, and the middle Atlantic region. The Trumpeter Swan is much more rare. Your best chance to see Trumpeters is a visit to Yellowstone National Park in Wyoming and Montana.

A Little Bird Told Me...

Mute Swans were first brought to America from Europe in the early 1900s. By 1919, a pair had escaped from captivity and was breeding in New York. Since then, Mute Swans have become well established in the wild. That's not necessarily a good thing. These very large birds can weigh in at 45 pounds. They're very aggressive and very strong—they've been known to attack and hurt humans—and they take over nesting territory from native waterfowl. They also destroy native habitat and pollute ponds and shorelines with their copious droppings. Despite the obvious damage these invading birds do, attempts to control them invariably raise howls of protest from local communities.

Loony Tunes

Technically, loons aren't waterfowl, but in the winter, they're so often seen with—and mistaken for—ducks that I thought I'd add something about them here.

Loons are large, heavy diving birds with long, thin, very unducklike bills. Loons have very short legs placed far back on their bodies; they are so awkward on land they hardly ever come ashore. To get into the air, loons need a long take-off run on the water. When they finally do get airborne, loons are strong fliers. They're also fabulous swimmers and divers; they can go down as deep as 180 feet and stay down for 15 minutes! Loons breed on the tundra and on lakes in the northern states. Their distinctive yodeling sounds are one of the real calls of the wild. All four North American loon species winter along coastlines and on rivers, estuaries, and large lakes. Unfortunately, in their winter plumage, they're hard to tell apart. Just call them loons and leave it at that.

Isn't That Just Ducky

All ducks swim, but not all swimming birds are ducks. There are a lot of other duck-like birds on the water. Coots, grebes, and cormorants are the ones you're most likely to see. I don't have room to discuss the details here; study your field guide to get the general idea for each of these families. Once you've gotten to know the ducks, geese, and swans, you'll immediately realize which birds aren't members of the waterfowl family. You might not know what they are, but at least you know what they aren't.

Waterfowl Migration

When you start seeing long, noisy Vs of migrating Canada Geese overhead, you know the seasons are changing. In the spring, the Canadas begin migrating through in

March (even earlier in the South) and when you see them in the early spring, you know. How and when waterfowl fly during migration gives you some useful clues to their identity. It's not that many waterfowl fly in the traditional V formation. Canada Geese do, but Brant fly in small groups. Among the ducks, Redheads fly in Vs, but Blue-winged Teals fly in small, tight flocks. Other birds, such as Glossy Ibises, also fly in Vs. I once interrupted a particularly dull editorial meeting to point out a V formation of these birds flying across Manhattan. Of course, by then the birds were out of sight and nobody believed me. Shortly after that, I became a freelance writer.

A Little Bird Told Me...

The usual explanation for why Canada Geese fly in V formation is that it's aerodynamically efficient. Studies have shown, however, that aerodynamics don't have much to do with it. More likely, the birds fly in a V to avoid collisions and keep in better visual contact. Why do Canada Geese honk so much during flight? It's probably to keep the members of the group in touch, but maybe it's just backseat driving.

Making a Difference

Birders and bird hunters have their difference, but they do agree on one crucial thing: habitat preservation. Organizations such as Ducks Unlimited are supported mostly by conservation-minded hunters. These groups have been important in the fight to preserve wetlands and other important waterfowl habitat. Your support helps them continue their work.

Another important way to support waterfowl conservation is through the federal Migratory Bird Hunting and Conservation Stamp, better known as the duck stamp program. By law, all waterfowl hunters have to purchase a federal duck stamp every year—and often a state stamp as well. The money is used to support refuges and conservation projects. Many birders collect duck stamps and prints of the stamp art as a way to show their support; plus, showing the stamp gets you free admission to all national wildlife refuges. The

Splat!

Like it or not, waterfowl hunting is a fact of birding life. During the fall hunting season, many refuges have specific days and hours for hunting; the refuge is closed to all other visitors. Avoid a wasted trip by calling ahead.

stamps themselves are beautiful. The federal design is based on a painting chosen in a nationwide contest; state designs come from local contests.

For more information on the federal duck stamp program, contact:

U.S. Fish and Wildlife Service
Federal Duck Stamp Program
1849 C Street, NW, Suite 2058
Washington, DC 20240
(888) 534-0400
Fax: (202) 208-6296
web_reply@fws.gov
www.fws.gov/r9dso/

Federal stamps cost $15 each and bring millions of dollars every year for wetlands preservation and waterfowl conservation.

The Least You Need to Know

➤ Ducks, geese, and swans are collectively known as waterfowl.

➤ Waterfowl are aquatic birds with broad, flattened bills, stout bodies, long necks, webbed feet, and short legs.

➤ The most common duck in North America is the familiar Mallard. You can see this duck anywhere there's a pond or stream.

➤ The Canada Goose and the Mute Swan are also common and widespread.

➤ The best time to see waterfowl is in the winter, when they are in their breeding plumage and often gather in large numbers along coastlines and in sheltered waters.

Chapter 19

Warblers, Warblers, Warblers!

In This Chapter

➤ The wonderful world of warblers

➤ Finding warblers

➤ Secrets of warbler identification

➤ Listening to warblers

Birders have a real problem with the spring, and it's called warblers. These little birds are so much fun to watch that when they arrive in April and May, we tend to forget about other things, like jobs. Why go to work when you can go warbler watching instead?

Welcome to Warbler World

Warblers are small, active, colorful, insect-eating birds with small, thin bills. They're birds of the New World; the 125 or so warbler species are found exclusively in South, Central, and North America. Only 57 of those species are commonly seen in North America—and even warblers that breed in North America head way south for the winter.

Warblers are among the most colorful birds. A lot of the species in Central and South America are very flashy. Among these species, as is usual among tropical birds, the males and females look a lot alike. The North American warbler species are brightly colored too—if they're male. The females and immatures tend to be lot duller.

The most widespread American warbler is the Yellow Warbler. Like all warblers, Yellow Warblers are small—only about five inches long. This little bird is a cheerful yellow all

Rappin' Robin

North American birders use the word **warbler** to mean the small, active, insect-eating birds in the *Parulinae* subfamily. We should really use the official term *wood warblers* to distinguish these little birds from the completely different and unrelated Old World warblers, which are all members of the *Sylviidae* family and are found almost exclusively in Europe (although our gnatcatchers are close relatives).

over; even the darker wings and upper parts have a yellowish cast, and the wing bars are yellow as well. The head is solid yellow; the breast has lovely chestnut streaks. Look for yellow patches on the tail when the bird flies. Listen for the "sweet, sweet, sweet" song—usually 6 or 7 notes, repeated about 10 times a minute.

Woods + Water = Warblers

I watch a lot of warblers, mostly because the environment right around my house in the Hudson Valley is very attractive to them. What's so great about the Buff estate? It's got a big pond surrounded by mixed woodland and a lot of undergrowth. A brush- and tree-lined stream runs from the pond right through the backyard. I do a lot of birding from the comfort of my back porch or by sitting on the bridge over the stream. Just across the quiet rural road is a large, overgrown pasture that has a big marshy corner. It's warbler heaven.

Almost all warblers are found in brushy or wooded areas, preferably areas that have some kind of fresh water. That's because areas like this are rich in shelter, nesting sites, and insects—and warblers eat insects almost exclusively. What warblers don't like is unsheltered open areas. They're also not too fond of wind, so they tend to stay inland. You can see warblers along coastlines, especially during migration, but they'll be low down in the scrubby vegetation behind the dune line, not on the beach.

The ideal time for warbler watching is early on a spring morning, especially from mid-April to mid-June. The birds are in their full breeding plumage and there's not too much foliage blocking your view. Warblers generally migrate during the night and come down at dawn to rest and feed during the day. During the summer, the birds tend to hide as they raise their young. They become a lot more visible in the fall as they head south.

A lot of warblers species disappear from the U.S. completely for the winter. They head to the warm, insect-rich tropics of Central and South America. Some (they must be the ones with offshore bank accounts) winter in the Caribbean.

Which Warbler?

The warblers go on for page after page in your field guide. The *Parulinae* subfamily is big, all right, but at least it's easy to get the birds into manageable categories. In fact, it's so easy that there are at least four good ways to do it:

1. **By genus:** Warblers in a particular genus have characteristics in common. The big genus of *Dendroica* warblers, for instance, usually have distinctive wing bars and

tail spots. The *Oporornis* warblers are a little larger and heavier by warbler standards and have "hoods" on their heads. Check the chart for a list of all 16 North American warbler genera. (There are 28 in all.)

2. **By wing bars:** Warblers either have wing bars or they don't. A bit more than half of all North American warbler species, including all the *Dendroicas*, have them.

3. **By habitat:** Some warblers, such as the Yellow-rumped Warbler, are very widespread. Others are found only in very specific habitats. The rare and endangered Kirtland's Warbler, for instance, nests only in large stands of jack pine trees that are between 6 and 20 feet tall—habitat that's found only in the pine woods of central Michigan. Some warbler species are found across North America, but most are either western or eastern species. Some, such as the Colima Warbler, just barely qualify as North American birds. This Mexican species is sometimes seen in the Chisos Mountains of Texas. A number of species, such as Lucy's Warbler and the Painted Redstart, are seen only in the Southwest.

4. **By layer:** Where the bird is within the habitat. This is such a help to warbler identification that I discuss the details a little later in this chapter.

North American Warbler Genera

Genus	Species
Vermivora	Bachman's (almost certainly extinct)
	Blue-winged
	Golden-winged
	Tennessee
	Orange-crowned
	Nashville
	Virginia's
	Colima
	Lucy's
Parula	Northern Parula
Dendroica	Yellow
	Chestnut-sided
	Magnolia
	Cape May
	Black-throated Blue
	Yellow-rumped
	Black-throated Gray
	Townsend's

continues

185

North American Warbler Genera   continued

Genus	Species
	Hermit
	Black-throated Green
	Golden-cheeked
	Blackburnian
	Yellow-throated
	Grace's
	Pine
	Kirtland's
	Prairie
	Palm
	Bay-breasted
	Blackpoll
	Cerulean
Mniotilta	Black-and-white
Setophaga	American Redstart
Protonotaria	Prothonotary
Helmitheros	Worm-eating
Limnothylpis	Swainson's
Seiurus	Ovenbird
	Northern Waterthrush
	Louisiana Waterthrush
Oporornis	Kentucky
	Connecticut
	Mourning
	MacGillivray's
Geothlypis	Common Yellowthroat
Wilsonia	Hooded
	Wilson's
	Canada
Cardellina	Red-faced Warbler
Myioborus	Painted Redstart
Icteria	Yellow-breasted Chat
Peucedramus	Olive

All warblers are small, active birds with thin bills and dark eyes, so clues such as bill size and body shape won't help you that much. To get down to species, you'll have to rely on field marks, behavior, and habitat.

A Little Bird Told Me...

Bachman's Warbler is the rarest warbler in North America. It's so rare, in fact, that it's probably extinct. In the late 1800s, this bird was common in the swampy forests of the Southeast. By the 1920s, habitat loss had made it rare. Bachman's Warbler was found in canebrakes (tangles of bamboo and vines) and wet woodlands in the Southeast; it spent its winters in Cuba and the nearby Isle of Pines. The last breeding records date back to the 1960s; the last sighting was in Cuba in 1981. No sighting of a Bachman's Warbler has been confirmed since then.

Watching Warblers

Actually getting your binoculars onto a warbler long enough to see a field mark or two can be a bit of a challenge to new birders. Warblers are very active. Most flit from branch to branch or through the underbrush, probing for bugs among the leaves. They'll often pop up into the clear for a second or two and then disappear again. The males tend to sing from sheltered spots, not from conspicuous perches. You'll spend a lot of time focusing on quivering twigs where the warbler was just a moment before. Keep at it; if you stick with the bird, the chances are good it will eventually pop up and give you a clear glimpse. Warblers fly a lot, but they don't usually fly very far; a lot of time they make short flutters from one branch or bush to another just a few yards away.

Be a Better Birder

Warblers tend to travel in little flocks during migration. If you see one warbler, then chances are good a few others of the same species and probably a few of other species as well, are nearby. When you see little flocks of chickadees, titmice, or kinglets in the spring or fall, look also for warblers.

Head Games

You might not have much time when you finally do get focused on a warbler. Make the most of it by looking at the head if at all possible. There's a reason for common names like Black-throated Green Warbler and Golden-cheeked Warbler. Look for the colors and patterns on the head. Do you see any vivid colors—orange, yellow, red, or blue—on the head? Is the color solid or broken up with bands of black or white? How about a hood or cap? Any colorful cheek or chin patches?

Next, try to spot the wing color and note the wing bars—or lack of them. The wings are helpful clues, as shown by the Blue-winged Warbler.

The tail also has some good field marks. Look for rump patches and tail spots. When the beautiful American Redstart fans its tail, you can see two red or yellow patches on it. If you see the bird fly, look for the colors on the rump.

Note where the bird is. Is it poking around in the underbrush or on the ground? Flitting around on the trunks and in the lower branches of trees? Hiding maddeningly high up in the upper branches of trees?

Warblers are one of the many reasons birders talk to themselves a lot; you don't have time to make notes of any field marks, much less flip through your guide looking for the bird. It's far better to keep watching, looking for field marks and behavior clues.

Layers of Warblers

Warbler species spread out vertically through their habitat. In other words, some species will usually be found feeding on the ground and in the lower underbrush, whereas others are usually found higher up. *Stratigraphic layering,* as birders call it, is a helpful way to narrow down your choices when you're facing a patch of woods full of warblers. It's not foolproof, of course, but take a look at the chart to get a rough breakdown of which birds are usually where.

Where the Warblers Are

Preference	Species
On or near the ground (below waist level)	Common Yellowthroat
	Connecticut
	Kentucky
	Louisiana Waterthrush
	MacGillivray's
	Mourning
	Northern Waterthrush
	Ovenbird
	Palm
	Swainson's
	Worm-eating
In mid-level trees and shrubs (eye level to waist level)	Bay-breasted
	Black-and-white
	Black-throated blue
	Blue-winged
	Canada

Preference	Species
High up in tree tops (above eye level)	Magnolia
	Orange-crowned
	Prothonotary
	Virginia's
	Yellow
	Yellow-rumped
	Blackburnian
	Blackpoll
	Black-throated Green
	Cape May
	Cerulean
	Chestnut-sided
	Grace's
	Hermit
	Nashville
	Tennessee
	Townsend's
	Yellow-throated

A Little Bird Told Me...

The great ecologist Robert MacArthur (1930–72) studied the way warblers share habitat. He looked at five species that all feed on insects found in conifers: Bay-breasted, Blackburnian, Black-throated Green, Cape May, and Yellow-rumped Warblers. What MacArthur discovered was that although the birds all fed in the same trees, they avoided competition with each other by feeding in different parts of the trees. The Yellow-rumped Warbler, for example, spent most of its time feeding in the area around the base and trunk of the trees, whereas the Cape May Warblers fed mostly in the outer parts of the upper-most branches.

Warblers by Ear

Warblers are pretty vocal. In fact, the family gets its common name from the quavering, trilled songs "warbled" by the various species. A lot of warblers do sing easily recognized, very distinct songs; the Yellow Warbler's song is easy to learn. Others aren't as easy. Because I can generally recognize the songs of nonwarblers such as robins and vireos, in the spring, I listen for songs I don't know. Chances are good the singer is a warbler of some sort.

Keep your ears open for rapid, trilling, high-pitched songs repeated frequently. Males tend to sing from sheltered spots instead of conspicuous perches. A singing male will move around a little bit, but you can often home in on the song and get a glimpse of the bird. Warblers make a lot of contact chips and chirps to keep the flock together. Listen for them as well.

Warbler Waves

One May morning when I was still fairly new to birding, I took my morning coffee and my binoculars out to the deck that overlooks our pond. The idea was to see whether the Wood Ducks that had been hanging around were still there. They were—and so were a few Yellow Warblers. That's nice, I thought, and started to go back to the house. A little flash of color caught my eye, though—a Yellow-rumped Warbler. Then, I noticed a tail-wagging, greenish little bird—a Prairie Warbler. Slowly, it dawned on me that this was a *warbler wave*. Without leaving the deck, I saw seven more warbler species and two Scarlet Tanagers before my coffee got cold.

Be a Better Birder

To track warbler migration and spot potential waves, check out the Warbler Watch pages at the BirdSource Web site (**birdsource.cornell.edu**). The site combines volunteer observations with state-of-the-art Internet technology to gather detailed information about migration pathways. The maps for the various migrating species are continuously updated as sighting reports come in.

To understand warbler waves and why they're such a birding bonanza, let's take a look at warbler migration. Almost all warblers head way, way south for the winter. The Yellow Warbler, which breeds as far north as the Arctic Circle, spends its winters anywhere from southern Mexico to as far away as Peru and Brazil.

When all these birds head north again in the early spring, they travel for long distances, often over open water. Not surprisingly, when they hit land, they dive down to rest and feed. As you'll remember from Chapter 6, "Birding Through the Year," the birds often land at predictable points along the coastlines and put on a show for the waiting birders. Sometimes, they get grounded there by bad weather; if you've ever been stuck at an airport by a blizzard, you know how the birds must feel. When the weather changes for the better, all the waiting birds take off. So many have backed up that they move out in waves, like ripples on a pond.

When a warbler wave arrives, the woods come alive with colorful little birds darting everywhere. You practically don't know where to look first; just as you get your bins on one bird, you catch sight of another. Calm down. The birds will probably hang around for at least the rest of the day, so you'll have plenty of time to try to identify them.

When do warbler waves come? Not often enough, but more or less according to this schedule:

➤ **South:** Most warblers arrive in southern Texas, the Gulf Coast, Florida, and southern California starting in the second week of April and continuing into early May.

➤ **Middle states:** By the third week of April, warblers are arriving in Virginia, the Midwest, Colorado, and central California.

➤ **North:** By the first week in May, warblers arrive in the Middle Atlantic states, New England, the prairie states, and the Pacific Northwest.

The true birder plans around these dates. Doesn't everyone's mother want to go birding on Mother's Day?

Confusing Fall Warblers

Roger Tory Peterson coined this term to describe warblers in autumn, when their vivid breeding colors have faded. As usual, Roger was right on the mark; these birds are confusing. Don't despair; you can still ID plenty of warblers in the fall. The colors may be faded, but the important field marks on the head and body are often still fairly distinct on the males. Take the Prothonotary Warbler, for instance. Summer or winter, this is still the only warbler to have a completely golden head and bluish-gray wings without wing bars; it's just a little less vivid by the fall. When I saw my first Cape May Warbler one day in late September, it still had traces of its distinctive chestnut cheeks.

What I find most confusing about fall warblers is identifying the females and immature birds born that summer. These birds really are drab; I usually end up making educated guesses based more on behavior and the nearby males.

Be a Better Birder

When warbler waves are on the move, the birding world swings into action. Check the rare bird alerts and online bulletin boards for updates on your area. Make plans for someone to cover for you when you call in sick.

Splat!

A few hours of peering through your binoculars at warblers in the trees can leave you with a bad case of "warbler neck." This common birdwatcher's ailment is no joke; you get a painful stiff neck and sometimes arm numbness and nasty headaches. Avoid suddenly tilting or jerking your head back, take breaks, and ask your birding friends for the name of a good chiropractor.

Every field guide has a few pages devoted to pictures of the warblers in autumn plumage. When you're studying these, keep a positive attitude. Focus on what's still visible or distinctive, not on what's missing. Behavior clues get to be more important because the birds won't be singing.

The Least You Need to Know

➤ Warblers are colorful, active little birds found mostly in wooded or brushy areas.

➤ About 57 warbler species are found in North America.

➤ Warblers are highly migratory. Many species spend the winter in Central and South America.

➤ The best time of year for warblers is the spring, especially between early April and mid–May. Fall is also a good time for seeing warblers.

➤ Warblers are so active that they're hard to spot, but identifying them is one of the most enjoyable challenges in birding.

Chapter 20

Hummingbirds: Tiny Terrors

In This Chapter

➤ Hummingbirds: Good things come in small packages

➤ Understanding hummingbird behavior

➤ How hummingbirds fly

➤ Unusual hummingbirds

➤ Places to see hummingbirds

The first Europeans to see hummingbirds were Christopher Columbus and his crew. At first, they didn't realize that these tiny, agile birds were birds at all. Hummingbirds were so alien to their idea of what a bird should be that they thought they were some sort of feathered insect. It all goes to show that when it comes to hummingbirds, you need to keep an open mind. These astonishing birds do a lot of things no other bird can do.

Life in the Fast Lane

Hummingbirds are extremely small birds with very long, slender bills. They feed by hovering over flowers and using their very long tongues to lap up the nectar. Hummingbirds get their name because their rapidly beating wings make a humming or buzzing sound. Male hummingbirds have *gorgets,* patches of beautifully colored, iridescent feathers on their throat. They sometimes also have *helmets,* vivid feathers on the forehead and crown.

All hummingbirds are members of the family *Trochilidae*, a big family that's found only in the Western Hemisphere. The family has about 320 species. (Some experts say there are about 340 species.) Almost all of them are found in Central and South America. Some 26 hummingbird species have been spotted in North America, but only 15 species breed on the continent.

A Little Bird Told Me...

The feathers on a male hummingbird's gorget are iridescent, with a beautiful metallic sheen to them when the light hits just right. Why? Each feather has a complex pattern of little colored platelets and air bubbles arranged in layers. When the light hits the feather, it's broken up into its component colors, just like light that passes through a prism. When the light's reflected and refracted back through the layers, some colors are canceled out, and others are intensified.

The best word to describe a hummingbird is *fast*. Just look at these hummingbird stats:

➤ A typical hummingbird's wings beat 50 times a second—so fast that all you can see is a blur.

Rappin' Robin

Hummingbirds are tiny, very active, nectar-eating birds with long, thin bills. Found only in the New World, hummingbirds are members of the family *Trochilidae*. A **gorget** (pronounced GOR-jet*)* is the patch of brightly colored feathers found on the throat of a male hummingbird. **Helmets** are colorful patches on the forehead and crown.

➤ During courtship displays, male hummingbirds may beat their wings as fast as 200 times a second.

➤ At rest, a hummingbird's heart beats about 500 times a minute. In flight, it can beat double that.

➤ The Ruby-throated Hummingbird can fly at speeds of up to 60 miles per hour.

➤ Hummingbirds move so fast that they have to eat about two-thirds their body weight in a day, feeding about once every 20 minutes or so.

➤ A hummingbird's normal body temperature is 104°F.

➤ Hummingbirds have the highest metabolic rate—they use energy faster—of any animal. Hummingbirds burn energy about 100 times faster than elephants and about 10 times faster than any other birds.

It's no wonder so many birders are fascinated by these zippy little birds. They're so unusual, and their colors are so brilliant, that they've been given a lot of evocative and even whimsical common names. Check the chart for some of my personal favorites.

Unusual Common Names for Hummingbirds

Chilean Firecrown
Berylline Hummingbird
Bahama Woodstar
Blossomcrown
Blue-crowned Woodnymph
Buff-tailed Coronet
Charming Hummingbird
Festive Coquette
Fiery-tailed Awlbill
Flame-rumped Sapphire
Glowing Puffleg
Green-breasted Mountain-gem
Horned Sungem
Lazuli Sabrewing
Magnificent Hummingbird
Marvelous Spatuletail
Plain-capped Starthroat
Rainbow-bearded Thornbill
Rainbow Starfrontlet
Red-tailed Comet
Shining Sunbeam
Snowcap
Sooty Barbthroat
Spangled Coquette
Sparkling Violet-ear
Tourmaline Sunangel
Velvet-browed Brilliant

Slow Down, You Move Too Fast

Hummingbirds are so tiny that they lose body heat quickly, especially when the weather's cold. Amazingly, however, hummingbirds are found high in mountains, where altitude makes the weather chilly at night even in the summer. The Chilean

Firecrown nests in Tierra del Fuego, the harsh region at the windy tip of South America. How do they survive? By going into *torpor* at night and when the weather is cold or too bad for the birds to feed. They slow their normal metabolism down to about a third of usual and let their body temperature drop, sometimes by as much as 50 degrees.

Rappin' Robin

Torpor is a state of slowed metabolism and lowered body temperature. Hummingbirds (and also some other birds such as poorwills and swifts) go into torpor for hours at a time to conserve energy at night, in cold weather, or when they can't feed for other reasons, such as bad weather.

Hummingbirds are as small as a bird can be; any smaller, and it would be impossible to eat fast enough to maintain its body temperature. As it is, most hummingbirds are only a few hours away from starvation. Torpor lets them slow down and conserve energy when they can't eat.

Living Dynamos

A lot of the hummingbird species seen in North America are found only in southernmost Arizona; they're really strays who are at the northernmost end of their range. Only about a dozen hummingbird species are fairly common in North America.

If you live in the eastern U.S., the only hummer you're likely to see is the Ruby-throated Hummingbird. This makes it easy to impress your friends by just glancing at the bird and announcing its identity. If you're west of the Mississippi, however, you'll have to work a little. In the western U.S., you have more variety: Rufous, Anna's, and Black-chinned hummers are fairly common. You're most likely to see a Rufous; this species nests as far north as the southern coast of Alaska, which makes it the northernmost of all the hummingbirds.

In recent years, Rufous Hummingbirds have been turning up regularly in the East, and some, along with some Ruby-throats, have even been overwintering along the Gulf Coast. Other hummingbird species have also been turning up where they're not supposed to be. Many researchers believe that the increase in the number of backyard hummingbird feeders is helping these birds expand their range. Check the chart to see which hummers are found where during the breeding season.

Common Hummingbirds in North America (Breeding Season)

Species	Region
Allen's	Coastal California
Anna's	Coastal California, Oregon, Washington
Black-chinned	West of the Rockies
Blue-throated	Southeastern Arizona
Broad-billed	Southern California, deserts of the Southwest

Species	Region
Broad-tailed	Rocky Mountains
Buff-bellied	Rio Grande Valley, Texas
Calliope	Rocky Mountains, Pacific Northwest, Idaho, Nevada
Costa's	Southern California, deserts of the Southwest
Lucifer's	Southeastern Arizona
Magnificent	Southeastern Arizona
Ruby-throated	East of the Mississippi
Rufous	Pacific Northwest, western Canada, Alaska, Southeast in winter
Violet-crowned	Southeastern Arizona

Hummingbird identification is fairly easy, at least when it comes to the males. When the light strikes a male bird the right way, the brilliant, iridescent colors in the gorget and on the head show up boldly. Unfortunately, when the light doesn't strike them the right way, the gorgeous reds, purples, and greens are hard to see; they can look almost black. Check out the colors on the back and tail; Rufous Hummingbirds, for instance, are reddish-brown on the back and tail, whereas the Black-chinned Hummingbird is metallic green on the back with a whitish underbody. Check out the tail. Note the shape. If the tail is forked, how deeply? Do you see white tips or spots on the tailfeathers? Also, look at the color and shape of the bill. Most hummers have black bills, but a few, such as the broad-billed, have red bills. The Calliope Hummingbird has a relatively short bill.

Female and immature hummers are another matter. Their plumage is duller, and they don't have colorful gorgets. Not only that, the different species look a lot alike. It's almost impossible to tell the difference between a female Rufous Hummingbird and a female Allen's, or between a female Ruby-throat and a female Black-chinned, for example. Study your field guide, study the birds, think about where you are, and make an educated guess.

Be a Better Birder

The best way to get good looks at hummingbirds is to stake out a nectar feeder. You get to sit comfortably and watch as the birds zoom in, hover for a few seconds while they feed, zoom away, and then come back again a few minutes later. You can easily get your binoculars on them while they feed and follow as they fly off.

Nectar of the Gods

Hummingbirds feed almost exclusively on flower *nectar*. They also eat some tiny insects and spiders, usually ones that are caught in the nectar. Long, tubular, brightly colored flowers are generally rich sources of nectar, so you're most likely to see hummingbirds near these plants. In the wild, plants such as trumpet vine, day lilies, cardinal flower, and many others are all highly attractive to hummers. Hummingbirds are also easily attracted to human-provided nectar in feeders. (I discuss gardening to attract hummingbirds in Chapter 28, "Gardening for the Birds;" I cover nectar feeders in Chapter 24, "In the Good Old Summertime.")

To find nectar, hummingbirds home in on any flower that's red, orange, or even yellow. They're so attuned to these colors, in fact, that they'll home in on anything. If I wear anything red or orange when I'm working in my garden, I'm likely to get buzzed by a Ruby-throated Hummingbird.

When the bird finds a nice, tubular flower full of nectar, it hovers by it and inserts its long, thin beak into the base, where the nectar is. Using their long, flexible, grooved tongues, they lick up the nectar, much as a cat licks up water. It all happens very fast, at a rate of about 13 licks a second. If you watch carefully as a hummingbird approaches a flower or feeder, you can sometimes see the tongue flicking out.

Rappin' Robin

Nectar is a sweet juice secreted by many plants as a way to attract insects that will pollinate them. Hummingbirds eat the nectar and also play a role in pollinating plants; in fact, some flowers, such as penstemons, probably rely on hummingbirds for pollination. Nectar-bearing flowers usually have tubular shapes and are brightly colored.

A Little Bird Told Me...

The Swordbill Hummingbird has the longest bill of any hummingbird. It's four inches long—about twice as long as the bird's body. In a textbook example of coevolution, the Swordbill feeds almost exclusively on nectar from a type of passion flower that's 4.5 inches deep. In return, the flower depends on the hummingbird for pollination. For an example closer to home, take the trumpet creeper, a common woodland vine in eastern North America. This plant relies mostly on Ruby-throated Hummingbirds for pollination.

Hummingbirds also eat bugs and feed them to their chicks. A lot of times, they're bugs caught in nectar, but sometimes, hummingbirds go after them. In southern Arizona, I once watched as a hummingbird perched on a wire fence and caught passing insects by shooting out its tongue.

When a hummingbird finds a reliable food source—your garden or feeder, for instance— it gets very territorial. The bird will perch nearby and guard the food source fiercely, chasing away or even tussling with any other hummingbird that dares to approach. The bird might even fly out at you or a pet if you get too near, but don't worry: The old myth that a hummingbird's beak is poisonous is a bunch of baloney. (In case you're wondering, there's only one bird that's definitely poisonous: the Hooded Pitohui, found in New Guinea. The feathers and skin of this bird contain a toxin very similar to the one found in the poison dart frogs of South America. How do you pronounce pitohui? Say pah-TOO-ee, as if you were spitting out something awful.)

Hum a Few Bars

Why do hummingbirds hum? Because they don't know the words! (Sorry if that caused a flashback to fourth grade.) Actually, the humming or buzzing noise a hummingbird makes comes from its rapidly beating wings. Experienced hummingbird watchers can tell species apart by the sound of the hum and by the whistling noises some hummingbirds make with their wings.

Anna's Hummingbird makes weak, scratchy noises that could charitably be called songs, but the other North American species don't really sing. (Most of the hummingbirds in Central and South America do sing, although not very well.) Hummingbirds mostly make a variety of unmusical chips and chirps. Some make sputtering noises, much like the sound an electric current makes when it arcs or the sounds made by a welding torch. When they're defending their territory, a lot of hummingbirds make a sort of chattering sound; it's surprisingly loud for such a small bird.

Hot-Dogging Hummers

When a male hummingbird courts a mate, he doesn't try to impress her by being a sensitive New Age guy. He takes a more old-fashioned approach and tries to impress her with how great his body is. The pick-up lines may vary a little, but all hummingbird courtships follow this basic pattern:

➤ **Gorget display:** The male displays the colorful feathers of his gorget, sometimes while making shrill chirps. He makes sure to line himself up with the sun so that the light hits his gorget at the right angle to show off the colors.

➤ **Shuttle flights:** No, he doesn't catch a plane from LaGuardia to D.C. Instead, he flies rapidly back and forth in front of the female in short arcs. Shuttle flights can be very in-your-face; they're usually done just inches in front of the female, and the width of the arc is only about a foot. The female may also do a shuttle flight.

Rappin' Robin

A **lek** is any area where male birds gather to perform complex courtship displays to an audience of females. Some hummingbird species, especially the more tropical ones, gather in leks. Lek behavior is also common among grouse, prairie chickens, and woodcocks.

➤ **Dive display:** The dive display is spectacular to watch; the birds may flap their wings as fast as 200 times a second. In some species, such as Anna's Hummingbird, the male makes repeated J-shaped dives in front of the female, often starting from treetop height. Male Ruby-throats fly rapidly back and forth like a pendulum. Some species make buzzing, whistling, or popping noises with their wings as they dive.

The female doesn't always just sit back and watch. Females sometimes make shuttle flights. They also do tail displays; they perch and spread out their tailfeathers to show off the white tips.

Some hummingbirds—including the Blue-throated, White-eared, and Berylline—gather in *leks* to do their courtship displays. They sing loudly to lure in the ladies. When they have a good enough audience, they start showing off. The more dominant a bird is, the better his chances of impressing a female into being his mate. If you've ever been to ladies' night at a sports bar, you have a pretty good idea of what happens at a hummingbird lek.

Love 'em and Leave 'em

Once the male hummingbird gets what he wants, he takes off for good and immediately starts looking around for another mate. No child support here—female hummingbirds make the nest and raise the young entirely on their own.

A Little Bird Told Me...

Did William Shakespeare know about hummingbirds? Probably not, but I wonder. *The Tempest,* one of Shakespeare's last plays, is set in the New World. Ariel's song in Act IV has always reminded me of hummingbirds. You remember, it's the one that goes: Where the bee sucks, there suck I/In a cowslip bell I lie;/.../Merrily, merrily shall I live now/Under the blossom that hangs on the bough.

Hummingbird nests are tiny, delicate cups. The Ruby-throated Hummingbird, for example, makes a nest about the size of a small walnut shell, just big enough to hold two bean-sized eggs. She uses dandelion and thistle down, held together with silk snatched from spider webs. The outside of the nest is often shingled with bits of lichen for camouflage. The nest is generally built on a thin tree branch, often where it's sheltered by leaves, and often over water.

The Calliope Hummingbird builds a nest that's a dead ringer for a pine cone. The bird makes its nest in the middle of a cluster of real cones, usually on a spruce or lodgepole pine. The nest of the Cuban Bee Hummingbird is less than an inch across; you could cover it with the cap from a milk jug.

How Hummers Hover

Of all the amazing things hummingbirds do, the most amazing is the way they fly. How do hummingbirds fly? Any way they want, including sideways, backward, and upside-down—the Harrier jump jets of the bird world. (Or is it that the jets are the hummingbirds of the aircraft world?)

To do all this, hummingbirds have wings that are very different from other birds. Remember the discussion of how birds fly in Chapter 7, "Understanding Bird Behavior?" Don't flip the pages back, just remember that birds get their lift from the downstroke of their wings. Hummingbirds get their lift from both the downstroke and the upstroke; that's how they can fly with such agility. Hummingbirds can also *hover* in place, like helicopters.

Hummingbirds are such good flyers that their feet have become almost useless. Hummingbird feet are so tiny and weak that they can't walk on them; they can only perch. For a hummingbird to move even a couple of inches, it has to fly.

Rappin' Robin

Hummingbirds can **hover** because they can also pivot their stiff wings at the shoulder and move them backward and forward, through a sort of figure eight shape. When the bird moves its wing backward and forward that way, the upstroke and the downstroke cancel each other out. The bird stays motionless in the air under its own power.

Heading South

If you depend on flowers to get your food, you'll have to head south when the weather gets cold and the flowers die off. With a few exceptions (Anna's Hummingbird doesn't migrate), hummingbirds leave North America for the winter and head to the flower-filled tropics. The distances these teeny birds fly during migration are awesome. The Ruby-throat, for instance, winters in Central America. To get there, at least some of the birds fly nonstop across the Gulf of Mexico—a distance of 500 miles or more. Here's another hummingbird myth that's not true: Hummingbirds do not migrate on the backs of geese!

In the spring, male hummingbirds return north a week or two ahead of the females; likewise, they head south a week or two earlier.

Hummers Far from Home

Sometimes, hummingbirds wander far from where they ought to be. Every year, a few hummers seem to turn up far enough from home to set the birding hotlines buzzing.

A Green Violet-ear Hummingbird spent the summer and fall of 1998 visiting a feeder in Wisconsin. This bird is ordinarily a fairly rare visitor to central and south Texas! Sometimes, these birds are nurtured through the winter by bird lovers.

What do vagrant hummingbirds tell us? Two things: First, birds have wings and they use them. Second, it's possible that some birds have bigger ranges than we thought or that they're expanding their ranges because so many people now plant hummingbird gardens and put out nectar feeders. Anna's Hummingbirds have been expanding their range northward and eastward from California and Arizona over the past few decades. Recently some serious banding work (using teeny, teeny little bands) has shown that Rufous Hummingbirds regularly overwinter in southern Louisiana. It's possible that these are actually a separate permanent population from the Rufous hummers that are found further west. The banding work has also shown that Black-chinned and Buff-bellied hummers regularly overwinter in Louisiana.

The World's Smallest Bird

The tiniest bird in the world is the Cuban Bee Hummingbird. Weighing in at 2.2 grams (about $1/10$ of an ounce, or just under the weight of a penny), this minuscule bird is less than 2 inches long. On the other end of the hummingbird scale is the Giant Hummingbird, found in the Andes mountains. This bird weighs in at about 20 grams (about $7/10$ of an ounce) and is about 8.5 inches long. The Calliope Hummingbird is the smallest in North America. It's only a touch over three inches long and weighs around half an ounce. (The smallest flying animal is Kitti's hog-nosed bat; it weighs only 1.5 grams, or about 0.05 of an ounce.)

Where to See Hummingbirds

Hummingbirds are surprisingly easy to see, mostly because they're absolutely fearless. No skulking in the underbrush for these little guys—they dart straight out to feed on their favorite flowers and then zoom on to the next one. They basically ignore you; I've had hummingbirds sip from flowers when I've been standing right next to them.

If you want to see hummingbirds, go where the nectar-bearing flowers are—or go where someone has a nectar feeder. For the more widespread species such as Rufous, Black-chinned, or Ruby-throated Hummingbirds, that's anywhere with flowers in bloom or an attractive backyard. For the southern Arizona specialties, that's any one of several hotspots, including my favorite place, Madera Canyon south of Tucson. I discuss details in Chapter 29, "Hotspots and Rare Birds."

A Little Bird Told Me...

Hummingbirds are beautiful to look at and have a lot of interesting behavior; it's no wonder they're popular among birders. If you'd like to contribute to hummingbird conservation and research, check out these organizations:

Hummer/Bird Study Group, Inc.
P.O. Box 250
Clay, AL 35048-0250
(205) 681-1339
E-mail: **HummerBSG@aol.com**
home.judson.edu/hbsg.html

The Hummingbird Society
249 East Main Street, Suite 4
Newark, DE 19711
(800) 529-3699
Fax: (302) 369-1816
info@hummingbird.org
www.hummingbird.org

The Least You Need to Know

➤ Hummingbirds are very small, active birds with long, thin bills. They feed chiefly on nectar gathered from flowers, but feed their young insects.

➤ Male hummingbirds have brilliantly colored feathers on their necks and heads.

➤ About 15 hummingbird species are found regularly in North America.

➤ The most common hummingbird in eastern North America is the Ruby-throated Hummingbird. West of the Rockies, Rufous, Black-chinned, and Anna's Hummingbirds are the most common.

➤ Hummingbirds are amazingly good fliers; they can hover or fly forward, backward, sideways, and even upside-down.

Chapter 21

Sparrows: Little Brown Birds

> ## In This Chapter
>
> ➤ Understanding the sparrow family
>
> ➤ Towhees, juncos, longspurs, buntings—they're all sparrows
>
> ➤ Identifying those little brown birds
>
> ➤ Which sparrows are where
>
> ➤ Sparrows in danger

You catch a glimpse of a little brown bird with streaks on its breast in an overgrown field. What is it? Well, even if you're an experienced birder, chances are good you're going to identify it as a little brown bird with streaks on its breast. In fact, it's most likely a sparrow; these birds can be tough to identify. But if you could identify every bird you see all the time, birding wouldn't be anywhere near as much fun.

Sparing Time for Sparrows

Now that I've got you thoroughly intimidated, let's get started on the *sparrows*. First, let's try to define the sparrow family. The problem is that the common name sparrow is applied to a lot of bird species without much regard to their taxonomy. That's because the word has deep Anglo-Saxon roots and has been used for centuries to mean just about any small bird. To complicate matters, North American sparrows are in a completely different family than the Old World sparrows.

Rappin' Robin

Sparrows are small, drab, seed-eating birds with conical beaks. In North America, sparrows are members of the family *Emberizidae*, which includes towhees, New World sparrows, juncos, longspurs, and buntings.

Rappin' Robin

Finches are small- to medium-sized birds with conical bills. In general, they're more brightly colored than sparrows and have a more varied diet. Finches are members of the family *Fringillidae*, which includes finches, siskins, crossbills, redpolls, and some grosbeaks.

With me so far? Okay, now for the members of the sparrow family, according to the most recent thinking. In North America, these members of the family *Emberizidae* are considered sparrows: towhees, New World sparrows, juncos, longspurs, and buntings. What makes them sparrows? They have conical beaks, mostly eat seeds, and usually skulk around in the underbrush. The New World sparrows have streaked backs. Broadly speaking, sparrows prefer open, grassy habitat and spend most of their time on the ground in small flocks.

How many sparrow species are there? Good question. The answer depends a lot on who you ask—a lumper or a splitter—so let's just say about 45.

On the Fringe

Now, I'll shake your confidence even more. Are you sure the bird you're seeing is a sparrow at all? Maybe it's a member of the closely related finch family.

Finches are a little easier to grasp. The finches are members of the *Fringillidae* family, which includes finches, siskins, crossbills, redpolls, and some grosbeaks. What makes these birds finches? Like sparrows, they have conical bills, but they're more colorful than the sparrows and they usually have solid colors, not streaks, on their backs. Finches eat a lot of seeds, but they'll also happily eat bugs. Finches generally prefer brushy or wooded habitat and spend more time in trees.

The Spurious Sparrow

One of the most familiar birds in the world is the House Sparrow, also sometimes called the English Sparrow (*Passer domesticus*). This little bird isn't a sparrow at all; it's a weaver, a member of a large Old World family. It sure looks like a sparrow, though; it's small, with a stout bill and a streaky back. House Sparrows have shorter legs and thicker bills than other sparrows, and they also behave a little differently. For one thing, they're aggressive, and for another, they're perfectly happy living anywhere, including crowded urban areas. I've seen House Sparrow nests in all sorts of weird places, including in street lights, under air conditioners, and on top of ventilating fans—and every House Sparrow nest I've ever seen has had some sort of fast-food wrapper in it. House sparrows will eat just about anything grain-based, and they also have a real taste for insects. Most "real" sparrows insist on seeds. It's fair to say that

House Sparrows are real pests that crowd out native birds. As non-native birds, they're not protected by federal or state law, so don't feel guilty about removing nests or trying to keep these birds away from your feeder.

A Little Bird Told Me...

House Sparrows are natives of Europe. The first House Sparrows in North America were deliberately introduced back in the 1850s in Brooklyn. The idea was that these little birds would help control insect pests. The idea made some sense in an era that depended on horsepower, because House Sparrows were known to hang around stables and eat the spilled grain and numerous flies that go with horses. In the larger environmental sense, of course, it was complete idiocy. The birds spread so quickly that by 1900, they were everywhere across North America.

Sorting Out the Sparrows

Think you've got a grasp on the sparrows? Good. Let's sort them out in family groups. Once you've got an idea of the different families, getting a handle on those little brown birds will become a lot easier.

Tea for Two: Towhees

I get a lot of Eastern Towhees (until recently the common name for this bird was Rufous-sided Towhee) in my backyard. I enjoy listening to their "drink your tea" calls; every bird seems to have its own individual variation on the theme. A towhee at a birdfeeder is a good example of sparrow behavior. It comes skulking out from the underbrush or brush pile to the ground under the feeder. Then, it kicks backward with both feet to stir up any seeds on the ground, eats a few, and walks or flutters back into the underbrush. I've never seen a towhee actually land on a feeder.

Birds in the towhee family are medium-sized ground lovers with long tails. Look for them in dense underbrush. You'll probably hear them first as they scratch around on the ground and make a lot of contact calls. In the east, the Eastern Towhee is your only choice. Out west, the choices are Spotted Towhee, California Towhee, Canyon Towhee, and Green-tailed Towhee. In the deserts of the Southwest, you might see an Abert's Towhee.

Towhees are a good example of why you should always use an up-to-date field guide. The Rufous-sided Towhee was recently split into the Eastern and Spotted towhees, and the Brown Towhee was recently split into the California and Canyon towhee. (I gained two life birds from those splits!)

The White-throated Sparrow gets its name from the easily seen white patch under the chin. Another good ID clue is the striping on the head. (Photo by Richard Day/ Daybreak Imagery.)

Bye, Baby Bunting

Were you starting to think that this sparrow business wasn't so bad? Hah! Let's talk about buntings. Part of the confusion is caused by the New World clashing with the Old. In England, when they say "sparrow," they actually mean weavers, like the House Sparrow, and when they say "bunting," they mean any New World sparrow. Here in North America, we use the word bunting not only for several members of the sparrow family, but also for several brightly colored New World species that are members of the *Cardinalinae* subfamily. (I don't have room to go into the *Cardinalinae* buntings, which is too bad, because the painted bunting is really gorgeous and I wanted to put in a picture of it. Look at the picture in your field guide instead.)

Got it? Good. Because this chapter covers sparrows, let's talk about Snow Buntings and Lark Buntings because they're the only sparrow-family buntings you're likely to see. Despite the common names, however, these birds are in separate genera.

Snow Buntings nest the furthest north of any songbird; they breed on the Arctic tundra. In the winter, they come south, but south is a relative term. In the Hudson Valley, not noted for its mild winters, I often see flocks of these birds on snow-covered corn fields. They're fairly large birds with conspicuous white wing patches. In the early fall, the males might still be in their white-and-black breeding plumage, but you're more likely to see these birds in their tan-and-black winter plumage.

The other likely sparrow bunting is the Lark Bunting. This stocky, short-tailed bird looks a lot more like a typical sparrow than the Snow Bunting does, especially among female and winter birds, but the big white wing patches give it away.

Longing for Longspurs

A few members of the sparrow family have extra-long claws on their hind toes. These birds are called longspurs. Three species are found only in North America: Chestnut-collared, McCown's, and Smith's. The Lapland Longspur is found across the Arctic region, including in Europe. In England, it's called the Lapland Bunting. Look for them on open grasslands. A good field mark is white feathers in the tail.

Wiping the Slate Clean: Juncos

When I was a very new birder, I had a chance to do some birding in the Vancouver area. In the underbrush near a roadside pullout, I saw some birds in the shrubs. Eventually, one popped up and gave me a good look. It seemed familiar, but at first I couldn't place it. Then, it flew and I saw two white tailfeathers. I can still remember the sensation as that field mark, along with the bird's overall appearance, its behavior, and the geographic location clicked into place in my brain and I realized I was seeing an "Oregon" Junco. For the first time, I had seen a new bird and identified it for sure without having to look it up in my field guide. What a feeling!

Even though I'd seen a new bird, it didn't count on my life list. The Oregon, the Slate-colored, the Pink-sided, and a couple other juncos are only subspecies of the Dark-eyed Junco. You'll still run across a lot of references to Slate-colored Juncos; that's the most widespread subspecies. Juncos are common birds at feeders in the winter. Look for the pink bill and two white tailfeathers.

Be a Better Birder

Females of some other species can look a lot like sparrows; take a look at the pictures of female House Finches and Rose-breasted Grosbeaks in your field guide to see what I mean. The female Rose-breasted Grosbeak is drab, with brown and white streaks. It's larger than a typical sparrow, though, and has a much larger conical beak.

Little Brown Birds: Separating the Sparrows

That mysterious little brown bird isn't a junco or towhee. You're sure it's a sparrow, but which one? Watch the bird as long as you can, and then ask yourself some questions to narrow down the possibilities.

Streaks on the Breast?

About a dozen sparrow species have streaky breasts; the others are plain. Check the pictures in your field guide, but use these two common sparrows for reference: The Song Sparrow has a streaked breast with a central spot, or "stickpin"; the White-throated Sparrow has a plain breast.

Male and female sparrows generally look a lot alike. Juvenile birds are even harder to identify because pretty much all of them have streaked breasts.

Head Markings?

Every sparrow species has different head markings. Some are a lot more obvious than others. Most of the birds with streaky breasts have fairly plain heads. Among the plain-breasted sparrows, the head markings are more distinct. The White-throated Sparrow, as the name suggests, has a well-defined white patch at the throat. Other sparrows have giveaway names: Black-chinned, White-crowned, Golden-crowned, Black-throated, Rufous-crowned. While you're looking at the head, check the color and size of the bill.

What Kind of Tail?

Look at the length and shape of the tail. Is it short or long, broad or narrow, notched or rounded? Do you see any white feathers when the bird flies? Check the color. Why do you think it's called the Green-tailed Towhee?

What's the Habitat?

Sparrows are fairly fussy about where they like to be. The White-throated Sparrow likes thick underbrush, whereas the Song Sparrow prefers shrubs and bushes near moist areas. A lot of sparrows are also found only in certain geographic regions. The Black-throated Sparrow is found in the desert areas of the Southwest, whereas the Sharp-tailed Sparrow is found mostly in short-grass salt marshes. Habitat is such a big help for identifying a sparrow that I've done a chart showing which ones are usually found in which environments.

Sparrows and Their Habitats

Grasslands and Prairies

Baird's Sparrow	Lark Sparrow
Chestnut-collared Longspur	McCown's Longspur
Chipping Sparrow	Savannah Sparrow
Dicksissel	Vesper Sparrow
Lapland Longspur	

Fields and Meadows

American Tree Sparrow	Harris' Sparrow
Brewer's Sparrow	Henslow's Sparrow
Cassin's Sparrow	Lark Sparrow
Chipping Sparrow	Savannah Sparrow
Clay-colored Sparrow	Snow Bunting
Dark-eyed Junco	Song Sparrow
Field Sparrow	Tree Sparrow
Grasshopper Sparrow	White-throated Sparrow

210

Brush and Thick Undergrowth

California Towhee

Clay-colored Sparrow

Eastern Towhee

Field Sparrow

Fox Sparrow

Green-tailed Towhee

Lincoln's Sparrow

Rufous-winged Sparrow

Song Sparrow

White-crowned Sparrow

White-throated Sparrow

Marshes and Wetlands

Golden-crowned Sparrow

LeConte's Sparrow

Lincoln's Sparrow

Nelson's Sharp-tailed Sparrow

Savannah Sparrow

Song Sparrow

Swamp Sparrow

Tree Sparrow

Woodlands

Bachman's Sparrow

Chipping Sparrow

Dark-eyed Junco

Fox Sparrow

Harris' Sparrow

Yellow-eyed Junco

Seashores and Salt Marshes

Saltmarsh Sharp-tailed Sparrow

Savannah Sparrow

Seaside Sparrow

Snow Bunting

Song Sparrow

Deserts

Abert's Towhee

Black-chinned Sparrow

Black-throated Sparrow

Canyon Towhee

Five-striped Sparrow

Rufous-winged Sparrow

Sage Sparrow

How Does It Sound?

Remember what I discussed back in Chapter 11, "Birding by Ear?" In the spring, listen for songs. You can easily recognize the songs of the White-throated and Song Sparrows, Eastern Towhees, and some other sparrows. When it comes to the various chips and chirps of most sparrows, however, I admit that sound isn't always much help, especially when you're starting out. Then, there's the Grasshopper Sparrow, which really does sound a lot like a grasshopper. Of course, you might be hearing a real grasshopper...

A Little Bird Told Me...

Song Sparrows (and some other species) sing different songs in different parts of the country. These dialects, as they're called, are variations on the basic song—sort of like regional accents in people. Why the birds have dialects isn't really clear. In some cases, researchers think it's to help females pick males from their own local region—but in other cases, it could be to help the females pick males from *outside* the region. Maybe dialects don't really mean anything; we've still got a lot to learn about birds.

What's the Season?

Sometimes, a sparrow is just passing through during migration. The only time I ever see Fox Sparrows in my yard is for a day or two in March, when they're on their way north to their breeding grounds in northern Alaska and Canada. I never see them on their way back south again. In general, sparrows aren't long-distance migrants like warblers, but many species do move with the seasons.

Spotting Sparrows

To put it politely (the only way I'm allowed to in a family book), sparrows can be challenging. Some are pretty easy to spot and identify, but a lot of them are real skulkers, scurrying around in the underbrush and never coming out long enough to give you a good look. That's frustrating enough, but then add in their natural camouflage and the lack of bright colors. These birds are just plain tough to tell apart—if all you're relying on is field marks. Keep watching (or listening for the scuffling, scratching noises the bird is making in the scrub). If you watch long enough, it will pop out. Most sparrows aren't especially strong flyers. A lot of times, they come out of the grass, fly a short way just above the grasstops, and drop down again—all too fast and unpredictably for you to see much. Sparrows are usually found in small flocks, so if you lose sight of one bird, keep watching. There's bound to be a few more around.

Sparrows are a wary bunch. They'll usually shut up and disappear if they see you coming. If they're feeding in an open area, they'll run for cover. Move slowly, with a lot

Be a Better Birder

In the spring, look for male sparrows singing from mid-level perches such as fence posts and the tops of shrubs and small trees. They rarely sing from points any higher than that.

of pauses. Conceal yourself by squatting down next to a shrub or leaning against a tree. Stay quietly in one spot and keep watching; the birds will get active again in a few minutes once they're sure you're no threat.

As you watch and wait, think about the habitat and geographic region; they're good clues that will help you eliminate a lot of possibilities.

Just when you think you might have a handle on the bird, a horrifying thought hits you: Maybe it's a subspecies. Many sparrow species, such as the Sharp-tailed Sparrow, have at least one subspecies. The Fox Sparrow is the champ, with 18. (Actually, some researchers say the Fox Sparrow is really three different species and a bunch of sub-species. Keep your life list ready for some changes in the future.) The Song Sparrow has a lot of regional variations. The birds look and sound different, but not enough to qualify as subspecies. The White-crowned Sparrow has five separate races.

Spaced-Out Sparrows

The most recent North American bird to become extinct was the Dusky Seaside Spar-row, a subspecies of the Seaside Sparrow. This dark, tiny bird lived in the salt marshes near Cape Canaveral in Florida. In the 1950s, as the area became the center of the space race, the bird's habitat began to disappear. The marshes were diked and flooded for mosquito control, and more of what was left became part of the space center, with all its roads, buildings, and housing. By 1979, only six male birds were left—all in captivity. Between habitat loss and some questionable management of the remaining birds, by 1987, the last dusky was dead.

Today, three other sparrow subspecies are on the federal endangered species list: the San Clemente Sage Sparrow, Cape Sable Seaside Sparrow, and Florida Grasshopper Sparrow. Another subspecies, the Belding's Savannah Sparrow, is on the state endan-gered list in California. The problem for all these birds? Habitat loss.

The Least You Need to Know

➤ Sparrows are small, inconspicuous birds with conical beaks; most have streaked backs and eat seeds.

➤ The North American sparrows include the towhees, New World sparrows, juncos, longspurs, and buntings.

➤ Most sparrows prefer open, grassy habitat. Because they spend most of their time on or low to the ground, they're hard to spot.

➤ You can't always get good looks at sparrows. Use other clues, such as habitat and location, along with field marks, to identify the bird.

Chapter 22

Birds of the Ocean Blue

In This Chapter

➤ Understanding the seabirds

➤ Shearwaters and petrels

➤ Puffins, auks, and other ocean birds

➤ Birding by boat

Pelagic birding—it's a tough job, but someone's got to do it. Somebody's got to go look at all those albatrosses, shearwaters, puffins, and all the other birds that spend most of their life on the ocean, far from shore. If that somebody's you, you're in luck. You get to spend a long day on a boat being cold, wet, quite possibly seasick—and seeing fabulous birds.

Far-Out Birds

Some bird species are found only far out at sea. *Pelagic* birds—birds of the ocean or seabirds—include albatrosses, shearwaters, petrels, fulmars, gannets, and boobies. Some gulls, jaegers, and skuas are highly pelagic. Puffins and auks also fall into the pelagic category.

Pelagic birds spend most of their lives on the ocean, feeding on fish, squid, crustaceans, and other sea critters. That sort of food is found most abundantly where cold ocean currents cause upwellings of the microscopic plankton and krill that the critters feed on. Where the fish are, so are industrial fishing boats. And where the fishing boats are, so are the pelagic birds. They're perfectly happy to scavenge the waste products the boats dump overboard.

Pelagic birds are found on all the world's oceans, but they're most abundant in the colder regions, especially the chilly subarctic and Arctic waters of the northern hemisphere and the South Atlantic and Antarctic region of the southern hemisphere. During the breeding seasons, the birds are concentrated here, but during the rest of the year, they tend to wander over the oceans.

Rappin' Robin

Pelagic is a general term for anything relating to the open ocean—salt waters far from shore. Pronounced peh-LAJ-ick, the word comes from the Greek word *pelagos,* meaning sea. Pelagic birds are birds such as albatrosses that spend most of their life at sea.

Rappin' Robin

Tubenose is a general term for pelagic birds that have two tubular extensions on their nostrils. Albatrosses, fulmars, gadfly petrels, storm-petrels, and shearwaters are all tubenoses, members of the order *Procellariiformes.*

To sleep or rest, pelagic birds roost on the water—although some albatrosses sleep on the wing and might not land for days or even longer. The only time these birds really come ashore is for the breeding season. Pelagic birds generally nest in colonies on isolated oceanic islands or rocky cliffs. Most tubenoses nest in the southern hemisphere. The birds we see off the coasts of North America are usually just visiting or are migrating south.

Seeing pelagic birds, needless to say, isn't as simple as just taking a walk in your local bird sanctuary. As I explain a little later in this chapter, the best way to fill in a lot of holes in your life list is to take a boat trip to see pelagic birds.

Taking in the Tubenoses

Take a good look at any of the pictures of shearwaters and petrels at the beginning of your field guide. You'll see two parallel tubes on the top of their bills; they look a little like a double-barreled shotgun. The tubes (albatrosses have them on the sides of the bill) are actually enlarged nostrils. They give these birds the overall name of *tubenoses.* In scientific terms, the tubenoses are members of the order *Procellariiformes.*

Why are the tubes there and what do they do? I answer those questions by asking another. How does a bird that spends all its life on the ocean get fresh water to drink? The answer is it drinks sea water and uses highly specialized glands at the base of the bill to remove the salt. The bird gets rid of the excess salt by dribbling out a waste fluid from the gland. In tubenoses, the fluid goes out through the tubes. In other pelagic birds, it flows along the bill and drips off the tip.

A Little Bird Told Me...

Albatrosses and other tubenoses often live 20 or 30 years. They don't reach breeding age until about eight or nine years. A typical albatross female lays one egg in a nest that's part of a massive colony that can contain thousands of birds. During the months the chick takes to mature, the parent birds leave it alone for days as they go to sea to feed. When they return, they regurgitate an oily and malodorous mixture of fish to feed the chick and then depart again. How do the birds know which chick among the many thousands on the island is theirs? In the case of the tubenoses, it might be by their sense of smell.

Flying over the Sea

One of the joys of pelagic birding is watching these birds in flight. How do albatrosses, shearwaters, and petrels manage to soar effortlessly for so long? How can they do it even on a windless day? The answer is *dynamic soaring.* Here's how it works: The motion of the waves on the surface of the water makes updrafts of air on the windward side. The birds catch the updrafts on their long, narrow, pointed wings and let themselves be lifted up. As they rise in the air, the wind speed picks up and raises them higher; you can experience this yourself on a boat by comparing the wind speed on a lower deck to the wind speed higher up. When the bird decides it's time to head down to the water again, it glides down on a gentle slope and then lets the wave updraft and its own momentum send it soaring up again.

Shearwaters don't always soar; often, they skim along rapidly just above the surface of the waves. They're looking for food in the most aerodynamically efficient way. Air resistance is low very close to the water—but it increases sharply just a few inches higher. That's why the birds follow the contours of the waves.

Rappin' Robin

The word **albatross** comes from the Spanish word *alcatraz,* which originally was applied to pelicans and eventually ended up meaning any large bird in the *Diomedeidae* family.

ABC's of Albatrosses

Albatrosses are huge birds with very long, narrow, pointed wings. In terms of wing span, albatrosses are among the largest birds on earth—on average, more than 10 feet wide. With such huge wings, it's not surprising that these birds are fabulous soarers, able to fly for days with barely a wing flap.

Generally, albatrosses are found in the cold waters of the southern oceans, in the subantarctic and Antarctic regions. Worldwide, there are 13 albatross species. Only two species—the Black-Footed and Laysan—are seen regularly in North America off the west coast, but occasional strays from other species sometimes turn up, causing great excitement.

A Little Bird Told Me...

Whenever the conversation turns to albatrosses, somebody's bound to bring up Samuel Taylor Coleridge's famous poem, "Rime of the Ancient Mariner." For the record, the Ancient Mariner shot the albatross with a crossbow. Also for the record, here are the two famous and most frequently misquoted lines from the whole poem: "Water, water every where,/nor any drop to drink." The Gray-beard Loon in Line 11 isn't a bird; it's the Ancient Mariner, who should not be confused with the bird known as the ancient murrelet.

The Short-tailed Albatross is one of the world's most endangered birds. This bird once bred in massive numbers on a number of islands in the Ryukyu Islands of Japan and Taiwan, and perhaps some islands off the coast of China. Because these albatrosses are slow and clumsy on land and have little fear of humans, between the late 1800s and 1930, feather hunters killed some five million birds. By the 1940s, fewer than 50 birds were left. Today, the population is up to about 600, but the Short-tailed Albatross is still at great risk of extinction. The birds breed only on the volcanic island of Torishima off the coast of Japan and range throughout the north Pacific.

Sheer Pleasure: Shearwaters

Shearwaters are a group of 17 tubenose species in the *Procellariidae* family. These birds are roughly the size of gulls but have longer, narrower wings and shorter tails. Their bills have distinct hooks on the ends; the nostril tubes are easily seen.

Shearwaters get their name from the way they fly. Generally, these birds flap rapidly for a bit and then glide very close to the surface of the water. They have a sort of stiffness to their wings that's very distinctive; although the Sooty Shearwater is about the size of a large gull, it flies in a completely different way. If you watch carefully, you might see one shear through the edge of a wave with a wingtip.

The Sooty Shearwater is one of the most abundant seabirds in the world. Flocks sometimes contain thousands of individuals, and researchers estimate that there are more than a billion of these birds worldwide.

Peeking at Petrels

Petrels are the smallest tubenoses. They fall into two groups: the gadfly petrels and the storm-petrels.

Gadding About

The gadfly petrels are actually shearwaters, despite their name. These little birds have short, rounded tails and wings that angle back sharply at the wrist. The only gadfly petrel regularly seen in North America is the Black-capped Petrel, which is a fairly regular sight off the West Coast. Other gadfly petrels occasionally turn up far offshore. These birds are called "gadfly" not because they're pesky, but because they fly erratically; they flutter and swoop, soar and dive.

Stormy Weather

The storm-petrels are true *petrels*—small seabirds no bigger than robins. They hover and flutter over the water, often pattering along the surface with their feet as they feed. They get their name from the way they tend to show up suddenly. Old-time sailors believed they came in advance of storms and used to call them "Mother Carey's chickens." Who was Mother Carey? I have no idea.

All told, there are about nine storm-petrel species likely to be seen off the coasts of North America. You'll have better luck on the West Coat; on the East Coast, the only species that's commonly seen is Wilson's Storm-Petrel.

Rappin' Robin

Petrel is a general name for the smaller pelagic tubenoses. The name comes from the way these birds feed by flying along the surface of the water with their legs dangling down. They seem to be "walking" on the water, just as St. Peter did. Petrel is a version of Peter.

A Little Bird Told Me...

To sailors in the age of sail, albatrosses meant good luck. The superstition probably goes back to the way an albatross might steadily follow a whaling ship in the southern hemisphere for days or weeks, feeding on whatever went over the side. Storm-petrels, on the other hand, were said to bring bad luck, and not just because they supposedly foretold storms. These fluttery little birds were believed to represent the souls of sailors lost at sea.

Puffins!

You may never have seen an Atlantic Puffin in person, but you've seen a lot of pictures of it. You know the shot: an upright, black-and-white bird with a large, triangular, colorful bill full of little fish. You've seen it on calendars and greeting cards and in magazines. You may even have read your kid a storybook about puffins or bought the kid a stuffed puffin toy.

Don't let all that cute stuff fool you. Puffins are really interesting, but they're not exactly cuddly. In fact, if you get too close to a puffin, it's likely to dive-bomb you. Because these stocky birds beat their wings between 300 and 400 times a minute, and reach flight speeds of more than 45 miles an hour, you'll want to keep your distance.

Transplanted Puffins

Atlantic Puffins used to nest in seven large colonies on islands in the Gulf of Maine, but by 1908, bird hunters had wiped out the colonies. After puffin hunting was banned, the birds slowly returned and were breeding again on Machias Seal Island and Matinicus Rock by the 1960s. In the 1970s, ornithologist Steven Kress began a reintroduction effort to Eastern Egg Rock. Because no puffins were imprinted on Eastern Egg Rock as a breeding site, in 1973 Dr. Kress transferred 53 very young birds (pufflings) to the island, made burrows for them, and fed them. The chicks fledged and left the island to spend two years at sea. The problem was that young birds don't come back to their birthplace to breed until after the older adults arrive. Because there hadn't been breeding adults on Eastern Egg Rock for more than a century, Dr. Kress put wooden decoys all over the island to make it look like it was a thriving colony. He also put out mirrors, so the birds would see their reflections and think they were other "birds." (Nobody ever said a puffin was smart.) He played tape recordings of the puffin's unusual "growl" call, which sounds a lot like a chain saw. The first transplanted birds returned on schedule in June 1977. Puffins don't reach breeding age until they're about eight—and sure enough, in July 1981, a few of the transplanted puffins began to raise chicks. By 1985, 20 pairs of puffins were nesting; today more than 3,000 birds breed on the island.

All About Alcids

Puffins are members of the larger *Alcidae* family, which includes razorbills, murres, dovekies, guillemots, murrelets, and auklets. Alcids, as birders call this group of birds, are denizens of the cold oceans. Of the 22 or so alcids found worldwide, most breed in North America. In general, they're smallish birds with narrow wings and black-and-white colors. Some, such as the puffins and auklets, have colorful bills and head plumage during the breeding season. Most alcids breed in very large, dense colonies on steep cliffs or islands in the Arctic region. They come ashore only for the breeding season, however, and during the rest of the year, they scatter up and down the coasts.

West Coast birders have a definite edge on the alcids. The murrelets and auklets are West Coast birds, and there are two puffin species—Horned and Tufted. The East Coast, however, gets Dovekies and Razorbills.

A Little Bird Told Me...

Alcids nest colonially on islands or cliffs—with one exception. For years, nobody knew where the Marbled Murrelet went to breed. Ornithologists searched for more than a century until a nest was finally located in 1974. Where was it? High up in a Douglas fir in northern California. The Marbled Murrelet, it turns out, nests in the old growth forests of the Pacific Northwest. The nest itself is just a depression in the thick moss that grows on the branch. Marbled Murrelets are fairly common birds, but to date, only about 160 nests have actually been located.

One bird you won't see on either coast is the Great Auk. This large, flightless bird has been extinct since 1844. At one time, the Great Auk was abundant in the North Atlantic, breeding in massive colonies on islands and cliffs. From the 1600s onward, more humans were in the same area, fishing for cod. Because the Great Auk was big, flightless, and tame, the fishermen hunted it for bait. By the early 1800s, the bird had become scarce, and it got even scarcer as collectors killed them off. In fact, the last two living Great Auks were killed by collectors. Today, the only Great Auks are stuffed ones in museums.

Spotting Sea Birds

A lot of sea birds look alike. The shearwaters, for instance, are pretty much all darkish birds. They don't have a lot of flashy field marks. Like the gulls, tubenoses and alcids go through plumage changes as they grow up. Even experienced birders sometimes have trouble telling species apart. In general, a good approach is to watch the flight pattern; each species has its own way of flying. With enough practice, you can get the birds into their families by the way they fly. Beyond that, you—and plenty of more experienced birders—will have to watch carefully to pick up some field marks and behavior clues. Pay attention to the time of year as well. Some pelagic birds are more seasonal than others.

The problem with pelagic birding is that it does take a lot of experience to learn the birds well—but unless you live near a coastline and have a lot of time to spend on boat trips, you won't get to do it very often. Don't let that stop you. On the beach or on the boat, there are always a lot of enthusiastic birders who will call out the birds they see and help you learn them.

Sea Birds from the Shore

Because the continental shelf drops off quickly on the West Coast, pelagic birds such as fulmars and Sooty Shearwaters often come in close enough to be seen from shore, especially if you're on the cliffs above the beach. On the East Coast, where the continental shelf extends much further offshore, you need to pick your time and place if you want to see these birds without a boat. The place has to be a coastal area that juts out into the ocean—Montauk Point on the tip of Long Island or Race Point at the tip of Cape Cod, for instance. The time has to be the late fall, when the seabirds are migrating. Shearwaters and petrels do a sort of reverse migration; they head to the Antarctic regions to breed in our winter, which is the Antarctic summer. Generally, the migration happens far out at sea. When a storm hits, however, the birds are blown in toward land, where eager (and slightly mad) birders await. If you want to try this kind of birding, be warned: It's very, very cold out there—and it's probably wet, too. Dress for the weather and then some.

Even if you don't want to brave a nor'easter or hurricane, places such as Montauk Point are well worth a visit for pelagic birds. You'll usually be able to see gulls, gannets, and perhaps a Sooty Shearwater or Northern Fulmar, along with some sea ducks, loons, and maybe grebes. Because these are beaches, you can also work on your shore`ärd IDs.

Boat Trips for Birders

The great thing about a pelagic boat trip is the number of species you'll see. On a typical winter trip from the East Coast, you could see five or six gull species, gannets, shearwaters, a fulmar or two, and possibly even a puffin. On the way out, you've got a good chance of seeing a variety of sea ducks and some loons.

Pelagic boat trips can be as simple as birdwatching from a ferry or fishing boat or as elaborate as an overnight trip on a chartered boat that takes you a hundred miles offshore.

The best way to see a lot of pelagic birds is to go on an organized boat trip. You have a lot of choices here, depending on the season and your location. In the northeast, a number of regularly scheduled commercial trips go out to bird islands and nesting cliffs in the late spring and summer. Numerous trips are available out of ports in Maine, Nova Scotia, and Newfoundland. Other good sites for pelagic birds, such as Monterey Bay in California, southern New Jersey, the Gulf Coast of Texas,

Be a Better Birder

The American Birding Association publishes a thorough directory of pelagic trips every January in its fascinating monthly newsletter *Winging It.* (See Chapter 32, "Volunteer Birding," for more on the ABA.) Also, check the classified ads in *Winging It* and the birding magazines for upcoming boat trips.

and the Cape Hatteras region, also offer a number of commercial operators. Sometimes, local bird societies arrange trips for their members, either through a commercial operator or by chartering a fishing boat.

The great advantage to going on an organized pelagic trip is that there will be a group leader and many other knowledgeable birders who will spot the birds and identify them. They'll be delighted to explain the birds to you, perhaps in more detail than you really want to know. At any rate, you'll learn a lot in a hurry.

As boat trips for pelagic birds become more popular, more rare pelagic birds are being reported. It's possible that these birds aren't quite so rare as we once thought; we haven't seen them more often because we weren't looking.

Sailing, Sailing, Over the Ocean Blue

Going on a pelagic trip is a fairly big deal. The trips fill up quickly, so you'll need to plan in advance and make your reservation early. Because it can take several hours to get far enough offshore for pelagic birds, the trips usually leave very early in the morning. Unless you happen to live close to the departure point, that means getting up very, very early or spending the night somewhere nearby. The trip itself will be at least half a day. Most are much longer; you'll be on the boat for 12 hours or more. If you want to go to the Dry Tortugas in the Gulf of Mexico, be prepared for a three- or four-day trip.

On most pelagic trips, you'll have to bring everything you need with you. What do you need?

➤ **Binoculars:** Bring your biggest and best. If you have a shoulder stock for your spotting scope, bring it along. Otherwise, leave your scope at home; you can't really use a tripod on a moving boat.

➤ **Warm clothing:** I can't stress this enough, especially for a winter trip. Dress in layers and bring at least one extra sweater, even in the summer. You might also want to bring a waterproof jacket or rain slicker and waterproof pants to keep rain and sea spray from soaking you. (Refer to Chapter 3, "Your First Field Trip," for more about this.)

➤ **Towel:** Handy for wiping spray off your face and your binocs.

➤ **Sunglasses, sunblock, and lip balm:** Glare on the water can put a real strain on your eyes. Wear sunglasses, even on an overcast day. Ditto for sunblock; you can get a burn even in the winter. Lip balm keeps your lips from being irritated by the sun, wind, and salt.

➤ **Hat with brim:** The brim shades your eyes and keeps rain off your face. Make sure it fits snugly; it can be very windy on the ocean.

➤ **Food and drink:** There's something about a boat trip that makes people really hungry. Bring *a lot* of food and drink; don't count on food being sold on the boat. In cold weather, be sure you have a big thermos (or two) of something hot. Avoid greasy, smelly, or highly spiced foods. If you get seasick, you'll regret that Limburger sandwich with raw onion.

There's no need to travel light on a boat trip. After all, you don't have to carry all that stuff around with you all day; it gets stowed in the cabin instead.

Chumming

To attract the birds, the group leader may toss chum—a disgusting mixture of fish guts and other stuff—overboard. In birder talk, chumming means either putting out chum or getting seasick and tossing your cookies overboard. Chances are good that you'll do some chumming of both kinds on a pelagic trip.

Don't let the fear of seasickness keep you from adding birds to your life list. Just follow these pointers and you'll enjoy your trip:

➤ **Sleep well:** Get a good night's sleep before the trip.

➤ **Eat breakfast:** Fasting doesn't keep you from getting seasick; in fact, it makes it more likely. Eat a good breakfast, but stick to easily digested foods such as oatmeal, toast, and cereal.

➤ **Eat crackers:** If you feel yourself getting queasy, nibble on some plain crackers or maybe a pretzel. Salty foods seem to help, but stay away from sweet stuff such as cookies.

➤ **Drink plenty of uncarbonated liquids:** Sip all day long. Stay away from soda pop, coffee, and anything alcoholic.

➤ **Stay on deck looking forward:** The boat's motion always seems worse inside the cabin. (The bathroom is the absolute worst.) You can fend off seasickness by getting fresh air and keeping your eyes on the horizon. Steer clear of the back of the boat; the diesel fumes will definitely not help. If food is sold, chances are it's stuff like hot dogs. Stay far, far away from that part of the boat.

➤ **Take seasickness medication:** If you know from bitter experience that you're a chumming champ, try an over-the-counter antinausea medication or ask your doctor for a prescription. The trick is to take the drug *before* you get sick.

➤ **Try ginger:** This really works—and it doesn't have the side effects of drugs. Buy ginger capsules at the health-food store. Swallow a couple before the trip begins and take more if you start to get nauseous.

➤ **Try acupressure:** This also really works. If you start to feel nauseous, place your right thumb on the inside of your left wrist, about an inch from the base of your hand. Squeeze hard for 20 seconds and then release. Repeat a couple more times and then switch hands and squeeze your right wrist three times. Repeat again a few minutes later. You'll be amazed at the way the nausea disappears.

➤ **Try wrist bands:** If you know you get seasick, wear acupressure wrist bands. These are elasticized bands with a bead that presses constantly on the wrist point; you can get them in health-food stores. Put them on before the trip begins.

➤ **Keep eating and drinking:** If you throw up despite all my good advice, remember that you need to replace the fluids you're losing. Otherwise, you'll feel even worse. Keep sipping water, diluted fruit juice, weak tea, herbal tea, or those old standbys—flat cola or ginger ale. Nibble on crackers, pretzels, plain rolls, an apple, or a banana.

Splat!

Over-the-counter antinausea drugs such as Dramamine (dimenhydrinate) and Bonine (meclizine hydrochloride) work well, but they can make you drowsy. Don't drink alcohol at the same time, and don't drive if possible. If you need stronger medication, ask your doctor about scopalamine skin patches; they don't make you drowsy.

If all else fails, remember to throw up over the rail on the lee side; that's the side *sheltered* from the wind. Don't be embarrassed. You won't be the only one getting sick, especially if the ocean is rough. Even experienced sailors do. Lord Nelson, England's greatest admiral, was famous for getting seasick even in calm seas. I once got very queasy on a boat at anchor!

Bonus Points: Marine Mammals

You might see a lot of neat marine mammals, such as seals, whales, dolphins, and sea otters, on a pelagic birding trip. Likewise, you'll see a lot of good birds on a whale-watching trip. In my experience, the birders on a bird trip will know a lot about the marine mammals as well. The same isn't true on a whale-watching trip. But what do you have against whales? Enjoy the trip.

The Least You Need to Know

➤ Pelagic birds are birds of the open ocean.

➤ Albatrosses, shearwaters, petrels, puffins, auklets, and others are all pelagic birds.

➤ Many pelagic birds, such as albatrosses, are magnificent fliers.

➤ You can sometimes see pelagic birds from shore, but the best way to see them is on an organized birding boat trip.

➤ Pelagic boat trips are a lot of fun—even if you get seasick. If you get the chance to take one, do it.

Part 6
Your Backyard Bird Habitat

Feeding birds is one of the most popular hobbies in America. Some 65 million people—nearly half the households in the country—put out food for the birds, to the tune of at least $2.5 billion bucks every year. That's not counting all the landscaping that people do to attract birds. With the right plants or just a simple birdbath, the smallest backyard—even an apartment house terrace—can become a haven for the birds.

Why do it? To help the birds, of course, but also because a backyard full of the activity, color, and sounds of birds is a backyard full of life.

Chapter 23

The Backyard Bird Buffet

> **In This Chapter**
>
> ➤ Enjoying backyard bird feeding
>
> ➤ Birds that like backyards
>
> ➤ Choosing the right feeder
>
> ➤ What to put in your bird feeder

According to the U.S. Fish and Wildlife Service, 52 million Americans feed their backyard birds. Every year, they spend about $2.8 billion just on wild bird food and another $832 million on feeders and other stuff for the birds. Can 52 million people be wrong? Not in this case. Feeding backyard birds is the most popular of all wildlife-watching activities because it's fun and easy.

Best Backyard Birds

Why do we feed the birds? Not because they need the food, although it can be a help in the winter. No, we feed them because a backyard full of birds is a backyard full of color and life.

Not every bird will come to the food you put out. Warblers, for instance, are mostly insect eaters. The birds that are most likely to come to your feeders are the ones that eat seeds or suet. In general, that means finches, sparrows, chickadees, titmice, woodpeckers, doves, jays, and some other species. A few warblers will also come to bird feeders. Pine Warblers, for instance, will come to suet and peanut butter. Take a look at the chart to see which ones to expect.

Common Feeder Visitors

Fowl-Like Birds
Wild Turkey
Ruffed Grouse
Ring-necked Pheasant
Gambel's Quail
California Quail
Northern Bobwhite

Woodpeckers
Downy Woodpecker
Hairy Woodpecker
Red-bellied Woodpecker
Northern Flicker

Doves
Rock Dove
Mourning Dove
Inca Dove

Titmice, Chickadees, and Nuthatches
Tufted Titmouse
Black-capped Chickadee
Carolina Chickadee
White-breasted Nuthatch

Grosbeaks
Rose-breasted Grosbeak
Northern Cardinal

Sparrows
Eastern Towhee
Dark-eyed Junco
American Tree Sparrow
Song Sparrow
Harris' Sparrow
Golden-crowned Sparrow
White-throated Sparrow
White-crowned Sparrow

Finches
Pine Siskin
American Goldfinch
Red Crossbill
Common Redpoll
Purple Finch
House Finch
Evening Grosbeak

Other Species
Blue Jay
Brown-headed Cowbird
American Crow
Common Grackle
House Sparrow
European Starling

Be a Better Birder

Whenever I give talks on bird feeding, someone always tells me how inspiring it is to watch the birds at the feeder on a winter morning. They insist that the busy birds inspire them to get to work themselves. As a writer, the birds inspire me to have another cup of coffee and watch some more—all in the name of research, of course.

Of all the birds on the chart, the one you're most likely to see is the Dark-eyed Junco; it's the most widespread bird visiting feeders in America.

As I discuss in the next chapter, "In the Good Old Summertime," you can attract some migratory birds, such as hummingbirds and bluebirds, with the right foods. And as I discuss in the other chapters in this section, providing water, nesting sites, and the right sorts of plants will attract a lot of species that won't go near your feeders no matter what you do.

What if you don't have a backyard? Maybe you can put up a feeder at your workplace or school. If you live in an apartment, you might be able to put a feeder on your terrace or window, but be careful. Your neighbors below might not appreciate birds as much as you do, especially if seed hulls and bird droppings are landing on them.

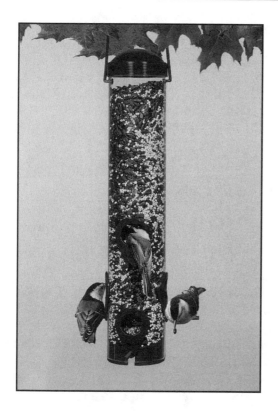

A typical tube feeder, made of sturdy clear plastic. The chickadees love it. (Photo courtesy Perky Pet.)

Eating Like a Bird

Birds eat all sorts of things, but you don't necessarily want to attract the ones that prefer to dine on road kill. Because most of the birds that come to feeders eat seeds, seeds are what you should give them. You have a lot of choices here, so let's take a closer look.

Let the Sun Shine In

Big birds, little birds, and all the birds in between love black-oil sunflower seeds. If you can offer only one food, this is the one. These small sunflower seeds have thin shells, so they're easy for smaller birds to break open. The seeds have a high nut-to-shell ratio, and they're rich in energy-giving protein and oil. Gray-striped sunflower seeds, the kind sold for people to eat, are bigger, with thicker shells. The birds like them fine, but they like the easier-to-handle black-oil sunflower seeds even better.

Be a Better Birder

Here's how to tell the difference between a Purple Finch and a House Finch: The male Purple Finch is purplish red all over, like a raspberry. House Finches are strawberry-colored. They have brown caps, aren't as red overall, and have their color mostly on the head and breast; the underparts are white streaked with brown. (To see the difference, check out the pictures in the color inserts.)

231

The only drawback to sunflower seeds is the hulls. They make a mess under the feeder and clog up the seed trays. The way around this is to buy hulled black-oil sunflower seeds, sometimes called sunflower hearts or chips. Right now, black-oil sunflower seeds cost about a dollar a pound or a little less; the hearts cost about a dollar fifty. The hulled seeds are definitely more expensive, but think of it this way: About half the weight of a 50-pound sack of sunflower seeds is in the hulls, so the edible part is really costing you two dollars a pound. If you buy a 50-pound sack of hulled seeds, you're getting nothing but the seeds, so there's no waste; the hearts are actually the better buy.

A Little Bird Told Me...

How do we know which seeds birds prefer? Back in 1980, the U.S. Fish and Wildlife Service did a study of seed preferences that showed black-oil sunflower was the top choice overall and that white proso millet was second, especially for smaller seed-eating birds. In 1994, the Cornell Laboratory of Ornithology did a seed preference test that showed pretty much the same results, but with a different breakdown. Ground-feeding birds such as sparrows preferred millet about half the time, whereas perch-feeding birds such as chickadees and finches preferred black-oil sunflowers almost all the time. The third choice was red milo. Ground feeders liked it, but perch feeders would barely touch the stuff.

White Proso Millet

When you think of bird seed, you're thinking of white proso millet—the stuff you give your parakeet. Millet seeds are small and round. Sparrows, doves, and other ground-feeding birds love these seeds. In fact, they seem to prefer them over black-oil sunflower seeds.

Red Milo

The seeds of red milo, also known as grain sorghum, are medium-sized and round. They're inexpensive, so red milo is often used as a filler in commercial seed mixes. They're not very popular with the birds. Ground feeders will eat them, but perch-feeding birds such as finches and chickadees don't.

Niger Seeds

Tiny niger seeds look a little like caraway seeds, the kind you find in rye bread. They're also sometimes called thistle seeds, and they're expensive; right now, they cost between one and two bucks a pound. On the other hand, their sweet taste attracts colorful finches and other birds like crazy. Niger seeds work best if you put them into their own separate feeder; I explain more later in this chapter.

Safflower Seeds

Safflower seeds are the same seeds used to make safflower oil, so you know they're rich in nutrition. They're usually recommended to attract cardinals, but in fact, just about all the birds love them almost as much as sunflower seeds. Even better, crows, grackles, and squirrels don't like them. Safflower seeds aren't really any more expensive than black-oil sunflower hearts, but you do get hulls.

Cracked Corn

The most economical food for the birds is cracked corn; a 50-pound sack costs only about six dollars, or about 12 cents a pound. Just about all birds will eat cracked corn. In fact, it's the best way to attract Wild Turkeys, quail, pheasants, Ruffed Grouse, and even mallards and Canada Geese. Be sure you're buying cracked corn, not whole kernels or the finely cracked corn that's sometimes sold as chick corn. If you're spreading the corn on the ground or a platform feeder, put out only as much as the birds will eat in a day. Cracked corn left out overnight will attract unwanted rodents such as mice and raccoons. Wet cracked corn can turn into a moldy, smelly mess.

Peanuts

Perch- and clinging-feeding birds such as jays, chickadees, titmice, woodpeckers, nuthatches, and Evening Grosbeaks enjoy peanuts—in the shell, whole, or broken up. Peanuts—and other nuts, for that matter—are nutritious and the birds like them, but they attract squirrels in no time.

Mix Your Own

To attract the maximum number of birds, you want to mix and match your seeds. You could buy sacks of commercial feed mixtures that contain a variety of seeds, but be careful. The mixtures sold in five-pound plastic bags in supermarkets contain mostly millet and inexpensive filler seeds such as wheat, red milo, and cracked corn. The sunflower seeds tend to be few and far between. These blends are no bargain. Remember how you used to eat the filling in your Oreos and toss away the cookie parts? That's what the birds do with these mixes. They pick out the millet and sunflower seeds and flick aside the filler seeds. They'll eventually eat them if you don't put out anything else, but in the meantime, some may rot or attract undesirable rodents. Even worse, the birds will find someone who's putting out better food and go there instead.

Some seed companies make good seed mixtures that are designed to attract specific types of birds. A mixture for cardinals, for instance, combines safflower and sunflower seeds. A finch mixture might combine sunflower hearts, millet, and niger.

I like to mix my own blends. It's not really any more economical, but it is a lot of fun. My goal is to find the perfect mixture for my particular backyard. So far, two parts sunflower hearts, one part millet, and one part cracked corn seems to be ideal.

Buying and Storing Your Seed

Birdfeeding is such a popular hobby that you can buy seed in just about any supermarket or hardware store. These stores usually sell only low-grade mixes. You'll do a lot better if you go to a well-stocked garden center, nature shop, or feed store. The selection will be broader and the seeds will be fresher.

In the movie *Mary Poppins*, there's a song about feeding the birds for just tuppence a bag. That was then; this is now. Bird feeding isn't as expensive a hobby as say, scuba diving or collecting Impressionist paintings, but the costs do add up. You could easily spend a few hundred dollars a year or more on seeds and other stuff. Some stores and mail-order companies offer frequent-buyer discounts and bird-feeding clubs.

Once you've got your bird seed home, store it in a sturdy, tightly covered container. Anything that keeps the seeds dry and mice and insects out is fine. I use a 30-gallon trash container. A friend who works in a deli brings home empty gallon-size pickle jars. She fills the jars with the seeds and stacks them in her garage, ready to take out to fill her gallon-size feeder.

Splat!

To avoid getting a lot of cheap filler seeds such as red milo or wheat, buy your seed mixes only from a reliable source.

Be a Better Birder

One of my neighbors once called me in October to ask what had happened to the American Goldfinches that used to come to her feeder. She also wanted to know the name of those little khaki-colored birds she was seeing. In fact, they were the same American Goldfinches she'd been seeing all along. In the fall, American Goldfinches molt into their duller winter plumage.

Buy from the Best

If you can, buy your bird-feeding seeds and gear from experts; you'll get good advice and the best value for your money. Check your area for local nature stores. If there's no independent retailer near you, contact these companies to find the closest franchise store:

Wild Birds Unlimited, Inc.
1711 North College Avenue, Suite 145
Carmel, IN 46032
(800) 326-4WBU
Fax: (317) 571-7110
webmaster@wbu.com
www.wbu.com

(A very useful feature of this web site is the Ask the Experts page. Submit your birdfeeding questions by email and get a quick response.)

Wild Bird Centers of America, Inc.
7370 MacArthur Boulevard
Glen Echo, MD 20812
(301) 229-9585
Fax: (301) 320-6154
info@wildbirdcenter.com
www.wildbirdcenter.com

If you don't want to wrestle home big sacks of bird seed, have it delivered instead. The best mail-order source for bird food and other stuff is

Duncraft
P.O. Box 9020
Penacook, NH 03303-9020
(800) 593-5656
Fax: (603) 226-3735
info@duncraft.com
www.duncraft.com

Bird seed is much cheaper when you buy it in bulk. If you don't have room to store a couple of hundred pounds of sunflower seeds, ask around among your birdfeeding friends and neighbors. Someone might want to split a bag or two with you.

Favorite Feeders

Go to any nature store or get any catalog, and you'll see all kinds of bird feeders. How can you pick the right one for your yard? It's not that hard. Before we get to the feeders, however, let's talk about the birds that will come to them. They fall into three basic groups:

➤ **Ground feeders:** Most sparrows, including juncos and towhees, feed on the ground; they don't usually fly up to a feeder. Ditto for doves, quails, and other larger birds like Wild Turkeys.

➤ **Perchers:** Finches, cardinals, jays, and other birds such as Evening Grosbeaks like to perch on a hanging feeder to eat.

➤ **Clingers:** Small, clinging birds such as chickadees, titmice, nuthatches, and woodpeckers don't need a perch; they can cling directly to the feeder.

To attract a variety of birds, then, you need a variety of feeding arrangements. Let's sort the feeders into some basic categories:

➤ **Platform feeders:** Think of these as little picnic tables for the birds. Platform feeders are generally flat surfaces raised slightly above the ground. You spread the seeds on the surface; the birds land on the platform to eat. Ideal for the ground-feeding birds.

➤ **Tube feeders:** Round tubes with feeding ports cut into them. Ideal for clingers, only fair for perchers; the perches are often too small for larger birds such as cardinals.

➤ **Hopper feeders:** Square (usually) feeder with perches running the length of the base. These feeders come in an amazing range of shapes, sizes, and designs—some very attractive. Good overall choice for clingers and perchers.

➤ **No-perch feeders:** Designed to attract only clinging birds such as chickadees.

Clear plastic window feeders that attach with suction cups are simple and fun. (Photo courtesy Aspects.)

More elaborate window feeders are attractive and give you great close-up views of the birds. (Photo courtesy Nature Products.)

Traditional wooden hopper feeders are natural-looking and attract a lot of different birds. (Photo courtesy Wild Birds Unlimited.)

➤ **Niger feeders:** These are tube feeders with very small openings for the tiny niger seeds. You can also buy niger "stockings," mesh bags with small holes. Fill the bag with niger seeds, hang it up, and watch the goldfinches come flocking.

➤ **Window feeders:** These range from simple hoppers that attach to the window with suction cups to elaborate designs that fill a window. Kids love them; you get great close-up views of a wide range of birds.

There are the specialized feeders for suet and nectar. I talk about suet a little later in this chapter. I discuss nectar feeders for hummingbirds and other birds in Chapter 24.

A Little Bird Told Me...

Here's how to make a temporary bird feeder: Rinse out an empty quart milk or juice carton. Using a sharp knife or razor blade, carefully slice off a small piece—about half an inch—of the bottom corners to make feeding ports. Make a small hole in each side of the carton near the feeding ports and poke in pencils or twigs to make perches. Fill the carton with seeds and staple it shut. Poke a hole in the top of the carton and run a loop of strong string through it. Hang up the feeder and hope the birds find it before the squirrels get it.

No matter what style you choose, buy a feeder only if it's well made from good materials. Tube and no-perch feeders should be made of heavy-duty polycarbonate plastic, the kind squirrels need a lot of time to chew through. Metal parts should be made of cast aluminum, galvanized steel, or solid zinc.

In an emergency, you can improvise a bird feeder out of almost anything. This one's made from a milk carton. (Photo by Sheila Buff.)

What's Your Hang-Up?

Once you've decided which kind of feeder to get, you need to put it outside. You have two basic choices: You can hang it from a branch (or anything else), or you can mount it on a post. Hanging the feeder from a branch, using a sturdy hook or chain, is the simplest method, if you happen to have a convenient tree. If not, a mounting post is handy, but you may have to dig a hole for the ground socket. You'll also have to move the feeder every time you mow the lawn.

Where you put the feeder makes a big difference in how many birds will come. The ideal spot is a sunny, sheltered area with a lot of nearby vegetation. Of course, you want the spot to be where you can see the birds easily. You also want it to be fairly close to the house and not too high up. If you have to slog through the snow with a stepladder to refill the feeder, it's time to move it some place more convenient. If you can't see the birds from the comfort of your kitchen window, what's the point?

When you look around your yard, you'll probably see at least one spot that would be a good place for your feeder. If you don't, check out Chapter 28, "Gardening for the Birds," for ways to make your yard more bird-friendly.

Here, Birds!

You've put up your feeder and filled it with mouthwatering sunflower hearts—and nobody's coming to it! Now what?

Give it a few more days. The birds probably just haven't noticed the feeder's there yet. You might be able to speed things along by scattering some seeds on the ground around the feeder. Keep an eye on the seed level; if it's going down, the birds are probably coming in. They're just not coming when you happen to be watching.

If you're definitely not getting any action, it could be the feeder's not in a good spot. To get the bird's-eye perspective, stand by the feeder and look around. Is the feeder more than 10 feet from any bushes or trees? If it is, the birds will be reluctant to come; they're too exposed to predators such as hawks and cats. However, don't put the feeder too close to the bushes, or cats can hide in the bushes and jump out. Is the feeder so close to the house that it's under the eaves? The birds might not be seeing it. Move the feeder to a more open spot. If everything seems fine but you still don't have birds, move the feeder somewhere else anyway; you might never know why, but it'll probably fix the problem.

Brushing Up Your Feeder

There's an easy way to make your feeder a lot more attractive in a hurry: Put a *brush pile* 5–10 feet from it. Even though my yard was already full of natural vegetation and I was getting a lot of birds at my feeder, I was amazed at how many more came when I made a brush pile about eight years ago. The number of birds seemed to double overnight, and I had Eastern Towhees come in for the first time that spring. The same brush pile is still there; I just toss on new branches whenever I tidy up the yard.

Making a brush pile is simplicity itself. Gather up some branches that have been pruned from trees and shrubs or blown down and pile them up like a teepee near your feeder. (This works well near birdbaths, too.) The pile will settle a bit over the winter, but you'll probably find plenty of branches and twigs to toss onto it over the course of the year.

You can clear the pile away in the spring if you want, but I leave mine in place and just mow around it. The shelter it provides is attractive to birds even when the feeder's empty. (Brush piles attract other wildlife as well. I'm pretty sure a chipmunk had an entrance hole to its burrow under there last summer.)

Rappin' Robin

A **brush pile** is just that: a heap of old branches piled up by your bird feeder. The branches provide shelter and perches for the birds waiting their turn at the feeder. A brush pile is especially good for bringing in ground-feeding birds such as juncos. They lurk in the brush and dart out for seeds.

Keep On Feedin'

People often think of bird feeding as something you do only in the winter. It's certainly true that the birds appreciate our help when the ground is covered with snow, but there's no reason to stop feeding once the weather warms up. In fact, the time when the birds really need help the most is in the early spring, when natural food is scarcest and the weather is still cold and wet. Keep those feeders up until summer—and the insect food that comes with it—has really arrived.

A Little Bird Told Me...

If you start feeding the birds in the winter, do you have to keep doing it? In other words, do the birds get dependent on the food? Absolutely not. Several careful studies have shown that even birds that visit feeders a lot still get most of their food from foraging in the wild. The real reason to refill your feeder regularly is to keep the birds coming. If the feeder runs dry, the birds won't come by your yard as often.

You do have to change your feeding strategy in the summer. I discuss that in the next chapter.

Chewing the Fat: Suet Feeders

Birds that ordinarily eat insects are powerfully attracted to suet, the hard white fat found around the kidneys of a cow. It's ideal for cool-weather birdfeeding because it's a rich source of nutrition for the birds, and it doesn't go bad even after days outside. Rendered suet lasts longer and has all of the impurities cooked out of it.

Chickadees, titmice, nuthatches, and woodpeckers are the birds most attracted by suet. They'll flock to your suet if you put it out in something they can cling to. The best approach is a suet basket—a container made of plastic-coated wire spaced about an inch apart. You can also buy suet prepackaged in plastic mesh containers, or you can put some into an old plastic-mesh onion bag yourself.

The best way to feed suet is in a wire-coated basket hung from a tree branch. (Photo courtesy Perky Pet.)

Chef's Specials

Birds love suet just by itself, but you can have a lot of fun making special suet mixtures for them. It's easy because suet melts quickly and mixes well.

Begin by cutting the suet into small pieces. Put the pieces into a large, heavy pot or skillet (cast-iron works great) over low heat. Cook until the suet melts, which takes only about 10 minutes or so.

Once you've got melted suet, you can mix in just about anything and it will stay there. Try these:

➤ Seeds such as sunflower and millet
➤ Bits of fruit, berries, and raisins
➤ Nuts and peanut butter
➤ Cracked corn

Mix and match any combination you want, but keep the ratio of suet to whatever at about one to one. In other words, for each cup or so of suet, stir in about a cup of the other stuff. If the mixture doesn't seem to be holding together well once it solidifies, melt it again and add some more suet.

Suet cakes are a great way to clean out the pantry and the fridge. Take all those dried-up raisins, stale nuts, wrinkled apples, old crackers, soggy breakfast cereals, and whatever else (pieces of stale doughnuts, for instance) and mix them into the suet.

Once you've got it all mixed in, pack the mixture into any sort of shallow container. Old aluminum pie tins work well; so do muffin tins lined with paper. Freeze the suet cakes until you need them.

Frankly, the aroma of melting suet can be a little much. If you can't stand it (or if they're out of suet at the store), make dough cakes instead. Here's my recipe, which uses cornmeal and peanut butter:

Bird Dough

1 1/2 cups peanut butter
1 cup solid shortening
4 cups cornmeal

Combine the peanut butter and shortening in a heavy pot or skillet, and cook over low heat until melted. Stir in the cornmeal a cup at a time. Pack into shallow containers and freeze.

As with suet cakes, you can add anything you want to the basic recipe. Buy the cheapest ingredients for this; the birds will never know the difference.

Egg Heads

Laying an egg is a lot of work for a female bird. Among other things, she has to get a lot of calcium from her diet to make the eggshell. You can help by putting out eggshells from your kitchen. Starting in the late winter, I rinse out eggshells, let them dry overnight, and crush them coarsely by putting them between two paper towels and squashing them with my fist. I save them up until it's time to refill the feeder, then mix the accumulated shell bits in with the seeds.

If you don't want to bother with saving eggshells, you can buy bird grit made from ground oyster shells and put that into the seed instead.

Because eggshells or grit attract all kinds of birds, not just the usual feeder visitors, I also put some on an old stump at the edge of our woods (you can use a shallow dish if you don't have a stump). I'm not always sure which birds take them, but over a few days, the shells disappear.

Keeping a Backyard Journal

Keeping some notes about your backyard birds is always a good idea. It's interesting for its own sake, and it also helps you plan ahead. I keep track of how much bird seed and other stuff I buy, for instance, and how often I have to fill my feeders. I also keep a backyard bird list (now up to 96 species). Most interesting to me is the appearance list; that's the one that tracks which species show up when. I like to note when I see the first Dark-eyed Juncos of the winter and when the Rose-breasted Grosbeaks turn up in the spring.

Backyard Biology

The next step in backyard record-keeping is to sign up with Project FeederWatch. Sponsored by the Cornell Laboratory of Ornithology, Project FeederWatch was started in 1986 and has been going strong ever since. (See Chapter 32, "Volunteer Birding," for more information about the Cornell Lab.) Feeder watchers across North America count the birds at their feeders during specific periods over the winter and send their tallies to the lab to be analyzed. The vast amount of information provided by the volunteers has led to some important discoveries about backyard birds. Range expansions and contractions, declines in some species and increases in others, irruptions—they've all been documented by the information from the volunteers.

Being in Project FeederWatch is fun and easy; it doesn't take much time at all. Most feeder birds are easy to recognize, so you can help even if you're a beginner.

Recently, the Cornell Lab has begun another great volunteer research project in cooperation with the National Audubon Society, the Great Backyard Bird Count. For four days in February, volunteers count all the birds they see at their feeders, in their yards, and in other local places. The counts are sent in to the BirdSource Web site and interpreted immediately, so you can get an instant "snapshot" of the whereabouts of the most common bird species in North America. Again, you don't need to be an expert birder to help out; you just need to know the most common backyard birds.

For more information on how you can participate in these really fun and important programs, contact:

Cornell Laboratory of Ornithology
159 Sapsucker Woods Road
Ithaca, NY 14850
(607) 254-2440
Fax: (607) 254-2415
feederwatch@cornell.edu
http://birdsource.cornell.edu

The Least You Need to Know

➤ A wide variety of colorful birds will come to your backyard feeder, including sparrows, finches, cardinals, jays, chickadees, titmice, woodpeckers, and nuthatches.

➤ The favorite food of backyard birds is black-oil sunflower seeds. The next favorite food is millet.

➤ Insect-eating birds such as woodpeckers and chickadees love suet.

➤ Platform feeders are a good choice for ground-feeding birds such as sparrows and doves.

➤ Tube feeders and hopper feeders attract perch-feeding birds such as finches, cardinals, and Evening Grosbeaks.

➤ Perchless feeders are good for small, agile, clinging birds such as chickadees, woodpeckers, titmice, and nuthatches; larger birds can't use these feeders.

➤ You can help scientists learn more about birds by participating in Project FeederWatch and other volunteer research programs.

In the Good Old Summertime

Feeding the birds in your backyard is a lot of fun in the wintertime. Why stop there? Feeding in the summer is a little different, but it's just as much fun—if not more. That's because in the summer you can attract those fascinating little flying jewels, the hummingbirds. You can also feed birds, such as bluebirds and orioles, that are only summertime visitors.

The Sweet Taste of Success

Feeding the hummingbirds is one of the things I like best about the summertime. These little birds are surprisingly easy to attract if you take a two-pronged approach: Plant hummer-friendly flowers and put out nectar feeders. I discuss the plants in Chapter 28, "Gardening for the Birds." In this chapter, I focus on nectar feeders.

As I'm sure you remember from my brilliant discussion in Chapter 20, "Hummingbirds: Tiny Terrors," these birds feed almost entirely on *nectar*. They usually get the nectar from tubular, red- or orange-colored flowers, but hummingbirds are open-minded. They'll happily come to red-colored feeders filled with sugar water.

Several manufacturers make good, solid hanging hummingbird feeders. They all have the same basic design: A bottle-shaped container for the nectar tops a red plastic base with feeding holes. (A few models have the nectar containers underneath.) The hummingbirds hover above the feeder and plunge their bills into the holes.

The important thing isn't really the feeder itself; it's what you put inside. Natural plant nectar is about 25 percent sugar, so you want your artificial nectar to be just as sweet—no more and no less. Here's the recipe to follow:

Rappin' Robin

Nectar is a sweet juice secreted by many plants as a way to attract insects that will pollinate them. Nectar-bearing flowers usually have tubular shapes and are brightly colored.

Splat!

Use *only* sugar and water in a one-to-four ratio to make your hummingbird nectar. Don't use honey; a fungus that can kill hummingbirds can grow in it. Don't use artificial sweeteners; they have no nutritional value.

Hummingbird Nectar

1 cup sugar
4 cups water

Boil the water in a medium pot, then add the sugar to dissolve. Stir well to dissolve the sugar, and then bring the mixture to a boil again. Immediately turn off the heat and let the nectar cool. Store in the refrigerator until ready to use.

The next most important thing is to keep the nectar feeder filled with fresh sugar water. In hot weather, that means emptying out the old mixture, washing the feeder, and refilling it with fresh nectar every couple of days. If you don't do this, the leftover nectar will ferment and the hummingbirds won't touch it.

You'll notice that my recipe doesn't include red food coloring. Opinion is divided about whether red-colored nectar attracts more hummers. Personally, I think if you're mixing your own nectar, you don't need to bother. If you want to use a prepared nectar mix with coloring, however, go ahead. There's really no evidence one way or the other that the dye is harmful.

To avoid waste, fill the feeders only about a third full, at least until your hummingbirds discover them. After that, fill them to the max; it's amazing how much nectar birds that small can drink.

To help your local hummers find your feeder, hang it up in the shade near some attractive plants—fuchsia or bee balm, for instance—or near a birdbath or mister. (I discuss the details about plants for hummingbirds in Chapter 28, "Gardening for the Birds." Check Chapter 26, "Wet and Wild," for more on water for the birds.)

The hummingbirds might take a few days to find your feeder, but when they do, they'll become regular visitors. In fact, they might start to fight over the feeder; male hummingbirds can be very territorial and pugnacious. The best way to deal with the problem is to put out another feeder at the other end of the yard.

Your hummingbird feeder might attract ants, bees, yellow jackets, and other insects. Pick a feeder with an anti-ant cap that fits between the hanger and the feeder. Ignore the bees and yellow jackets unless they're really getting out of hand. If they do, take the feeder down for a couple of days. Smaller bugs might actually attract hummers. These birds get the protein they need from the little spiders, fruit flies, and other tiny insects they pick up along with the nectar.

It's crucial to keep your nectar feeders clean. Otherwise, all sorts of really gross crud starts to grow in them—and that could be harmful to the birds. Take down your nectar feeders every few days and wash them thoroughly. Use only very hot water (no detergent) and a bottle brush. Sometimes the crud is in a hard-to-reach part of the feeder. In that case, try putting a handful of uncooked rice grains into the feeder and adding a little water. Shake well—the rice grains will scour off the crud. If stubborn mold builds up inside the feeder, add some white vinegar to the washing water.

You can keep your hummer feeders up from early spring through the end of November. (Replace the nectar at once if it freezes.) It's a myth that the hummingbirds won't migrate south on schedule if you keep feeding them!

Note to dwellers on the Great Plains: If you're not attracting any hummingbirds, don't blame yourself. Sadly, your part of the country just doesn't get that many.

Hummingbirds are easily attracted by feeders filled with nectar (sugar water). The little cup on the top of this feeder keeps ants out of the nectar. (Photo courtesy Aspects.)

Sweet Surprises

You might be surprised to see orioles, Downy Woodpeckers, and other birds sneaking a drink from your hummingbird feeder. They're attracted by the sweet taste of the water. To make it easier for the orioles, you can get a separate nectar feeder with a perch and bigger feeding holes. Orioles will also eat grape jelly; put out a little dish of that.

The Baltimore Oriole is one of my favorite birds. I love its brilliant orange color and its jaunty, individual song. This poor bird has been through some tough times recently. Back in 1994, it was lumped with the Bullock's Oriole into one species, the Northern Oriole. In 1997, the species was split again and the original names—Baltimore for the eastern species and Bullock's for the western—were restored.

All orioles are members of the *Icterid* family, the same family that includes the black-birds, meadowlarks, and grackles. Nine oriole species are found in North America, but only four species—Scott's, Orchard, Baltimore, and Bullocks—are common. Scott's Oriole is found mostly in the dry regions of the Southwest; I saw my first at Madera Canyon in southern Arizona. The Orchard Oriole is really an eastern bird; it's found mostly in orchards and wooded areas. Baltimore Orioles and Bullock's Orioles both like open woodlands, orchards, and shady suburbs. If you live east of the Rockies, you're seeing the Baltimore Oriole at your nectar feeder, although Orchard Orioles have been known to come in for a snack as well. (Orchard Orioles have chestnut-colored, not orange, bodies. They're also noticeably smaller than Baltimore Orioles.) If you live west of the Rockies, you're seeing Bullock's.

Orioles enjoy fruit and nectar. They'll come to sip from hummingbird feeders, but they prefer their own larger feeder. (Photo courtesy Perky Pet.)

In the summer of 1998, Baltimore Orioles nested in my backyard. I didn't realize the nest was there until I noticed a female oriole flying back and forth between a mulberry tree full of ripe fruit and a big maple about 200 yards away. I eventually spotted the nest—a deep, beautifully woven pouch made of plant fibers and some of the yarn I put out every spring. The rim of the nest was woven onto the branch and some nearby twigs. I'm pretty sure at least two and possibly three chicks fledged from the nest.

I was amazed to learn, when I looked it up, that the nest is made entirely by the female bird—and that she manages to do it in only eight or nine days.

Fruitful Ideas

A lot of the migratory birds that are in your yard in the summer are insect-eaters who won't really try your seed feeders or even suet. However, birds such as orioles, tanagers, Cedar Waxwings, catbirds, mockingbirds, woodpeckers, and robins are attracted to fresh fruit. This sort of feeding is simplicity itself; just spear half an orange or apple cut-side up on a twig or nail driven into a tree trunk. These are perching, not clinging birds, so place the fruit where the birds can perch to eat it. If you want to get a little more elaborate, you can make or buy a hanging fruit feeder that has a spike for the fruit and a perch for the bird. You can also put grapes, berries, diced apples, sliced bananas, raisins, and other small pieces of fruit on a platform feeder. If the fruit's not eaten, however, it will go bad quickly in the summer heat. Check the feeder every evening and remove any uneaten fruit.

Bringing Up Baby

There's no reason to stop offering your usual foods in the summer; it's not true that the baby birds won't learn to fend for themselves if you feed them. In fact, if you take your feeders down, you'll miss the fun of seeing the adult birds introduce their chicks to the food you provide. I was once watching as a parent Black-capped Chickadee landed on my suet basket, followed closely by a chick. The chick crash-landed onto the parent and grabbed on. Another chick flew in and landed on top of the first one. While it was clinging to its sibling, yet another chick flew in and landed on the second chick; for a few hilarious moments, a little chain of fluttering chickadees hung down from the basket.

You can easily see the begging behavior of young birds at the feeder. I've often seen newly fledged birds fly in with a parent bird, sit on the perch right next to the food, and still beg to be fed. Reminds you of your own kids, doesn't it?

Got Those Hungry Blues

Bluebirds don't ordinarily come to seed feeders, but you can attract them with mealworms or a mixture of suet, peanuts, and fruit. Use my recipe for bluebird crumble and spread it on the ground, a tree stump, or a platform feeder near your bluebird boxes. The bluebirds love it—and so do other birds and raccoons. Put out only a handful or two at a time.

Bluebird Crumble

1 cup peanut butter
4 cups cornmeal
1 cup flour
1 cup sunflower hearts
1 cup chopped nuts
1 cup chopped raisins
1 cup melted rendered suet

Combine the peanut butter, cornmeal, and flour in a big mixing bowl. Stir until a crumbly mixture forms. Stir in the sunflower hearts, nuts, and raisins.

Drizzle the melted suet over the mixture, stirring now and then as you do. Let cool. Store in the refrigerator until ready to use.

The idea is to get a crumbly mixture of pea- and bean-sized lumps. If the mixture seems too sticky or doesn't form lumps, add some more flour. If it seems too dry and forms crumbs instead of lumps, add some more suet.

Putting out nesting boxes for the bluebirds is a great way to attract them so they're around to feed. I discuss the details of how to house the bluebirds in Chapter 27, "Equal Opportunity Housing."

Live Bait

Some insect-eating birds like their food live. Robins and bluebirds, for instance, prefer their food to wiggle a bit on the way down. You can attract these birds by putting out *mealworms* for them. Put a handful of the worms in a shallow dish (about an inch deep) and leave it where the birds can spot it easily—near your bluebird house or a robin's nest. (Use a scoop if you can't stand the idea of actually touching worms.)

You can buy mealworms inexpensively at birdfeeding specialty shops or bait shops, or you can order them through the mail. Store them in the refrigerator, but be sure to warn your family first. Be prepared for a certain amount of resistance; I can't think why, but some people object to having them in the fridge. (If you think that's gross, don't open the freezer at my friend Steve's house. It's full of dead rats he feeds to the injured owls and hawks he nurses back to health.)

Rappin' Robin

Mealworms aren't really worms like night crawlers or other earthworms. They're the larval form of a type of harmless black beetle. Mealworms are about half an inch to an inch long.

I do draw the line at raising the mealworms myself. My brother tells me it's easy to do (he raises them to feed his lizards), so I pass along his instructions:

1. Put a two-inch layer of wheat bran in a flat-bottomed plastic container with a lid.

2. Put half an apple on top of the bran for moisture.

3. Drop in a big handful of mealworms and cover the container, leaving the lid open a crack. (The worms can't crawl out—or so he says.)

4. Leave the containers in a warm, dark place.

5. Scoop out the worms with a slotted spoon as needed.

6. When half of the mealworms are gone, add another layer of wheat bran. Leave a few worms to pupate and turn into adult beetles. They'll lay eggs, and in a couple of months, you'll have a new crop of worms.

I warn you, these instructions come from the same brother who told me it's easy to repair your own camera.

So Suet Me

When the weather gets hot, suet feeding can be a bit of a problem. In really hot weather, the stuff melts and drips down; it's really gross. If it goes rancid, it's grosser still. That's why you should use rendered suet or suet dough—it lasts longer.

Stay away from suet in the summer. Your best bet is to switch to dough cakes made with cornmeal. In the spring, move the suet feeder to a shaded spot and take it down altogether in a heat wave. Some people take in the feeder at night and stick it in the fridge until the next morning, but at that point, I just stop putting out suet.

The Least You Need to Know

➤ In the summertime, you can feed all the usual birds, along with hummingbirds, bluebirds, and orioles.

➤ Hummingbirds are attracted to red-colored feeders filled with sugar water. Orioles are also attracted to sugar water.

➤ Birds such as orioles, mockingbirds, and robins will eat fruit such as oranges and grapes.

➤ Bluebirds and many other insect-eating birds can be attracted by putting out live mealworms.

Chapter 25

Feeder Pests and Problems

> **In This Chapter**
>
> ➤ Keeping your feeders clean
>
> ➤ What's all that squawking about?
>
> ➤ Chasing off squirrels and other feeder pests
>
> ➤ Cats!
>
> ➤ Windows and birds

Feeding the birds is basically a simple hobby. It's hard to go seriously wrong, but problems can happen. With a little knowledge, you can avoid most of the common problems and fix almost all the others if they turn up. With constant vigilance and a certain amount of low cunning, you can even keep the squirrels under control.

Keep It Clean

Let's start with the most important thing to remember about bird feeding: Keep your feeders clean. Whenever birds crowd together, at a feeder or anywhere else, they can spread disease among themselves. You can help keep this from happening by taking down your feeders—and the chains and hooks they hang from, if possible—every couple of weeks and cleaning them thoroughly. Start by removing any seeds and hulls stuck in the feeder or in the seed tray. Then, wash the feeder with hot water; use a stiff brush to get into the crevices. (You can put most small plastic feeders into your dishwasher.) If feeders are really dirty, kill off any germs by cleansing the feeder in a mixture of one part chlorine bleach to nine parts water. Rinse well.

Keep the area around the feeder clean, too. Rake up all those sunflower hulls every couple of weeks. If you put out stale baked goods, fruit, or other stuff, clean up every couple of days. Remove anything that's wet, moldy, or rotted.

In Sickness and in Health

Despite your best housekeeping efforts, you might notice a bird that doesn't look too good at your feeder. You'll probably be able to tell it's sick; it won't move around much and its feathers will be fluffed out. It's only natural that a sick bird would hang out near an easy food supply. Here, you can let nature take its course. The bird might get better, or it might not. Don't do anything.

If you start seeing a lot of sick birds near the feeder, or if you start seeing corpses, nature is taking its course, all right—but now, you're helping it along. The birds are spreading a disease around as they throng to your feeder.

Take the feeder down immediately. Discard the seeds and clean the feeder thoroughly. Clean up around the feeder as well. Don't put the feeder back up right away; wait about a week. If you're still seeing sick or dead birds by then, wait a few more days. Because whatever's causing the disease could be in the soil, move the feeder to the other side of the yard.

Splat!

Birds can spread disease when they crowd together at feeders. Wash your feeders with hot water every couple of weeks. If you notice sick or dead birds around your feeder, take your feeders down, wash them thoroughly, and don't put them back up for a few days.

Sick House Finches

Over the past few years, an epidemic of an eye disease called conjunctivitis has hit the House Finches in eastern North America. If you notice any house finches with swollen or runny eyes, they have it. Because this illness may be catching to other species, take your feeders down at once if you notice any sick or dead house finches. Remove the dead birds (use a plastic bag over your hand or wear disposable latex gloves) and report them to your local wildlife officials. You can also report the problem to the Cornell House Finch Disease Survey by calling (607) 254-2440 or visiting the Web site at **www.birds.cornell.edu/hofi.**

Duking It Out

As you watch the birds at your feeder, you'll see a certain amount of squabbling, squawking, and jockeying for position. You might see a chickadee land and chase off another before grabbing a seed and flying off, for instance. The chickadee that was chased off then returns for its seed, sometimes to be chased off several times more before it finally gets a seed.

What's going on here? The aggression among birds of the same species is part of the birds' *dominance hierarchy*—in other words, their *peck order*. The birds argue among themselves to decide who's the biggest, toughest bird on the block—and who's the second-biggest, third-biggest, and so on down the line. All that chasing and squawking might seem like a waste of energy, but it's not. The birds pretty much know who's who, and it's rare for them to fight with each other to the point of getting hurt. The most dominant bird gets first pick, and the least dominant bird might not get as much as it wants, but overall, each bird gets its turn at the feeder with a minimum of arguing.

On the other hand, you don't want large numbers of birds fighting for seeds and perch space at your feeder. This causes a lot of energy-wasting squabbling and even injuries, and the birds are more likely to spread diseases. If you can, reduce the crowding at any one feeder by adding another (or even two) elsewhere in your yard. You could put more food on the ground, but scatter only as much as the birds will eat in a day.

If mobs of birds are showing up in your yard, you might have to take the drastic step of not feeding at all for a week or so. Don't worry; the birds will spread out and find other sources of food. When you start feeding again, keep the crowds down by putting out only as much seed as the birds can eat in a morning.

Rappin' Robin

The birds in a flock have a **dominance hierarchy**, also called a **peck order**. Each bird knows where it stands relative to the other members of the flock. The most dominant bird gets first crack at any food, and so on down the line.

SQUIRRELS!

The most important thing to remember about keeping squirrels out of your bird feeders is that it can't really be done. The best you can hope for is to reach some sort of truce with your local squirrels. Let's take a look at your defenses.

Counter Measures

The best solution to the squirrel problem is feeders they can't get into. That eliminates most feeders; a determined squirrel can get into almost *anything*. Wooden feeders are easy targets, and anything that's not made of metal will eventually be gnawed to bits.

In my experience, the only feeders that are genuinely squirrel-proof are counterweighted, all-metal models such as the Absolute and Absolute II, made by Heritage Farms. (Call (800) 435-4525.) The Absolute is the Fort Knox of bird feeders. When a squirrel lands on the perch of a counterweighted feeder, its weight brings down a shutter that seals off the seeds. I've had my Absolute for 12 years now. It's covered with tooth marks and the squirrels gnawed off the wooden perch out of spite (you can get replacements), but they've never gotten into it. Even better, they've pretty much stopped trying. Counterweighted feeders are adjustable, so you can also keep out pigeons, crows, and other undesirable large birds.

A gray squirrel—the biggest feeder pest and the best reason to avoid platform feeders. (Photo courtesy of Connie Toops.)

The Fort Knox of bird-feeders: the Absolute II. When squirrels land on the perch bar, the counter-weight brings down a shutter that closes off the seed supply. (Photo courtesy Heritage Farms.)

A good alternative to a counterweighted feeder is a tube feeder with a plastic-coated wire cage around it. The smaller birds can easily get into the cage to feed, but the squirrels and larger birds are fenced out.

It's Baffling

Squirrels are very persistent; even if your feeder really is squirrel-proof, they'll still annoy you and chase off the birds by trying to get in. Baffles—large shields or domes that fit between the feeder and its support—-help keep the squirrels off. Some are designed to tilt when the squirrel lands on them and tip it harmlessly to the ground, but some are barriers that block the squirrel's way or domes that cover the feeder and keep the squirrel from reaching the seeds. Squirrels overcome obstacles by eating them. Pick a baffle that's made of metal or heavy plastic.

The domed Big Top feeder keeps squirrels and large birds out of the feeder. (Photo courtesy Droll Yankees.)

Bear in mind that squirrels can easily jump six feet or more in any direction from any convenient launching point—from the ground, from a railing, from a tree trunk or branch. They can even climb up brick walls and wooden siding. If they can get around the baffle by jumping, they will.

Yuck!

Squirrels like just about everything your birds like, with one exception: safflower seeds. Fill your feeder with these seeds instead of sunflower seeds. Pretty much all the birds will eat them—and cardinals love them.

You can also lace your usual seeds with hot pepper powder. This doesn't harm the birds and, in theory, the squirrels hate it. In practice, I think they actually like the stuff. If you want to try it, be careful; capsaicin, the chemical that gives hot peppers their sting, can burn your eyes, nose, and mouth.

Diversion Feeding

One good way to keep the squirrels off the birdfeeder is to give them a feeder of their own. Some people see this as a shameful capitulation to the enemy, but think of it this way: Harmony is nature's way. What's easier, constantly battling the squirrels or just giving them some inexpensive corn kernels in a far corner of the yard? Check out the squirrel-feeding devices at your local wild bird store. They're designed to make the squirrels work a little for their corn and give you some good laughs at the same time.

If you can't beat 'em, join 'em. The Squirrel-Go-Round is a diversion feeder in two ways; it keeps the squirrels away from your birdfeeder and it's diverting to watch the squirrels whirl harmlessly around as they chow down on the corn. (Drawing courtesy Heritage Farms.)

Other Solutions

There are a couple other things you can try before you decide to have squirrel stew for dinner. I let my dogs out, but the squirrels are on to them; they give them a sporting 10 yards or so before bothering to run. If you're the creative type, you can make elaborate arrangements of baffles, shields, and booby traps. They'll work for at least a few days, and then you can start all over. Every now and then, a real nuisance squirrel—one that's even more athletic and ingenious than most—shows up. You can try catching it in a humane live trap, taking it far, far away, and letting it go. Your problem squirrel is now someone else's, of course, so try not to be seen as you release it. Nature hates a vacuum. Another pesky squirrel will quickly arrive to take over.

Cat-astrophe

Before I start this section, let me just put on my skateboarding helmet and pads; I know from experience that what I'm about to say gets some people really, really upset. *Cats needlessly kill hundreds of millions of birds in North America every year.* Any cat, no matter how apparently fat and lazy, will kill birds if it gets the chance. I'm not saying this because I hate cats; I love them. I'm saying it because it's true—and many studies back it up.

There's an easy solution to the cat problem, but it also gets some people really, really upset. *Keep your cat indoors.* I don't understand why this bothers people so much. Keeping your cat indoors is good for the cat. Again, I'm not saying this because I hate cats; I love them. I'm saying it because it's true.

Here's why your cat is safer and happier indoors:

➤ Putting a bell on your cat won't keep it from catching and killing birds and other small wildlife. It also won't keep your cat from getting lost or being attacked by other animals, including dogs, coyotes, raccoons, and other predators.

➤ Millions of outdoor cats are run over by cars every year. Almost as many are injured.

➤ Outdoor cats get fatal diseases such as feline leukemia and feline immunodeficiency disease, to say nothing of abscesses, eye diseases, and other infections.

➤ Outdoor cats get all sorts of harmful parasites, including worms, mites, ticks, and fleas.

Be a Better Birder

The Humane Society of the United States, the nation's largest animal protection organization, and the American Humane Association, founded in 1877, feel it's so important to keep your cats indoors that they sponsor the American Birding Conservancy Cats Indoors! campaign.

➤ Unaltered free-roaming cats are the single most important cause of cat overpopulation. Every year, millions of homeless cats must be put to sleep at overburdened animal shelters.

There's nothing "natural" about cats eating birds. There weren't any domestic cats in North America until settlers brought them here just a few hundred years ago. What with habitat loss, pesticide use, and natural predators, birds have enough problems these days. You'll be helping both the cats and the birds if you keep your own cats indoors, catch stray cats and find good homes for them, and support local cat control and protection plans.

A Little Bird Told Me...

To learn more about the Cats Indoors! campaign and how you can help keep cats from killing birds, contact:

Cats Indoors! The Campaign for Safer Birds and Cats
American Bird Conservancy
1250 24th Street NW, Suite 400
Washington, DC 20037
(202) 778-9666
Fax: (202) 778-9778
abc@abcbirds.org
www.abcbirds.org

Bad Birds

I'm a broad-minded sort, so I don't really object to having larger birds such as Blue Jays, Red-winged Blackbirds, and even crows at my feeder. They may temporarily hog the feeder, but they don't usually stay long. I think their interesting behavior far outweighs any drawbacks. I draw the line, however, at seed-hogging, non-native birds such as pigeons, starlings, and House Sparrows. These birds can take over your feeder, scoffing down huge amounts of seed and keeping all the other birds away. Take these steps to keep them away:

➤ Use a counter-weighted or caged feeder to keep crows, pigeons, and starlings out of the seeds.

➤ These birds can't cling well, so they won't come to perchless feeders.

➤ Don't put food on the ground or on an uncaged platform feeder; it's an open invitation to unwanted birds.

➤ Starlings can't cling well, and they definitely can't cling upside down. To keep them out of suet feeders, choose the kind that have an opening only on the bottom.

Don't hesitate to banish these pest birds from your feeders; they're an unnatural blight on the landscape.

Hungry Hawks

I don't really see hawks as a problem at birdfeeders; after all, hawks are birds and they have to eat, too. Bird-eating accipiters such as Sharp-shinned and Cooper's Hawks are part of the natural environment for small birds. Every once in a while, one of these fierce hawks might pick off an unwary, injured, sick, or just unlucky bird from near your feeder. If you're fortunate, you'll get to see it happen. Don't interfere. Once the hawk has struck, the prey bird's chance of survival, even if you chase off the hawk, is basically none. Instead, see the hawk strike for what it is: a vivid reminder that in the natural world, very few creatures die of old age.

If you hear a commotion at your feeder and notice all the birds diving for cover, there might be a hawk around. It might be a false alarm, however. There's a Blue Jay in my backyard who does a pretty convincing imitation of a Red-tailed Hawk's scream. The birds at the feeder scram, and he flies down to feed in peace.

A Plethora of Pests

After squirrels and unwanted birds, rodents are probably the biggest pest problem at birdfeeders. The best way to keep chipmunks, mice, and rats away is to use only hanging feeders. Don't scatter any food on the ground, and keep the area under the feeder raked up. If you notice any rats, stop feeding immediately, clean up the area, and look around the neighborhood for areas where rats will thrive. Clean up the area, or organize a neighborhood cleanup. Do not put dog or cat food out, and do not start feeding the birds again until the rats are definitely gone.

People in rural areas may find deer, raccoons, and even black bears raiding their feeders. These pests can easily get into (or rip up) wooden hopper-style feeders. Switch to hanging, squirrel-proof feeders.

Every once in a while, I read in the paper about neighbors suing each other over birdfeeders.

Splat!

Wild animals such as raccoons and bears are cute at a distance, but up close, they can be dangerous. If you spot an unwanted visitor at your feeder, don't try to chase it off. Let it eat its fill and go away. Then, take down the feeder (or what's left of it).

The problem usually seems to be that the feeders are attracting pigeons. Much as I love birds, I think I might sue a neighbor who attracted pigeons. Of all the problem birds, pigeons are the worst. There's a reason why pigeons are called "rats with wings." They gobble your seeds and then hang around, perching on roofs, fences, and railings, and leaving droppings all over the place. If pigeons show up in your yard, pretty much the only way to get rid of them is to stop feeding seeds. (You can still leave up your suet feeders and feeders that limit large birds, such as hummer feeders.) In suburban areas, this will only work if you get your neighbors to stop feeding as well.

Even if you're not attracting bad birds, your neighbors might get upset with you if your feeding attracts too many squirrels or rats and mice. If you live in an apartment, your lease might ban you from putting a feeder on a terrace or window, especially if you live above ground level.

Unsafe at Any Seed

Most of today's birdfeeders are well designed and well made of good, durable materials. Even so, some feeders on the market today are downright dangerous to the birds. Watch out for feeders with feeding ports that are large enough for the birds to stick their heads all the way in. When the seed gets low, birds trying to reach the last seeds can get their heads stuck and end up injured or dead. In some feeders, the opening is large enough for a small bird such as a chickadee to squeeze all the way into the feeder. When this happens, the bird sometimes gets stuck and can't get out again.

Avoid feeders with holes larger than an inch across. If you don't want to get rid of a potentially dangerous feeder, fill it every day instead. The birds won't get into trouble as long as they can reach the seeds easily. But do take these feeders down if you're not going to be around to take care of them.

Window Strikes

When we moved into our house years ago, someone gave us a little wooden feeder as a house gift. I hung it up with a piece of string on the hickory tree near the house. Within an hour, birds were taking seeds from it. After two hours, a squirrel bit through the string and sent the feeder crashing to the ground. As I stood there contemplating the wreckage, a cute little chickadee swooped in, snatched up a seed, and flew off directly into a window. Then, I was contemplating both a wrecked feeder and a chickadee corpse. (That night, our first in the new house, we had a power failure and a bat in the living room. As we sat there by the fading light of the only flashlight we had, wondering how to get the bat out, the phone rang. It was my mother. "Well," she asked brightly, "How do you like country living?")

The awful thud of a bird hitting one of your windows is a sound you definitely don't want to hear. In just about every case, you can avoid or solve the problem, especially if you understand why the birds are hitting in the first place.

Reflected Gory

When a bird sees the sky or the plants and trees in your backyard reflected in a window, it can't tell the difference between the real thing and the glass. The best way to avoid this sort of window strike is to break up the reflections somehow. The best approach is to put something in front of the window, on the outside. Hang something decorative in front of the window such as wind chimes or a mobile. If all else fails, stretch netting (the kind sold to protect fruit trees works well) over the window. The birds may still hit, but at least they'll bounce off harmlessly.

Clear and Present Danger

Sometimes, the birds look right through the clear glass of one window and out the glass of another on the opposite side of the house. They think they have a clear passage to fly through—and they only find out they don't when they smack into the window. Show-throughs, as this situation is called, are easy to fix. Sometimes, all you have to do is close the curtains or draw the blind on one of the windows. You can break up the illusion by putting something on the inside of the pane. Hawk silhouettes are the traditional approach. They don't really scare the birds, but they do break up the show-through. Any sort of decal or decoration will do the trick.

Be a Better Birder

To prevent birds from flying into your windows, hang something in front of the window—such as a mobile, a flag, or a wreath. Potted plants in front of the window or a window box will also help. A less effective alternative is to apply stick-on decals to the inside of your window.

Take That!

During the breeding season, a male bird will sometimes see his reflection in a window and think it's a rival male intruding on his territory. (Birds aren't too smart sometimes.) He'll rush at the reflection and try to chase it away. I once had a male cardinal who flew along the windows of my workroom every morning chasing away his "rival." I solved the problem by putting window boxes in front of the windows. They broke up the reflections and convinced the cardinal he had vanquished his rival for good.

Dazed and Confused

Crashing into a window often kills a bird, usually by breaking its neck. If the bird isn't killed immediately, there's a chance that it's just dazed or stunned and will survive. Help it along by covering it with an empty box (shoe boxes work well) or a brown paper bag. In an emergency, you can use a kitchen colander. By covering the bird, you keep predators away. The darkness keeps the bird quiet as it recovers. Generally, dazed birds recover within 10 to 20 minutes. Lift the box and let the bird fly off.

Even though a dazed bird may fly off and seem okay, there's still a strong likelihood that it will die from a head injury within the next couple of weeks. Prevention is definitely the best approach to keeping the wild birds at your feeder safe.

The Least You Need to Know

➤ To keep the birds from spreading disease among themselves as they flock to your feeders, keep the feeders and the area underneath clean.

➤ If you notice sick or dead birds near your feeder, stop feeding at once, clean your feeders, and wait several days before you put them back up.

➤ It's almost impossible to keep squirrels out of your feeders. Your best bet is to select a squirrel-proof feeder.

➤ Outdoor cats are a real menace to birds. Keep your cats indoors, ask your neighbors to do the same, and remove stray cats from the area.

➤ By choosing feeders they can't hold onto, you can keep undesirable birds such as pigeons, crows, and starlings from getting your seeds.

➤ Keep birds from hitting your windows by breaking up reflections and blocking show-throughs.

Chapter 26

Wet and Wild

In This Chapter

➤ Attracting birds with water

➤ Ponds—natural and otherwise

➤ Birdbaths, misters, and other water

➤ Water for the winter

What's the best way to bring birds to your backyard? The same way that's also the easiest and cheapest: providing water. All birds—including birds that wouldn't dream of going to your feeder—need water. When you provide it year round, you help the birds with something they really need, and you attract more bird species than you would with only a feeder.

Taking a Bath

Nature's birdbath is a shallow puddle, the edge of a pond, or perhaps a flat rock partially submerged in a stream. It stands to reason, then, that any birdbath you provide should be something similar. Ideally, what the birds want is something shallow and sloping that reaches a maximum depth of only about two to three inches. If there's a flat rock in the middle or at one end, so much the better. What you want is a birdbath that's also attractive to look at and easy to keep clean.

Fortunately, just about any commercial birdbath on the market today is good for both the birds and you. You've got a wide choice of styles. The traditional pedestal style makes an attractive addition to your garden. Tripod- or pole-mounted birdbaths are lighter and easier to move around. The advantage of a raised birdbath is that you can see the birds easily—and the birds can see any lurking cats easily. Even so, the wide variety of birdbaths designed to fit on fence posts, terraces, or even flat on the ground are also fine, as long as you keep the area around them open.

Birdbaths can be improvised out of anything shallow. Those shallow dishes designed to go under potted plants work well. So do old glass pie plates, upturned trash-can lids, and just about anything else. If the surface seems slippery, put some flat rocks or gravel in the bottom. Fill the birdbath with just an inch of water.

Whatever you're using as a birdbath, put it in an open area that has plenty of natural shelter about 20 feet away. If you set the birdbath in an open area, the birds can spot any cats or other predators that might be creeping up. After a bird has splashed around in your birdbath, its feathers will be wet and it won't be able to fly well. The birds need to perch somewhere sheltered to dry off and *preen* their feathers.

Be a Better Birder

Watching the birds bathe is a lot of fun. They squat down in the water, splash around with their wings, and then duck their heads under a few times. After that, they shake themselves off and fly away to a nearby perch to preen their feathers. If you're really lucky, you'll get to watch a parent bird bring a chick to the birdbath for its first bath.

Water is the easiest and least expensive way to attract the maximum number of birds. Here, a Curve-billed Thrasher enjoys water from a dish equipped with a dripper. (Photo by Peter Gottschling/KAC Productions.)

Birdbaths get dirty quickly, especially in the summer. You can keep seeds and hulls out of the birdbath by placing it away from the feeder. Give the birdbath a rinse and fill it with fresh water every couple of days (daily in hot weather). Once or twice a week, scrub it out with a stiff brush and a solution of one part chlorine bleach to nine parts warm water.

Birds aren't the only critters attracted to water. A raccoon is enjoying the birdbath in this shot. (Photo by Kathy Adams Clark/KAC Productions.)

Hey, Mister

Birds are quickly attracted to birdbaths. To attract them even quicker, add a mister or a dripper. These inexpensive devices attach to a garden hose and provide a steady flow of water. There's something about the sight and sound of moving water that really brings in the birds. The misters spray a fine mist that's amazingly attractive, especially to hummingbirds. (Hummingbirds will also hover and dart in and out of your lawn sprinkler.) Drippers put out a steady flow of small drops that land in the birdbath and work like magic to attract birds. You can easily improvise a dripper by filling an empty milk jug with water, hanging it above the birdbath, and punching a tiny hole in the bottom or by draping a dripping hose over a branch above the birdbath.

Rappin' Robin

Birds **preen** their feathers to keep them clean and in good working order. You can easily see this behavior after a bird bathes. A bird uses its bill to "nibble" at its feathers, starting at the base and working out. Preening removes water, dirt, and parasites such as fleas and mites. It also realigns the barbs that hold feathers together.

Winter Water

Whenever we get a cold snap in the winter and most of the nearby natural water freezes up, I know I'll start seeing a flock of 30 to 40 robins in the yard every morning at around 10 a.m. They're coming in to drink and bathe where a small waterfall keeps the water open. (Despite all that stuff about the first robin of spring, a surprisingly large number of them overwinter.) When the cold snap breaks, the robins disappear again.

For the birds, water can be just as hard to find in the winter as it is in the summer. When everything is frozen solid, there's no place to drink or bathe. By providing winter water, you'll bring in a lot of extra birds to your yard, including birds that don't ordinarily visit your feeders.

The trick is to keep the water from freezing. Although the birds don't seem to mind bathing in really cold water, the water does need to be open.

Start by putting your birdbath in a sunny, sheltered location. If the water freezes overnight but the day gets warm, the sun will melt the ice quickly. Don't put alcohol or antifreeze in the water! (You'd think I wouldn't have to say something so obvious, but you'd be amazed at the things I hear when I give talks!)

Splat!

Don't use an ordinary indoor extension cord for your outdoor birdbath heater. Use only a heavy-duty, three-pronged cord designed for the outdoors.

If you've got a commercial birdbath with a hollow pedestal, you might be able to rig a light bulb inside, using an outdoor cord and fixture and a little ingenuity. The heat from the bulb will keep the water from freezing. Check out the range of inexpensive birdbath heaters and birdbaths with built-in heaters available at your local nature shop or garden center. The electric cords on these are short, so you'll almost certainly need a heavy-duty extension cord designed for outdoor use. The heaters themselves are perfectly safe; they're designed to shut off if they're not in the water. The better designs also have thermostats for energy efficiency. The heaters can make the water evaporate fast, so check the birdbath often and refill it as needed. Remember, birds don't mind the cold—as long as there's some open water, the heater is doing its job, even if there's ice in the water.

Dusting Off

Birds like to take dust baths almost as much as they like to bathe in water. They'll find a patch of dusty or sandy ground and flap around in it; their activity in the dust is exactly the same as it is in the water because they're doing very much the same thing. The dust absorbs excess oil from their feathers and also helps remove annoying parasites.

The birds will usually find a good dust bathing spot on their own; if you notice little hollows in a bare spot under the eaves of your house, the birds have been there.

A Little Bird Told Me...

Every once in a while, you might notice a bird crouching down in your yard and holding still for a while. Look more closely and you'll probably see that the bird is on top of an anthill—and the aggravated ants are swarming all over the bird. Sometimes, you'll see a bird pick up an ant and rub it on its wings and tail feathers. This mysterious behavior, known as *anting*, is believed to help the bird get rid of skin and feather parasites. It works because the ants give off formic acid, which kills the parasites.

It's a Natural

If you're fortunate enough to have natural water on your property, you're going to see a lot of birds. Any size natural pond, lake, or stream brings in a lot of birds. We've had dozens of species on our pond, including Green Herons, Great Blue Herons, Kingfishers, Louisiana Water Thrushes, Mallards, Wood Ducks, and Canada Geese, to say nothing of the warblers that pass through in the spring and stay for the summer.

Because we have natural water, we also have more birds all year round. Some come to the feeders, but we also get a lot of species, such as Wood Thrushes, that don't usually visit feeders. They come in for a drink and a bath.

Attractive as natural water is, you can make it even better. Add some partially submerged flat rocks and sheltering plants around the edges.

If You Build It, They Will Come

Natural water for the birds can be scarce, especially in built-up areas. In fact, it's so scarce that if you have a choice between feeders and water, I recommend the water.

For a beautiful addition to your garden that will also attract a ton of birds, try an artificial pond. Even a tiny pond no more than a foot in diameter will work. These are easy to make; just buy an inexpensive molded plastic liner from any garden center. If you make a pond, be sure it has a shallow end and some flat rocks or perches to make it safe and easy for the birds to bathe in.

You'd be amazed at how quickly the birds and other critters find it. When our neighbors down the road added one to their flower garden, they had birds at it within a day and five resident froggies within a week. With a little imagination, you can come up with all sorts of variations on the basic artificial pond idea. Be warned: Ponds can be addictive. Our neighbors are already planning a new, bigger pond with more water plants.

Be a Better Birder

If you have a wet or marshy area on your property, you're in luck. Instead of drying out the area, do what you can to keep it wet. Plant some native grasses or native wildflower mix in the area, and let it grow up naturally. You'll turn an eyesore into a great bird magnet.

To keep the water in your pond open during the winter, look into a floating de-icer. The models I've seen look like miniature flying saucers. They're attached to a long electrical cord and work well in small natural or artificial ponds.

Making a Difference

Decades ago, farmers routinely drained wetlands areas and turned them into farmland. Today, many of those fields are being restored back into wetlands as part of the Partners for Wildlife program of the U.S. Fish and Wildlife Service. When wetlands come back, so do the birds—and the wildflowers, the butterflies, and the other wildlife. At one marsh restoration in Pennsylvania, 213 bird species were seen just a few years after the project was finished.

For more information on wetlands restoration, check with the Partners for Wildlife Coordinator at your regional office of the U.S. Fish and Wildlife Service. To find your regional office, check your phone book or call your county extension agent.

The Least You Need to Know

➤ Birds need water for drinking and bathing. Even birds that don't come to feeders will come to your birdbath.

➤ Birdbaths should be shallow and sloping—no more than two inches at the deepest.

➤ The sound and sight of moving water is very attractive to birds. Misters and drippers will bring the birds flocking to your birdbath.

➤ Birds need water in the winter, too. Use an inexpensive birdbath heater to keep the water open.

➤ Natural or artificial ponds are a great addition to the garden and are also attractive to birds.

Superintendent

Chapter 27

Equal Opportunity Housing

In This Chapter

➤ Attracting birds with nesting sites

➤ Nesting box basics

➤ Nesting boxes for bluebirds and other special birds

➤ Bats in your backyard

If you've ever tried to find a decent apartment for a reasonable rent in a nice neighborhood, you have an idea of what the birds in your backyard are up against. Good housing is hard to find—and getting harder all the time. The natural nesting places birds depend on, such as thick bushes and hollows in dead trees, are scarce in cities and well-groomed suburbs. To attract more birds to your yard, then, try being an avian real-estate developer. Put up some housing, and you'll see a real increase in the number of bird species on your property.

Where Birds Nest

Birds nest in an amazing variety of ways, ranging from the simple scrape in the sand of many shorebirds to the elaborate hanging nest of the oriole. What all the birds look for—even the ones that don't seem to make much of a nest at all—is a sheltered spot safe from predators.

The birds that are most likely to nest in your backyard are passerines (songbirds) such as robins, catbirds, wrens, chickadees, cardinals, warblers, finches, sparrows, and other common birds. In areas with the right habitat, bluebirds, Purple Martins, Barn Swallows, and other birds will build nests. You can even provide housing for owls, Kestrels, and Wood Ducks.

Two basic approaches will bring nesting birds to your backyard: habitat and housing.

Habitat for Housing

Take a look at an old field that's grown up into a meadow dotted with trees and shrubs. It's full of nesting sites for birds. Ground-nesting birds such as bobolinks build nests in the tall grass; sparrows, warblers, finches, and many other species build their nests in the dense shrubs and among the vines and branches of the trees. Cavity-nesting birds such as chickadees and woodpeckers find or excavate holes in dead trees and branches.

Compare that rich nesting habitat with the typical suburban backyard. The manicured lawn and carefully trimmed shrubs and trees don't offer much in the way of nesting sites.

What can you do to add nesting sites to your property? I tell you a lot more about this in Chapter 28, "Gardening for the Birds." For now, what it all boils down to is being a little less neat in the garden. Don't be so quick to trim off those dead or broken tree branches or prune those hedges. Remember that from a bird's perspective, dead trees are almost as valuable as live ones.

Nesting Box Basics

Your backyard, unless it's a pretty unusual one, will never have as many possible nesting sites as a natural area will. You can make up the difference by putting up nesting boxes, also known as birdhouses or bird boxes.

Not every bird will move in to a nesting box. As a general rule, only birds that ordinarily nest in cavities—chickadees, wrens, titmice, woodpeckers, Tree Swallows, bluebirds, starlings—will use a nesting box. Birds such as robins and phoebes will use nesting shelves, but as a rule, most other birds won't use a nesting box.

Be a Better Birder

At some point, you're bound to get a gift of some adorable little birdhouse with hearts and flowers painted on it, a huge entrance hole, and a perch. Turn it into a planter or a garden ornament, but don't put it where the birds might use it.

I'm always amazed at the number of terrible nesting box designs I see. My rule of thumb is, the cuter or more whimsical the design, the further away you should stay. Here's what to look for in a nesting box:

➤ **Solid wood construction:** Keeping the eggs at the right temperature is crucial for nesting success. Solid wood—at least 3/4 inch thick—keeps the temperature steady. Nesting boxes made of metal, pottery, or ceramic will get too hot and too cold inside. The better made the box is, the longer it will last.

➤ **Natural wood:** Painted nesting boxes can get too hot inside, especially if a dark color is used. Skip the stains as well; untreated, natural wood is best. It blends in well and attracts the most birds with the least amount of upkeep.

➤ **Ventilation and drainage holes:** Ventilation holes at the top keep heat from building up inside the box. Drainage holes at the bottom let rainwater drain out.

➤ **The right size entrance hole:** Entrance holes that are too big let unwanted birds such as starlings take over the nesting house. They also let predators reach in easily.

➤ **The right size for the bird:** Nesting boxes that are too small or too large inside won't attract the birds you want.

➤ **No perch in front:** As I explain in a little bit, perches just let predators such as cats and raccoons reach in easily. Unwanted birds can sit on the perch and harass the birds you do want.

➤ **Slanted roof:** The rain will run off easily instead of getting into the box.

➤ **Cleaning panel:** To clean out the box and also check on the nest and chicks, the nesting box should have a cleaning and observation panel you can lift up easily.

A wren enters a small hanging birdhouse. Note that the wren has no need for a perch. (Photo courtesy Wild Birds Unlimited.)

Once you've got your nesting box, the time to put it up is over the winter or very early in the spring, before the birds start hunting around for a nesting site. If the box is there, chances are good a bird will use it.

Sizing Up Your Nesting Boxes

The dimensions of your nesting boxes are really important. You want the interior of the box to be the right size for the nest. House wrens, for instance, build messy nests out of twigs that nearly fill the space. You don't want the box to be too big, then, because the birds will have to work too hard to fill it up. The entrance hole should be just the right size to let in the birds you want and keep out the house sparrows, starlings, and other unwanted birds. The hole also needs to be the right distance above the floor of the box. If the distance from the nest to the hole is too high, the parent birds might not use the box. Even if they do, then the fledglings will have trouble climbing out.

Where you place the box is important to nesting success. In general, nesting boxes should go in sheltered areas away from driveways, swimming pools, and roads. Place the box with the entrance hole facing east; birds get up with the sun. Depending on the species the box is designed for, you might want to mount it on a post or fence post, hang it from a branch or bracket, or attach it to a tree. The height above ground should be right for the species you want to attract. Use the chart to check on the right dimensions and heights for nesting boxes.

Nesting Box Dimensions

Bird Species	Entrance Hole Diameter	Entrance Above Floor	Box Depth	Floor Area	Area Above Ground
Wood Duck	4"	17"	22"	12"×12"	10'–20'
Kestrel	3"	9"–12"	12"–15"	8"×8"	10'–30'
Barn Owl	6"	0"–4"	15"–18"	10"×18"	12'–18'
Red-headed Woodpecker	2"	9"	12"	6"×6"	10'–20'
Downy Woodpecker	1 1/4"	7"	9"	4"×4"	5'–15'
Hairy Woodpecker	1 5/8"	9"–12"	12"–15"	6"×6"	12'–20'
Northern Flicker	2 1/2"	14"–16"	16"–18"	7"×7"	6'–30'
Great Crested Flycatcher	1 9/16"	6"–8"	8"–10"	6"×6"	8'–20'
Purple Martin	2 1/4"	1"	6"	6"×6"	10'–20'
Tree Swallow	1 1/2"	4"–6"	6"–8"	5"×5"	4'–15'
Chickadees	1 1/8"	7"	9"	4"×4"	4'–15'
Titmice	1 1/4"	7"	9"	4"×4"	5'–15'
Nuthatches	1 1/4"	7"	9"	4"×4"	5'–15'
Wrens	1 1/4"	4"–6"	6"–8"	4"×4"	5'–10'
Eastern and Western Bluebirds	1 1/2"	6"–10"	8"–12"	4"×4"	3'–6'
Mountain Bluebird	1 9/16"	6"–10"	8"–12"	4"×4"	3'–6'

Source: U.S. Fish and Wildlife Service.

Building Boxes

Making your own nesting boxes is a fun project for a winter weekend. It's a good way to use up some scrap lumber and introduce a kid to woodworking. Building nest boxes makes a great scouting or school project. The boxes are easy and inexpensive to make, and the birds don't care if they're not exactly works of art. Use the dimensions in the chart as your guide; be sure to make the entrance hole the right size. For exact plans, check out any good book on the subject. I like *The Audubon Society Guide to Attracting Birds* by Stephen Kress (Scribners, 1985) and *The Complete Birdhouse Book* by Donald and Lillian Stokes (Little, Brown, 1990). You can also get plans on-line from the U.S. Fish and Wildlife Service at **www.fws.gov/r9mbmo/pamphlet/house.html.**

Slumming It

A few common problems can turn your luxury bird housing into a slum. Of all the problems, unwanted birds and predators top the list.

Unwanted Birds

House Sparrows and starlings are very aggressive birds that will try to take over nesting boxes and keep the other birds out. You could argue that these birds are part of the natural landscape and deserve housing just like any other bird. You'd be wrong. Starlings and House Sparrows are non-native birds that were introduced to North America more than a century ago and have since become real pests. Unlike all other birds, pigeons, House Sparrows, and starlings aren't protected by federal law.

The best way to keep these birds from squatting in your nesting boxes is to use boxes with the right size entrance hole and no perches. Boxes for smaller birds such as bluebirds and wrens need small holes to keep the pests out. When buying nesting boxes or building your own, make sure the entrance hole is exactly the right diameter.

Splat!

Keep an eye on your nesting boxes at the start of the nesting season in the early spring. If you notice House Sparrows or starlings entering a box, be firm. Open the box and remove any nesting materials they've put in. Even if they've already laid eggs, this isn't the time for sentimentality; remove the nest.

Leggo My Eggs

Critters such as raccoons, snakes, and cats are serious problems for nesting birds. Raccoons can climb up to a nesting box and reach in to grab the eggs or chicks. Snakes can slither in and swallow eggs or chicks. Cats generally can't get into the boxes—although they'll try—but they'll catch fledglings as they flutter around. By keeping the parent birds from the box, cats keep the chicks from being fed. Of course, if a cat kills a parent bird, that means almost certain death for the chicks. (For more on why cats are bad news for birds, refer to Chapter 25, "Feeder Pests and Problems.")

There's an unnatural number of raccoons in suburban areas with rich pickings from household trash. Raccoons demolish or damage nesting boxes and eat a lot of eggs and chicks. They're also hard to keep out. You can put baffles on pole-mounted boxes. Raccoons can't climb or jump as well as squirrels, so this usually keeps them off. Another approach is to nail a small block of wood about 1 1/4 inches thick under the entrance hole. Raccoons have short front legs, and the block keeps them from reaching in far enough to grab the eggs. You can also buy plastic guards that fit into the entrance holes.

Note the predator baffle around the entrance hole. (Photo courtesy Wild Birds Unlimited.)

Toxic Chemicals

Using insecticides, fungicides, weed killers, and other dangerous chemicals in your backyard can kill or seriously harm all the birds, to say nothing of your pets, your family, your neighbors, and the planet. Take the natural approach and stick to organic gardening techniques. Remember, a lot of birds in the yard means a lot fewer bugs. One Tree Swallow, for instance, can eat thousands of mosquitoes in a day.

Awkward Nesting Spots

My mother once returned home from being away for a couple of weeks in the spring and was startled to hear cheeping noises coming from somewhere in the kitchen. She finally tracked the sound down to the oven vent in the wall, where a robin had made a nest and hatched out four chicks. Rather than hurt the chicks or risk moving the nest, she just didn't use the oven until the chicks fledged about a week later.

Federal law says you can't interfere with a wild nesting bird, unless it's harmful in some way. Birds do sometimes make nests in awkward spots—on outdoor light fixtures or in potted plants, for instance—but ask yourself whether that's really harmful before you remove it. Couldn't you just not turn that light on for a few weeks? Remember, birds use the nest only for breeding. From the time the nest is built until the time the chicks fledge will only be about four to six weeks.

Sometimes, birds nesting near your house will dive-bomb anyone who comes near. Once again, can't you learn to live with that? Do you have to use that door to go out? An Eastern Phoebe nests on our front porch every year and raises two broods. Rather than disturb her, we just use one of the three other doors. It's hardly a major inconvenience, and we get to watch the nest activity from the living room window. Several times over the years, I've seen that magical moment when the chicks leave the nest, flying off one by one.

A Little Bird Told Me...

As part of his mating strategy, a male House Wren will busily build several messy nests, called cock nests, of twigs, grass, and other materials within a few days. The female wren inspects his efforts, decides which nest will be the real nest, and then helps the male improve that one. House Wrens will build nests in any sort of cavity—your mailbox, outdoor light fixture, and even in the pockets of clothing hung out to dry.

Fall Clean Up

When the nesting season is over, it's time for you, the landlord, to clean up the boxes and get them ready for the winter. Here's what you need:

➤ **Work gloves:** Much as I love birds, I have to admit that old nests are pretty gross. They're often kind of soggy and full of bugs you wouldn't want to touch.

➤ **A stiff brush:** Use it to brush out the remnants of the old nest. Be sure to clean out blocked drainage and ventilation holes.

As I discuss a little later in this chapter, some birds, such as Downy Woodpeckers, will use nesting boxes as nighttime roosts in the winter. By cleaning out the boxes, you make them more attractive as roosting sites. You're also getting rid of the old, insect-infested nesting material so that when the birds return in the spring, they'll have a cleaner, safer place to build a new nest.

Feathering the Nest

Birds use all sorts of stuff to make their nests. The traditional cup-shaped woven nest—the sort of nest a Cedar Waxwing makes—uses mostly vegetable fibers such as grass, twigs, roots, and plant down. Birds also use moss, lichens, bark, feathers, and even pine needles in their nests. Woodpeckers, not surprisingly, prefer to lay their eggs in a bed of wood chips.

Providing nesting materials is a fun way to help the birds. Cotton balls and short bits of yarn and string are good choices. (Photo by Richard Day/ Daybreak Imagery.)

Most birds will happily use any feathers, short bits of yarn or string, cotton, and other fibers you provide. In fact, they'll put a surprising range of man-made stuff into their nests. I once found a robin's nest that had a big piece of duct tape in it, and I've seen plenty of nests with pieces of paper, cloth scraps, dog hair, and even drinking straws in them.

I keep a plastic bag in a kitchen drawer to store all the string scraps, cotton from medicine bottles, feathers from outdoors and the feather duster, and other odds and ends that accumulate over the year. In the early spring, I drape the stuff over branches and watch the birds come in for it. If you're not the packrat sort, you can buy prepackaged nesting fibers at specialty bird shops.

A Little Bird Told Me...

The prize for most unusual nest has to go to the *Megapodidae* family, better known as the brush turkeys or megapodes. Most of the 22 species of this large, chicken-like bird, found in Australia, New Guinea and the many islands of southeastern Asia, make huge mounds of vegetation that are basically giant compost heaps. The female lays her unusually large eggs in the center of the mound, where heat from the decaying plants takes care of incubation. Once the eggs are laid, the parent birds check the mound temperature often, but have nothing more to do with the chicks. When they hatch, they dig their way out of the mound and are completely on their own after that.

Watch the Birdie

Birding takes on a whole extra dimension when you're watching a nesting site. It's a wonderful way to introduce kids to the joy of birding—and also to the whole birds and bees thing.

You can safely watch the activity at the nesting box from a nearby window, using your binoculars or spotting scope. At first, you'll see the birds checking out the box, going in and out of it, and flying around near it. Then, you'll see them carrying in nesting materials. It generally takes no more than a week to finish the nest; the eggs are laid very soon after. Most back-yard birds incubate their eggs for about 12 days. When you see the birds tirelessly carrying in insects, you'll know the eggs have hatched. Keep watching. In about two to three more weeks, you might be lucky enough to see the chicks *fledge* and leave the nest. After that, they'll be in the area, still being fed by their parents and learning to feed on their own, for another couple of weeks.

Every once in a while, you, or more likely your young child, will find a baby bird hopping around all by itself on the ground and making pitiful cheeps. Don't project your human ideas about babies onto the chick. Despite appearances, the bird has almost certainly not been "abandoned" by its parents. It probably has just fledged and is still

Rappin' Robin

To **fledge** means to leave the nest. Baby birds are born pretty much naked or covered with down. They start to grow feathers within a few days. When they've grown enough feathers to leave the nest on their first flight (usually within three weeks for most songbirds), they're said to have fledged. A young bird is a **fledgling** until it's completely independent of its parents.

Be a Better Birder

Nesting birds are secretive; they don't want to give away where the nest is. They take a roundabout route to and from the nesting box and enter it quickly. All that sneaking around makes it hard to spot the birds. Keep watching. After the chicks hatch, they need to be fed about once every 10 minutes. Sooner or later, you're bound to see the parent bird arrive.

Be a Better Birder

To see nesting and feeding birds live and round the clock, check out the great Webcam sites on-line. Here are a few to get started with:

Wild Birds Unlimited Bird FeederCam:
www.wbu.com/ feedercam_home.htm

Cornell Nestbox Network:
birdsource.cornell.edu/cnbn

The Canadian Peregrine Foundation
www.peregrine-foundation.ca

Mining Company BirdCam list:
www.birding.miningco.com

trying to figure out how to fly. The parent birds are hiding somewhere nearby, making encouraging noises—or they were until you came along and scared them into silence. Chase off any possible predators, such as pet cats, and *go away.* Watch through a window or from a distance, and you'll soon see and hear the parent birds taking care of the chick.

Sometimes, baby birds really are abandoned; the parent birds may have been killed somehow. But remember, just because you don't see the adults doesn't mean they're not there. If you're absolutely certain the parents are permanently gone, you might be strongly tempted to take in the chicks and attempt to raise them. This is a major undertaking that is probably doomed to heart-breaking failure—and is also technically illegal. Don't do it. A certain amount of nest failure is a sad but inevitable part of nature. By some estimates, only about 1 in 10 nests is completely successful.

With caution, it's safe to open the panel on a nesting box and check out what's happening inside. You can even take pictures. Wait until you see the parent bird leave. If you're not sure it's gone, stand to one side of the box and tap on it. The parent will fly out. Open the box and take a quick peek; keep the box open for only a few minutes, and check on it only once every few days. Do this early in the day, so your scent will diminish by evening when nighttime predators like raccoons come out. It's best not to check on nest boxes very often—in fact, there's no real need to check at all, and some good reasons not to. Your presence and your scent after you're gone can lead predators such as crows and raccoons to the nest box. You could also be stressing the chicks and parent birds by interrupting the incubation and feeding schedule.

On the Shelf

Robins, phoebes, and Barn Swallows build their nests on flat, shelf-like surfaces. That could be a rafter in your woodshed or a flat area on your porch. You might not want the birds that close to the house—or maybe you do want them, but you just don't have any good spots. Put up a nest shelf, also called a nesting platform. These L-shaped structures are nesting boxes without the box. They work surprisingly well. Phoebes love them.

The Bluebirds of Happiness

Bluebirds are members of the thrush family, closely related to robins. Three species are found in North America: the Eastern, the Western, and the Mountain Bluebirds. (You can figure out which parts of the country they're in by their names.) Bluebirds are cavity nesters. They prefer holes in older trees that border on open areas full of insects. Unfortunately, that sort of housing has been hard to find ever since suburbs began gobbling up open space and trees more than 50 years ago. Add to that competition for the remaining nesting sites and pesticide use, and it's no wonder the bluebird population, especially in the east, took a nosedive in the 1950s.

Bluebirds have been brought back from the edge by the efforts of thousands of birders. By putting up nesting boxes specially designed for these beautiful birds, you, too, can help them survive. To really help the bluebirds, however, the box has to be exactly right. Otherwise, all you're doing is giving the House Sparrows and starlings another handy place to nest.

Be a Better Birder

After the chicks hatch, watch closely as the adult birds enter the nesting box. You'll see them bringing in insects. As a parent leaves the box, you might notice something white in its bill. It's a fecal sac—waste from the baby birds. To keep predators from discovering the nest site, the parent bird drops the sac at a distance from the nest area.

What's crucial about your bluebird box is the entrance hole. For Eastern Bluebirds, it must be 1 inch wide and no wider; for Western and Mountain Bluebirds, it must be 1 $^9/_{16}$ inches wide and no wider. Anything bigger lets in the House Sparrows. The entrance hole should be six inches above the floor of the box. The baby bluebirds need to be able to climb out of the box, so look for a design that has a fledgling "ladder" built on the front panel. Some designs have a piece of wire mesh (hardware cloth) in the bottom of the box. The idea is that harmful insect larvae such as blowflies fall through the mesh and can't reach the chicks.

Put the bluebird box in an open area; an old pasture, golf course, or field is perfect. Ideally, the box should be about five to six feet off the ground, but I've had luck with boxes that were on top of four-foot fence posts.

All kinds of bluebird nesting boxes are sold. To make sure you're getting a design that provides everything the bluebirds need, look for boxes that have been approved by the North American Bluebird Society. For more information, contact:

North American Bluebird Society (NABS)
P.O. Box 74
Darlington, WI 53530
nabluebird@aol.com
www.cobleskill.edu/nabs

For more information about bluebirds, I recommend *Bluebirds Forever* by Connie Toops (Voyageur Press, 1997). This beautiful book has great color photos, solid information, and excellent nesting box plans.

Bluebirds often raise two or more broods over the nesting season from March through August. Keep an eye on your boxes. If you notice House Sparrows or starlings entering the box with nesting materials, immediately open it up and remove the nest. Tree Swallows also nest in bluebird boxes. These are very desirable birds—in fact, I talk more about how to attract them a little later—so you might not want to evict them. The decision is yours. If Tree Swallows do enter the box, place another bluebird box 10 to 20 feet away for the bluebirds.

After the first brood fledges, and again after the second, open the box and clean it out. Remove the old nest and use a stiff brush to remove any gunk; wear gloves.

Be a Better Birder

If you're interested in setting up a bluebird trail or working on an established trail, contact your local birding group or Audubon Society chapter, or contact the North American Bluebird Society for more information.

Happy Trails to You

If you've already got bluebirds on your property, all you need to do is put up a couple of boxes. However, to attract bluebirds where they've never been, or to help increase the bluebird population in your area, you might want to create a bluebird trail—a line of bluebird nesting boxes spaced about 300 to 400 feet apart. That might sound like more open space than your neighborhood has, but you'd be surprised how much good bluebird habitat is around.

You can string together a long trail with dozens of boxes along parks, power-line rights-of-way, backyards, golf courses, old fields, cemeteries, and other open space. You need permission from each landowner, of course, which is why setting up a bluebird trail can be a real project. Some bluebird trails now stretch for hundreds of miles and are maintained by organized groups of volunteers.

The Swallows of Summer

Tree Swallows and Violet-green Swallows are major insect-eating birds. They're the safest, cheapest, and most effective way to keep down the mosquitoes and other annoying bugs in your backyard. Tree Swallows, found across North America, and Violet-green Swallows, found west of the Rockies, are cavity nesters. They'll nest in bluebird boxes or in boxes you put up just for them. If you see a cup-shaped nest adorned with feathers inside the box, swallows are nesting.

Swallows like to be in a crowd, so the best way to attract them is to put up several boxes in a fairly small area. On the other hand, they tend to squabble over nest boxes, so you want to place the boxes out of sight from each other. A good way to do this is to put one box under the eaves on each side of your house. The birds actually seem to prefer nesting near people.

Martins Move In

Purple Martins are members of the swallow family. Like all swallows, they eat a lot of bugs and nest in cavities. They're very social—so much so that they nest in colonies. Purple Martin nesting boxes are really apartment houses for birds. A good martin house has 9 or more separate compartments; some models have 24 rooms and are about as big as a typical Manhattan studio apartment.

Purple Martins are really beautiful to look at. They're acrobatic in flight and they catch zillions of bugs. They're also fun to listen to; they make all sorts of delightful popping and clicking sounds, along with musical gurgles, chortles, and bubbling noises.

Being a Purple Martin landlord takes some doing. First, you need the right habitat. That means an open location that has some nearby fresh water. Ideally, you need an open area at least 50 feet square without many large trees nearby, but near your house. For some reason, Purple Martins like to nest near humans.

You'll also need to put the house (some people swear by hanging gourds instead and recent research the Purple Martin Conservation Association shows better results with gourds) up on a pole so that it's at least 10 to 15 feet off the ground. At the same time, you have to do constant battle with the House Sparrows that want to take over. That generally means some sort of pulley or telescoping pole arrangement so that you can reach the house or gourd and remove the interlopers. Martin houses should always be white to keep heat from building up inside.

Even assuming you have all the right habitat, attracting Purple Martins has an element of hit-or-miss to it. People put up houses in areas that would seem to be ideal for these birds and never attract a single one, whereas other people get a colony going almost immediately. Why? Who knows?

If you're interested in Purple Martins, you can get more information about the best houses and ways to attract the birds from:

Purple Martin Conservation Association
Edinboro University of Pennsylvania
Edinboro, PA 16444
(814) 734-4420
Fax: (814) 734-5803
pmca@edinboro.edu
www.purplemartin.org

Resident Raptors

Barn Owls, as their name suggests, like to make nests in barns. There aren't that many barns around anymore, however, so these birds could use some help. Barn Owl nesting boxes are fairly large, with entrance holes that are six inches wide. Barred and Screech-Owls will also sometimes nest in these boxes. To attract these birds, put the boxes high up in large trees, preferably trees that border open areas full of delicious mice, voles, and other small rodents.

The only other raptor that will nest in a box is the Kestrel. These fierce little hawks eat mostly grasshoppers and small rodents. They need boxes with smaller entrance holes, only about three inches wide. Place the box near an open, grassy area.

You'll often see Kestrels on wide, grassy median strips or along the grassy shoulders of highways. Some bird groups have arranged to put unobtrusive kestrel boxes on the poles supporting road signs. They've had good luck attracting the birds. Don't try this on your own; you need to have permission from whoever's in charge of the road.

Wood Ducks

The handsome male Wood Duck, with his brilliant colors and sleek head crest, is a beautiful sight. Wood Ducks are common on freshwater ponds, lakes, and rivers. They nest in tree cavities. If you haven't guessed by now, nowadays these birds have a hard time finding good homes. Wood Ducks cheerfully use nesting boxes; in fact, they seem to prefer them. Visit any wetlands preserve, and you're bound to see some placed on poles in the middle of ponds.

If you have the right habitat, you can put up a Wood Duck box. It is best not to put the pole in the pond—studies show that some ducks dump their eggs in the water in this case. It's okay to put the box about 10 feet up on a tree overlooking the water. After they hatch, the Wood Duck chicks leave the nest by jumping out. Amazingly, they make the leap and land on the ground far below without hurting themselves at all.

Rappin' Robin

A **roost** is a place where a bird goes to rest or sleep. Sometimes, the word is used to mean a **communal roost**—a place where many birds gather together. Communal roosts are sometimes very, very large. Starlings, for instance, sometimes gather in roosts that have many thousands of birds.

Roosting Sites

Birds generally use nests only to raise their young; the rest of the year, they simply perch somewhere sheltered to spend the night. When the weather is very cold, however, some birds species form *communal roosts*. They all crowd together into a tree cavity or the like and keep each other warm with their body heat. That's why you should leave your nesting boxes up over the winter. Bluebirds, nuthatches, chickadees, titmice, Downy Woodpeckers, flickers, and Carolina Wrens all use nesting boxes as winter roosting sites.

Going Batty

Birders should be open-minded about all flying creatures—including bats. These fascinating animals take over from the birds to do the night shift for insect-eating. They're attracted to much the same habitat as swallows. If you have plenty of bugs and some nearby natural water, you'll probably have bats. Like birds, bats need sheltered cavities for roosting and breeding. And like birds, they sometimes have a hard time finding good homes. You can help by putting up a bat house.

Because this is a book about birds, I don't have the space to provide the details here. For more information, contact:

Bat Conservation International
P.O. Box 162603
Austin, TX 78716
(800) 538-BATS
Fax: (512) 327-9724
batinfo@batcon.org
www.batcon.org

A bat condo with full occupancy will help keep your yard insect-free. (Photo courtesy of Nature Products.)

The Least You Need to Know

➤ Cavity-nesting birds such as wrens, chickadees, and bluebirds will use nesting boxes (birdhouses). Larger birds such as Barn Owls and Kestrels will also use nesting boxes.

➤ Choose nesting boxes that are made of solid wood, don't have perches on the front, and are the right size.

➤ House Sparrows and starlings will try to take over nesting boxes. Keep them out by using boxes with small entrance holes and by removing nests.

➤ Birds such as robins and phoebes will nest on artificial shelves or platforms.

➤ Bluebirds will nest in boxes in the right habitat. You can encourage them by making a bluebird trail with a series of boxes.

➤ In cold weather, birds such as nuthatches and Downy Woodpeckers roost together in nesting boxes to keep warm.

➤ Bats can be attracted with special bat houses.

Chapter 28

Gardening for the Birds

In This Chapter

➤ Why more plants equals more birds

➤ The right plants for your garden

➤ Plants for shelter and nesting sites

➤ Plants for hummingbirds and butterflies

➤ Bird-safe gardening

A few years ago, a Hudson Valley ice storm left some dangerous hanging branches on some trees near the house. I called in the tree surgeon to have them removed. While we walked around to see which trees needed work, he offered to cut down a tree that leaned over the pond. No, I said, the Belted Kingfisher perches there. As we headed back to the house, he offered to remove the rotted old apple tree by the side of the road. No, I said, and showed him the oblong holes made by the Pileated Woodpecker that comes by. He gave me a funny look. I knew that look; it was the same one the house painter gave me when I told him he couldn't start until the Eastern Phoebe nesting on the front porch had fledged her second brood. Then, he offered to cut down an old tree stub by the stream. No, I said, the flickers are nesting in there. He gave me that look again and struggled for words. Finally, he blurted out, "You have a very unusual approach to your property."

A Garden Spot for Birds

I don't think my approach to my property is unusual at all, although I can see how some people would think otherwise. My goal is to attract the maximum number of birds. That means I don't have a perfect lawn, trimmed hedges, barbered bushes, and

Be a Better Birder

Basically, what you want to do is provide the birds with plenty of what they need: natural food, protection from predators, nesting sites, and perching points. Birds also need water. Refer to Chapter 26, "Wet and Wild," for more on birdbaths, misters, and ways to add natural water to your landscape.

tidy flower beds. But it also means my property is environmentally friendly, easy to maintain, and fun to be in; there's plenty of room for us and the birds.

I'm fortunate that I live in a rural area where most people bush hog their fields instead of mowing their lawns, but I spent my formative gardening years in the suburbs, where things such as perfect lawns and trimmed hedges really do matter. With a little planning, it's easy to have an attractive, if a little unconventional, bird-friendly backyard without being hassled by the lawn police. And as a bonus, you'll have plenty of beautiful butterflies.

Elevated Thoughts

Remember the edge effect? (Refer to Chapter 5, "Location, Location, Location," if you don't.) That's the increase in birds you get wherever different types of vegetation—lawns and hedges, say—meet. It works because the edges provide a good mix of different foods and shelter. Provide more edges on your property, then, and you'll have more birds.

You'll also have more birds if you provide a good mix of elevations. Some birds like to be on the ground, some like to hang around in bushes, some prefer the lower branches of trees and others like to be at the top. The more levels your yard has, the more birds you'll attract.

A big expanse of open lawn and a few flower beds doesn't begin to provide the rich mixture of vegetation that's best for attracting birds. Your goal, then, is to provide edges and elevation through a good variety of plants.

Lose the Lawn

Face it: Your lawn is a real pain in the neck. You have to put a lot of time and money into keeping that perfect expanse of green grass looking so good. You have to mow it, water it, trim it, and weed it. You might even be using weed killers, pesticides, fungicides, and artificial fertilizers on it. And for what? A big, open field of the same grass variety, trimmed down to half an inch and poisoned with chemicals, is about as inviting to birds as a parking lot.

Wouldn't you just love to lose the lawn? You can—and you can still have an attractive, neat-looking yard with plenty of room for the swing set and barbecue. Here are some easy ways to cut down on the lawn and add to the edges:

➤ Let the corners of your yard grow up into a natural meadow. You can speed up the process by using a wildflower seed mix designed for your region.

➤ Replace some lawn with low-growing ground cover plants such as Bearberry, Crown Vetch, Cotoneaster, or Creeping Juniper.

➤ Plant a hedge instead of putting up a fence.

➤ Add flower beds around the rim of the lawn, in corners, and as islands.

➤ Ditto for shrubs and bushes; add them around the edge of the lawn or as clusters. Put them in as foundation plantings as well.

➤ Plant flowering and fruiting trees and shrubs.

➤ Plant evergreens and hardwoods.

➤ Add elevation by making a rock garden or building a stone wall.

➤ Plant vines that climb trees, trellises, arbors, and fences.

➤ Add water. Let a wet area grow up into a natural marsh, or add a small pond.

➤ Let dead leaves accumulate under trees and bushes. The leaves are a natural mulch, and birds love the insects and worms they find underneath them.

Get the idea? Look at your lawn and think about which areas you really use. Replace the grass in areas you don't use with other types of plants. You'll have more birds and a more attractive property with less maintenance work. Not only that, your yard will be nice to look at all year round because you'll have a variety of plants. They'll bloom at different times of the spring and summer, change color in the fall, and be interesting even in the winter. As an added benefit, you can save on home heating and cooling costs. A row of ornamental evergreens by the house, for instance, can cut your heating costs by blocking harsh winter winds; shade trees by the house reduce your summer air-conditioning bill.

A Little Bird Told Me...

The great secret to having both a less manicured property and happy neighbors is to make it *look* neat. You can make your garden seem like it's under control by adding borders and walkways along the areas you're letting grow up and by mixing cultivated and wild areas. You can also use evergreens and shrubs to screen off wild areas.

To attract more birds, you don't need to do a massive, expensive landscaping job all at once on your property. In fact, you don't even need a yard. Even a window box or some potted plants on a terrace will attract birds. Every little improvement helps. The steps I've suggested can happen over years, according to your time and budget. Once

289

you've planted a few flowering crab apples, for example, they'll reward your investment by blooming away for years.

In the Zone

The real trick to landscaping for the birds is picking the right plants—plants that not only attract birds but also will grow well in your region with the least amount of fuss. To do that, you need to know your *plant hardiness zone.* Choose trees, shrubs, and perennials that are right for your zone—in other words, plants that can survive the lowest temperatures in your region. If you live in Zone 6, and a plant is hardy to Zone 7, it should do well in your yard because your lowest temperature is still higher than what it can survive. You don't have to worry much about whether an annual flower is right for your zone because these plants die off in the winter.

Plant hardiness zone maps appear in just about every book on general gardening. You can also learn more about your local zone by checking with your local county extension agent.

Rappin' Robin

Plant hardiness zones are based on the average low temperatures in various regions of the country. The zones run from Zone 1, with average low temperatures of −50°F, up to Zone 10, with average low temperatures of 30 to 40°F.

Extending Yourself

The United States Department of Agriculture provides every gardener with a free source of excellent information: the Cooperative State Research, Education, and Extension Service, often called the County Extension Service for short. Extension agents staff more than 3,000 local offices across the country—at least one in just about every county. It's the job of extension agents to help you with all your gardening and environment questions. In my experience, they love their work. They'll help you in any way they can; our local agent even made a house call to discuss my pond. To find your local extension agent, check the blue pages of your phone book under U.S. government. Look for the Agriculture Department listing. You can also contact:

U.S. Department of Agriculture
Cooperative State Research, Education, and Extension Service
Washington, DC 20250
(202) 447-8005
webmaster@reeusda.gov
www.reeusda.gov

I've been able to get inexpensive wild flower seeds, bare-root nursery stock perennials, and even small trees through local Extension Service conservation programs.

Going Native

Logically, the best plants for attracting birds are native plants—those that are naturally found in your region. Those are the plants the birds are best adapted to find and eat. On the other hand, a lot of popular garden plants such as Autumn Olive aren't even native to North America, much less to your particular region, and they still attract plenty of birds. Still, introduced plants such as the Brazilian Pepper Tree, although attractive to birds, are also fast-growing nuisances. Kudzu, the plant that ate the South, is a good example of an exotic plant that's not only a major nuisance but also crowds out plants that are useful for wildlife. Check with your county extension agent before you plant something you'll regret.

The advantage of native plants is that they're usually very hardy; they'll do well in your garden without a lot of attention because they're in exactly the conditions they like. Native plants are generally more resistant to insects, fungi, and other pests. They also don't need much in the way of fertilizer, and they need a lot less watering—a major advantage in dry parts of the country. Save yourself some wear and tear by using native plant species wherever you can.

Plants for Birds

Okay, you're ready to start planting. Now comes the fun part: deciding what to plant. I can spend hours checking out my vast library of gardening books and leafing through the piles of plant catalogues that arrive every winter. (One of the few real perks of being a writer is getting a lot of free books from your friends in publishing.) You're looking for plants that provide food, so you want plants that provide nectar (for hummingbirds), seeds, berries, fruits, or nuts. You also want plants such as bushy evergreens and dense, thorny shrubs that will provide shelter and nesting sites.

To help you figure out the best choices, I've made some lists of bird-friendly plants. I don't have space to get too detailed, so the plants are listed by type: ground covers, annuals, perennials, shrubs, vines, and trees. Among the species, you can generally find a variety that will do well in your region. If you're not sure which variety to get, ask your county extension agent. He or she can also help you with other plant suggestions for your region.

Be a Better Birder

One person's weeds are another's wildflowers. Birds love the seeds from Goldenrod, Dandelion, Wild Chicory, Thistle, Pigweed, and other weedy plants. They adore the seeds of any kind of grass, including crabgrass. A great way to attract birds is to plant a wildflower (weed) meadow. You can get native seed and grass mixtures designed for your region from your local nursery or county extension agent.

Ground Covers for Birds

Bearberry

Bunchberry

Cotoneaster

Creeping Juniper

Partridgeberry

Strawberry

Wintergreen

Annual Plants for Birds

Ageratum

Aster

Bachelor's Button

Bush Lantana

Coreopsis

Cornflower

Cosmos

Evening Primrose

Forget-me-not

Impatiens

Indian Paintbrush

Lavender

Marigold

Petunia

Phlox

Poppy

Sage

Sunflower

Sweet Alyssum

Sweet Rocket

Valerian

Zinnia

Perennial Plants for Birds

Blazing Star

Butterfly Weed

Candytuft

Cardinal Flower

Coral Bells

Fire Pink

Lavender

Mexican Sunflower

Sweet William

Wild Columbine

Deciduous Shrubs for Birds

Arrowwood (Viburnum)

Barberry

Bayberry

Beautyberry

Blackberry

Blueberry

Buckthorn

Butterfly bush

Coralberry

Cotoneaster

Chokeberry

Dogwood

Elderberry

Firethorn (Pyracantha)

Holly

Lilac

Mahonia

Manzanita

Saltbush

Sand cherry

Serviceberry

Shadblow

Spicebush

Viburnum

Winterberry

Vines for Birds

Ampelopsis

Bittersweet

Euonymus (Winter Creeper)

Grape

Greenbrier (Smilax)

Honeysuckle (Lonicera)

Supplejack

Trumpet Creeper

Virginia Creeper (Boston Ivy)

Evergreen Shrubs for Birds

Bearberry

Buckthorn

California Holly (Toyon)

Holly

Juniper

Oregon Grape

Privet

Yew

Evergreen Trees for Birds

Arborvitae (Thuja)

Fir

Hemlock

Juniper

Pine

Red Cedar

Spruce

Wax Myrtle

White Cedar

Deciduous Trees for Birds

Ash

Alder

Aspen

Autumn olive

Beech

Birch

Cherry

Cottonwood

Crabapple

Dogwood

Hackberry

Hawthorn

Hickory

Holly

Hornbeam

Larch

Magnolia

Maple

Mountain Ash

Mulberry

Oak

Plum

Russian Olive

Sassafras

Staghorn Sumac

Sweet Gum

Tulip

Tupelo

Humming Along: Hummingbird Plants

Hummingbirds are attracted to hummingbird feeders filled with nectar, but what brings them to your yard in the first place? Flowers—especially red, orange, or yellow tubular flowers. Plants such as fuchsia, day lilies, trumpet vine, and many others have long, tubular flowers with delicious nectar deep inside at their base. The humming-bird's long, thin bill and brushy tongue are perfectly designed to reach in and lap it up. (For more on all this, refer to Chapter 20, "Hummingbirds: Tiny Terrors" and Chapter 24, "In the Good Old Summertime.")

The flowers that attract hummingbirds also happen to be easy to grow and beautiful to look at. Bee Balm, for instance, is so easy to grow it'll take over your garden if you let it. Check out the chart to see what I mean.

Flowers for Hummingbirds

Bee Balm (Monarda)	Indian Paintbrush
Bleeding Heart	Jewelweed (wild impatiens)
Butterfly bush	Orange Honeysuckle
Cardinal Flower	Penstemon
Columbine	Phlox
Coral Bells	Red-hot Poker
Cypress Vine	Sage
Day lilies	Scarlet Gilia
Fire Pink	Spider Flower
Fireweed	Trumpet Vine
Flowering Tobacco	Trumpet Honeysuckle
Fuchsia	

Float Like a Butterfly

If you like gardening for birds, why not try gardening for butterflies as well? The two go hand in hand (maybe I should say wing in wing). A lot of lovely flowers are attractive to butterflies when they're in bloom. Other insects are attracted as well, which is fine with the bug-eating birds. When the flowers go to seed, they bring in the seed-eating birds. One big difference between hummingbird plants and butterfly plants is their scent. Birds don't really use their sense of smell to find food, but butterflies do. The flowers they like best also usually smell great.

A Little Bird Told Me...

Butterflies and butterfly gardening are fascinating topics. For more information and advice, see *The Butterfly Book* by Donald and Lillian Stokes (Little, Brown, 1991), *The Butterfly Garden* by Jerry Sedenko (Villard Books, 1991), *The Butterfly Garden*, by Mathew Tekulsky (Harvard Common Press, 1986), and *Butterfly Gardening: Creating Summer Magic in Your Garden*, by the Xerces Society (Sierra Club Books, 1998). For a good general introduction to observing butterflies, see *Butterflies through Binoculars*, by Jeffrey Glassberg (Oxford University Press, 1993).

Butterflies are attracted to any sort of nectar-bearing flower. They especially like flat-topped composite flowers: flowers that are really multiple clusters of small, shallow florets. Think of wildflowers such as Queen Anne's lace, milkweed, or yarrow, and you have the right idea. The chart lists some favorite butterfly flowers.

Favorite Butterfly Flowers

Annuals	Perennials
Ageratum	Aster
Candytuft	Astilbe
Cosmos	Bee Balm (Monarda)
Heliotrope	Bellflower
Johnny-jump-up (Viola)	Blanketflower
Lantana	Butterfly Weed
Lupine	Coneflower
Mallow	Coreopsis
Marigold	Creeping Phlox
Mexican sunflower	Dame's Rocket
Nasturtium	Gazania
Sage (Salvia)	Hollyhock
Sweet Alyssum	Meadow Rue
Sweet William	Mexican Daisy
Thyme	Shasta Daisy
Verbena	Stonecrop
Zinnia	Valerian
	Wallflower
	Yarrow

Build your butterfly garden in a sunny, sheltered area away from the wind. For maximum attractiveness over the summer, plant a variety of flowers with different blossoming times.

Butterfly Feeders

Flowers are the best way to attract butterflies, but you can also draw them in with special nectar feeders. The feeders look a bit like hummingbird feeders and use a similar sort of nectar. The scent of decaying fruit attracts some butterfly species, so these feeders also have space for a few pieces of banana, peach, or other fruit.

A brush pile, water, and a sheltering tree make this backyard attractive to birds. (Photo by Connie Toops.)

Bird-Safe Gardening

When it comes to pesticides, fungicides, weed killers, and chemical fertilizers, birds are sitting ducks. Globally, more than five billion pounds of chemical pesticides are used every year—1.2 billion of them in the United States. DDT was banned in the U.S. in the early 1970s in part because it's so harmful to birds, but it's still widely used elsewhere in the world. The replacements for DDT aren't much better. Researchers believe that about 67 million birds in the U.S. are killed by pesticides every year. In 1995, pesticide use killed at least 20,000 Swainson's Hawks—about 5 percent of their total population—on their wintering grounds in Argentina.

Splat!

Using pesticides and other dangerous chemicals in your garden is bad for your garden, your birds, you, your family, and the planet. Why poison your environment when there are so many easy, natural ways to control pests and fertilize your soil? Organic gardening is inexpensive and safe.

A Little Bird Told Me...

The more birds you have in your backyard, the fewer pesky insects—and slugs, snails, and other annoying critters—you'll have. Birds love to eat bugs such as gypsy moths and mosquitoes. In fact, without birds to keep them under control, the bugs would take over. In the evergreen forests of the northeast, for instance, birds can eat up to 98 percent of the population of harmful spruce budworms.

Gimme Shelter

Trees, dense bushes, tangles of vines and shrubbery, and even tall grass all provide shelter and natural nesting sites for the birds. (Refer to Chapter 27, "Equal Opportunity Housing," for a discussion of nest boxes.) This is another good reason not to have a perfectly groomed backyard. I'm always amazed every winter when the leaves come down and I start seeing all the nests that were built over the summer in hedges, lilac bushes, ornamental evergreens, and in trees where vines twine around the trunk and branches. Broken tree branches and stubs provide anchoring points for nests.

Living trees are great for birds, especially if you don't trim off every little dead branch or cut down the vines that climb up the trunks.

Dead trees are almost as good. Cavity-nesting birds such as chickadees, flickers, wood-peckers, owls, Great Crested Flycatchers, and many others either dig out their own holes in the soft wood or take over old holes and natural cavities. In addition, dead trees are often infested with insects that attract woodpeckers and other birds. It's not true, by the way, that woodpeckers kill trees. Just the opposite—the birds are attracted to a tree that's dying from insect infestation. Once the tree is dead, a whole different set of insects moves in to be nature's cleanup crew. These bugs aren't interested in living trees, so there's no reason to cut down dead trees to keep the insects in them from infesting living trees.

As long as a dead tree isn't likely to fall over and crush your car, there's no real reason to cut it down. Vines and creepers of all sorts will eventually cover it—and that means a lot of fruit and shelter for birds and other wildlife.

Making a Difference

You've worked hard to make your backyard attractive to birds. Why not get some recognition for it? And why not have a nice certificate to show your block association if it gets on your case about your landscaping? Look into the National Wildlife Federation's Backyard Wildlife Habitat program. This program started in 1973 and has since certified more than 22,000 sites. You don't need a lot of land; even an apartment balcony can be certified. For information and advice about your backyard habitat, contact:

> National Wildlife Federation (NWF)
> 8925 Leesburg Pike
> Vienna, VA 22184
> (703) 790-4000
> **www.nwf.org**

There's also a NWF program for certifying wildlife habitats in the workplace.

Starting in 1999, the NWF will work with Wild Birds Unlimited on a new Habitat Stewards Initiative. The program will develop a nationwide volunteer network to assist in the development of Backyard Wildlife Habitats in homes, schools, community centers, and corporate sites.

Another interesting program for backyard habitat is called Backyard Conservation. It's a joint project of the National Association of Conservation Districts, the Wildlife Habitat Council, and the USDA's Natural Resources Conservation Service. For more information, contact:

> Natural Resources Conservation Service
> P.O. Box 2890
> Washington, DC 20013
> (888) LANDCARE
> **backyard@swcs.org**
> **www.nrcs.usda.gov**

The Backyard Conservation project helps people nationwide with information and advice about making property a haven for wildlife.

The Least You Need to Know

➤ By planting more trees, bushes, flowers, and other plants, you can greatly increase the number and variety of birds attracted to your property.

➤ Landscaping for the birds is easy and attractive; you can do it even if all you have is a terrace or window box.

➤ The best plants for birds are those that provide food—berries, seeds, fruits, nuts—or shelter and nesting sites.

➤ Stick to native plants in your landscaping. These plants are best adapted to your environment and will attract the most birds.

➤ Hummingbirds are attracted by nectar-bearing, tubular flowers such as Fuchsia or Bee Balm.

➤ Many of the same flowers that attract birds also attract colorful butterflies.

➤ Avoid using chemical pesticides and fertilizers. They poison the environment and kill birds.

Part 7

Beyond the Backyard

There's a big, wide world full of birds just waiting for you. North America has literally thousands of hotspots—places that are crammed with birds you might not be able to see at home. As birding becomes more popular, it's easier than ever to enjoy visiting a hotspot. Birding festivals and events abound; so do birding tours led by experienced guides. You can take a learning vacation by signing up for a birdwatching class or take a working vacation by volunteering for a bird research project.

You can't always be outdoors watching birds. When the weather is bad or it's too dark, watch them indoors—on your computer. There's an amazing amount of birding software and great stuff on the Web.

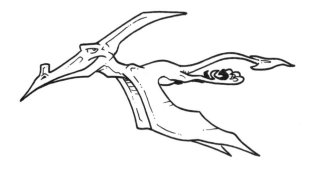

Chapter 29

Hotspots and Rare Birds

In This Chapter

➤ Hotspots: where a *lot* of birds are

➤ The best hotspots nationwide

➤ Finding rare birds

➤ Chasing rarities

Way back in 1975, a Ross's Gull turned up at Newburyport, Massachusetts—the first record of this bird south of Alaska. The news caused a sensation in the birding world. Thousands of birders flocked to the area from all over the country to catch a glimpse of the gull. The news media caught on, and stories about the gull and the birders were appearing everywhere, including a spread in *Time* magazine. The stories generally took the sort of amused, "Aren't birders crazy?" tone that seems to be usual in coverage of birding. Even so, the excitement over the Ross' Gull made many people realize how many serious birders are out there.

Where the Birds Really Are

What was really going on with the Newburyport Ross' Gull—and with all the rare and unusual birds that have been in the news since then? Two things: First, rare birds turn up at places such as Newburyport all the time; that's why they're called hotspots. Second, some serious birders are willing to drop everything and travel hundreds—even thousands—of miles to see a rare bird.

Let's deal with the hotspot end of things first. I've already talked about hotspots in a general way in the early chapters of this book, especially in Chapter 5, "Location, Location, Location," and Chapter 6, "Birding Through the Year." You already know that a hotspot is a geographic area that's particularly attractive to birds.

Hot Stuff

Most hotspots offer pretty good birding year-round and spectacular birding during particular parts of the year. Usually, the birding is best during the spring or fall migration period.

Be a Better Birder

There are many hundreds of hotspots across North America. Today, almost all of them are on some sort of public land—wildlife refuges, parks, and preserves run by federal, provincial, state, and local agencies, by nonprofit conservation organizations, and by local volunteer groups all across the continent.

Be a Better Birder

A valuable guide to finding rare birds in the U.S. is *America's 100 Most Wanted Birds,* by Steven G. Mlodinow and Michael O'Brien (Falcon Publishing, 1996). It gives detailed information on the best spots for finding rare but regularly occurring birds in the lower 48 states. For more information about hotspots around the world, check the Where Do You Want to Go Birding Today? Web site at **www.camacdonald.com/ birding/birding.htm**

What makes a good hotspot? Geographic location is one important factor. Point Pelee in Ontario, for instance, is a famous spring migration hotspot. That's because it's a finger of land that sticks out into Lake Erie, so it's the first landfall for tired birds migrating north across the lake. During the spring migration, Point Pelee is like a bird funnel. Large numbers of exhausted birds land there, rest and feed for a bit, and then spread out as they move farther north. Because the birds are concentrated into one small space, you can see a lot of different species in a short time. Because some of the species are just passing through on their way to breeding grounds far to the north, you can see birds that you would otherwise never see.

Cape May Point in New Jersey, perhaps the most famous hotspot in all North America, is another good example of how geographic location is important. The tip of Cape May is a landing point for birds flying over a big open stretch of Delaware Bay.

Habitat is the other crucial element in a good hotspot. Take Newburyport again. This is a fabulous place to see birds because it has a wide variety of habitats, including extensive mud flats, ocean beach, salt marsh, and fresh-water marsh. During migration, the area is a magnet for birds of all kinds—and the more birders out there scoping an area, the more likely it is that someone will spot an unusual bird.

A few hotspots are famous for one particular species, even though you'll also see plenty of other good birds while you're there. Loxahatchee National Wildlife Refuge in Florida, for instance, is just about the only place in the U.S. you can see the Snail Kite. The Platte River in Nebraska in March is the premier place to go to see sandhill cranes; in the winter, you can see them at Bosque del Apache National Wildlife Reserve in New Mexico.

I could rhapsodize about a lot of other hotspots, but I won't. (I can hear you breathing a sigh of relief.) Take a look at Appendix D, "Birding Hotspots," instead; that's where I give my personal list of 30 top North American hotspots.

Visiting a Hotspot

If you have a chance to visit a hotspot, by all means, take it. You're guaranteed to see good birds and interesting habitat, even if you don't add any lifers to your list. You'll get more from your visit if you can plan a little in advance. For instance, the birding is always good on the Gulf Coast of Texas, but it's a lot better in the winter when you can see the Whooping Cranes at Aransas National Wildlife Refuge and also enjoy the balmy weather.

Whenever possible, call, write, or visit the web site of a hotspot well in advance of your visit. You want up-to-the-minute information on current conditions. You also need to know about the open hours. Some sites are closed to the public one or two days a week; others are so environmentally sensitive that you need advance permission. (For more tips on getting the most from a birding trip, refer to Chapter 3, "Your First Field Trip.")

To help identify the birds you see, review the sections of this book on the different bird families, and check out the many great books devoted to bird families. (See Appendix F, "Your Basic Birding Bookshelf," for some suggestions.)

No matter which hotspot you're visiting, get the latest rare bird alert for the area before you go.

Be a Better Birder

Before you visit a hotspot, do a little homework. If the spot is famous for a particular bird family—Hawk Mountain in Pennsylvania, say—study the relevant sections of your field guide so you'll be better able to identify the birds.

Local Hotspots

You don't necessarily have to make a big trip to visit a hotspot. Local hotspots are everywhere. The birds might not be in huge concentrations, and they might not be especially rare, but they're close at hand and abundant. Local hotspots are great places to practice your birding skills and build your life list.

You might need some local knowledge or inside information to find the hotspots near you and to know the best times of year to visit them. Your local birding group will let you in on the secrets. With a little exploration of likely habitat, you might even find a hotspot of your own. You can get clues by checking the rare bird alerts in your region; some places will be mentioned over and over as hot birding areas.

Rare, Rarer, Rarest

When does a bird stop being just hard to find and start being rare? According to the U.S. Fish and Wildlife Service, a *rare bird* is one that is found "in such small numbers throughout its range that it may be endangered if its environment worsens." From a birder's perspective, that means a bird you're not very likely to see, even when you go to the appropriate habitat in the bird's range. The next step up from rare is threatened. A threatened bird is likely to become an endangered bird within the foreseeable future. The definition of an endangered bird is one "in danger of extinction throughout all or a significant proportion of its range." The definition of extinct is "gone forever."

From a practical birding standpoint, here's the breakdown of hard-to-find birds:

➤ **Uncommon:** The bird is present in its normal habitat during the proper season, but it might not be seen.

➤ **Occasional:** The bird is seen only a few times during a season.

➤ **Scarce:** The bird is seen only once every few seasons.

➤ **Rare:** The bird is usually not present and is seen only once every two to five years.

➤ **Accidental:** There's only one existing record of the bird at the site.

Even if a bird isn't uncommon to rare—in fact, even if it's common as dirt somewhere—it's a big deal if it's an accidental or just plain in the wrong place. An Anna's Hummingbird in upstate New York in the fall of 1998, to take a recent case, was the first record of that bird in the state. Birders by the hundreds made the trek to see the bird in a suburban backyard.

A Little Bird Told Me...

For information on endangered species in the U.S., contact:

U.S. Fish and Wildlife Service
Division of Endangered Species
4401 North Fairfax Drive, Room 452
Arlington VA 22203
(703) 358-2171
www.fws.gov/r9endspp/endspp.html

Rare Bird Alert!

Today, *rare bird alerts* (RBAs)—tape-recorded phone messages reporting local rarities—are so much a part of the birding scene that only old-timers remember when they didn't exist. The first RBA was begun in 1954 by the Massachusetts Audubon Society. Today, there are more than a hundred telephone RBAs in the U.S. and more than 20 in Canada. Almost all are now also available by email through one of the birding listservs. (See Chapter 33, "Virtual Birding," for more on this. For a complete list of phone numbers for North American rare bird alerts, see Appendix C, "Rare Bird Alerts.")

Actually, calling them rare bird alerts is a little misleading; I think they should really be called interesting bird alerts. Sure, the messages list rare and unusual birds, but they also often mention things such as huge rafts of sea ducks or a warbler that's not rare but is hanging around long after it should have migrated south.

A Little Bird Told Me...

If you're truly dedicated to rarities, look into NARBA, the North American Rare Bird Alert. This nonprofit subscription service, sponsored by the Houston Audubon Society, provides rare bird sighting information for the U.S. and Canada via telephone and email. For more information, contact:

North American Rare Bird Alert (NARBA)
Houston Audubon Society
440 Wilchester Boulevard
Houston, TX 77079
(713) 932-1639
Fax: (713) 461-4911
staff@narba.org
www.narba.org

All proceeds support Houston Audubon's extensive nature sanctuary program.

An interesting web site for rare birds is the Unofficial List of Current Rarities (ULCR), at **www.erols.com/gregorym/rarities.html.**

Another interesting web site for rare birds around the world is Worldwitch, at **www.geocities.com/RainForest/Vines/9684/.**

Rare bird alerts are maintained by dedicated volunteers through local birding groups. They rely on sightings reported by birders in the field. Most are updated weekly or more often if something exciting happens.

Rappin' Robin

A **rare bird alert** (RBA) is a weekly (or more frequent) list of rare and unusual birds in a particular state or local region. RBAs are tape-recorded phone messages produced by volunteers; today most RBAs are also available on email.

Of course, you'll want to check your local RBA every week for updates. If you're planning a birding trip somewhere, checking the RBA for the area lets you know what to expect.

RBA tapes sometimes assume a certain amount of local knowledge, saying things such as "The bird is in the trees on the north end of the lake" and not giving you much in the way of directions. Usually, however, the RBAs give detailed information, including driving directions where needed. Have a pen and your birding notebook handy when you call.

To report a sighting to an RBA, call the number listed on the tape. Provide as much information about the bird as you possibly can. Remember that the person on the other end is a volunteer and you're probably calling a home number. Do not call too early or late in the day.

Help! I've Seen a Rare Bird!

Let's say you're out birding on a beach somewhere, and you happen to notice an interesting bird. You think it might be something rare, but you're new to birding. Uh oh. Now what? First, do what you came to do: Watch the bird. Stay with it, observing as much as you possibly can about its appearance, field marks, and behavior. Take notes. Be sure to note the time of day, the weather, the names and phone numbers of all observers, how long you saw the bird, how far away you were, the optics you used, and most important, *exactly* where the bird was. Make sketches (no matter how crude), and take pictures if possible. Point out the bird to any other birders in the area. If you're lucky, someone experienced will be able to identify it as a common bird and you'll be off the hook.

What if it really does turn out to be a rarity? Good call—congratulations. Phone in your report, with all the details, to the local rare bird alert. If your bird is really rare or unusual for the state, report it to your state record committee. This august group of experienced birders decides, on the basis of past sightings and the evidence you provide, whether the bird is a record for the state.

Whoever runs the local rare bird alert can put you in touch with the state record committee. The names are also listed in the annual directory put out by the American Birding Association.

Cut to the Chase

Okay, you've heard about a rare bird you'd really like to see—a Kelp Gull off the coast of Maryland, to take a recent example. You cancel all your plans, get up Friday at 4 a.m., pack your spotting scope, kiss your family goodbye, and jump in the car for a five-hour drive to the spot. Somewhere along the way, you stop to call in sick to work.

You arrive, see the rare bird (not always) and see some other good birds (usually) while you're at it. You drive home and spend most of Saturday recuperating. Then, you go in to the office on Sunday to catch up on your work.

Welcome to the world of *chasing*.

A lot of serious birders are enthusiastic chasers. To them, it's a really enjoyable part of the hobby, something they get a kick out of spending a weekend doing.

It's fun to chase a new bird, especially if it means visiting a new hotspot. I've been known to do it myself, even though I'm not a big fan of chasing. Here's why: Interesting and rare as the bird may be, and as much as I'd like to fill in that blank on my life list, the bird is probably wherever it is by mistake. Maybe it's been blown off course by a storm, or maybe it's sick or just terribly mixed up. Whatever the reason, you're seeing the bird out of context, even if it's in a habitat close to its natural one. Somehow, to go all that way to see a forlorn, genetically doomed bird seems like a waste. You could have spent that time and energy volunteering at a local bird refuge instead.

On the other hand, you could be seeing a pioneer bird, one that's blazing the way for a range extension or setting a state record for the first appearance of the species. Maybe you'll never have another chance to see that species. How can you know? You can't—which is why people chase rare birds.

I've reached a compromise position. I'll chase a bird if it means no more than two hours' driving. Fortunately, as a self-employed writer I don't have to call in sick; I just have to make feeble excuses to my editor.

Rappin' Robin

Chasing means traveling, usually on short notice, for a long distance to an inconvenient place in order to see a rare or unusual bird. When you're chasing a bird, your own personal rain cloud is likely to go along.

The Least You Need to Know

➤ Hotspots—areas that are particularly attractive to birds—are the best places to see rare and unusual birds. There are thousands of hotspots nationwide.

➤ Birds that aren't especially rare still cause a lot of excitement when they turn up in the wrong place.

➤ To find out about rare and unusual birds in a particular state or region, call the rare bird alert phone message.

➤ Chasing—traveling on short notice to see a rare bird—is an aspect of the hobby many birders enjoy.

Chapter 30

Birders on Tour

In This Chapter

➤ Choosing a birding tour

➤ Getting the most from your tour

➤ Arranging your own birding trip

➤ Tips for traveling birders

➤ How to keep nonbirders happy

You've got a couple of weeks of vacation coming. What will you do? Go birding, of course. Maybe you've decided on that dream trip to Costa Rica, or maybe you'll have to be content with a trip much closer to home. No matter where you go, with some basic planning, you'll have a great time and see a ton of birds—and even manage to keep the nonbirders in your family happy.

Why Tour?

You have two basic choices when it comes to planning a birding trip: Go with a tour group or do it yourself. There's advantages and disadvantages to both approaches. For now, let's concentrate on the touring option. (I discuss the do-it-yourself side a little later in this chapter.)

Why go on a birding tour? It's the best way to be sure of seeing the most birds, especially if you're visiting some place you've never been before. It's also the most convenient way to go. Someone else organizes all the details, makes the reservations, and arranges the transportation and box lunches. Most important of all, the tour leader is familiar with the area and knows where the birds are. All you have to do is watch them.

Finally, if you're visiting someplace exotic—the Peruvian Amazon, for instance—you need the help of an experienced tour operator to have a reasonable chance of getting there and back in one piece. (Birders on their own in some countries have been kidnapped and held for ransom. This sort of experience makes a great story, but only if you live to tell it.)

You can't get to some places, such as the Antarctic or Attu, the westernmost island of the Aleutian chain off the coast of Alaska, unless you're in a tour group.

Choosing the Best Trip for You

Birding tours abound; just check the classified listings in any birding magazine. There's a tour to just about any place worth visiting. There's also a tour to fit just about any budget. The two aren't always the same, but hey, the world's not a perfect place. Within reason, you can easily find a good trip to take, even on a tight budget.

Once you figure out more or less where you want to go and about how much you can spend, here's what to look for in a birding tour:

➤ **Small groups:** You'll see the most birds in a small group of no more than about 10 or 15 people. There should be enough guides so that large groups can divide into smaller groups.

➤ **Expert guides:** Tour guides should know the area and the birds well. Your group should have at least one expert guide at all times.

➤ **Photography:** In some ways, photography and birding are two sides of the same hobby. Some birding tours are much more oriented toward photography than others. Ask before you sign up.

➤ **Skill level:** Some birding tours are designed for intensive birding; beginners might have a hard time keeping up.

➤ **Exertion level:** Let's face it: Some of us aren't up to 10 straight days of running around in rough terrain.

➤ **Comfort level:** There's usually not a lot of nightlife or gourmet restaurants in good birding spots, and the accommodations are generally less—sometimes a lot less—than four star. Are

Splat!

When you contact a tour company, ask a lot of questions; you want a trip that's good for your level of birding skills and physical ability. Look for a "relaxed" tour. This generally means a trip that offers leisurely birding over easy to moderate terrain, which gives you a chance to appreciate the natural and cultural attractions of the area and *is* suitable for a nonbirding companion.

Splat!

Nothing will ruin your birding faster than getting sick. If you're traveling to the less developed world, you might need to take medication, starting well before you go, to prevent malaria and other diseases. Check with the tour operator, your doctor, and the Federal Centers for Disease Control and Prevention (CDC) in Atlanta. Call the CDC at (404) 639-3311 or check its Web site pages on travelers' health at **www.cdc.gov/travel.htm.**

you so interested in birding that you're prepared to spend a vacation in a part of the world without cable? Think that over carefully before you write the check.

➤ **Beyond birds:** A lot of birding tours are just that: all birds, all the time. You're reading Chapter 30 of this book, so you must really like birds, but are you sure you want to spend your whole vacation that way?

Your next step is to contact all the tour companies operating in the region you want to visit. I suggest checking the classified ads in *Winging It*, the monthly newsletter of the American Birding Association (ABA), for the most comprehensive listing of available tours. Read the brochures carefully. Don't hesitate to ask for references to satisfied customers and for trip lists from previous tours.

Ecotourism and the Environment

Are you taking a nature tour? Join the crowd. According to the World Tourism Organization, *ecotourism* is the fastest-growing area of the tourism industry. That's a mixed blessing. Too many people visiting a fragile habitat destroys the very environment they come to see. When you choose a tour operator for a birding trip, be sure it's one that's aware of environmental issues. Right now, there's no industry-accepted rating of ecotourism operators, so you'll have to ask some questions before you sign up. When you contact a tour operator, ask for the company's ecotourism code of ethics. A good set of guidelines is the National Audubon Society's Travel Ethic for Environmentally Responsible Travel. (See Appendix A, "Birding Organizations," for more information about the NAS.) If the company doesn't have a code, skip the trip.

Rappin' Robin

Ecotourism is responsible travel to natural areas that conserves and respects the environment and sustains the well-being of local people.

Service Trips

Want a cheap vacation in an exotic, faraway place? There's a way, if you're willing to work for it. Try a service trip, where you help an environmental research project in exchange for cheap or even free room and board and possibly a charter airfare to the site.

You won't get to do much lounging on the beach on a service trip. The work is usually hard and sweaty, and the accommodations are far from luxurious. On the other hand, you'll get to participate in real science with working scientists and learn something in exchange for your blisters. Two nonprofit organizations offer service tours of interest to birders:

Earthwatch Institute
680 Mt. Auburn Street
P.O. Box 9104
Watertown, MA 02471
(800) 688-1822
Fax: (617) 926-8532
info@earthwatch.org
www.earthwatch.org

Earthwatch was founded in 1972. Since then, it has sponsored more than 2,000 projects in 118 countries and 36 states.

Oceanic Society Expeditions
Fort Mason Center, Building E
San Francisco, CA 94123
(800) 326-7491
Fax: (415) 474-3395
info@oceanic-society.org
www.oceanic-society.org

OSE focuses on researching and protecting aquatic habitats. The organization also offers nature expeditions to interesting sites around the world.

Doing It Yourself

Organizing your own travel is usually pretty easy, especially if you stick more or less to the beaten birding paths in North America. Planning ahead is the most important step. If you don't, you might have a hard time getting a motel or campground reservation at the more popular birding sites, especially if you want to go to one of the birding festivals these areas sponsor. (See Chapter 31, "Birding Events," for more information.)

When you're planning your trip, get as much information as possible. Fortunately, that's easy. Start by contacting the various government and business organizations for the area.

Be a Better Birder

Finding guides, the books I talked about in Chapter 3, "Your First Field Trip," are invaluable. Get the latest edition and use it. Remember, however, that things change. Be sure to check any directions against an up-to-date map. Call the site if possible before you go. Natural events such as droughts or hurricanes can damage or close trails.

Tourism Agencies

Every state and province—and country—has an agency that promotes tourism. So do most cities and many smaller regions. For example, there's a tourism office for the Jersey Cape region, which includes Cape May. (See Appendix D, "Birding Hotspots," for details.) These agencies have a lot of different names: tourism offices, chambers of

Feeder Styles

The classic tube feeder, made from heavy plastic with metal feeding ports and perches. Photo courtesy Droll Yankees, Inc.

Goldfinches adore thistle seeds. This tube-style thistle feeder has small holes to keep the tiny seeds from falling out. Photo courtesy Wild Birds Unlimited.

Traditional wooden hopper feeders, like this handsome example, have hinged roofs for easy refilling. Photo courtesy Wild Birds Unlimited.

Suet feeders made from plastic-coated wire are very sturdy. This selective suet feeder keeps away starlings and crows. Photo courtesy Heritage Farms.

This selective feeder lets small birds in but keeps large birds, squirrels, and cats out. Be sure to clean out the seed tray daily. Photo courtesy Heritage Farms.

This gazebo-style feeder lets you offer different kinds of seeds in different compartments and has a seed tray to keep hulls and spilled seed off the ground. If you go for this style, clean out the seed tray every day. Photo courtesy Aspects.

Drink Up!

The sound of dripping water is irresistible to birds. A simple dripper, as shown here, will bring the birds flocking to your birdbath. Photo courtesy Wild Birds Unlimited.

You may not get quite so many hummingbirds at one time, but nectar feeders like the HummZinger are a good way to attract these little birds. Photo courtesy Aspects.

While you're at it, why not attract butterflies? This one lets you offer two sure-fire attractants: nectar and bananas. Photo courtesy Nature Products.

Orioles love nectar and juicy fruit such as oranges. Specially designed oriole feeders offer them both. Photo courtesy Nature Products.

Birds at Home

An Eastern Bluebird stands on its new home with nesting material in its mouth. This house is part of a bluebird trail at Antietam National Battlefield in Maryland. Photo by Connie Toops.

Checking the nest boxes on a bluebird trail. Chances are there's a bluebird trail near you— ask if you can help out. Photo by Connie Toops.

Birds that nest in cavities will happily nest in boxes you provide. Here a Carolina Chickadee enters a box. Note that no perch is needed. Photo by Connie Toops.

Tree Swallows and bluebirds use the same kind of nest box. In this shot, a female Tree Swallow arrives to feed a very hungry nestling. Photo by Richard Day/Daybreak Imagery.

A few owl species will use nest boxes. Here a red-phase Eastern Screech-Owl peers out of the box. Photo by Richard Day/Daybreak Imagery.

Feeder Freeloaders

Squirrels aren't the only freeloaders from your birdfeeders. Here a white-tail deer gets a free meal. Photo by Connie Toops.

Most of us aren't likely to have coatimundis (relatives of raccoons) ransacking our feeders, but watch out if you live in the Southwest. Photo by Connie Toops.

Beautiful Birds in Beautiful Places

Visitors along the Anhinga Trail boardwalk in Everglades National Park. Although the birder on the boardwalk doesn't seem to be noticing, the bird that gives the trail its name is posing just in the center of this shot. Photo by Connie Toops.

Birding can be strenuous, but more often it's like this: An easy stroll along an easy path in a beautiful place. Photo by Connie Toops.

Sights like this—Snow Geese at unspoiled Bosque del Apache National Wildlife Refuge in New Mexico—are why birders skip theme parks and go for the real thing. Photo by Cliff Beittel.

Birding the really easy way—drive right up and unload the scopes. Photo by Connie Toops.

Beyond Basic Birding

Helping out at a banding station is a great way to learn more about birds close up. Here a White-throated Sparrow gets its leg band. Photo by Connie Toops.

If you're interested in bird photography, get ready for some major equipment purchases, like this heavy-duty tripod and really long, really expensive lens. Photo by Susan Day/Daybreak Imagery.

Competitive birding can be fun, if you have the stamina. Here a van full of birders barrels down the road on the way to the next stop. Photo by Kathy Adams/KAC Productions.

Visitors to an offshore island head toward the bird blinds. From inside, they'll be able to see the birds close up without disturbing them—and without being bombarded by whitewash. Photo by Richard Day/Daybreak Imagery.

Being in a birdathon is a team effort. Team members peer into the bushes of South Padre Island in pursuit of one more check on the list. Photo by Kathy Adams Clark/KAC Productions.

commerce, convention and visitors bureaus, and economic development offices. Check the ads in the birding and travel magazines for phone numbers. You can also call directory assistance for the state capital or nearest big town or county seat.

Tourism agencies exist for the sole purpose of getting you to visit. The helpful staff will be delighted to send you tons of great—and usually free—information, including maps, accommodation guides, campground information, and brochures about all the local attractions, natural and otherwise.

Wildlife Offices

Every state has an agency that deals with fish, game, and wildlife. The name of the agency varies a bit from state to state, but it usually includes the words conservation, game, or wildlife somewhere in the title. When you're planning a birding trip, contact the wildlife office and ask to speak to an ornithologist or nongame biologist. This person will be a font of information about the state's bird life and can provide free (or inexpensive) maps, checklists, and brochures about state and local parks, refuges, and other birding sites. He or she can probably also give you a lot of information about local birding, such as the best places to see state or regional specialties and programs of interest to visiting birders.

Local Birding Groups

Local Audubon societies and bird clubs almost always have regularly scheduled field trips to nearby birding areas. Call ahead and find out what's happening. The names and numbers are listed in the ABA's annual directory, *A Birder's Resource Guide*. In my experience, local birders are helpful about sharing hotspots and directions to the best spot to find local specialties (both birds and food).

Bear in mind that these groups are run entirely by volunteers. The phone for the group probably rings in the home of a volunteer. Don't call early in the morning or late at night. If you get an answering machine, say you'll call back or you'll accept a collect call. Try not to take up too much of the volunteer's time.

Be a Better Birder

When you contact other birders or birding groups for information, be courteous. If you're writing, enclose a stamped, self-addressed envelope for the reply. If you're calling, don't call too early or too late in the day. Keep time zone differences in mind!

Guiding Lights

To get the most from a birding trip, you might want to hire a local guide. Working with a guide is especially helpful if you only have a short time available or if you're in pursuit of a particular bird. A number of guides advertise their services in *Winging It* and the birding magazines. Some rely on word of mouth, so ask around. Call and schedule your trip as much in advance as possible.

Mommy, Can't We Go to the Mall?

As a birder, your idea of a fun vacation involves going some place remote, staying at a motel or campground, and getting up very early in the morning. The rest of your family might think that a fun vacation involves a beach resort, room service, and nightlife.

With a little compromising, you can come up with a vacation that's fun for everyone. If your family wants to visit Mickey Mouse and all his friends in Florida, for instance, you're in luck. Excellent birding awaits you at the nearby Merritt Island National Wildlife Refuge. You can combine a visit there with a visit to the Kennedy Space Center—fun, educational, and even inspiring for everyone.

A Little Bird Told Me...

A visit to New York City will let you enjoy everything about the Big Apple, including outstanding birding at half a dozen places in Manhattan, to say nothing of the other four boroughs and nearby areas. One of the best-kept secrets in birding is Inwood Hill Park at the northern tip of Manhattan. It has 140 acres of untouched natural woodland; more than 150 bird species are regularly seen there. You can get to Jamaica Bay National Wildlife Refuge in Queens, a fabulous birding spot, on the subway. Trust me on this; I'm the author of *Nature Walks in and Around New York City* (Appalachian Mountain Club, 1995).

Sadly, there are some wonderful birding destinations that don't really have anything else aside from great natural beauty. To keep the family peace, you might have to visit them on your own or spend only a day when you could happily spend a week.

Squeezing in Some Birding

Hate to travel on business? Once you get into birding, you might change how you feel. With some careful timing, you can use those business trips to squeeze in some great birding. If you schedule a three-day business trip to end on a Friday, for instance, you can stay over for an extra day or two, bird in the area, and still be back at your desk Monday morning. The beauty part is, you can actually save money. That's because a lot of round-trip airfares are cheaper if you stay over a Saturday night. It's the perfect reason to spend a day birding instead of traveling. You might even persuade your company to pick up the extra nights at the hotel because you're saving so much money on the plane ticket.

You might not be able to extend your trip, but you might still be able to manage some birding. I've seen a lot of good birds while going to conferences at posh resorts. Why not? The hotels have nicely landscaped grounds with attractive water and are often right on a beach. If you can get away even for a morning, you're often close enough to a natural area to do some serious birding.

The Least You Need to Know

➤ Going on a birding trip with a tour group is a great way to spend a vacation. There's a tour for every budget and level of birding ability.

➤ Organized tours are the easiest, safest, and often least expensive way to visit exotic areas.

➤ If you're traveling on your own, plan well in advance and make your reservations early. Some popular birding areas fill up fast.

➤ State, provincial, and local tourism offices and wildlife agencies are a good source of free information about areas you'd like to visit.

➤ Avoid family conflict by visiting areas that have both good birding and other activities.

Chapter 31

Birding Events

In This Chapter

➤ Enjoying birding festivals

➤ Being in a birdathon

➤ Big Days and other events

➤ Counting the birds

As birding has become more popular, more great festivals for birders are springing up. Usually timed around a migration period, festivals are a fabulous way to see a lot of birds, learn more about them, and meet other birders. If you have a more competitive streak, you can participate in one of the many birding events that challenge you to see as many birds as possible in a single day. Laid back or leading the charge, it doesn't matter; birding events are *fun*.

Flocks of Birders

Hang around in a parking lot at a birding hotspot, and you'll see license plates from all over the country. (Keep an eye out for birding vanity plates; you'll see some pretty good ones.) Hotspots attract birds, and birds attract birders—nowadays, *a lot* of birders. That means a lot of tourism dollars for the nearby communities as visiting birders stay in local lodgings, eat in local restaurants, and buy stuff locally. In other words, birders bring in big bucks.

Birding Festivals

To attract more birders to their region at the peak seasons, many areas around the country have started annual birding festivals. You can visit the Attwater's Prairie

Chicken festival in Texas every April and see these endangered birds on their breeding grounds. You can go to the oldest birding festival in America, the Klamath Basin Bald Eagle conference held in Oregon every February. You can attend one of the famous birding spring or autumn weekends held at Cape May, New Jersey. You can enjoy all sorts of fun birding events at the Wings Over Water festival in Manteo, South Carolina every November.

All told, well over a hundred birding festivals are held every year in the U.S. and Canada—and more are starting all the time. Birding festivals are great events. You get to see a lot of birds while promoting bird and habitat conservation in the most effective way possible: by putting your money where your binoculars are.

Generally, birding festivals take place over a weekend that coincides with a peak migration period or other spectacle. The festival organizers usually arrange for self-guided or guided field trips; sometimes, they even organize vans or buses to take you right to a hotspot. In the evenings, there are workshops, lectures, art exhibits, photography contests, and other fun activities, to say nothing of the chance to meet birders from all over the country and abroad.

You can get information about upcoming festivals by checking the articles and ads in the birding magazines. The National Fish and Wildlife Foundation publishes a free annual directory of birding festivals. Lodgings and campgrounds fill up fast; make your reservations as far in advance as possible.

Be a Better Birder

For an excellent—and free—annual directory of birding festivals, write to:

National Fish and Wildlife Foundation (NFWF)
1120 Connecticut Avenue NW, Suite 900
Washington, DC 20036
(202) 857-0166
Fax: (202) 857-0162
info@nfwf.org
www.nfwf.org

The complete directory with updated information is posted on the NFWF Web site.

International Migratory Bird Day

International Migratory Bird Day (IMBD) is the premier event of Partners in Flight, an international coalition whose mission is to restore populations of migratory birds. Founded in 1992, IMBD is sometimes called "Earth Day for birds." Early in May every year, hundreds of federal, state, and local agencies, along with organizations and businesses, hold events to raise awareness of migratory birds and the need to conserve them and the habitat they depend on. IMBD has become so popular that in 1998, more than 150 events were held to celebrate it.

The American Birding Association and Wild Birds Unlimited are major sponsors of IMBD Online!, a Web site that covers upcoming events, helps you start your own site, and links to many other organizations and agencies in the world of bird conservation. Visit the site at **www.americanbirding.org/imbdgen.htm.**

To find out more about IMBD, contact:

> International Migratory Bird Day
> U.S. Fish and Wildlife Service
> Office of Migratory Bird Management
> 11510 American Holly Drive
> Laurel, MD 20708
> (703) 358-2318
> **IMBD@mail.fws.gov**
> **www.fws.gov/r9mbmo/homepg.html**

Competitive Birding

Think birding is a nice, relaxing hobby? You've obviously never been in a *birdathon*. Talk about competition—the goal of a birdathon is to see the largest possible number of species in a given area over 24 hours.

The first organized birdathon was started in 1984 by the inimitable Pete Dunne of the New Jersey Audubon Society. He set up the World Series of Birding as a fund-raising event that has since become the premier birdathon in the country. Teams of birders from all over the country compete every May, scouring New Jersey from end to end for the most species in 24 hours. As you might expect, the logistics of being in a birdathon are awesome. Months of planning go into getting sponsorship and putting a team in the field. Despite that—or maybe because of it— a number of birdathons are held every year during the spring migration at major hotspots, including the week-long Great Texas Birding Classic in April. These events attract a lot of media attention and get free publicity for the corporate sponsors. More importantly, they raise a lot of money for habitat conservation and other bird-related activities. The 47 teams participating in the 1998 World Series of Birding raised more than $500,000 in pledges for bird conservation.

Every May, local chapters of the National Audubon Society sponsor a birdathon where local teams compete to see which can spot the most birds. Every year, more than 100,000 birders in some 300 chapters compete—and raise more than a million dollars in pledges for local projects as well as an international project to purchase rainforest land.

Rappin' Robin

A **birdathon** is a birding event where teams of birders compete to see the most bird species in a particular area over a single 24-hour period.

Big Days

A birding *Big Day* is like having your own personal birdathon. During a Big Day, you try to do what a birdathon does: See as many different bird species as possible in one

24-hour period. You may be competing against other birders, trying to set a local or state record, or just having fun with some friends. Whatever—the goal is to see the most possible birds, which takes the same sort of planning and endurance that goes into organizing an invasion of a small country. Big Days are definitely not for wimps.

To be officially accepted by the American Birding Association, a Big Day needs to follow some fairly strict rules. I won't go into the details, but here are the highlights:

➤ The Big Day must take place within a single 24-hour period.

➤ Any geographic area may be covered.

➤ Team members must stay within voice contact distance of each other.

➤ No help from outside sources (people not members of the team) is allowed.

➤ Heard birds count.

Rappin' Robin

A **Big Day** is an organized effort, usually by a team of birders, to see as many bird species as possible in a single 24-hour period.

If your Big Day qualifies, you can send your tallies to the American Birding Association and have them published in *Birding* magazine.

A Little Bird Told Me...

The idea of a Big Day goes back to the famed ornithologist Ludlow Griscom (1890–1959), who started them in the 1930s. Griscom made many contributions to ornithology, but his real contribution was in popularizing birdwatching as a sport. I mention all this in part because Griscom's Big Days took place in Dutchess County, New York—where I live now. The birding around here is still pretty good.

North American Migration Count

Held every year on the second Saturday in May, the North American Migration Count (NAMC) is a way to take a snapshot of the birds across North America at the peak of the spring migration. Volunteer birders cover their county, counting the birds and keeping track of where they see them. The results are reported to the NAMC and local bird clubs and are posted on a number of web sites.

The count is organized by local or state coordinators. To find out how to participate, contact:

North American Migration Count
P.O. Box 71
North Beach, MD 20714
(410) 257-9540
jlstasz@aol.com

Christmas Bird Counts

The annual *Christmas Bird Count (CBC)* is a birding tradition that dates back more than a century. Every year, some time between December 15 and January 3 (not necessarily on the 25th of December), local bird clubs and Audubon societies set aside a single day to take a snapshot of the birds in their area. Teams of birders are assigned to cover count circles with a 15-mile diameter (about 177 square miles). Feeder watchers count the numbers of birds visiting their yards. At the end of the day, the total numbers of species and the total numbers of individual birds are added, usually at a fairly festive gathering in someone's house or a nearby restaurant. The tallies are sent in to BirdSource, a joint project of the National Audubon Society and the Cornell Laboratory of Ornithology. You can get the results on the BirdSource Web site at **www.birdsource.cornell.edu.** The results are also available as a report put out by the National Audubon Society. To order a copy, call (800) 690-1669.

The goal of a Christmas Bird Count is to get an overall picture of the birds in the area. It's not a contest, but that doesn't keep people from trying hard to see the most number of species in their count area, to see more than they saw last year, or to see more species than the rival club in the next town.

If you'd like to participate in a Christmas Bird Count, check with your local birding club or contact:

NAS Christmas Bird Count
National Audubon Society
700 Broadway
New York, NY 10003
(212) 979-3000
glebaron@audubon.org
www.audubon.org

Not only is being in CBC a lot of fun, you're contributing in an important way to bird science. Long-term trends in bird populations are documented by data from CBCs going back to 1900.

Rappin' Robin

A **Christmas Bird Count** (CBC) is an annual winter event. Thousands of birders around the country (and in some other parts of the world) tally the birds in their count regions on a single day and send in their results to BirdSource, a joint project of the National Audubon Society and the Cornell Laboratory of Ornithology.

A Little Bird Told Me...

The first Christmas Bird Count was held in 1900. It was organized by Frank Chapman, one of the founders of the Audubon movement in America, as an alternative to hunting on Christmas Day. Twenty-seven birders took up the idea that first year; a few years later, more than 100 participated. Today, the Christmas Bird Count is the largest and longest-running wildlife survey ever undertaken; and it's all done by volunteers. Some 50,000 people participate in nearly 1,800 annual CBCs. Counts are held in every state of the U.S., every province of Canada, and in the Caribbean, Central America, South America, and some Pacific islands—anywhere that North American birds go to spend the winter.

The Big Sit

Doing a Big Sit is the most relaxed way possible to count birds. As far as I know, it's also an unofficial way; I don't think anybody except the people who do it keeps track of the numbers.

Here's how a Big Sit works: Stake out a good spot for seeing birds. (The spot should be easy to get to, shady but with good sight lines, and conveniently close to a bathroom.) Draw a circle with a 15-foot radius and put your lawn chair and picnic cooler in the center. Sit in the chair and keep track of all the birds you see and hear within your circle over a defined period—six hours, say—or until you run out of iced tea or experience some other insurmountable discomfort.

The New Haven Bird Club in Connecticut is behind a Big Sit event that happens nationwide every October. If you're interested in sitting the sit, contact:

John Himmelman
17 Hunter's Ridge Road
Killingworth, CT 06419
jhimmel@connix.com

Great Backyard Bird Count

A newcomer on the counting scene, the Great Backyard Bird Count began on February 20, 1998. This event, sponsored by BirdSource, a joint project of the National Audubon Society and the Cornell Laboratory of Ornithology, aims to take a snapshot of 100 common birds in the backyards, parks, and other areas of North America. The information is reported to BirdSource via the Internet and compiled instantly.

More than 14,000 people took part in the first Great Backyard Bird Count weekend, over 16,000 took part in the second in 1999. The results are made into distribution maps for each species. In 1998, the maps revealed some interesting information about the birds, including an irruption of crossbills in the Northeast.

Participating in the Great Backyard Bird Count is easy, even for brand new birders. For more information, visit the BirdSource Web site at **www.birdsource.cornell.edu/gbbc.**

The Least You Need to Know

➤ Dozens of great birding festivals are held at hotspots all over the country every year. More festivals are getting started all the time.

➤ International Migratory Bird Day is an annual event every May that encourages interest in migratory birds.

➤ Birdathons are competitive events where teams of birders try to see the most number of species in 24 hours.

➤ On a Big Day, you try to see as many bird species as possible within 24 hours.

➤ The Christmas Bird Count is an annual event that has taken place every winter since 1900. Participants count the species and numbers of birds in defined areas across the continent.

➤ One of the newest birding events is the Great Backyard Bird Count, which takes place every February.

Chapter 32

Volunteer Birding

In This Chapter

➤ Make a difference by volunteering

➤ Feeder watching and other fun volunteer research

➤ Atlas projects: learn about the world of birds

➤ Helping with bird banding

Every time I go birding in a preserve, a park, a refuge—whatever it's called—I think of the dedicated volunteers who made it possible. From the great American national park system to the smallest local preserves, the actions of individuals made all the difference. As the asphalting and sodding of America continue, the actions of individuals—people just like you—become even more important. It's up to you personally as a birder to do everything you can to preserve and protect your local environment so that the birds you love will still be there to watch.

Making a Difference

As a birder, you have a lot of great volunteer opportunities right in your own community. You can lead bird walks, conduct birdfeeding workshops, teach about birds to kids, Scouts, and community groups, and participate in all sorts of local birding activities, such as maintaining bluebird trails. Your local birding group might be active in helping at a local preserve; in fact, it might even own one. As a birder you have an overall interest in the outdoors and your community's environment. You can also work on other volunteer projects, such as maintaining hiking trails, greenways, and refuges.

Once you start getting involved with local birders and community projects, you'll discover other ways to be an active volunteer and make a real difference in your own neighborhood. You'll also meet a lot of really great people, have a lot of fun, and get a lot of personal satisfaction out of the work you do.

Finding Volunteer Opportunities

There are hundreds of volunteer opportunities for birders. The projects range from maintaining bird blinds and staffing the information desk at a local refuge for a few hours every few weeks to serious research projects that last for weeks or months. (I get into the details of some of the larger, ongoing projects nationwide later in this chapter.) I couldn't possibly detail all the volunteer projects at the state and local level. Fortunately, someone else does exactly that every year. The American Birding Association issues an annual directory of volunteer opportunities for birders. The comprehensive listings include an indication of how much physical effort and birding expertise each project needs. To get a copy of the directory, contact:

American Birding Association
P.O. Box 6599
Colorado Springs, CO 80934
(719) 578-9703
Fax: (719) 578-1480
member@aba.org
www.americanbirding.org

The price of the directory is $2.00.

Another way to find state and local volunteer jobs is through your state fish and wildlife office. The nongame biologist or staff ornithologist is the person to contact.

Project FeederWatch

Project FeederWatch, sponsored by the Cornell Laboratory of Ornithology, is one of the most interesting bird research projects around. Why? It relies completely on information provided by volunteer feeder watchers across North America. Anyone with a birdfeeder can participate—and each year, more than 14,000 volunteers do. You need only two skills: First, you have to be able to identify your backyard birds—which you should certainly be able to do by now if you're up to this chapter. Second, you need to be able to fill in the little circles on the reporting form with your trusty number-two pencil. Anyone who's survived the American educational system should be able to do that.

The long-term data from Project FeederWatch is incredibly valuable. It's been used to show, for instance, that more accipiter hawks such as Sharp-shins and Cooper's are spending the winter in the north rather than heading south. It's also documented the population declines of some species, such as the Painted Bunting and Field Sparrow.

A Little Bird Told Me...

Project FeederWatch began in 1987 as a winter survey of the birds that visited backyard feeders in North America. The information collected each year helps ornithologists track changes in the abundance and distribution of bird species that use feeders in the winter. Among other things, the reports are used to gather long-term data on the winter bird populations throughout North America, to detect significant population declines and expansions, and to track the movements of irruptive and nomadic species during the winter months.

Project FeederWatch is volunteer citizen science at its best. If you're interested in participating, here's how to get more information if you're in the U.S.:

PFW/Cornell Laboratory of Ornithology
159 Sapsucker Woods Road
Ithaca, NY 14850
(607) 254-2440
feederwatch@cornell.edu
www.birds.cornell.edu

A Little Bird Told Me...

Many teachers find Project FeederWatch to be a great classroom project for students at any age—even at the college level. It's an excellent introduction to birds, nature study, and the scientific method. If you're a teacher and you want more information, you can get a brochure about the Classroom FeederWatch curriculum kit by calling the Cornell Lab at (800) 843-BIRD.

If you're in Canada, contact:

> PFW/Bird Studies Canada
> P.O. Box 160
> Port Rowan, Ontario N0E 1M0
> (519) 586-3531
> **pfw@nornet.on.ca**
> **www.bsc-eoc.org**

There is a modest $15 fee for participating in Project FeederWatch. The money is used to produce the kits and an enjoyable and informative newsletter.

Cornell Nest Box Network

To study the breeding success of cavity-nesting birds such as bluebirds, Tree Swallows, and House Wrens, the Cornell Nest Box Network organizes volunteers to put up nesting boxes and keep track of the birds that use them. This is an enjoyable project that doesn't require a lot of bird knowledge and teaches you a lot about bird biology. It's an excellent student or Scout project. For more information, contact:

> The Cornell Nest Box Network
> Cornell Laboratory of Ornithology
> 159 Sapsucker Woods Road
> Ithaca, NY 14850
> Phone: (800) 843-BIRD
> **cnbn@cornell.edu**
> **www.birds.cornell.edu**

Important Bird Areas

The Important Bird Areas (IBA) project is a major, nationwide project that aims to identify and conserve key areas of bird abundance and diversity. The project is part of the Partners in Flight Bird Conservation Plan. At the state level, it's coordinated by local birding and environmental groups, often working with a PIF coordinator at the state fish and wildlife office. Nationally, it's coordinated by the National Audubon Society. For more information or to find your state coordinator, contact:

> Fred Baumgarten
> IBA National Coordinator
> National Audubon Society
> 700 Broadway
> New York, NY 10003
> (212) 979-3081
> **fbaumgarten@audubon.org**

If you live near a great birding area, now's the time to nominate it for IBA status. The site could be eligible for a wide range of conservation programs and funding.

Atlas Projects

A *bird atlas* is a set of maps showing bird distribution in a particular area—usually a state or geographic region. Atlases show the range of bird species, where they're found, where they breed (if they do), and in what numbers. They're invaluable research tools, and they're a huge amount of work to put together. Right now, volunteer atlas projects are underway in just about every state and province.

You need to be a fairly experienced birder to identify and count the birds in each map region, but even new birders can help with some aspects of a bird atlas, especially with data entry and scouting trips. Check with your local birding group, state fish and wildlife office, or Audubon Society chapter for more information.

Rappin' Robin

A **bird atlas** is a set of maps that shows how the birds are distributed in a particular area. **Atlasing** projects to record the locations of breeding birds and other information are important for research. Almost all atlasing projects rely heavily on volunteers.

Breeding Bird Survey

The Breeding Bird Survey (BBS) run by the U.S. Geological Survey (USGS) is a research project that's been going on since 1966. The survey tracks long-term population trends and distribution patterns for more than 400 North American breeding bird species. The survey is done once a year at the peak of the breeding season, which for most of North America is some time in June.

To do the survey, a volunteer follows a preplanned route of 24.5 miles along quiet back roads. Every half mile, the volunteer stops, watches and listens for birds for exactly three minutes, and records all the birds seen and heard during that time—what's called a point count survey. Then, he or she goes on to the next stop, until all 50 have been covered.

Right now, there are more than 4,100 active BBS routes across North America. Volunteers with good birding skills are always needed to cover the routes. For more information, contact:

> Breeding Bird Survey
> Patuxent Wildlife Research Center
> 12100 Beech Forest Road
> Laurel, MD 20708
> (301) 497-5843
> Fax: (301) 497-5784
> **Keith_Pardieck@nbs.gov**
> **www.mbr.nbs.gov/bbs/bbs.html**

A similar BBS program operates across Canada. For information, contact:

Connie Downes
Canadian Wildlife Service
National Wildlife Research Centre
Hull, Ontario K1A 0H3
(819) 953-1425
Fax: (819) 953-6612
downesc@msm1s6.sid.ncr.doe.ca

Breeding bird surveys and atlases are essential conservation tools. Other sorts of monitoring and counting projects are also extremely important. These sorts of projects always need volunteers:

➤ **Censuses** (also called inventories): A bird census counts the number of species and the number of birds in an area, including nonbreeding birds.

➤ **Surveys:** A bird survey locates and monitors specific bird species, especially if they're rare or threatened, in an area. For example, volunteers might conduct a survey of the birds in a particular wetlands preserve to document which species are present and which are breeding. They might survey just the raptors or warblers in an area.

➤ **Monitoring:** In a monitoring project, volunteers keep an eye on something specific, such as noting the activity at nest boxes and nesting sites or tracking the movements of migratory birds.

The information from all these counting and monitoring projects gets put to good use. It's used to make checklists, to document the effects of development and habitat loss, and perhaps most important of all, to make the case for preserving habitat.

Bird Banding

Bird banding is one of the most fascinating things you can do as a volunteer birder. You get to see the birds really close up—even hold them in your hand—and also make an important contribution to scientific knowledge.

The goal of bird banding is to capture a bird harmlessly, attach a numbered, lightweight aluminum ring to its leg, and release it. With luck, the bird will be recaptured or found dead at some later date and the band will be recovered, giving researchers some idea of where the bird has traveled in the meantime. Over the years, banding has provided important information about bird longevity and migration patterns. It's completely harmless to the bird.

Under federal law, setting up a banding station and putting the bands on the birds can only be done by a licensed bird bander. (I explain how to become one in a little bit). At any banding station, plenty of willing volunteers are needed to help with recording data about each captured bird. It's a great way to get involved with birds up close and personal, even if you're brand new to birding.

If you're interested in helping, there's probably a local banding program near you that needs some volunteers. You can look into helping at one of nearly 500 banding stations of the Monitoring Avian Productivity and Survivorship Program (MAPS). This program, coordinated by the Institute for Bird Populations (IBP) at Point Reyes, California, has been tracking long-term trends in bird populations across North America since 1989. During the breeding season, each station safely traps birds in mist nets (very fine nets that harmlessly entangle the birds) 6 hours a day for 10 days. The birds are identified and banded and have their vital statistics recorded, including sex, age, and weight. They're then released, usually minutes after they were captured.

To learn more about MAPS, contact:

Institute for Bird Populations
P.O. Box 1346
Point Reyes Station, CA 94956
(415) 663-1436
Fax: (415) 663-9482
dfroehlich@birdpop.org
ourworld.compuserve.com/
homepages/birdbanding

Rappin' Robin

Bird banding (ringing if you're British) is the placement of a numbered ring on the leg of a bird in order to keep track of its movements over time.

You can also get MAPS information from BirdSource, the joint National Audubon Society/Cornell Laboratory of Ornithology Web site, at **www.birdsource.cornell.edu.**

Most people who become licensed bird banders start by working as an apprentice with another licensed bird bander. Training courses in bird banding are offered by the IBP and by:

North American Banding Council
For more information, check their web site:
www.purc.gov/bbl/resources/nabc.htm

To get a license, you need not only banding skills, but also a specific, well-defined research project—the sort in which results would be published in a serious birding journal. Permits to do bird banding are issued by the U.S. Geological Survey Bird Banding Laboratory in Laurel, Maryland and by the Canadian Wildlife Service.

The Least You Need to Know

➤ Working as a volunteer on a birding research project is a great way to make a contribution and learn more about birds.

➤ Volunteer birding projects abound, ranging from local activities to nationwide studies. Birders at all levels can make valuable contributions.

➤ Project FeederWatch is an important long-term project for backyard birders.

➤ Atlasing projects to record breeding birds are good opportunities for volunteers.

➤ Bird banding is a valuable research tool. Volunteers are always needed to help with banding projects.

Chapter 33

Virtual Birding

> **In This Chapter**
>
> ➤ Listing software
>
> ➤ Getting the most from other birding software
>
> ➤ Birding online with chat groups
>
> ➤ The best Web sites for birders
>
> ➤ Around the world with virtual birding

When it's too dark to bird outdoors, what can you do? Bird indoors—on your computer. Virtual birding is an amazingly fast-growing area, with new stuff coming out just about every day. From listing software to interactive birding CDs, using your computer to keep track of your sightings and learn more is easier than ever. When it comes to birding online, there's a vast worldwide community of birders out there to share your information and experiences through cyberspace bulletin boards and mailing lists. And there's a fantastic amount of bird information out there waiting for you on the World Wide Web.

Computers and Listers: the Perfect Match

Birders were among the first people to see the possibilities in spreadsheet software for personal computers. The reason should be pretty obvious to you by now: You can use these programs to keep track of your birding lists.

Today, listing software is extremely sophisticated yet easy to use. The software keeps track of all your birding lists and also creates target lists for you. Let's say you're planning a birding trip somewhere and you want to know which of the birds you're likely to see in the area are already on your life list. Your listing program will tell you and create a target checklist of birds to look for. Most programs also come with checklists for countries, states, and provinces. Listing software lets you keep notes on your sightings and trips and organize them in all sorts of different ways. You can create reports, organize your life list into all sorts of sublists, and keep all your other lists as well. If you're into listing, this sort of software is endlessly fascinating.

Even if you're not a major lister, the software is convenient. Among other features, listing programs will automatically update all your lists when you add a new bird. Say you spot a life bird; the listing program will add it to your life list and also any other relevant lists, such as your state or regional list. Let's say you're planning a trip somewhere. The program can tell you what birds you're likely to see there and which ones are already on your life list.

There's one hitch to all this: The more features a particular listing program has, the more sophisticated your computer has to be to run it. To find the software that's best for you—and will run best on your computer—check with the manufacturers. Here's an alphabetical list of the most popular programs:

AviSys
Perceptive Systems
P.O. Box 3530
Silverdale, WA 98383
(800) 354-7755
support@avisys.net
www.avisys.net

BirdBase
Santa Barbara Software Systems
1400 Dover Road
Santa Barbara, CA 93103
(805) 963-4886
sbsp@aol.com
members.aol.com/sbsp/

Bird Brain
Ideaform Inc.
908 East Briggs
Fairfield, IA 52556
(800) 779-7256
dporter@fairfield.com
www.birdwatching.com

Birder's Diary
Thayer Birding Software
P.O. Box 770463
Naples, FL 34107
(800) 865-2473
webmaster@birding.com
www.birding.com

Birding for Dodos Avian Notebook
Chaos Management/Wildlife Habitat
1000 Old Marion Road NE
Cedar Rapids, IA 52403
(800) 728-4927
Fax: (800) 728-0843
info@chaosman.com
www.chaosman.com/aviannotebook

If you're already online, I strongly recommend visiting the Web sites for the software producers. You can get all the information you need and also see the program in action by looking at the demonstration pages.

Name That Bird

Remember flash cards? Well, nowadays, even elementary school students use computers instead. So do birders who want to practice their bird identification. Comprehensive multimedia CD-ROMs with fabulous bird photos, bird calls, range maps, and much more—even pop quizzes—are a great way to improve your birding skills. As with listing software, make sure your computer has the system requirements to play these interactive discs.

New birding CDs come out all the time, so take this alphabetical list as a starting point:

Birds of North America
Thayer Birding Software
P.O. Box 770463
Naples, FL 34107
(800) 865-2473
webmaster@birding.com
www.birding.com

Birdstar
LJB Expert Systems
96 Craig Drive
Kitchener, Ontario N2B 2J3
(519) 894-9308
lbond@birdstar.com
www.birdstar.com

National Audubon Society Interactive
CD-ROM Guide to North American Birds
Knopf Publishing Group
201 East 50th Street
New York, NY 10022
(800) 733-3000
Fax: (212) 572-8700
webmaster@randomhouse.com
www.randomhouse.com

Know Your Birds series
Axia Knowledge Products
600-1040 Seventh Avenue SW
Calgary, Alberta T2P 3G9
(403) 265-0812
Fax: (403) 264-2705
info@axia.com
www.axia.com

Peterson Multimedia Guides:
North American Birds
Houghton Mifflin Interactive
120 Beacon Street
Somerville, MA 02143
(800) 829-7962
Fax: (617) 503-4900
hmi@hmco.com
www.petersononline.com

YardBirds
Ramphastos
P.O. Box 310
Dover, NH 03821
(888) 221-BIRD
www.ramphastos.com

Singin' on the Web

In Chapter 11, "Birding by Ear," I talked about how birdsong tapes and CDs help you learn. Birdsongs are an integral part of the identification CD-ROMs discussed earlier; there are also interactive CD-ROMs that combine photos and sound to teach you birdsongs. Again, this is an area where new products appear all the time, so take this list as a good starting point:

AviSys Song
Perceptive Systems
P.O. Box 3530
Silverdale, WA 98383
(800) 354-7755
support@avisys.net
www.avisys.net

Bird Song Master
Micro Wizard
5277 Forest Avenue
Columbus, OH 43214
(614) 846-1077
microwizard@prodigy.net
pages.prodigy.net/microwizard/

Know Your Common Bird Songs
Axia Knowledge Products
600-1040 Seventh Avenue SW
Calgary, Alberta T2P 3G9
(403) 265-0812
Fax: (403) 264-2705
info@axia.com
www.axia.com

A Little Bird Told Me...

For an excellent selection of birding software and interactive CD–ROMs, check the sales catalog of the American Birding Association. Many nature and birding stores also carry some of these products. You can also contact the manufacturers and either buy directly from them or find a retailer near you. Birding software and CDs can be on the pricey side, but in my opinion you learn so much from them that they're worth every penny and then some.

Birding Online

The world of birding is a big, big place—but it's getting a lot smaller. That's because birders today can communicate instantly and cheaply across the country and around the world through the magic of email, newsgroups, and mailing lists (also called listservs). Instead of expensive phone calls to rare bird alerts, for example, you can sign up to have them delivered to you electronically the instant they're available. If you have a birding question, need information, have a trip report, or just want to share an observation, you can reach thousands of your fellow birders instantly.

Mailing Lists and Newsgroups

Nationally, there are two major mailing lists of interest to birders:

1. BIRDCHAT: This mailing list covers birds, birding, and birders. To subscribe, send email to **listserv@listserv.arizona.edu** with the message **subscribe BIRDCHAT**, followed by your name.

2. ORNITH-L: This mailing list contains discussions on ornithology, ecology, conservation, and other scientific topics. Some of the discussion is pretty serious, but anyone with a real interest in birds can follow along and learn something. To subscribe, send email to **listserv@uafsysb.uark.edu** with the message **subscribe ORNITH-L**, followed by your name.

The lists are based in the U.S., but they have subscribers from all over the world. This makes the list a lot of fun because it puts you in contact with the international birding community. A word of warning: These groups focus on wild birds and birdwatching. Don't sign up if your primary interest is pet birds or bird feeding.

A good newsgroup for birders is **rec.birds**, a sort of cyberspace bulletin board. How you access this will depend on your software.

Young birders can subscribe to *Teen BirdChat* by sending an email to **teenbirdinfo@nbhc.com**.

Rare Bird Alerts

Several mailing lists provide rare bird alerts from across the U.S. via email:

➤ BIRD_RBA: An alert for really rare birds across North America. To subscribe, send email to **listserv@listserv.arizona.edu** with the message **subscribe BIRD_RBA**, followed by your name.

➤ BIRDCNTR: Rare bird alert for the central U.S. and Canada. To subscribe, send email to **listserv@listserv.arizona.edu** with the message **subscribe BIRDCNTR**, followed by your name.

➤ BIRDEAST: Rare bird alert for the eastern U.S. and Canada. To subscribe, send email to **listserv@listserv.arizona.edu** with the message **subscribe BIRDEAST**, followed by your name.

➤ BIRDWEST: Rare bird alert for the western U.S. and Canada. To subscribe, send email to **listserv@listserv.arizona.edu** with the message **subscribe BIRDWEST**, followed by your name.

You can subscribe to any or all of these RBAs when you sign up for BIRDCHAT. If you're interested in European birds, sign up for EBN (EuroBirdNet), which provides European bird news and alerts. To subscribe, send an email request to **Martin.Helin@otax.hut.fi**.

Regional Mailing Lists

Keep track of what's happening in your state—or somewhere you're planning to visit—by subscribing to regional mailing lists. There are way too many local lists to list them all here, so I stick to statewide or regionwide lists:

➤ ARBIRD-L: Arkansas birds. To subscribe, send email to **listserv@uafsysb.uark.edu** with the message **subscribe arbird-l**, followed by your name.

➤ AZ-NM CHAT: Arizona and New Mexico birds. To subscribe, send email to **listserv@listserv.arizona.edu** with the message **subscribe BIRDWG05**, followed by your name.

➤ CALBIRD: California birds. To subscribe, send email to **listserv@pterodroma.kiwi.net** with the message **subscribe Calbird**, followed by your name.

➤ Carolinabirds: North and South Carolina birds. To subscribe, send email to **majordomo@acpub.duke.edu** with the message **subscribe carolinabirds**, followed by your name.

➤ COBIRDS: Colorado birds. To subscribe, send email to **listprod@lists.Colorado.edu** with the message **subscribe cobirds**, followed by your name.

➤ GABO-L: Georgia birds. To subscribe, send email to **listserv@listserv.uga.edu** with the message **subscribe GABO-L**, followed by your name.

➤ IBET: Illinois birds (stands for Illinois Birders Exchanging Thoughts). To subscribe, send email to **majordomo@lists.enteract.com** with the message **subscribe ibet**, followed by your email address.

➤ IN-BIRD: Indiana birds. To subscribe, send email to **listserve@list.audubon.org** with the message **subscribe IN-BIRD**, followed by your name.

➤ LABIRD-L: Louisiana birds. To subscribe, send email to **listserv@listserv.lsu.edu** with the message **subscribe labird-l**, followed by your name.

➤ MARVADEL: Maryland, Virginia, and Delaware birds. To subscribe, send a request to **maravdel-request@osi.ncsl.nist.gov**.

➤ MDOsprey: Maryland birds. To subscribe, send email to **majordomo@ari.net** with the message **subscribe MDOsprey**, followed by your name, city, and email address.

➤ MissBird: Mississippi birds. To subscribe, send email to **listserv@sunset.backbone.olemiss.edu** with the message **subscribe missbird**, followed by your name.

➤ Missouri Birds Listserv: Missouri birds. To subscribe, send email to **mo-birds@show-me.com**.

➤ **MnBirdNet**: Minnesota birds. To subscribe, send email to
   MnBird-request@linus.winona.msus.edu with the message **subscribe
   MnBirdNet**, followed by your name.

➤ **MOBirds**: Missouri Birds. To subscribe, send email to
   majordomo@proteus.mig.missouri.edu with the message **subscribe mobirds-l.**

➤ **NYSBirds-L**: New York birds. To subscribe, send email to **listproc@cornell.edu**
   with the message **subscribe NYSBirds-L**, followed by your name.

➤ **OBOL**: Oregon birds. (Did you guess?) To subscribe, send email to
   majordomo@-mail.orst.edu with the message **subscribe obol**, followed by your
   email address.

➤ **OKBIRDS**: Oklahoma birds. To subscribe, send email to **listserv@listserve.ou.edu**
   with the message **subscribe Okbirds**, followed by your name.

➤ **ONTBIRDS**: Ontario birds. To subscribe, send email to **majordomo@hwcn.org**
   with the message **subscribe ontbirds**, followed on the next line by the word end.

➤ **PABirds**: Pennsylvania birds. To subscribe, send email to **listproc@ship.edu** with
   the message **subscribe pabirds**, followed by your name.

➤ **SIBA**: Southwest Idaho birds. To subscribe, go to **www.eGroups.com/list/siba.**

➤ **TEXBIRDS**: Texas birds. To subscribe, send email to **majordomo@igc.apc.org**
   with the message **subscribe AUDUBON-TEXAS-BIRDS**, followed by your name.

➤ **TWEETERS**: Washington state birds. (Bet you'd never have guessed this one!) To
   subscribe, send email to **listproc@lists.u.washington.edu** with the message
   subscribe tweeters, followed by your name.

➤ **Utah Birding Listserve**: Utah birds. To subscribe, sent email to
   birdnet-listrequest@utahbirders.org.

➤ **Virginia Valley Bird Network:** Virginia, Tennessee, northern Georgia, and
   northern Alabama birds. To subscribe, send email to **jwcoffey@tricon.net** with a
   brief message describing yourself.

Bird Subjects

As with local mailing lists, lists abound on specific bird subjects, some pretty specialized or highly scientific. Don't sign up unless you're serious. Here are just a few:

➤ **BIRDHAWK**: Raptors. To subscribe, send email to **birdhawk@listserv.arizona.edu.**

➤ **BLUEBIRD**: Bluebirds and other cavity nesters. To subscribe, send email to
   listproc@cornell.edu with the message **subscribe bluebird-l**, followed by your
   name.

➤ **HMANA**: Mailing list for the North American Hawk Migration Association. To
   subscribe, send email to **majordomo@virginia.edu** with the message **subscribe
   HMANA**, followed by your name.

➤ **HUMMER:** Hummingbirds. To subscribe, send email to **mailthing@chattanooga.net** with the message subscribe hummer, followed by your name.

➤ **HUMNET-L:** Hummingbirds. To subscribe, send email to **listserv@listserv.lsu.edu** with the message **subscribe humnet-l**, followed by your name.

➤ **SEABIRD-L:** Seabirds. To subscribe, send email to **listserver@uct.ac.za** with the message **subscribe SEABIRD**, followed by your name.

➤ **NW-Pelagics:** Pelagic birding from California to British Columbia. To subscribe, send email to **majordomo@teleport.com** with the message **subscribe nw_pelagics-L**, followed by your name.

➤ **PELAGICS:** Pelagic birds. To subscribe, send email to **pelagics-subscribe@egroups.com**.

Birding on the Web

Today, there are so many cool Web sites for birding that I couldn't possibly list them all. (I'd like to; surfing the Web for interesting bird sites is absolutely the best way I know to pretend I'm working.) Besides, if I did, you wouldn't have the fun of discovering them for yourself.

Because the World Wide Web has become such an integral part of birding, and because birders as a group seem to be more wired than most, I've listed site addresses throughout this book wherever I've given a mailing address or wherever a particular site was relevant. What I do here is list my personal top 20 general birding sites. You can use these sites as jumping-off points for your own explorations:

Backyard Birding
www.bcpl.lib.md.us/~tross/by/backyard.html

Birding in Canada
www.interlog.com/~gallantg/canada/

Birding on the Web
www.birder.com/

Birding on the Web, the Next Generation
www-stat.wharton.upenn.edu/~siler/birding.html

BirdNet
www.nmnh.si.edu/BIRDNET

BirdSource
birdsource.cornell.edu

Birdwatch America
www.birdwatchamerica.com

Birdwatching.com
www.birdwatching.com

Electronic Resources on Ornithology
www.chebucto.ns.ca/Environment/NHR/bird.html

GORP—Bird Watching
www.gorp.com/gorp/activity/birding.htm

Mining Company Birding Home Page
birding.miningco.com

National Audubon Society
www.audubon.org

Noel's Very Birdy Web Site
www.users.nac.net/nwamer/index.htm

The Ornithological Web Library (OWL)
www.aves.net/the-owl

The Ornithology Website
mgfx.com/bird

Partners In Flight
www.PartnersInFlight.org

Patuxent Wildlife Research Center
www.pucr.usqs.gov

Peterson Online
www.pwrc.usgs.gov

Smithsonian Migratory Bird Center
web2.si.edu/smbc/smbchome.htm

The Virtual Birder
www.virtualbirder.com

Did you find that some of these sites didn't exist when you went to visit them? Did you find some really cool sites that I didn't mention? I'm not surprised; the Web changes a lot faster than a book can be printed.

The Least You Need to Know

➤ Computers have become extremely important for today's birders.

➤ Listing software keeps track of your life and other lists; it also lets you create target lists and use your listing data in creative new ways.

➤ You can learn more about birds and bird songs—and have a lot of fun—by using interactive software.

➤ Electronic mailing lists and forums use email to send rare bird alerts and exchange information among fellow birders.

➤ Many cool sites on the World Wide Web provide great information about birds.

Learning More

What, you're not tired of reading about birds yet? You want to learn even more? You're in luck. Birders tend to be an educated group with an insatiable desire to learn more. You can take a birding vacation and a course at the same time—or you can study at home. You can read all about birding in fabulous magazines with gorgeous pictures, borrow and buy books from specialized libraries and bookstores, and watch birds on video. You can see bird exhibits at museums and see living birds at aviaries and zoos. Why? Because in birding, an educated watcher sees the most birds.

Classy Birding

If you want to learn more about birds and birding, you have a lot of interesting options. Start by checking with your local adult education programs and nearby colleges. You might be able to take college-level ornithology as a non-credit student. Also, check with local natural history museums; they often offer courses about birds and other interesting subjects. Don't forget that your local Audubon society may well offer a short course in introductory birdwatching.

Participating in a bird-study program is a great way to spend a long weekend or a vacation, although it might take some fast talking to get the nonbirders in your family to agree. Many environmental organizations sponsor interesting seminars. The New Jersey Audubon Society, for instance, offers its famous Cape May weekends in the spring and fall. Hundreds of birders from around the country and even around the world come to enjoy the fabulous birding and interesting programs.

Be a Better Birder

I strongly recommend a bird-study weekend to you as a beginner; you'll be amazed at how much fun you can have and how much you can learn in two days.

Adults over 55 years of age (and their companions) can participate in the many interesting birding courses offered by Elderhostel. This nonprofit organization offers low-cost learning adventures around the country and around the world. I'm a ways off from being old enough to do an Elderhostel, but I have it on good authority (my mother—would she lie?) that they're great programs. To find out more, contact:

> Elderhostel
> 75 Federal Street
> Boston, MA 02110
> (800) 895-0727
> **www.elderhostel.org**

Dr. Eldon Greij, Founding Editor of *Birder's World* magazine, offers a three-day course on birds and birdwatching called An Appreciation of Birds. Participants learn basic birding skills and get an introduction to ornithology through field and classroom sessions. The only requirement is an interest in birds. For more information on dates and locations, contact:

> Dr. Eldon Greij
> 240 South River Avenue
> Holland, MI 49423
> (888) 973-2473

Several other well-known bird centers offer a variety of courses for birders at all levels. Some of the longer courses are ideal for teachers on their summer break. For more information, contact:

> Field Biology Training Program
> Manomet Center for Conservation Sciences
> P.O. Box 1770
> Manomet, MA 02345
> (508) 224-6521
> Fax: (508) 224-9220
> **www.manomet.org**

> Institute for Field Ornithology
> University of Maine at Machias
> Nine O'Brien Avenue
> Machias, ME 04654
> (207) 255-1289

Fax: (207) 255-1390
ifo@acad.umm.maine.edu
www.umm.maine.edu/ifo

Pocono Environmental Education Center
R.D. 2, Box 1010
Dingmans Ferry, PA 18328
(717) 828-2319
Fax: (717) 828-9695
peec@ptd.net
www.peec.org

The Cornell Home Study Course

Courses in ornithology aren't that easy to find, especially if you don't live near a college. For years now, birders have had an excellent home-study alternative from the Cornell Laboratory of Ornithology. For more information, contact:

Cornell Laboratory of Ornithology
Home Study Course in Bird Biology
159 Sapsucker Woods Road
Ithaca, NY 14850
(607) 254-2452
Fax: (607) 254-2415
hstudy@cornell.edu
birds.cornell.edu

The Cornell home-study course has recently been revised and updated. It's better than ever.

Sweet Bird of Youth

I've been talking about programs for adult birders, but what about kids and teenagers? For the younger kids, check out the many excellent environmental programs offered at your local nature centers on weekends and in the summer. Teenage birders can participate in some outstanding summer camps that introduce them to serious scientific birding:

On the Wing Summer Camp
Colorado Bird Observatory
13401 Picadilly Road
Brighton, CO 80601
(303) 659-4348
Fax: (303) 659-5489
cboeducate@aol.com
members.aol.com/CBOEducate/camp.html

VENT/ABA Birding Camps
Victor Emanuel Nature Tours
P.O. Box 33008
Austin, TX 78764
(800) 328-VENT
Fax: (512) 328-2919
ventbird@aol.com
www.ventbird.com

Teens can also go to Camp Machias at the Institute for Field Ornithology in Maine.

The American Birding Association has been active in promoting youth birding. Among other things, the ABA offers scholarships to deserving young birders to attend the summer camps.

Read All About It

To keep up on the birding news and learn more about birds, you'll want to subscribe to at least one of the popular birding magazines. The articles are well-written, informative, and easy to follow—and the photographs are beautiful:

Birder's Journal
Eight Midtown Drive, Suite 289
Oshawa, Ontario L1J 8L2
(905) 668-1449
Fax: (905) 668-1626
holder@netcom.ca

Birder's World
Box 1612
Waukesha, WI 53187
(800) 446-5489
Fax: (414) 796-1615
customerservice@kalmbach.com
www.birdersworld.com

Birding
American Birding Association
P.O. Box 6599
Colorado Springs, CO 80904
(800) 850-2473
Fax: (719) 578-1480
member@aba.org
www.americanbirding.org
Note: Subscription is part of an ABA annual membership.

Bird Watcher's Digest
P.O. Box 110
Marietta, OH 45750
(800) 879-2473
ReadBWD@aol.com
www.petersonsonline.com

Field Notes
P.O. Box 6599
Colorado Springs, CO 80904
(800) 850-2473
Fax: (719) 578-1480
member@cba.org
www.americabirding.org

The Living Bird
Cornell Laboratory of Ornithology
159 Sapsucker Woods Road
Ithaca, NY 14850
(607) 254-BIRD
Note: Subscription is part of annual membership.

WildBird
P.O. Box 6050
Mission Viejo, CA 92690
(949) 855-8822
wildbird@fancypubs.com
www.petchannel.com

For breaking news, bird-finding information, and a lot of interesting tidbits, I suggest reading *Winging It,* the lively monthly newsletter of the American Birding Association, and *The BWD Skimmer,* an informative monthly newsletter from *Bird Watcher's Digest.*

Serious scientific articles and research studies appear in ornithological journals such as *The Auk,* a quarterly published by the American Ornithologists' Union or *Wilson Bulletin,* published by the Wilson Ornithological Society. The average birder can generally follow these articles, even when the finer points are technical or mathematical, but I don't have space to list all the journals here. Unless you're really interested, you wouldn't want to

Be a Better Birder

Don't know what to give a birding friend? How about a subscription to a magazine? To get a gift subscription for yourself, work on your family. As your birthday nears, leave your favorite birding magazine on the kitchen table, folded open to the bound-in subscription card. This works for books, too. Leave the catalog on the table, with the book you want circled in red.

subscribe to them, mostly because they're pretty pricey. Many large public libraries carry the journals or can arrange for you to get them through interlibrary loans; I discuss that later in this chapter.

Books for Birders

When you start birding, you'll have a handful of useful books: this one, a field guide or two, and some basic reference books such as *The Birder's Handbook*. (Check Chapter 2, "Getting Started," and Appendix F, "Your Basic Birding Bookshelf," for more suggestions.) As you get into the hobby, your bookshelves will get crammed with all sorts of birding books, such as finding guides, specialized field guides, books of birding essays, and reference works on bird families. You'll also find yourself accumulating books on many other aspects of natural history, such as butterflies, wildflowers, fungi, and the environment in general.

Your average bookstore—even your average superstore—doesn't carry all the titles you want. You need a specialty bookstore that carries a broad selection of current titles and also out-of-print and even rare birding books.

Throughout this book, I've often mentioned the American Birding Association as an excellent source for current birding books and multimedia tools. To get the ABA sales catalog, contact:

ABA Sales
P.O. Box 6599
Colorado Springs, CO 80934
(800) 634-7736
Fax: (800) 590-2473
abasales@abasales.com
www.americanbirding.org/abasales/salescatal.htm

Specialty nature and birding stores such as Wild Birds Unlimited, Wild Bird Marketplace, and Wild Bird Centers generally carry a good selection of current books and magazines.

Several independent booksellers offer a wide range of birding books—new and used—through the mail. Here's a list of well-known sources:

Buteo Books
Route 1, Box 242
Shipman, VA 22971
(804) 263-8671
Fax: (804) 263-4842
allen@buteobooks.com
www.buteobooks.com

Patricia Ledlie Bookseller, Inc.
One Bean Road
Buckfield, ME 04220
(800) 791-1028
Fax: (207) 336-2778
ledlie@ledlie.com
www.ledlie.com

Marcher's Books
6204 North Vermont
Oklahoma City, OK 73112
(405) 946-6270

Russ's Natural History Books
Box 741071
Orange City, FL 32774
(305) 293-9818
Fax: (305) 293-9818

Snowy Egret Books
1237 Carroll Avenue
St. Paul, MN 55104
(800) 349-4707
snowy@mr.net

Raymond M. Sutton, Jr.
430 Main Street
Williamsburg, KY 40769
(606) 549-3464

As a writer, I always check the bookshop at whatever nature center I happen to visit. Some bookshops are better than others, and some are very good (not just because they happen to carry my books). Check them out; if you're visiting from out of town, these stores are usually a good place to get books about local birds and birding spots.

Libraries for Birders

Your local public library is a convenient source for general books about natural history and will probably have at least a few of the standard bird reference works. If you live in or near a big city, the main branch of the public library will probably have a better collection, including some of the serious ornithological journals. If your local library doesn't have the books or journals you want, you can often arrange to get them through your state interlibrary loan system. Your librarian will be delighted to help you.

There are also other sources. A lot of birding clubs have libraries of donated and purchased books; as a member, you have access. Natural history museums usually have libraries that are open to museum members. You can also sometimes arrange to use the library at a college or university.

One of the best fringe benefits of joining the Wilson Ornithological Society is the right to borrow books and journals from the Van Tyne Library at the University of Michigan—the best ornithological library in the country—for the cost of the return postage. The WOS welcomes all birders—about half the membership are amateurs. For more information, contact:

> Wilson Ornithological Society
> Museum of Zoology
> University of Michigan
> Ann Arbor, MI 48109
> (734) 764-0457
> **www.ummx.lsa.umich.edu/birds/wos.html**

A Little Bird Told Me...

What if your problem isn't finding birding books but getting rid of your surplus? Your local library can come to the rescue again. The librarians will be delighted to accept any reasonably current titles and back issues of magazines you want to donate. You can also donate birding books to the Birder's Exchange program, which will send them to naturalists in Central and South America. (Check Chapter 10, "Optics: Binoculars and Spotting Scopes," for more information.)

Get Stuffed

You can't count a dead bird on your life list, but they're still worth seeing. And where can you see a lot of dead birds? At a natural history museum. Actually, there are two ways to see dead birds at a museum. One is in the exhibit area, where you can see informative displays and get close-up views of the birds. The other is behind the scenes. Any natural history museum will have extensive collections of specimen birds filling drawer after drawer in the back rooms. These study specimens are a little depressing to examine, but they're very valuable. Ornithologists measure them, compare them, and study them to learn more about the species. In some cases, you might be able to see the specimens, especially if you've got a serious research question.

It's All Happening at the Zoo

The birds in zoos and *aviaries* are alive, but you still can't count them on your life list because they're not free. Go see them anyway. Realistically speaking, how likely are you to ever see a penguin or an emu in its natural habitat? Seeing one in a zoo is the closest most of us will ever get. If you are planning a trip to the South Atlantic, you wouldn't want to misidentify the penguins you see. Studying them in the zoo is good preparation for your trip.

Today's zoos usually have open aviaries for the birds, where they live in a natural environment, not in cages. That makes zoos excellent places to practice your ID skills; bring your binocs. In the open environment, you also get to see a lot of natural behavior. I'll never forget seeing a mother hummingbird feeding her nestlings at the hummingbird aviary at the Sonora Desert Museum near Tucson. That's something I've never seen in the wild—and probably never will.

I've been to a lot of zoos across North America. They all have good bird exhibits. However, some rate four stars, meaning they're worth a special trip. The stand-out in my experience is the San Diego Zoo, with nearly 500 species. It's followed closely by the New York Zoological Park (better known as the Bronx Zoo), with more than 300 species. The National Aviary in Pittsburgh has more than 200 species, as does Busch Gardens in Tampa. I also like the National Zoo in Washington, D.C., but that's as much for the pandas as the birds.

Rappin' Robin

An **aviary** is an enclosure for captive birds that's large enough to let them fly freely and behave naturally.

The Least You Need to Know

➤ Courses in basic and advanced birding are a good way to improve your skills.

➤ Birding courses are offered by many organizations, including local birding clubs, environmental associations, natural history museums, and others. Teenage birders can attend summer birding camps.

➤ Keep up with the birding news by subscribing to one or more of the many good magazines for birders.

➤ Books about birding are available from a number of specialty bookstores. Your local library can help you get some books and journals through interlibrary loan.

➤ You can learn a lot by "birding" at museums and zoos.

Birding Organizations

Birders are a well-organized bunch at every level. In fact, they're so well-organized that I only have room to list national organizations. There are hundreds of regional, state, and local organizations, as well as many organizations for people with a particular birding interest, such as hawks or hummingbirds. I've mentioned some special interest groups throughout this book. For up-to-date information on state and local birding groups, look in *A Birder's Resource Guide,* published annually by the American Birding Association.

American Birding Association
Box 6599
Colorado Springs, CO 80934
(800) 850-2473
Fax: (719) 578-1480
member@aba.org
www.americanbirding.org

American Ornithologists' Union
c/o Division of Birds, MRC 116
National Museum of Natural History
Washington, DC 20560
aou@nmnh.si.edu

Association of Field Ornithologists
c/o Allen Press
P.O. Box 1897
Lawrence, KS 66044

Audubon Naturalist Society
8940 Jones Mill Road
Chevy Chase, MD 20815
(301) 652-9188
learn@AudubonNaturalist.org
www.AudubonNaturalist.org

Cornell Laboratory of Ornithology
159 Sapsucker Woods Road
Ithaca, NY 14850
(607) 254-BIRD
member@cornell.edu
birds.cornell.edu

Massachusetts Audubon Society, Inc.
208 South Great Road
Lincoln, MA 01773
(800) AUDUBON
Fax: (781) 259-7928
kquirk@massaudubon.org
www.massaudubon.org

National Audubon Society
700 Broadway
New York, NY 10003
(212) 979-3000
www.audubon.org

National Bird-Feeding Society
P.O. Box 23
Northbrook, IL 60065
(847) 272-0135
Fax: (847) 498-4092
feedbirds@aol.com
www.birdfeeding.org

National Wildlife Federation
8925 Leesburg Pike
Vienna, VA 22184
(703) 790-4434
Fax: (703) 790-4468
wildlife@nwf.org
www.nwf.org

New Jersey Audubon Society
Nine Hardscrabble Road
P.O. Box 126
Bernardsville, NJ 07924
(908) 204-8998
www.nj.com/audubon

North American Butterfly Association
39 Highland Avenue
Chappaqua, NY 10514
www.naba.org

Western Field Ornithologists
6011 Saddletree Lane
Yorba Linda, CA 92886
(714) 779-2201
Fax: (714) 779-2202
ouzelm@aol.com
www.wfo-cbrc.org

Wilson Ornithological Society
Museum of Zoology
University of Michigan
Ann Arbor, MI 48109
(734) 764-0457
www.ummz.lsa.umich.edu/birds/wos.html

American Birding Association Code of Ethics

PRINCIPLES OF BIRDING ETHICS

Everyone who enjoys birds and birding must always respect wildlife, its environment, and the rights of others. In any conflict of interest between birds and birders, the welfare of the birds and their environment comes first.

CODE OF BIRDING ETHICS

1. Promote the welfare of birds and their environment.

1(a) Support the protection of important bird habitat.

1(b) To avoid stressing birds or exposing them to danger, exercise restraint and caution during observation, photography, sound recording, or filming. Limit the use of recordings and other methods of attracting birds, and never use such methods in heavily birded areas, or for attracting any species that is Threatened, Endangered, or of Special Concern, or is rare in your local area.

Keep well back from nests and nesting colonies, roosts, display areas, and important feeding sites. In such sensitive areas, if there is a need for extended observation, photography, filming, or recording, try to use a blind or hide, and take advantage of natural cover.

Use artificial light sparingly for filming or photography, especially for close-ups.

1(c) Before advertising the presence of a rare bird, evaluate the potential for disturbance to the bird, its surroundings, and other people in the area, and proceed only if access can be controlled, disturbance minimized, and permission has been obtained from private land-owners. The sites of rare nesting birds should be divulged only to the proper conservation authorities.

1(d) Stay on roads, trails, and paths where they exist; otherwise keep habitat disturbance to a minimum.

2. Respect the law, and the rights of others.

2(a) Do not enter private property without the owner's explicit permission.

2(b) Follow all laws, rules, and regulations governing use of roads and public areas, both at home and abroad.

2(c) Practice common courtesy in contacts with other people. Your exemplary behavior will generate goodwill with birders and non-birders alike.

3. Ensure that feeders, nest structures, and other artificial bird environments are safe.

3(a) Keep dispensers, water, and food clean, and free of decay or disease. It is important to feed birds continually during harsh weather.

3(b) Maintain and clean nest structures regularly.

3(c) If you are attracting birds to an area, ensure the birds are not exposed to predation from cats and other domestic animals, or dangers posed by artificial hazards.

4. Group birding, whether organized or impromptu, requires special care.

Each individual in the group, in addition to the obligations spelled out in Items #1 and #2, has responsibilities as a Group Member.

4(a) Respect the interests, rights, and skills of fellow birders, as well as people participating in other legitimate outdoor activities. Freely share your knowledge and experience, except where Code 1(c) applies. Be especially helpful to beginning birders.

4(b) If you witness unethical birding behavior, assess the situation, and intervene if you think it prudent. When interceding, inform the person(s) of the inappropriate action, and attempt, within reason, to have it stopped. If the behavior continues, document it, and notify appropriate individuals or organizations.

Group Leader responsibilities [amateur and professional trips and tours].

4(c) Be an exemplary ethical role model for the group. Teach through word and example.

4(d) Keep groups to a size that limits impact on the environment, and does not interfere with others using the same area.

4(e) Ensure everyone in the group knows of and practices this code.

4(f) Learn and inform the group of any special circumstances applicable to the areas being visited (e.g. no tape recorders allowed).

4(g) Acknowledge that professional tour companies bear a special responsibility to place the welfare of birds and the benefits of public knowledge ahead of the company's commercial interests. Ideally, leaders should keep track of tour sightings, document unusual occurrences, and submit records to appropriate organizations.

PLEASE FOLLOW THIS CODE AND DISTRIBUTE AND TEACH IT TO OTHERS

Rare Bird Alerts

Rare bird alerts (RBAs) are tape-recorded messages listing rare and unusual sightings for a particular state or region. Most RBAs are also available online through one of the birding listservs. RBAs are usually maintained by volunteers working with state and local birding groups. Please respect any restrictions on when to call.

This listing is up-to-date as of January 1999. The phone numbers and email addresses sometimes change, and new RBAs are sometimes added. Changes are published monthly in *Winging It*, the newsletter of the American Birding Association, and are listed on the Web site at **www.americanbirding.org**.

United States

Alabama
Statewide (205) 987-2730

Alaska
Statewide (907) 338-2473
Fairbanks (907) 451-9213
Kachemak Bay (907) 235-7337
Seward (907) 224-2325

Arizona
Phoenix (602) 832-8745; **www.amug.org/~drowley/mas**
Tucson (520) 798-1005
To report: (520) 696-4461; **AZBirding@aol.com**

Arkansas
Statewide (501) 753-5853

California
Arcata (707) 822-5666
Los Angeles (213) 874-1318; **www.netcom.com/~laas**
Monterey (408) 375-9122; updates (408) 375-2577

Morro Bay (805) 528-7182; **tedell@aol.com**
Northern region (415) 681-7422
Orange County (949) 487-6869
Sacramento (916) 481-0118
Southeastern region (909) 793-5599; **johnfgreen@aol.com**
San Diego (619) 479-3400
San Joaquin/South Sierra (209) 271-9420
Santa Barbara (805) 964-8240
Southern region (818) 952-5502

Colorado
Statewide (303) 424-2144

Connecticut
Statewide (203) 254-3665

Delaware
Statewide (302) 658-2747

District of Columbia
Districtwide (301) 652-1088; **voice@capaccess.org**

Florida
Statewide (561) 340-0079; **www.audubon.org/chapter/fl/tas/flarba.html**
Miami (305) 667-7337
Lower Keys (305) 294-3438
Northern region (912) 244-9190
Northwest region (850) 934-6974

Georgia
Statewide (770) 493-8862; **www.hitt.com/~jhitt/audubon.html**
Southern region (912) 244-9190

Idaho
Northern region (208) 882-6195; **dumroese@uidaho.edu**
Southeast region (208) 236-3337
Southwest region (208) 368-6096

Illinois
Central region (217) 785-1083

Chicago (847) 265-2118
Dupage (708) 406-8111;
ourworld.compuserve.com/homepages/jimfrazier/dupage.htm
Northwestern region (815) 965-3095

Indiana
Statewide (317) 259-0911; **www.indianaaudubon.org**

Iowa
Statewide (319) 338-9881; **storm.simpson.edu/~birding**

Kansas
Statewide (316) 229-2777
Kansas City (913) 342-2473
Wichita (316) 681-2266

Kentucky
Statewide (502) 894-9538; **www.biology.eku.edu/kos/rarebird.htm**

Louisiana
Baton Rouge (225) 768-9874
Southeastern region (504) 834-2473
Southwestern region (318) 988-9898

Maine
Statewide (207) 781-2332; **www.maineaudubon.org**
Reporting: **birdalert@maineaudubon.org**

Maryland
Statewide (301) 652-1088; **voice@capaccess.org**
Baltimore (410) 467-0653

Massachusetts
Boston (781) 259-8805
Cape Cod (508) 349-9464; **www.capecodconnection.com**
Nantucket Island (508) 228-8818
Western region (413) 253-2218

Michigan
Statewide (616) 471-4919
Detroit (248) 477-1360
Sault Ste. Marie (705) 256-2790

Minnesota
Statewide (612) 780-8890
Duluth (218) 525-5952

Mississippi
Mississippi coast (228) 435-RBA7

Missouri
Statewide (573) 445-9115
Kansas City (913) 342-2473
St. Louis (314) 935-8432

Montana
Statewide (406) 721-9799
Big Fork (406) 756-5595

Nebraska
Statewide (402) 292-5325; **storm.simpson.edu/~birding**

361

Nevada
Northwestern region (702) 324-2473
Southern region (702) 390-8463

New Hampshire
Statewide (603) 224-9900

New Jersey
Statewide (908) 766-2661; **www.nj.com/life/audubon**
Cape May (609) 861-0466

New Mexico
Statewide (505) 323-9323

New York
Albany (518) 439-8080
Buffalo (716) 896-1271
Ithaca (607) 254-2429
Lower Hudson Valley (914) 666-6614; **www.cyburban.com/~anneswaim**
New York City (212) 979-3070
Rochester (716) 425-4630
Syracuse (315) 668-8000

North Carolina
Statewide (704) 332-2473

North Dakota
Statewide (701) 250-4481; 5 p.m. to 7 a.m. weekdays, 24 hours weekends and holidays.

Ohio
Statewide aves.net/obr/
Blendon Woods Park (614) 895-6222
Cincinnati (513) 521-2847
Cleveland (216) 526-2473
Columbus (614) 221-9736
Northwestern region (419) 877-9640
Southwestern region (937) 277-9640
Youngstown (330) 742-6661

Oklahoma
Statewide (918) 669-6646
Oklahoma City (405) 373-4531

Oregon
Statewide (503) 292-0661; **hnehls@teleport.com**
Klamath Basin (541) 850-3805
Northeastern region (208) 882-6195

Pennsylvania
Central region (717) 255-1212, ext. 5761
Eastern region (610) 252-3455
Greater Pocono Region (717) 622-2342
Lehigh Valley Audubon Society Web site: **www.lehigh.edu/~bcm0/lvas.html**
Philadelphia (215) 567-2473
Reading/Berks County (610) 376-6000, ext. 2473
Schuylkill County (717) 622-6013
Western region (412) 963-0560
Wilkes-Barre (717) 825-2473

Rhode Island
Statewide (401) 949-3870; reporting (401) 949-5454

South Carolina
Statewide (704) 332-2473

South Dakota
Statewide (605) 773-6460
West River (605) 584-4141; **tallmand@wolf.northern.edu**

Tennessee
Statewide (615) 356-7636
Chattanooga (423) 877-1129

Texas
Statewide (713) 369-9673; **www.birdware.com/lists/rba/_us/tx/statewide/rba.htm**
Abilene (915) 691-8981
Austin (512) 926-8751
Central region (254) 299-8170
Corpus Christi and Coastal Bend (512) 883-7410
Heart of Texas (409) 694-9850; **bafa@acs.tamu.edu**
Lower Rio Grande Valley (956) 969-2731
Lubbock (806) 797-6690
Northcentral region (817) 329-1270
Northeastern region (903) 234-2473
San Antonio (210) 308-6788
West Texas **dsarkozi@infocom.net**
Upper Texas Coast texasbirding.simplenet.com

Utah
Statewide (801) 538-4730; reporting to **westwings@sisna.com**

Vermont
Statewide (802) 457-2779;
www.uvm.edu/~smorrica/sightings.html; treefrog@sover.net

Virginia
Statewide (757) 238-2713; **cwillis@infi.net**
Statewide (301) 652-1088, **voice@capacess.org**

Washington
Statewide (425) 454-2662
Lower Columbia Basin (509) 943-6957
Southeastern region (208) 882-6195
Western region (206) 933-1831
Washington BirdBox (206) 454-2662;
weber.u.washington.edu/~dvictor/digest.html

West Virginia
Statewide (304) 736-3086
Morganstown (304) 284-8217

Wisconsin
Statewide (414) 352-3857
Madison (608) 255-2476 (except 9 a.m. to 3 p.m., Monday through Friday)
Northeastern region (Green Bay) (414) 434-4207

Wyoming
Statewide (307) 265-2473

Canada

Alberta
Calgary (403) 237-8821
Edmonton (403) 433-2473

British Columbia
Vancouver (604) 737-3074
Victoria (250) 592-3381; **www.islandnet.com/~boom/birding/bc-home.htm**

New Brunswick
Provincewide (506) 382-3825
Shediac/Moncton (in French) (506) 532-2873; **personal.nbnet.nb.ca/tingley/**

Nova Scotia
Provincewide (902) 852-2428

Ontario
Hamilton (905) 648-9537; **www.hwcn.org/link/hamnature/hncblin.html**
Oshawa (905) 576-2738
Ottawa (613) 825-7444
Sault Ste. Marie (705) 256-2790
Toronto (416) 350-3000, ext. 2293
Windsor/Detroit (810) 477-1360
Windsor/Pt. Pelee (519) 252-2473

Quebec
Eastern region (in French) (418) 660-9089
Coeur-du-Quebec (in French) (819) 370-6720
Sagueny/Lac St. Jean (in French) (418) 696-1868
Bas St. Laurent (in French) (418) 725-5118
Western region (in French) (819) 778-0737
Montreal (in English) (514) 989-5076
Montreal (in French) (514) 978-8849

Saskatchewan
Regina (306) 949-2505

Birding Hotspots

North America is full of fabulous birding hotspots—places where the birding is really special. I couldn't begin to give them any sort of ranking, although I do have a few personal favorites. Here, I list alphabetically the 30 hotspots (with contact addresses) in North America that are, in my humble opinion, definitely worth a visit if you're within a hundred miles. Apologies if I've left off a hotspot that's *your* personal favorite.

The addresses given here are for the administrative offices, not necessarily the sites themselves. Bear in mind that the entire region around a hotspot usually has other good birding spots; the site I mention specifically is usually just a good starting point. If you're planning a visit to a hotspot, call ahead not only to the site but also to the local and state tourism offices for more information.

Arkansas National Wildlife Refuge
P.O. Box 100
Austwell, TX 77950
(512) 286-3559
Fax: (512) 286-3722
r2rw_ar@fws.gov
sturgeon.irm1.r2.fws.gov/refuges/texas/aransas.html

Big Bend National Park
P.O. Box 129
Big Bend National Park, TX 79834
(915) 477-2251
bigb@us-national-parks.net
www.big.bend.national-park.com

Block Island National Wildlife Refuge
c/o Ninigrat Refuge Complex Office
P.O. Box 307
Charlestown, RI 02813
(401) 364-9124
Fax: (401) 364-0170
r5rw_ninwr@fws.gov

Bombay Hook National Wildlife Reserve
Whitehall Neck Road
Smyrna, DE 19977
(302) 653-9345
Fax: (302) 653-0684
r5rw_bhnwr@fws.gov

Bosque del Apache National Wildlife Refuge
Socorro, NM 87801
(505) 835-1828
Fax: (505) 835-0314
r2rw_bda@fws.gov
www.nmt.edu/mainpage

Cape May Bird Observatory
701 East Lake Drive
Cape May Point, NJ 08212
(609) 884-2736
Fax: (609) 884-6052
cmbo@njaudubon.org
www.njo.com/audubon

Columbia National Wildlife Refuge
735 East Main Street
Othello, WA 99344
(509) 488-2668
Fax: (509) 488-0705
r1rw_cmb@fws.gov

Corkscrew Swamp Sanctuary
375 Sanctuary Road West
Naples, FL 33964
(813) 657-3771

J. N. "Ding" Darling National Wildlife Refuge
One Wildlife Drive
Sanibel, FL 33957
(941) 472-1100
Fax: (941) 472-4061
r4rw_fl.jnd@fws.gov
www.fws.gov/r4eao/wildlife/nwrjnd.htm

Dauphin Island Sanctuary
P.O. Box 848
Dauphin Island, AL 36528
(205) 861-2882

Elkhorn Slough National Marine Estuary
c/o Elkhorn Slough Foundation
Box 267
Moss Landing, CA 95039
(831) 728-5939
Fax: (831) 728-1056
esf@elkhornslough.org
www.elkhornslough.org

Everglades National Park
40001 State Road 9336
Homestead, FL 33030
(305) 242-7700
ever@us-national-parks.net
www.everglades.national-park.com

Hawk Mountain Sanctuary
1700 Hawk Mountain Road
Kempton, PA 19529
(610) 756-6000
Fax: (610) 756-4468
info@hawkmountain.org
www.hawkmountain.org

Jamaica Bay National Wildlife Refuge
Gateway National Recreation Area
Floyd Bennett Field
Brooklyn, NY 11234
(718) 318-3575

Maine Coastal Islands Sanctuary
12 Audubon Road
Bremen, ME 04551
(207) 529-5828 (June through September)

Malheur National Wildlife Refuge
P.O. Box 245
Princeton, OR 97721
(541) 493-2612
Fax: (541) 493-2405
diana_king@fws.gov

Montezuma National Wildlife Refuge
3395 Route 5/20 East
Seneca Falls, NY 13148
(315) 568-5987
Fax: (315) 568-8835
r5rw_mznnwr@fws.gov

369

Parker River National Wildlife Refuge
Northern Boulevard
Plum Island
Newburyport, MA 01950
(978) 465-5753
Fax: (978) 465-2807
r5rw_prnwr@fws.gov

Patagonia-Sonoita Creek Preserve
P.O. Box 815
Patagonia, AZ 85624
(520) 394-2400

Pawnee National Grassland
600 O Street
Greeley, CO 80631
(970) 353-5004
jadams/r2_arnfpng@fs.fed.us
fs.fed.us/arnf/png

Point Pelee National Park
118 Point Pelee Drive
Leamington, Ontario N8H 3V4
(519) 322-2365
Fax: (519) 322-1277
Pelee_Info@pch.gc.ca
parkscanada.pch.gh.ca/parks/ontario/Point_Pelee

Point Reyes National Seashore
Point Reyes, CA 94956
(415) 663-1092

Ramsey Canyon Preserve
27 Ramsey Canyon Road
Hereford, AZ 85615
(602) 378-2785

George C. Reifel Migratory Bird Sanctuary
5191 Robertson Road
Delta, British Columbia
(604) 946-6980

Rowe Sanctuary
44450 Elm Island Road
Gibbon, NE 68840
(308) 468-5282
rowe@nctc.net

Sabine National Wildlife Refuge
3000 Holly Beach Highway
Highway 27 South
Hackberry, LA 70645
(318) 762-3816
Fax: (318) 762-3780
r4rw_la.sbn@fws.gov
www.fws.gov/r4eao/wildlife/nwrsbn.html

Salton Sea National Wildlife Refuge
906 West Sinclair Road
Calipatria, CA 92233
(760) 348-5278
Fax: (760) 348-7245
clark_bloom@fws.gov
www.r.1.fws.gov/news/saltbgrd/htm

Santa Ana National Wildlife Refuge
Route 2, Box 202A
Alamo, TX 78516
(956) 787-3079
Fax: (956) 787-8338
r2rw_sta@fws.gov
sturgeon.irm1.r2.fws.gov/u2/refuges/texas/santana.html

Snake River Birds of Prey Natural Area
The Nature Conservancy
Idaho Field Office
P.O. Box 64
Sun Valley, ID 83353
(208) 726-3007

Tijuana Slough National Wildlife Refuge
c/o Sweetwater Marsh National Wildlife Refuge
301 Caspian Way
Imperial Beach, CA 91932
(619) 575-2704
Fax: (619) 575-6913
rebecca_young@fws.gov

Optics Manufacturers

If you're a birder, by definition, you're always thinking of buying new binoculars or a new spotting scope. To find out more about the model you're interested in, contact the manufacturer and request information. The companies are always happy to send it to you.

Bushnell/Bausch & Lomb Binoculars
9200 Cody
Overland Park, KS 66214
(800) 423-3537
Fax: (913) 752-3550
custserve@bushnell.com
www.bushnell.com

Canon U.S.A., Inc.
One Canon Plaza
Lake Success, NY 11042
(800) OKCANON
www.usa.canon.com

Celestron International
2835 Columbia Street
Torrance, CA 90503
(310) 328-9560
Fax: (310) 212-5835
www.celestron.com

Docter-Optic Technologies, Inc.
4685 Boulder Highway, Suite A
Las Vegas, NV 89121
(800) 290-3634
Fax: (702) 898-3737

Eagle Optics
2120 West Greenview Drive, #4
Middleton, WI 53562
(800) 289-1132

Fax: (608) 836-4416
webmaster@eagleoptics.com
www.eagleoptics.com

Fujinon Inc.
Ten High Point Drive
Wayne, NJ 17470
(973) 633-5600
Fax: (973) 694-8299
www.fuginon.co.jp

Kowa Optimed, Inc.
20001 South Vermont Avenue
Torrance, CA 90502
(800) 966-5692
Fax: (310) 327-4177
scopekowa@kowa.com
www.kowascope.com

Leica Camera Inc.
156 Ludlow Avenue
Northvale, NJ 07647
(800) 222-0118
Fax: (201) 767-8666
www.leica-camera.com/usa

Leupold & Stevens/WindRiver
Box 688
Beaverton, OR 97075
(503) 526-5196
www.leupstv.com

Meade Instruments Corporation
6001 Oak Canyon
Irvine, CA 92620
(949) 451-1450
Fax: (949) 451-1460
www.meade.com

Minolta USA
101 Williams Drive
Ramsey, NJ 07446
(800) 528-4767
otherphoto@minolta.com
www.minoltausa.com

Mirador Optical Corporation
Box 11614
Marina Del Rey, CA 90295
(800) 748-5844

Nikon Sport Optics
1300 Walt Whitman Road
Melville, NY 11747
(800) 247-3464
Fax: (516) 547-0309
allen@nikonincmail.com
www.nikonusa.com

Olympus America Inc.
Two Corporate Center Drive
Melville, NY 11747
(800) 622-6372
Fax: (516) 844-5930
www.olympus.com

Optolyth
Box 7518
San Diego, CA 92167
(800) 225-9407
Fax: (619) 692-8199
deutoptik@aol.com
www.deutscheoptik.com

Pentax Corporation
35 Inverness Drive East
Englewood, CO 80112
(800) 709-2020
Fax: (303) 790-1131
pentaxmc@rmii.com
www.pentax.com

Questar Corporation
6204 Ingham Road
New Hope, PA 18938
(215) 862-5277
Fax: (215) 862-0512
questar@erols.com
www.questar-corp.com

Swarovski Optik
One Wholesale Way
Cranston, RI 02920
(800) 426-3089
Fax: (401) 946-2587
webmaster@swarovskioptik.com
www.swarovskioptik.com

Swift Instruments, Inc.
952 Dorchester Avenue
Boston, MA 02125
(617) 436-2960
Fax: (617) 436-3232
swift1@tiac.net
www.swift-optics.com

Tasco
2889 Commerce Parkway
Miramar, FL 33025
(888) 438-8272
info@tascosales.com
www.tascosales.com

TeleVue Optics
100 Route 59
Suffern, NY 10901
(914) 357-9522
www.televue.com

VERNONscope & Company
Five Ithaca Road
Candor, NY 13743
(607) 659-7000
Fax: (607) 659-4000

Carl Zeiss Optical
1015 Commerce Street
Petersburg, VA 23803
(800) 338-2984
Fax: (804) 862-3734
optical@zeiss.com
www.zeiss.com

374

Your Basic Birding Bookshelf

It's a fact of birding life; you can't have too many books. Be prepared for bulging shelves. Here, I've tried to stick mostly to current titles, but I've also listed some classics that are inexplicably out of print. If you ever see a used copy of *The Audubon Society Encyclopedia of North American Birds,* by John Terres, grab it.

Field Guides

Griggs, Jack. *American Bird Conservancy's Field Guide to All the Birds of North America* (HarperCollins, 1997).

National Geographic Society, *Field Guide to the Birds of North America,* Third edition (National Geographic Society, 1999).

National Audubon Society, *The Audubon Society Field Guide to North American Birds* (Knopf, 1994).

Peterson, Roger Tory. *Field Guide to Western Birds* (Houghton Mifflin, 1990).

———. *Field Guide to Birds East of the Rockies,* Fourth edition (Houghton Mifflin, 1980).

Robbins, Chandler, et al. *Birds of North America* (Golden Press, 1983).

Stokes, Donald and Lillian. *Stokes Field Guide to Birds* (Eastern and Western regions) (Little, Brown, 1996).

Essential References

American Ornithologists' Union and The Academy of Natural Sciences of Philadelphia. *The Birds of North America: Life Histories for the 21st Century*, 10 vols. to date (Allen Press, 1995–).

Bent, Arthur Cleveland. *Life Histories of North American Birds,* Reprint edition (Dover Books, 1988).

Ehrlich, Paul, David S. Dobkin, and Darryl Wheye, *The Birder's Handbook* (Simon & Schuster, 1988).

Farrand, John, editor. *The Audubon Society Master Guide to Birding,* 3 vols. (Knopf, 1983).

Forshaw, Joseph, et al. *The Nature Company Guides: Birding* (Time-Life Books, 1994).

Harrison, Hal H. *A Field Guide to the Birds' Nests* (Houghton Mifflin, 1975).

Kaufman, Kenn. *Advanced Birding* (Houghton Mifflin, 1990).

————.*Lives of North American Birds* (Houghton Mifflin, 1996).

Palmer, Ralph S., editor. *Handbook of North American Birds,* 5 vols. to date (Yale University Press, 1990–).

Sibley, Charles G. and Burt L. Monroe, Jr. *Distribution and Taxonomy of Birds of the World* (Yale University Press, 1991).

Terres, John. *The Audubon Society Encyclopedia of North American Birds* (Knopf, 1980).

Checklists

American Ornithologists Union. *AOU Checklist of North American Birds,* Seventh edition (AOU, 1998).

Clements, James. *Birds of the World: A Check List,* Fourth edition (Ibis Publishing, 1991).

Howard, Richard, and Alick Moore. *A Complete Checklist of the Birds of the World,* Second edition (*Academic Press,* 1994).

Monroe, Burt L. and Charles G. Sibley, *A World Checklist of Birds* (Yale University Press, 1993).

General Reference

Buff, Sheila. *The Birder's Sourcebook* (Lyons & Burford, 1994).

Choate, Ernest A. *The Dictionary of American Bird Names,* Revised edition (Harvard Common Press, 1985).

Cohen, Sharon. *Bird Nests* (Collins Publishers, 1993).

Cox, Randall. *Birder's Dictionary* (Falcon Publishing, 1996).

Cronin, Edward W., Jr. *Getting Started in Bird Watching* (Houghton Mifflin, 1986).

Dunne, Pete, and Clay Sutton. *Hawks in Flight: A Guide to Identification of Migrant Raptors* (Houghton Mifflin, 1988).

Elliott, Lang, and Marie Read. *Common Birds and Their Songs* (Houghton Mifflin, 1998).

Feduccia, Alan. *The Origin and Evolution of Birds* (Yale University Press, 1996).

Freethy, Ron. *Secrets of Bird Life: A Guide to Bird Biology* (Blandford, 1990).

Goodnow, John. *How Birds Fly* (Periwinkle Books, 1992).

Jones, John O. *Where the Birds Are* (William Morrow, 1990).

Kerlinger, Paul. *How Birds Migrate* (Stackpole Books, 1995).

Leahy, Christopher. *The Birdwatcher's Companion* (Bonanza Books, 1984).

McElroy, Thomas P., Jr. *The Habitat Guide to Birding* (Lyons & Burford, 1974).

Pyle, Peter, et al. *Identification Guide to North American Passerines* (Slate Creek Press, 1997).

Sutton, Patricia and Clay. *How to Spot an Owl* (Chapters Publishing, 1994).

Terres, John K. *The Audubon Society Encyclopedia of North American Birds* (Knopf, 1980).

———. *How Birds Fly* (Stackpole Books, 1994).

Books About Bird Families

Enticott, Jim, and David Tipling. *Seabirds of the World* (Stackpole Books, 1997).

Grant, P.J. *Gulls: A Guide to Identification,* 2nd edition (Academic Press, 1997).

Harrison, Peter. *Seabirds: An Identification Guide* (Houghton Mifflin, 1991).

———. *Seabirds of the World: A Photographic Guide* (Princeton University Press, 1997).

Hayman, Peter, John Marchant, and Tony Prater. *Shorebirds: An Identification Guide* (Houghton Mifflin, 1991).

Johnsgard, Paul A. *The Hummingbirds of North America,* Second edition (*Smithsonian Institution Press*, 1997).

Johnsgard, Paul A. *North American Owls* (*Smithsonian Institution Press*, 1997).

Todd, Frank. *Handbook of Waterfowl Identification* (Ibis Publishing, 1997).

———. *Natural History of the Waterfowl* (Ibis Publishing, 1996).

Toops, Connie. *Bluebirds Forever* (Voyageur Press, 1994).

Weidensaul, Scott. *Raptors: The Birds of Prey* (Lyons & Burford, 1996).

Wheeler, Brian K. and William S. Clark, *A Photographic Guide to North American Raptors* (Academic Press, 1995).

Birdwatching and Bird Essays

Connor, Jack. *The Complete Birder: A Guide to Better Birding* (Houghton Mifflin, 1988).

Dunne, Pete. *The Feather Quest* (Dutton, 1992).

————. *More Tales of a Low-Rent Birder* (University of Texas Press, 1994).

————. *Tales of a Low-Rent Birder* (Fireside, 1986).

Kastner, Joseph. *A World of Watchers* (Knopf, 1986).

Kaufman, Kenn. *Kingbird Highway* (Houghton Mifflin, 1997).

Stap, Don. *A Parrot Without a Name* (University of Texas Press, 1990).

Bird Photography

Gallagher, Tim. *Wild Bird Photography* (Lyons & Burford, 1994).

Heiberg, Milton. *The Essentials of Nature Photography* (Tern Book Company, 1997).

Morris, Arthur. *The Art of Bird Photography* (Watson-Guptill, 1998).

Shaw, John. *John Shaw's Business of Nature Photography: A Professional's Guide to Marketing and Managing a Successful Nature Photography Business* (Amphoto, 1997).

Birdfeeding and Backyard Birding

Adler, Bill, and Heidi Hughes. *The Expert's Guide to Backyard Birdfeeding* (Crown, 1990).

Burton, Robert. *The National Audubon Society North American Birdfeeder Handbook* (Dorling Kindersley, 1992).

Dennis, John V. *A Complete Guide to Bird Feeding* (Knopf, 1994).

————. *A Guide to Western Bird Feeding* (Bird Watcher's Digest Press, 1991).

Kress, Stephen W. *The Audubon Society Guide to Attracting Birds* (Scribner's, 1985).

Newfield, Nancy, and Barbara Nielsen. *Hummingbird Gardens* (Chapter Publishing, 1996).

Editors of *Sunset Magazine. An Illustrated Guide to Attracting Birds* (Sunset Publishing, 1990).

Stokes, Donald and Lillian. *The Bird Feeder Book* (Little, Brown, 1987).

Terres, John K. *Songbirds in Your Garden* (Algonquin Books, 1994).

Warton, Susan, editor. *An Illustrated Guide to Attracting Birds* (Sunset Publishing, 1990).

Magazines, Newsletters, and Journals

Backyard Bird News
P.O. Box 110
Marietta, OH 45750
(800) 879-2473
ReadBWD@aol.com
www.petersonsonline.com

Bird Conservation
American Bird Conservancy
1250 24th Street NW
Washington, DC 20037
(888) BIRD-MAG
abc@abcbirds.org
www.abcbirds.org
Note: This is the newsletter of Partners in Flight.

Birder's Journal
Eight Midtown Drive, Suite 289
Oshawa, Ontario L1J 8L2
(905) 668-1449
Fax: (905) 668-1626
holder@netcom.ca

Birder's World
Box 1612
Waukesha, WI 53187
(800) 446-5489
Fax: (414) 796-1615
customerservice@kalmbach.com
www.birdersworld.com

Birding
American Birding Association
P.O. Box 6599
Colorado Springs, CO 80904
(800) 850-2473
Fax: (719) 578-1480
member@aba.org
www.americanbirding.com

Birds & Blooms
540 South 60th Street
Greendale, WI 53129
(800) 344-6913
www.reimanpub.com

Bird Watcher's Digest
P.O. Box 110
Marietta, OH 45750
(800) 879-2473
ReadBWD@aol.com
www.petersonsonline.com

The BWD Skimmer
P.O. Box 110
Marietta, OH 45750
(800) 879-2473
ReadBWD@aol.com
www.petersonsonline.com

Field Notes
P.O. Box 6599
Colorado Springs, CO 80904
(800) 850-2473
Fax: (719) 578-1480
kennk@ix.netcom.com
www.americanbirding.org/fldngen.htm

The Living Bird
Cornell Laboratory of Ornithology
159 Sapsucker Woods Road
Ithaca, NY 14850
(607) 254-BIRD
birds.cornell.edu
Note: Subscription is part of annual membership.

WildBird
P.O. Box 6050
Mission Viejo, CA 92690
(949) 855-8822
wildbird@fancypubs.com
www.petchannel.com

Butterflies

Glassberg, Jeffrey. *Butterflies Through Binoculars* (Oxford, 1993).

Pyle, Robert Michael. *Handbook for Butterfly Watchers* (Houghton Mifflin, 1992).

Stokes, Donald and Lillian. *The Butterfly Book* (Little, Brown, 1991).

State and Provincial Birds

Do you really need to know this? You'll be surprised at how often it comes up.

State	Birds
Alabama	Northern Flicker (yellowhammer)
Alaska	Willow Ptarmigan
Arizona	Cactus Wren
Arkansas	Northern Mockingbird
California	California Quail
Colorado	Lark Bunting
Connecticut	American Robin
Delaware	Blue Hen Chicken
District of Columbia	Wood Thrush
Florida	Northern Mockingbird
Georgia	Brown Thrasher
Hawaii	Nene
Idaho	Mountain Bluebird
Illinois	Northern Cardinal
Indiana	Northern Cardinal
Iowa	American Goldfinch
Kansas	Western Meadowlark
Kentucky	Northern Cardinal
Louisiana	Brown Pelican
Maine	Black-capped Chickadee
Maryland	Baltimore Oriole
Massachusetts	Black-capped Chickadee
Michigan	American Robin
Minnesota	Common Loon
Mississippi	Northern Mockingbird

continues

continued

State	Birds
Missouri	Eastern Bluebird
Montana	Western Meadowlark
Nebraska	Western Meadowlark
Nevada	Mountain Bluebird
New Hampshire	Purple Finch
New Jersey	American Goldfinch
New Mexico	Greater Roadrunner
New York	Eastern Bluebird
North Carolina	Northern Cardinal
North Dakota	Western Meadowlark
Ohio	Northern Cardinal
Oklahoma	Scissor-tailed Flycatcher
Oregon	Western Meadowlark
Pennsylvania	Ruffed Grouse
Rhode Island	Rhode Island Red Chicken
South Carolina	Carolina Wren
South Dakota	Ring-necked Pheasant
Tennessee	Northern Mockingbird
Texas	Northern Mockingbird
Utah	California Gull
Vermont	Hermit Thrush
Virginia	Northern Cardinal
Washington	American Goldfinch
West Virginia	Northern Cardinal
Wisconsin	American Robin
Wyoming	Western Meadowlark

Canadian Province	Birds
Alberta	Great Horned Owl
British Columbia	Steller's Jay
Manitoba	Great Gray Owl
New Brunswick	Black-capped Chickadee
Newfoundland	Atlantic Puffin
Northwest Territory	Gyrfalcon
Nova Scotia	Osprey
Ontario	Common Loon

Canadian Province	Birds
Prince Edward Island	Blue Jay
Quebec	Snowy Owl
Saskatchewan	Sharp-tailed Grouse
Yukon Territory	Raven

Glossary

Accipiter   Woodlands hawk built for speed and maneuverability, with long tails and short, rounded wings.

Alarm calls   Loud, urgent noises birds make to warn each other of danger.

Allopreening   Preening of one bird by another of the same species.

Atlasing   Discovering and recording on maps the locations of specific birds in a specific area, usually to record breeding or distribution.

Aviary   Enclosure for captive birds that's large enough to let them fly freely and behave naturally.

Banding   See *bird banding*.

Big Day   An effort to see as many bird species as possible over a 24-hour period.

Binoculars   Two small telescopes arranged side-by-side so that you can look through them with both eyes. Your most important birding tool.

Birdathon   Birding event where teams of birders compete to see the most bird species in a particular area over a single 24-hour period.

Bird atlas   Set of maps that shows how the birds are distributed in a particular area.

Bird banding   Placing a numbered ring on the leg of a bird in order to keep track of its movements over time.

Bird box   Artificial nesting structure for birds; birdhouse.

Birder   Someone whose hobby is watching birds; birdwatcher.

Birding   The art and science of observing bird life. Synonymous with birdwatching.

Birdsong   The complex, loud, musical sounds made by birds.

Birdwatcher   Someone whose hobby is watching birds. Synonymous with birder.

Birdwatching   The art and science of observing bird life. Synonymous with birding.

Blind   Small, hutlike structure designed to let you view the birds close up without scaring them off.

Brush pile   Heap of old branches piled up by your birdfeeder to provide shelter and perches for the birds waiting their turn at the feeder.

Buteo   Soaring hawk with a chunky body, broad, rounded tail and large, broad wings.

Buzzard   In Europe, a word for soaring hawks, or buteos. In the U.S., commonly and incorrectly used for vultures.

Calls   Short, simple sounds made by almost all birds.

Ceres   Leathery "saddle" at the base of the upper mandible, as in many raptors.

Chasing   Traveling, usually on short notice, to see a rare or unusual bird.

Checklist   Preprinted booklet listing all the birds known to occur in a particular region or birding site.

Christmas Bird Count (CBC)   Annual winter event where birders around the country tally the birds in their count regions on a single day and send in their results to BirdSource, a joint project of the National Audubon Society and the Cornell Laboratory of Ornithology.

Colonial nesters   Birds that breed in large groups, or colonies, of the same species. Many water birds, such as gulls, terns, pelicans, herons, and cormorants, are colonial nesters.

Commensal feeding   Finding food as a result of another bird's activity.

Communal roost   Place where many birds gather together, usually to rest or sleep, sometimes in very large numbers.

Contact calls   Short, simple sounds birds make to keep in touch with each other.

Decurved   Describing a bill that curves downward, as in curlews and whimbrels.

Diopter adjustment   Device on the right eyepiece of binoculars used to adjust the image to accommodate individual eyesight.

Distraction display   Luring a predator away from the nest by pretending to be injured or imitating a rodent. Often done by ground-nesting birds.

Diurnal raptors   Birds of prey active during the day—basically, all the raptors except for the owls.

Dominance hierarchy   See *peck order.*

Eclipse plumage   In ducks, the dull plumage of the male in winter before he molts and grows brighter breeding plumage.

Ecotourism   Responsible travel to natural areas that conserves and respects the environment and sustains the well-being of local people.

Edge effect   The greater abundance of bird species that occurs where different habitats—a field and woods, for instance—meet.

Falconry   Hunting with tamed raptors, especially peregrine falcons.

Field guide   Compact, illustrated book designed to help you identify birds in the field through the pictures, descriptions, and range maps.

Field card   See *checklist*.

Field mark   Fairly obvious aspect of a bird's appearance, such as color, bill shape, wing bars, head markings, and so on, that identifies the bird as that species and no other.

Field trip   An outdoors excursion to see birds.

Finches   Small- to medium-sized birds with conical bills. Finches are members of the *Fringillidae* family, which includes finches, siskins, crossbills, redpolls, and some grosbeaks.

Finding guide   Book listing the places to see birds in a particular area, along with discussions of the sites, the birds you can expect to see, and detailed directions for getting there.

Fledging   Flying away from or leaving the nest for the first time.

Fledgling   A young bird that has flown from the nest but is still being cared for by the parent birds.

Flushing   Making a bird fly suddenly because you've disturbed it in some way. Avoid doing this if at all possible.

Frontal shield   Flat extension of the bill up onto the forehead, as in coots and gallinules.

Getting on   Seeing the bird through your binoculars.

Global Positioning System (GPS)   Array of navigation satellites used to locate your position on land or sea.

Gorget   Patch of brightly colored feathers found on the throat of a male humming-bird. Pronounced GOR-jet.

Habitat   The preferred environment of a particular bird species (or any other living thing).

Hawking   Catching insects on the wing, usually by darting out from a perch.

Helmet   Colorful patch on the forehead and crown of a hummingbird.

Hotspot   Particular geographic area that's especially attractive to birds.

Hummingbirds   Tiny, very active, nectar-eating birds with long, thin bills. Found only in the New World, hummingbirds are members of the family *Trochilidae*.

Hybrid   Product of interbreeding between birds of two species; a crossbreed.

Kettle   Group of hawks (not always the same species) using a thermal to climb upward; also, any large group of hawks. The word is used because a bunch of hawks soaring up on a thermal look a lot like the bubbles in a pot full of boiling water.

Lek   Area where male birds gather to perform complex courtship displays to an audience of females. Some hummingbird species, especially the more tropical ones, gather in leks. Lek behavior is also common among grouse, prairie chickens, and woodcocks.

Life bird   Bird you've seen and identified for the first time.

Life list   List of all the bird species you have ever seen.

Listing   The practice of keeping ongoing permanent records of the birds you have seen.

Lobed or **lobate**   Describing flat, paddle-shaped toes, as in grebes and coots.

Lumping   Combining two species into one.

Mandibles   Loosely, another way of saying jaws. The top part of the bill is often called the upper mandible; it's really the maxilla. The lower part is the mandible.

Mealworms   Larval form of a type of harmless black beetle. Mealworms are about half an inch to an inch long.

Molting   Normal process of losing and replacing feathers. Just before the breeding season begins, birds molt into their brightly colored breeding plumage. When the breeding period is over, they molt again, usually into duller colors.

Morph   Normal variation in color or some other aspect of appearance or anatomy within a species. It's enough to be noticeable but not enough to count as a subspecies.

Nail   The hard, hooked tip on the upper mandible of the flattened bill of a waterfowl.

Nares   Nostrils. Pronounced NAIR-eez.

Nectar   Sweet juice secreted by many plants as a way to attract insects and birds that will pollinate them.

Nesting box   Artificial nesting structure for birds; birdhouse.

Niche   The role a bird plays within its habitat. More loosely, the bird's preferred place within the habitat.

Ornithologist   A scientist who studies birds.

Ornithology   The scientific study of birds.

Owl   Bird of prey active mostly at night or twilight. In general, owls are stocky birds with forward-facing eyes, large heads, short bills, and short tails. Owls fly silently.

Palmated   Having webbing between the forward-facing three toes, as in ducks, geese, and gulls.

Pamprodactyl   Having all four toes facing forward—as in the swifts.

Passerines   Loose term for the very large group of perching birds, also loosely known as songbirds.

Peck order   The dominance order in a flock of birds, or which birds are submissive or dominant.

Peeps   General term for small shorebirds such as plowers and sandpipers.

Pelagic   General term for anything relating to the open ocean—salt waters far from shore. Pelagic birds are birds such as albatrosses that spend most of their life at sea. Pronounced peh-LAJ-ick.

Pellets   Regurgitated digested food from owls. Pellets are dry, compact, and rough; they're often gray or whitish. They vary in size from tiny (Screech-Owls) to huge (Great Horned Owls) and contain obvious bits of fur, bones, and feathers.

Petrel   General name for the smaller pelagic tubenoses.

Phase   See *morph*.

Pishing   Attracting birds by making squeaking or hissing noises with your mouth or with a bird call. Some shy birds will pop up out of the vegetation in response to pishing. Synonymous with spishing.

Preening   Using the bill to remove water, dirt, and parasites from the feathers to keep them clean and in good working order. Preening also reattaches the barbs that hold feathers together.

Race   See *subspecies*.

Raptors   Birds of prey, members of the hawk, falcon, eagle, and owl families.

Rare bird alert (RBA)   Weekly (or more frequent) listing of rare and unusual birds in a particular state or local region. RBAs are tape-recorded phone messages produced by volunteers; today most RBAs are also available via email.

Recurved   Describing a bill that curves upward, as in avocets.

Reference bird   Any bird that you can instantly recognize and use as a basis of comparison for other birds.

Roost   Place where a bird goes to rest or sleep.

Semipalmated   Having partial webbing between the forward-facing toes, as in plovers and sandpipers.

Serrate   Describing a bill that has "teeth" along the edges, as in mergansers.

Shorebird   General term used mostly for birds in the plover (*Charadriidae*) and sandpiper (*Scolopacidae*) families—birds found mostly along ocean and bay shorelines.

Sparrows   Small, drab, seed-eating birds with conical beaks. In North America, sparrows are members of the *Emberizidae* family, which includes towhees, New World sparrows, juncos, longspurs, and buntings.

Species   The fundamental unit of taxonomy. A bird species is one that is closely related to other members of its genus but can't interbreed with them.

Speculum   Patch of colorful secondary feathers on the wings of a waterfowl.

Spishing   See *Pishing.*

Splitting   Dividing a species into two or more separate species.

Staging ground   Area where birds gather in large numbers to rest and feed during migration.

Subspecies   A population within a species that shows some variation, usually because of geographic separation. The differences aren't enough to keep the subspecies from interbreeding where they meet.

Talons   The strong, sharp, curved claws of birds of prey.

Taxonomy   Standard hierarchical system used to classify and arrange the birds (and other animals and plants), based on their similarities and differences and their degree of evolutionary closeness. Pronounced tax-ON-oh-mee.

Territory   An area a bird stakes out and defends against other birds of the same species. Territories are usually used as feeding and breeding areas.

Thermal   Column of warm air that rises up from the ground as it's warmed by the sun. Soaring birds such as hawks use thermals as an easy way to gain altitude.

Throat pouch   A leathery pouch hanging from the lower mandible, as in pelicans.

Torpor   State of slowed metabolism and lowered body temperature. Hummingbirds (and also some other birds such as poorwills and swifts) go into torpor for hours at a time to conserve energy at night, in cold weather, or when they can't feed for other reasons, such as bad weather.

Totipalmated   Having webbing between all four toes, as in cormorants and pelicans.

Tribe   Taxonomic grouping that falls between a subfamily and a genus. Tribe names are used to group related species within a varied subfamily. Names for tribes always end in the suffix *-ini.*

Tubenose   General term for pelagic birds that have two tubular extensions on their nostrils. Albatrosses, fulmars, gadfly petrels, storm-petrels, and shearwaters are all tubenoses, members of the order *Procellariiformes.*

Warblers   Small, active, colorful, insect-eating birds with small, thin bills. The 125 or so warbler species are found exclusively in South, Central, and North America.

Warbler wave   During migration, the movement northward of large numbers of warblers, usually after a delay caused by bad weather.

Waterfowl   Aquatic birds that have flattened, blunt-tipped bills, webbed feet, and stout bodies covered with thick coats of dense, waterproof feathers. Ducks, geese, and swans are all waterfowl.

Whitewash   The polite way of saying bird droppings, whitewash looks just like it sounds—like splashes of thick white paint.

Zygodactyl   Having two toes pointing forward and two pointing backward—as in woodpeckers, parrots, and owls.

Index

I-J-K

L-M-N

405

Now add to your birdwatching library with

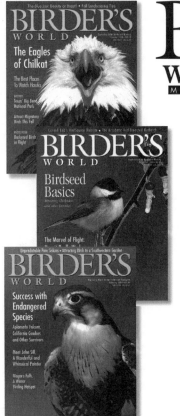

BIRDER'S
WORLD
MAGAZINE

It brings out the birdwatcher in you!

Now that you know the basics, enjoy birds even more with a subscription to this premier publication, *Birder's World* Magazine! Whether you're a beginning birdwatcher or a seasoned birder, you'll marvel at the hundreds of bird facts and beautiful photography you'll see in every issue! Order today and receive a year of birdwatching fun.

- ■ **Enjoy beautiful full-color bird photos**
- ■ **Discover details about backyard bird feeding habits**
- ■ **Learn bird-friendly gardening and landscaping tips**
- ■ **Explore travel destinations for birding vacations**
- ■ **Meet birding experts, authors, and artists**

1 year/6 issues for only $14.95!

Ordering is easy! Mail your completed order form below to

Birder's World, P.O. Box 1612, Waukesha, WI 53187-9950 or
Call 1-800-533-6644, Dept. A991B • Outside the U.S. and Canada, call 414-796-8776, Dept. A991B
Mon-Fri, 8:30 am-5:00 pm Central Time • Visit us online at www.birdersworld.com